Mobile Cloud Computing

Mobile Cloud Computing

Foundations and Service Models

Dijiang Huang
Huijun Wu

MORGAN KAUFMANN PUBLISHERS

AN IMPRINT OF ELSEVIER

Morgan Kaufmann is an imprint of Elsevier
50 Hampshire Street, 5th Floor, Cambridge, MA 02139, United States

Library of Congress Cataloging-in-Publication Data
A catalog record for this book is available from the Library of Congress

British Library Cataloguing-in-Publication Data
A catalogue record for this book is available from the British Library

ISBN: 978-0-12-809641-3

For information on all Morgan Kaufmann publications
visit our website at https://www.elsevier.com/books-and-journals

Working together
to grow libraries in
developing countries

www.elsevier.com • www.bookaid.org

Publishing Director: Jonathan Simpson
Acquisition Editor: Romer Brian
Editorial Project Manager: Charlotte Kent
Production Project Manager: Punithavathy Govindaradjane
Designer: Mark Rogers

Typeset by VTeX

To Lu, Alex, and Sarah:

love,

— Dijiang/Dad

To my family:

love and regards,

— Huijun

Contents

About the Authors

Dijiang Huang

Why should I have been the person to write this book? Well, I seem to have accumulated the right mix of experience and qualifications over the last 22 years. I graduated in Telecommunications from Beijing University of Posts and Telecommunications (China) with a Bachelor degree in 1995; my first job was that of a network engineer in the computer center of Civil Aviation Administration of China (CAAC); having four-year industry working experience, I came to the University of Missouri-Kansas City (UMKC) in the United States to pursue my graduate study in the joint computer and telecommunication networking program of Computer Science; and I earned my MSc and PhD degrees in Computer Science in 2001 and 2004, respectively. During my study at UMKC, I became interested in the research areas of mobile computing and security, and focused my research on securing Mobile Ad Hoc Networks (MANET).

LinkedIn QR Code

After graduating with my PhD, I joined the Computer Science and Engineering (CSE) department at Arizona State University (ASU) as an Assistant Professor to start my independent academic life. One of my early research focus areas was securing MANET communication and networking protocols. Later, I realized that the cross-layer approach is extremely important to make a MANET solution more efficient and practical. Gradually, I looked into the research problem on how to build a situation-aware solution to better support MANET applications considering various instability issues due to nodes' mobility and intermittent communication. Considering mobiles trying to utilize all reachable resources to support their applications, this situation is very similar to the resource management scenario for cloud computing; of course, with different context, running environment, programming and virtualization capabilities and constraints.

In 2010, I was awarded the Office of Naval Research (ONR) Young Investigator Program (YIP) award for working on a research project to establish a secure mobile cloud computing system. The main task of the award is to develop a secure and robust mobile cloud computing system to support trustworthy mission-critical MANET operations and resource management considering communication, networking, storage, computation, and security requirements and constraints. With the booming of Internet of Things (IoT), SDx (i.e., Software Defined Everything) in a mobile application scenario such as mobility powered and focused applications for the future smart city, mobile cloud computing has been refocusing its research agenda on a broader definition of "mobile" including cloud infrastructure, software, and services. I hope this book can share my past research and development outcomes and provide a starting point to ride on the next research and development wave for mobile cloud computing, which can benefit both research communities and practitioners.

In summary, my current research interests are in computer and network security, mobile ad hoc networks, network virtualization, and mobile cloud computing. I am currently an Associate Professor in the School of Computing Informatics Decision Systems Engineering (CIDSE) of ASU, and I am currently leading the Secure Networking and Computing (SNAC) research group. Most of my current and previous research is supported by federal agencies such as National Science Foundation (NSF), ONR, Army Research Office (ARO), Naval Research Lab (NRL), National Science Foundation of China (NSFC), and North Atlantic Treaty Organization (NATO); and industries such as Consortium of Embedded System (CES), Hewlett-Packard, NCI Inc., and China Mobile. In addition to ONR Young Investigator Award, I was also a recipient of HP Innovation Research Program (IRP) Award and JSPS Fellowship. I am a cofounder of two start-up companies: Athena Network Solutions LLC (ATHENETS) and CYNET LLC. I am a senior member of IEEE and member of ACM. For more information about my research publications, teaching, and professional community services, please refer to http://www.public.asu.edu/~dhuang8/. By the way, I love all kinds of sports, play guitar, and like traveling :-).

Huijun Wu

Huijun Wu is now an engineer at Twitter Inc. He received his PhD from Arizona State University.

In 2007, Huijun graduated from Huazhong University of Science & Technology, after which he showed interest in database and data processing. He worked on a database kernel project named CacheDB which is an in-memory real-time database kernel. CacheDB was adopted by the China Southern Power Grid to collect meter metrics in Guangzhou, China. When Huijun was working on the CacheDB project, he invented a log merging method and a parallel recovery method, which were patented. For the accomplishments in the database and data processing area, he received his MS degree.

LinkedIn QR Code

In 2009, Huijun joined Alcatel-Lucent Shanghai Bell to work on the 5060 Wireless Call Server (WCS). The 5060 WCS has served multiple areas worldwide, playing pivotal role in the backbone communication network. Huijun's work helped the 5060 WCS to work reliably.

Huijun did not stop progressing. He joined the SNAC research group and started his PhD journey in 2011. The 5 years spent at SNAC research group were the best time in his life. He worked with the intelligent SNAC colleagues in the mobile cloud area. His research includes mobile cloud application, mobile cloud service framework, and cloud computing. He developed a mobile cloud service framework called POEM, which was awarded the best student paper at the 4th IEEE International Conference on Mobile Services. Besides mobile cloud system, he published several offloading algorithms to optimize computation performance. For the accomplishments in the mobile cloud area, he received his PhD degree.

Huijun joined Twitter Inc. in 2016, working on the Heron project. Heron is a realtime, distributed, fault-tolerant stream processing engine to substitute Apache Storm, and Heron is moving to Apache Incubator. Huijun contributed several new components for Heron, including MetricsCacheManager. Besides developing Heron, he is a technique article author to promote the Heron project.

Foreword

Today personal computing devices such as smart phones and tablets have become the most popular means to access the Internet. They feature processing, storage, and communications power that increase exponentially, almost doubling each year. They are also equipped with a growing number of sensors, making them ideal for environmental monitoring, activity recognition and recording, health monitoring, navigation, and social match making. However, many emerging applications require independent, personal devices to coordinate the inputs, e.g., to analyze photos from a variety of cameras or to route data through multiple radios. Enabling these applications will require new services for efficient and secure sharing of data and resources.

Equally impressive has been the evolution of another utility, the vehicle, from its function as a basic means of transport to that of a sophisticated sensor platform. On-board vehicular routers have enormous processing, storage, and communication resources. Vehicle processing and communications resources coupled with sophisticated lasers, infrared sensors, and cameras have brought us the autonomous driving cars. In this area, a major contribution has been to intelligent transport by facilitating cruise control, detecting pedestrians, and assisting impaired drivers. Even bigger gains are expected from Vehicle-to-Vehicle communications, e.g., informing other vehicles of road conditions ahead, exchanging pedestrian sightings and collaborating to resolve congestion.

These examples are a part of a growing trend in **mobile computing**. Technologies are leading to a shift away from a backbone centric Internet scenario (in which personal and vehicular platforms communicate exclusively with the Internet Cloud), towards a mobile Internet dominated by mobile node interactions. Keeping the data local produces two important benefits – reducing wireless access traffic and easing Internet Cloud load. It is appropriate then to view a cluster of collaborating mobile devices as a Mobile Computing Cloud (MCC). One can borrow from the Internet Cloud the notion of "service", initially provided to local cloud members only, but now extensible to Internet customers as well. The Mobile Computing Cloud shares one aspect with the Internet Cloud: the access to massive resources (storage, processing, communications, and applications). However, resources are scattered over heterogeneous, and often intermittently connected, personal and vehicular platforms. They cannot be aggregated and harnessed for supercomputer type computations. This scattering of resources is a major challenge in MCCs. On the other hand, pervasiveness and mobility are also their main assets: mobility makes the MCCs the ideal observatories over the physical world in which they operate.

Given the phenomenal growth of Mobile Data and Mobile Applications, there is no question that Mobile Cloud Computing will be one of the fastest growing themes in Mobile Internet research and development. While there are many excellent articles and books that cover Mobile Computing platforms, protocols, security and applications in depth as separate topics, it is far more difficult to find a comprehensive source of information that captures and interrelates the various components together in a consistent way. The Book "Mobile Cloud Computing: Foundations and Service Models" by Dijiang Huang and Huijun Wu takes on the challenge of providing a unified view of Mobile Cloud Computing design from Foundation to Services. The book is appropriate for beginners as it goes through the various steps of the MCC design. It is also very valuable for practitioners, for its ample references and implementation examples.

The book is organized in three parts. Part 1 covers the fundamentals. After an extremely helpful taxonomy, mobile platforms including iOS and Android are introduced, and computation offloading, the most popular mobile cloud service, is described. Next, Virtualization is introduced as the most important enabling technology for mobility. Besides virtualization concepts developed for the Internet Cloud such as computation, network, storage virtualization and Hypervisor, Mobile device virtualization techniques (e.g., BYOD and KVM over ARM) are presented. Finally, MCC service models are described, starting as usual from Internet Cloud services – (IaaS), (PaaS), (SaaS) – and moving next to existing mobile cloud service models with plenty of use-case examples, and concluding with mobile IoT microservices.

Part 2 reports on current research and development of mobile cloud computing leveraging the author's own work, in particular POEM, an open service framework based on OSGi and XMPP and offering an offloading and composition system for MCCs. Next, offloading is defined as an optimization problem (to minimize energy and latency) and it is solved using a mobile cloud directed acyclic graph model. Finally, service offloading/composition is tested on several MCC application scenarios including hedge and fog platforms. Noteworthy is the service demonstration on IOT microservice platforms for popular use cases like personal health management, smart building, and platooning of autonomous vehicles.

Part 3 is dedicated to security. First, Access Control is demonstrated using ABE (Attribute Based Encryption) and is illustrated on an Information Centric Networking (ICN) naming scheme and a secure offloading application. Next, a secure BYOD solution based on KVM-based virtualization of ARM devices is presented. Two essential components are hardware assisted virtualization and Open vSwitch. An SDN remote controller is used to provide SDN functionalities.

The four Appendices cover advanced topics of significant interest to implementers. The Cloud resource management section provides an excellent survey on management techniques in the Internet Cloud. It is contrasted to mobile cloud management of mobile resources, still in its infancy, but nonetheless critical. The Mobile Cloud Programming Platform is an initiative by the authors to develop a platform based on XMPP and OSGi compatible with the existing mobile OS implementation. If offers a valid open environment for developers with excellent example illustration. Cryptographic Constructions covers the theoretical aspects of ABE and together with the Part 3 section makes the topic self-contained in the book. The Bring Your Own Device (BYOD) section complements the Part 1 BYOD coverage with an interesting implementation and evaluation.

Hopefully, I have successfully highlighted the content of this book and convinced you to examine it personally. Practicing mobile computing engineers as well as beginners will enjoy and benefit from this reading as much as I did.

Mario Gerla
CS Dept. UCLA

Preface

A Little History

The project of working on a research-oriented book on mobile cloud computing has been laid out since 2010, when the first author was awarded the Office of Naval Research (ONR) Young Investigator Program (YIP) award for working on a research project on how to establish a secure mobile cloud computing system. The main task of the YIP award was to develop a secure and robust mobile cloud computing system to support trustworthy mission-critical Mobile Ad Hoc Networks (MANET) operations and resource management in terms of communication, networking, storage, computation, and security. The primary focus of the project was to develop a secure mobile cloud computing infrastructure to host and manage all these resources.

The project encountered a very interesting research issue on how to manage mobile and cloud resources in a more coherent and systematic way. To this end, our research group has been looking into mobile cloud computing research, particularly in computation workload offloading. Inspired by earlier work such as CloneCloud [80] and Maui [89], our initial work focused on how to build a program transition system to provide real-time workload offloading. Towards this end, we adopted the OSGi [222] framework, which is a Java-based Service-oriented Architecture (SoA) that has been targeted at both Internet- and mobile-based application running environment. The initial work was mainly limited to one-on-one, i.e., from a mobile to a cloud server, computation workload offloading with the targeting goal of minimizing the battery's energy consumption on mobiles. Later, we expended the offloading models by considering one-to-many and many-to-many offloading, and the offloading entities that are not limited to cloud servers but also incorporate other mobiles or nearby computing devices. Additionally, we also developed new cost models considering communication/networking reliabilities and transmission overhead.

The offloading focused research for mobile cloud computing had attracted many researchers to present various mathematical models and software prototypes. To promote the research in mobile cloud computing, the first author worked with Professor Mario Gerla from University of California Los Angeles (UCLA) and started the Mobile Cloud Computing (MCC) workshop in conjunction with ACM Sigcomm 2012 and 2013. Later, the first author served as the Technical Committee (TPC) cochair for IEEE International Conference on Mobile Cloud Computing, Services, and Engineering (MobileCloud) in 2014 and served as a general cochair of the conferences in 2015 and 2016. My effort to lead the mobile cloud computing workshops and conferences is intended to bring together researchers, developers, and practitioners in current mobile computing and cloud computing from academia, industry, and service providers, to share ideas, experiences, and practical implementations related to new mobile cloud technologies and applications, and thus promote research efforts, attention from the research community, and initiate new mobile applications. For example, the 2014 IEEE MobileCloud conference had attracted research articles covering fairly broad research topics related to mobile cloud computing. The following figure presents the research areas that were covered by accepted articles published in the IEEE MobileCloud 2014.

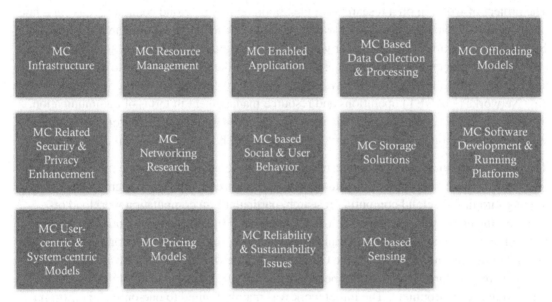

Mobile cloud computing research focus areas in the IEEE MobileCloud 2014.

With the development of mobile cloud computing research, the focus had been shifted from mathematical workload offloading models to software systems that can really implement the research outcomes and demonstrate the benefits of offloading. Based on many year research and development efforts in mobile cloud computing, the first author has been motivated to provide a comprehensive view of the research and development that can be used by researchers and mobile cloud computing application developers.

It must be noted that the book has been greatly influenced by Huijun Wu's, the second author's, research and development during his PhD study at Arizona State University. Huijun joined my research group as a PhD student in 2011 and earned his PhD degree in 2016. Hui-jun's research work had been focused on mobile cloud computing, especially the new service models built on workload offloading and functions' composition in a mobile application running environment. In this book, Chapters 4 and 5 are mainly based on his PhD dissertation. Additionally, he had worked with the first author and put significant efforts to compose other chapters and appendices.

With the research and development since 2010 in the area of mobile cloud computing, we strongly feel that the original focus and definitions of mobile cloud computing have their limitations, where the term "mobile" is usually considered as a smart phone or a similar mobile device that have some level of computing, networking, and storage capabilities. When using Internet cloud computing infrastructures, the research is mainly focusing on how to utilize Internet cloud computing and storage resources to support mobile applications using smart phones as the interfaces allowing end users to interact with the cloud. We have witnessed the research and development trends of mobile cloud computing, which has been geared up to a new level due to the emerging mobile applications powered by Internet of Things (IoT), microservices, smart infrastructures, and data-driven applications, etc. Moreover, new networking and security models must be designed to support mobile cloud computing applications to meet application scenarios that have various integrated and interconnected models that we traditionally see with clearly separated boundaries. One of the main goals of this book is to systematically lay out the R&D history and new trends.

Audience

Our goal has been to create a book that can be used by a diverse audience, and with various levels of background. It can serve as a reference book for college students, instructors, researchers, and software developers who are interested in developing mobile cloud computing applications. It can serve as a good reference book for undergraduate and graduate courses focusing on mobile computing, cloud computing, computing networking, and applied cryptography. Specifically, we set out to create a book that can be used by professionals as well as students and researchers. In general, this is intended as a self-study. We assume that the reader already has some basic knowledge of computer, networking, and software-based service models. Among professionals, the intent has been to cover two broad groups: software developers, including mobile and web-based services, and cloud computing services, with the overall goal to bring out issues that one group might want to understand that the other group faces. For students, this book is intended to help learn about virtualization for cloud computing and networking in depth, along with the big picture and lessons from operational and implementation experience. For researchers, who want to know what has been done so far and what critical issues are to address for next generation cloud computing for IoT, smart cities, vehicular networks, etc., this is intended as a helpful reference. In general, this book has been intended as a one-stop treatise for all interested in mobile computing and cloud computing.

Organization and Approach

The organization of the book is summarized as follows:

In the first part of this book, we focus on the foundation of MCC. Particularly, we first present concepts of Mobile Cloud Computing (MCC) in Chapter 1, covering definitions, taxonomy, and applications of cloud computing, mobile computing, and mobile cloud computing. Their characters and differences are presented. Mobile platforms including iOS and Android are introduced and compared. Besides mobile platforms, cloud-based mobile service platforms are described. The computation offloading, which is the typical mobile cloud computing form, is described and similar composition and migration concepts are described and compared. The definition of "Mobile" in mobile cloud computing has also transited from its original meaning of a "Mobile Device" to "mobile capability/features." In modern mobile devices involving services/applications, such as software, physical resource, location, service composition, etc., all can be "mobile" to meet a mobile cloud application's need. In this chapter, the definitions of CC, MC and MCC are discussed. The state of art mobile cloud computation offloading framework and decision strategies are presented as well.

To support such a mobility, virtualization is the most important enabling technology. Thus, in Chapter 2, we provide a comprehensive view of existing virtualization solutions to support such a mobility. This chapter focuses on virtualization concept and technologies including computation, network, and storage virtualization. Several computer-based virtualization classifications will be presented. The first virtualization approach is based on a computer internal process model. The second classification covers most of virtualization techniques at a different level of implementation within a computer. The third classification discusses two types of hypervisors. Besides computer-based virtualization, lightweight virtualization will be discussed as well, including Docker and OSGi. Mobile device virtualization is one special type of virtualization to be presented, including BYOD and KVM over ARM. Popular virtual networking protocols will be presented, including L2TP, PPP, VLAN, VXLAN, GRE, SSL, and IPSec. Two storage virtualization types, block store and file store, will be introduced as well.

Finally, in the first part, Chapter 3 presents a survey of existing MCC service models. We will first review cloud service models, including Infrastructure-as-a-Service (IaaS), Platform-as-a-Service (PaaS), and Software-as-a-Service (SaaS), as well as their service examples. Then we will move to existing mobile cloud service models. We will discuss three scenarios, including mobile as service consumer, mobile as service provider, and mobile as service broker. For each scenario, we will present several use-case examples. In the end, we will discuss IoT that can connect an incredible diversity of devices and each device may serve a microservice that can be composed to a more complicated service.

In the second part of this book, we will focus on the current research and development of mobile cloud computing. In Chapter 4, we present a Personal On-demand Execution environment for Mobile cloud applications (POEM) [278] service framework to realize the functional collaboration feature. We will discuss design principles of user-centric mobile cloud computing. In addition, we will present POEM, i.e., a service offloading and composition mobile cloud system. The system design, implementation, and evaluation of the POEM system will be described in details. The POEM system leverages OSGi and XMPP techniques. The offloaded code is encapsulated in OSGi bundles and hosted in OSGi framework. The POEM system demonstrates three execution patterns, such as service discovery, service composition, and service offloading.

In Chapter 5, we provide detailed analysis and decision models on two-party (one-to-one) service offloading and multiparty (one-to-many and many-to-many) service offloading scenarios. This chapter will present several mobile cloud offloading models. Using them, the mobile cloud application is modeled as a directed acyclic graph where computation tasks as vertexes are connected by data channel as edges. The offloading objectives are usually saving mobile device energy or decreasing execution time. The offloading can be essentially modeled as an optimization problem. We will start from offloading to one virtual machine, then we will discuss offloading to multiple surrogate sites. In the end, we will present how to optimize the offloading objective in a continuous time domain.

In Chapter 6, several MCC application scenarios will be studied by focusing on how to use mobile cloud computing service offloading/composition approaches. We will first discuss the edge cloud concept and compare it with existing Internet clouds. We will then present examples of edge cloud platforms such as fog computing, Nebula, and FemtoClouds. In addition, we will present a mobile cloud computing service model based on microservices. The microservices solutions will be compared with existing SOA approaches. Micro-service architectural style will also be presented. In particular, a microservice pattern for IoT will be presented including microservices, API gateway, distribution, service discovery, containers, and access control. Three cases studies demonstrate microservices in three application scenarios: personal health management, smart building, and platooning of autonomous vehicles.

In the third part of this book, we will focus on security research and development in mobile cloud access control and Bring Your Own Device (BYOD) solutions. Particularly, in Chapter 7, we provide the foundation of ABAC, particularly, the presentation will focus on using Attribute-Based Encryption (ABE) as the building block to establish ABAC for mobile cloud computing. We will review the current state-of-the-art of ABE, present an ABAC reference model and the ABE-based ABAC realization. In addition, we will discuss how to use ABE for Information Centric Networking (ICN) naming scheme as a new mobile cloud computing networking solution. To manage attributes (or policies) across multiple administrative domains, we will present how to use an ontology-based attribute management scheme. Finally, we will present the secure computation offloading with ABE and a use-case study for an attribute-based data storage solution.

In Chapter 8, we present a resource isolation approach based on ARM architecture-based mobile devices. A BYOD solution based on KVM-based virtualization approach will be presented. The BYOD solution is implemented through KVM-based virtualization for ARM devices. Two essential components of this framework are hardware assisted virtualization and Open vSwitch. The presented BUOD solutions have three main features: (a) the host OS has hardware assisted virtualization enabled; (b) Open vSwitch is run on top of host platform; and (c) a guest OS can be booted using the bridged network provided by Open vSwitch. In the presented solution, an SDN remote controller can be used for managing and monitoring the network traffic, and achieve the functionality of an SDN network.

In addition to presented eight chapters in three partitions, four appendices are presented at the end of the book to cover additional learning materials related to the eight chapters, including an overview of mobile cloud resource management, our developed POEM mobile cloud programming and application running platform, the cryptographic constructions and proofs for attribute-based encryption schemes, and the BYOD implementation and guidance.

Bonus Materials and Online Resources

The book, in its printed form, has 8 chapters and 4 appendices, where additional support materials (for example, source codes and implementation instructions) for POEM and BYOD implementations are available at https://github.com/MobileCloudComputingCode and https://github.com/ankur8931/Secure-Mobile-SDN, respectively. The first site provides OSGi-based source codes of the implementation of POEM; and the second site provides source codes of the basic implementation of BYOD solution using KVM on ARM architecture. Both projects are open source and free for downloading.

Acknowledgment

The Secure Networking And Computing (SNAC) group is formed by graduate students who are working on various research and development projects in the areas of computer networking security, cloud computing security, applied cryptography, and IoT security, etc. SNAC hosts regular meeting for group members to share research results and discuss research issues. Many mobile cloud computing related work had been studied through SNAC meetings. The authors would like to thank all past and current SNAC members who had contributed to the research outcomes of our previous work. Special thanks to SNAC alumni: Bing Li (Google), Zhijie Wang (General Electric Research Laboratory), Chun-Jen Chung (Athena Network Solutions LLC), Tianyi Xing (Wal-Mart Research Lab), Zhibin Zhou (Huawei), Yang Qin (Facebook), Janakarajan Natarajan (AMD), Qingyun Li, Pankaj Kumar Khatkar (CAaNES), Zhenyang Xiong (Omedix), Ashwin Narayan Prabhu Verleker (Microsoft), Xinyi Dong (Amazon), Yunji Zhong (Microsoft), Kadne, Aniruddha (F5), Sushma Myneni (Microchip), Nirav Shah (Intel), Arasan Vetri (Garmin), Le Xu (Microsoft), Elmir Iman (Hassan 1st University, Morocco), Xiang Gu (Nantong University, China), Bo Li (Yunnan University, China), Zhiyuan Ma (UESTC, China), Weiping Peng (Henan Polytechnic University, China), Jin Wang (Nantong University, China), Aiguo Chen (University of Electronic Science and Technology, China), Jingsong Cui (Wuhan University, China), and Weijia Wang (Beijing Jiaotong University, China).

This book could not have been written without the days and nights hard-work from several SNAC members: particularly Bing Li and Janakarajan Natarajan who contributed their thesis work related to ICN, attribute-based naming, and ontology-based federation schemes; parts of BYOD solutions are derived from Ankur Chowdhary's thesis work; Duo Lu contributed his original thoughts of microservices for IoT, etc. The authors also gratefully thank other current SNAC members: Abdullah Alshalan, Sandeep Pisharody (MIT Licoln Lab), Yuli Deng, Adel Alshamrani, Qiuxiang Dong, Zeng Zhen, Bhakti Bohara, Shilpa Nagendra, Fanjie Lin, Oussama Mjihil (Hassan 1st University, Morocco), and Chunming Wu (Southwest University, China). One individual deserves special note – Sandeep Pisharody helped proof-read the entire book.

We are honored that Prof. Mario Gerla (UCLA) gladly accepted our request to write the foreword for this book. The first author also gratefully thanks him for his collaboration in organizing ACM MCC workshop and sharing research ideas of mobile cloud computing in the past few years.

The first author would like to thank the Office of Naval Research (ONR), the National Science Foundation, China Mobile, and HP for supporting his networking and security research.

The second author would like to thank SNAC members who had inspired him a lot through discussions, seminars, and project collaborations, and he would like to thank the following people for their valuable interactions: Chun-Jen Chung, Yuli Deng, Abdullah Alshalan, Ankur Chowdhary, Sandeep Pisharody, Duo Lu, Fanjie Lin, Weijia Wang, Bing Li, Zhijie Wang, Pankaj Kumar Khatkar, Tianyi Xing, Le Xu, Xinyi Dong, Yunji Zhong, Yang Qin, Bo Li, Zhiyuan Ma, Jingsong Cui. Over the years, many friends and colleagues have provided him very helpful suggestions, insightful comments, support and encouragement during his PhD journey. He would like to thank Yiming Jing, Guohua Hu, Yang Cao, Jingchao Sun, Shaobo Zhang, Xiaowen Gong, Mengyuan Zhang, Kerem Demirtas, Jane Perera, Wei Zhou, and Ahmet Altay.

It has been a pleasure to work with Brian Romer, Amy Invernizzi, and Charlotte Kent of Morgan Kaufmann Publishers/Elsevier. From the initial proposal of the book to final production, they provided guidance in many ways, not to mention the occasional reminders and patience due to our delay. We appreciate their patience with us during the final stages of the manuscript preparation.

Our immediate family members suffered the most during our long hours of being glued to our laptops. Throughout the entire duration, they provided all sorts of support, entertainment, and "distractions":-) Dijiang would like to thank his wife, Lu, and their son Alexander and daughter Sarah, for love and patience, and for enduring this route. He would also like to thank his father Biyao and mother Zhenfen, brother Dihang for not being able to call them regularly and postponed several trips to China to have a family reunion. He would also like to acknowledge his family members, Shan and Yicheng. Finally, he would like to thank his many friends for numerous support.

Dijiang Huang
Tempe, Arizona, USA

Huijun Wu
San Francisco, CA, USA

PART 1

Mobile Cloud Computing Foundation

After the Millennium, witnessed by milestone events such as Amazon's Elastic Computing Cloud (EC2) service online in 2006, Utility Computing (2007), and a glut of active parties in the increasingly popular field of Cloud Computing (2008), etc., today, Cloud Computing generates over 100 million matches on Google. The scope of Cloud Computing grew from simple infrastructure services such as storage and calculation resources to include applications. However, this meant that forerunners such as application service providing and Software-as-a-Service (SaaS) would also henceforth be included under the designation of Cloud Computing.

At the bottom of these developments was the eventual shifting of IT services away from local computers to the Internet or, generally speaking, in networks. Eventually, Cloud Computing realized an idea that had already been hit upon by Sun Microsystems long before the Cloud Computing hype, i.e., *The network will be the computer.*

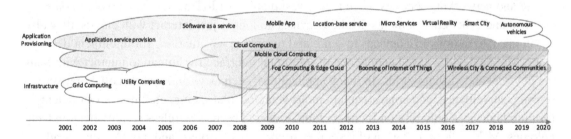

History of Cloud Computing.

As shown in the above figure, existing technology such as grid computing, utility computing or adaptive computing marks the infrastructure path leading to Cloud Computing; application service providing and SaaS signifies the growth towards provision of programmes.

In present discussions about Cloud Computing, it is often ignored that high-performance networks represent an essential basis of the cloud construct. Consequently, the starting point of

Cloud Computing would have to be linked with the development of the Internet. The various accesses to and views of Cloud Computing, and its respective origins led to differing definitions and to its strongly diverging public perception.

Cloud computing, including its offspring Mobile Cloud Computing (MCC), Fog Computing, Edge Clouds, etc., has a strong technical feature, known as "on-demand computing", which is a kind of Internet- and mobile-based computing, where shared resources, data and information are provided to computers, mobiles, and other devices such as Internet of Things (IOT) on-demand. It is a model for enabling ubiquitous, on-demand access to a shared pool of configurable computing, storage, and networking resources. Cloud computing, storage, and networking solutions provide users and enterprises with various capabilities to store and process their data in third-party data centers. MCC emerged with the proliferation of smart mobile devices 3/4/5G and ubiquitously accessible WiFi networks, and it was originally promoted by enabling cloud computing applications for mobile devices. Later Fog Computing and Edge Clouds target at establishing cloud services by harvesting edge networking devices, mobile devices, and IoT devices with a short communication distance, in which they mostly communicate through direct wireless communication channels and highly rely location-based services.

Recently, MCC has been evolved into a new paradigm compared to traditional Internet clouds, where MCC devices become more distributed and heterogeneous including not only high performance smart mobile devices but also lightweight IoT devices in home, vehicles, shopping centers, grocery stores, working places, etc. It brings out new challenges, especially for computing and networking services when facing vast number of IoT devices spread out in our physical and cyber environments. Mobile devices no longer just interact with clouds, they also can connect to various IoT devices to sense and recognize its situations for intelligent decisions. Mobile devices have become one of important interface for human to interact with both the physical and virtual worlds. In many applications, such as virtual reality, collaborative sensing, surveillance, and control, autonomous vehicles' platooning, etc., it is not sufficient for mobile devices only rely on Internet cloud. Powered by new wireless communication technologies, MCC relies on sharing of resources from Internet clouds, and neighboring mobile, sensing, computing, and storage devices, to achieve coherence and economies of scale, break barriers among different service communities, similar to a utility (like the electricity grid), however, over a heterogeneous networking environment. If we consider that each (or collective) IoT device provides a microservice, at the foundation of MCC is the broader concept of converged infrastructure and shared services.

In the first part of this book, we will focus on the foundation of MCC. Particularly, we first present concepts of MCC in Chapter 1, covering definitions, taxonomy, and applications of MCC. The definition of "Mobile" in MCC has also transited from its original meaning from

"Mobile Device" to "mobile capability/features" in modern mobile devices involved services/applications, such as software, physical resource, location, service composition, etc., all can be "mobile" to meet an MCC application's need. To support such a mobility, virtualization is the most important enabling technology. Thus, in Chapter 2, we provide a comprehensive view of existing virtualization solutions to support such a mobility. Finally, in Chapter 3, a survey of existing MCC service models is presented.

CHAPTER 1

Mobile Cloud Computing Taxonomy

Mobile cloud computing is not a simple math by adding mobile devices into cloud computing. Mobile cloud has extended its computation model from centralized to distributed, from Internet cloud to edge cloud, and from mobile devices to mobile services.

Dijiang Huang

MCC has originated from mobile computing and cloud computing, but there are significant differences between MCC and cloud computing, and between MCC and mobile computing. This chapter presents an overview of MCC, cloud computing, and mobile computing. The two pivot topics about mobile cloud are mobile cloud infrastructure and mobile cloud offloading, which will be discussed after the overview of MCC. Mobile cloud applications, including application programming platforms, will be presented at the end.

1.1 Overview of Cloud Computing

Cloud computing is a model for enabling ubiquitous, convenient, on-demand network access to a shared pool of configurable computing resources (e.g., networks, servers, storage, applications, and services) that can be rapidly provisioned and released with minimal management effort. The present availability of high-capacity networks, low-cost computers, and storage devices, as well as the widespread adoption of hardware virtualization, service-oriented architecture, and autonomic and utility computing, have led to a growth in cloud computing. Cloud computing has now become a highly-demanded service or utility due to the advantages of high computing power, cheap services, high performance, scalability, accessibility, as well as availability. Cloud vendors are experiencing growth rates of 50% per annum. After several years building-up cloud services, Amazon Web Services (AWS) has been historically generating profit and approached a $1 billion-a-year profit in 2016.

Based on cloud computing, companies can scale up as computing needs increase and then scale down again as demands decrease. Cloud computing allows companies to avoid upfront infrastructure costs, and focus on projects that differentiate their businesses instead of on infrastructure. Moreover, cloud computing allows enterprises to get their applications up and running faster, with improved manageability and less maintenance, and enables IT to more rapidly adjust resources to meet fluctuating and unpredictable business demand.

Mobile Cloud Computing
DOI: 10.1016/B978-0-12-809641-3.00002-8
Copyright © 2018 Elsevier Inc. All rights reserved.

In this section, we present several important definitions and concepts for MCC. We first present the definition of cloud computing, then we describe what mobile computing is, and finally, we summarize the terms and concepts of mobile cloud computing.

1.1.1 NIST Definition of Cloud Computing

The National Institute of Standards and Technology (NIST), which is an agency of the US Department of Commerce, gives its definition of cloud computing [200]:

> *Cloud computing is a model for enabling ubiquitous, convenient, on-demand network access to a shared pool of configurable computing resources (e.g., networks, servers, storage, applications, and services) that can be rapidly provisioned and released with minimal management effort or service provider interaction.*

The NIST definition of cloud computing is composed of five essential characteristics, three service models, and four deployment models. The essential characteristics are:

On-demand self-service. A consumer can unilaterally provision computing capabilities, such as server time and network storage, as needed automatically without requiring human interaction with each service provider.

Broad network access. Capabilities are available over the network and accessed through standard mechanisms that promote use by heterogeneous thin or thick client platforms (e.g., mobile phones, tablets, laptops, and workstations).

Resource pooling. The provider's computing resources are pooled to serve multiple consumers using a multitenant model, with different physical and virtual resources dynamically assigned and reassigned according to consumer demand. There is a sense of location independence in that the customer generally has no control or knowledge over the exact location of the provided resources but may be able to specify location at a higher level of abstraction (e.g., country, state, or datacenter). Examples of resources include storage, processing, memory, and network bandwidth.

Rapid elasticity. Capabilities can be elastically provisioned and released, in some cases automatically, to scale rapidly outward and inward commensurate with demand. To the consumer, the capabilities available for provisioning often appear to be unlimited and can be appropriated in any quantity at any time.

Measured service. Cloud systems automatically control and optimize resource use by leveraging a metering capability at some level of abstraction appropriate to the type of service (e.g., storage, processing, bandwidth, and active user accounts). Resource usage can be monitored, controlled, and reported, providing transparency for both the provider and consumer of the utilized service.

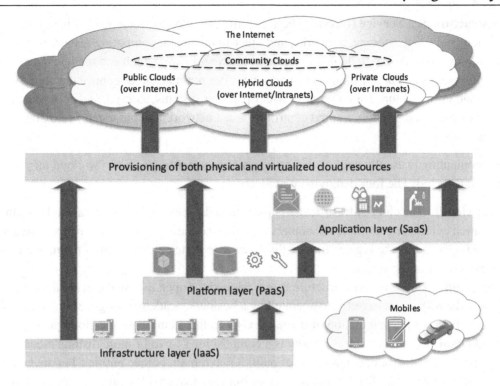

Figure 1.1: Cloud computing classification.

Cloud computing can be classified as presented in Fig. 1.1. The three service models categorize cloud computing into three layers according to the provided service types. The service models are:

Software as a Service (SaaS).   The capability provided to the consumer is to use the provider's applications running on a cloud infrastructure. The applications are accessible from various client devices through either a thin client interface, such as a web browser (e.g., web-based e-mail), or a program interface. The consumer does not manage or control the underlying cloud infrastructure including network, servers, operating systems, storage, or even individual application capabilities, with the possible exception of limited user-specific application configuration settings.

Platform as a Service (PaaS).   The capability provided to the consumer is to deploy onto the cloud infrastructure consumer-created or acquired applications created using programming languages, libraries, services, and tools supported by the provider. The consumer does not manage or control the underlying cloud infrastructure including network, servers, operating systems, or storage, but has control over the deployed applications and possibly configuration settings for the application-hosting environment.

Infrastructure as a Service (IaaS).   The capability provided to the consumer is to provision processing, storage, networks, and other fundamental computing resources where the consumer is able to deploy and run arbitrary software, which can include operating systems and applications. The consumer does not manage or control the underlying cloud infrastructure but has control over operating systems, storage, and deployed applications; and possibly limited control of select networking components (e.g., host firewalls).

Cloud computing is usually deployed in four scenarios according to how the cloud infrastructure is constructed. The four deployment models are:

Private cloud.   The cloud infrastructure is provisioned for exclusive use by a single organization comprising multiple consumers (e.g., business units). It may be owned, managed, and operated by the organization, a third party, or some combination of them, and it may exist on or off premises.

Public cloud.   The cloud infrastructure is provisioned for open use by the general public. It may be owned, managed, and operated by a business, academic, or government organization, or some combination of them. It exists on the premises of the cloud provider.

Hybrid cloud.   The cloud infrastructure is a composition of two or more distinct cloud infrastructures (private, community, or public) that remain unique entities, but are bound together by standardized or proprietary technology that enables data and application portability (e.g., cloud bursting for load balancing between clouds).

Community cloud.   The cloud infrastructure is provisioned for exclusive use by a specific community of consumers from organizations that have shared concerns (e.g., mission, security requirements, policy, and compliance considerations). It may be owned, managed, and operated by one or more of the organizations in the community, a third party, or some combination of them, and it may exist on or off premises.

1.1.2 Mobile Computing

The idea of mobile computing has only been around since the 1990s. Since then, mobile computing has evolved from two-way radios that use large antennas to communicate simple messages to today's mobile phones that can do almost everything a regular computer does. People cannot go to their local Starbucks and not see a laptop linked up to a hot-spot WiFi network. Two-way radios used by police officers were also considered mobile technology, but now, it means that human associated or operated mobile devices can connect wirelessly to the Internet or to a private network almost anywhere. As long as a person has one of the devices capable of wirelessly accessing the Internet, he/she is capable of participating in mobile computing. Today, smart phones and tablets are becoming the main approach to conveniently

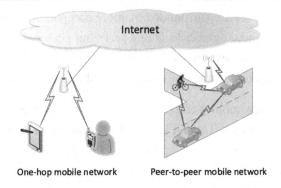

Figure 1.2: Networking examples of mobile computing.

access the Internet; they have been developed for mobile computing and have taken over the wireless industry.

WiFi network is the most popular wireless access technology, supporting one-hop mobility between mobile devices and stationary access points as shown in Fig. 1.2. The portable and smart mobile devices have changed computing world dramatically, from huge machines that could not do much more than word processing to tiny handheld devices. It offers the opportunity to bring people together and give everyone access to a greater wealth of information and knowledge, and to share their knowledge with others. Peer-to-Peer (P2P) mobile ad hoc network has been promoted in military application scenarios; however, recent booming of Vehicle-to-Vehicle (V2V), communication solutions introduced P2P wireless networking solutions into civilian uses. Mobile computing can be generally defined as follows:

> *Mobile computing focuses on device mobility and context awareness considering networking and mobile resource/data access. Mobile computing applications usually rely on mobile devices to create, access, process, store, and communicate information without being constrained to a single location. Mobile computing usually considers similar types of mobile devices that offers many otherwise unattainable benefits to organizations that choose to integrate it into their fixed information system.*

During the past three decades, mobile computing has expanded from being primarily technical to now also being about usability, usefulness, and user experience. This has led to the birth of the vibrant area of mobile interaction design at the intersection between mobile computing, social sciences, human-computer interaction, industrial design, and user experience design, among others. Mobile computing is a significant contributor to the pervasiveness of computing resources in modern western civilization. In concert with the proliferation of stationary and embedded computer technology throughout society, mobile devices such as cell phones and other handheld or wearable computing technologies have created a state of ubiquitous and pervasive computing where we are surrounded by more computational devices than people. Enabling us to orchestrate these devices to fit and serve our personal and working lives is a huge challenge for technology developers, and "as a consequence of pervasive computing, interaction design is poised to become one of the main liberal arts of the 21st century" [166].

From this angle, we can view mobile computing as the root of pervasive computing and even today's popular IoT technologies. Thus, it is important to understand the difference between mobile computing, pervasive computing, and IoT technologies. We can also view IoT applications as extensions of using mobile computing solutions, in which devices are heterogeneous (e.g., mobile vs. stationary, computer-grade smart phones vs. lightweight sensors), and they may belong to different administrative domains, where their computation and networking models are more distributed or decentralized, and the scale of the IoT system can be much larger than mobile computing application scenarios.

From the functionality and application per se, the history of mobile computing can be divided into a number of eras, or waves [166], each characterized by a particular technological focus, interaction design trends, and by leading to fundamental changes in the design and use of mobile devices. Thus, the history of mobile computing has, so far, entailed seven particularly important waves. Although not strictly sequential, they provide a good overview of the legacy on which current mobile computing research and design is built:

Portability. The era of focus on portability was about reducing the size of hardware to enable the creation of computers that could be physically moved around relatively easily.

Miniaturization. Miniaturization was about creating new and significantly smaller mobile form factors that allowed the use of personal mobile devices while on the move.

Connectivity. Connectivity was about developing devices and applications that allowed users to be online and communicate via wireless data networks while on the move.

Convergence. Convergence was about integrating emerging types of digital mobile devices, such as smart phones, music players, cameras, games, etc., into hybrid devices.

Divergence. Divergence took an opposite approach to interaction design by promoting information appliances with specialized functionality rather than generalized ones.

Applications. The latest wave of applications is about developing matter and substance for use and consumption on mobile devices, and making access to this fun or functional interactive application content easy and enjoyable.

Digital ecosystems (e.g., IoT). Finally, the emerging wave of digital ecosystems is about the larger wholes of pervasive and interrelated technologies that interactive mobile systems are increasingly becoming a part of.

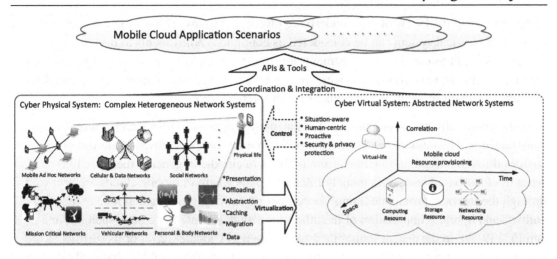

Figure 1.3: Mobile cloud computing: a view of virtual and physical world interactions.

1.1.3 Mobile Cloud Computing

Mobile Cloud Computing (MCC) is initially built on concepts of cloud computing and mobile computing, where it relies on wireless networks to bring rich computational resources to mobile users. The goal of MCC is to enable execution of rich mobile applications on a plethora of mobile devices, with a rich user experience. MCC provides business opportunities for mobile network operators as well as cloud providers. For example, from a business aspect, people usually consider MCC as "*a rich mobile computing technology that leverages unified elastic resources of varied clouds and network technologies toward unrestricted functionality, storage, and mobility to serve a multitude of mobile devices anywhere, anytime through the Internet, regardless of heterogeneous environments and platforms based on the pay-as-you-use principle.*" This definition is a combination of cloud computing and mobile computing by describing MCC's service features focusing on how mobile devices acquire and then use cloud computing based services through mobile networks.

Traditional client–server type of service model considers a thin client device requiring services from a powerful server. When replacing the powerful server with a cloud, the computation paradigm is not fundamentally changed, where the resource provisioning approach is based on cloud computing technologies. In the new paradigm of MCC, we can view the computing model as a virtual–physical interactive model, where the virtualized system and the physical system are interactively providing services to each other, which is shown in Fig. 1.3. The virtual system can be simply viewed as a mobile cloud application built on interfaces and APIs virtualized on top of a physical system composed by computing, networking, and storage devices, and humans. Through virtualization and abstraction approaches, the virtual system is a simplified view of their underlying physical systems. The interactions between virtual and physical system can be considered as continuous adjustments to best serve the humans' need. Physical system adjustments are changes such as location, protocols, communications methods, networking, services, etc., and the humans' need can also be changed due to changes of their location and job functions (or interests), etc.

Researchers usually use a computational augmentation approach, by which resource-constrained mobile devices can utilize computational resources of varied cloud-based resources through offloading functions from mobiles to clouds. In general, there are four types of cloud-based resources, namely Internet clouds where immobile clouds are accessed through the Internet, proximate immobile computing entities, proximate mobile computing entities, and hybrid (combination of the other three models). Internet clouds such as Amazon EC2 [9] are in the distant immobile groups, whereas Cloudlet [237] or its surrogates are members of proximate immobile computing entities. Smartphones, tablets, handheld devices, and wearable computing devices are part of the third group of cloud-based resources, which is proximate mobile computing entities.

In the MCC landscape, an amalgam of mobile computing, cloud computing, and communication networks (to augment smartphones) creates several complex challenges such as mobile computation offloading, seamless connectivity, long WAN latency, mobility management, context-processing, energy constraint, vendor/data lock-in, security and privacy, elasticity that hinder MCC success and adoption. As shown in Fig. 1.4, although significant research and development in MCC is available in the literature, efforts in the following domains still need significant investigation:

- *Situation-awareness issues.* Situation-aware computing possesses inseparable traits of contemporary handheld computers. To achieve the vision of mobile computing among heterogeneous converged networks and computing devices, designing resource-efficient, use-behavior sensing, and secure/privacy-aware MCC application running environment is an essential need.
- *Architectural issues.* A reference architecture for heterogeneous MCC environment is a crucial requirement for unleashing the power of mobile computing towards unrestricted ubiquitous computing. A current trend is to transit from a cloud- and network-centric service model to a user-centric model, where situation-awareness on real-time sensing and supporting users' need is the key factor to make MCC applications success.
- *Function and service migration issues.* Executing resource-intensive mobile application via function/service offloading involves encapsulation of functions and services, and migrating them from mobiles to the cloud or other mobiles, which is a challenging task due to additional overhead of deploying, managing, and interfacing for different application/service providers.

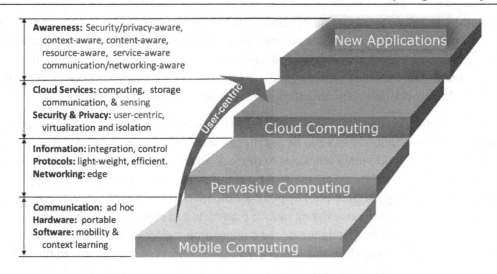

Awareness: Security/privacy-aware, context-aware, content-aware, resource-aware, service-aware communication/networking-aware

Cloud Services: computing, storage communication, & sensing
Security & Privacy: user-centric, virtualization and isolation

Information: integration, control
Protocols: light-weight, efficient.
Networking: edge

Communication: ad hoc
Hardware: portable
Software: mobility & context learning

New Applications

Cloud Computing

Pervasive Computing

Mobile Computing

User-centric

Figure 1.4: Mobile cloud computing technologies.

- *Energy-efficient transmission.* MCC requires frequent transmissions between cloud platform and mobile devices, due to the stochastic nature of wireless networks, the transmission protocol should be carefully designed.
- *Mobile communication congestion issues.* Mobile data traffic is tremendously hiking by ever increasing mobile user demands for exploiting cloud resources, which impact on mobile network operators and demand future efforts to enable smooth communication between mobile and cloud endpoints.
- *Trust, security, and privacy issues.* Trust is an essential factor for the success of the burgeoning MCC paradigm. The challenge is how to enable mobile devices and cloud services to collaboratively build new MCC applications by composing resource, functions, and services. Federated identity administration and management (IDM) should be established for MCC applications. In addition, security and privacy sharing the similar challenge when running MCC application across multiple administrative domains.

1.2 Mobile Cloud Solutions

The mobile cloud technology has been growing for decades. One of the major aspects of the mobile cloud technologies is infrastructure and framework. The mobile cloud infrastructure consists of the mobile devices and the cloud resources. Typically, smart phones are the common mobile devices which can host mobile applications and the cloud provides almost unlimited resources for the mobile applications to consume. Mobile devices can interact with the Internet cloud or a small cloud nearby the mobile device, e.g., Cloudlet [237], for caching the computation and communication. The mobile cloud framework, based on the mobile cloud infrastructure, provides the programming interface for the developers to build the mobile applications. The framework should handle the resource management including the mobile resource and the cloud resource, and usually provides the computation offloading feature. Some framework also provides offloading decision function.

The mobile application can run on both mobile device and cloud virtual servers since the application or the computation tasks can be partitioned into parts. The partitioned code and data are migrated to the cloud virtual machines to run and computation results are composed eventually and feedback to the user. Due to the various infrastructure and scenarios, the application partition and offloading decision is a key point for the mobile cloud application to earn benefit. This section first discusses existing mobile platforms and cloud-based mobile service platforms; then the offloading, migration, and composition concepts are introduced; existing work on how to partition applications and offloading frameworks are presented in the end.

1.2.1 Mobile Platforms

The mobile applications are developed on various platforms. Two platforms comprising the largest share of the current market are Apple iOS and Google Android.

Apple iOS

Apple iOS (originally iPhone OS) is a mobile operating system created and developed by Apple Inc. and distributed exclusively for Apple hardware. It is the operating system that presently powers many of the company's mobile devices, including the iPhone, iPad, and iPod touch. It is the second most popular mobile operating system platform in the world by sales, after Android.

Originally unveiled in 2007 for the iPhone, it has been extended to support other Apple devices such as the iPod touch (September 2007), iPad (January 2010), iPad mini (November 2012) and second-generation Apple TV onward (September 2010). Apple's App Store is the second largest app store. As of January 2017, the store had 2.2 million mobile apps available for download.[1] Games are by far the most popular category on Apple's App Store, accounting for about a quarter of all apps available on the platform. Business, education, lifestyle, and entertainment are also popular categories in terms of availability of apps. In late 2016, Apple announced that 140 billion apps had been downloaded from its App Store.

The iOS user interface is based on the concept of direct manipulation, using multitouch gestures. Interface control elements consist of sliders, switches, and buttons. Interaction with the

---

[1]   https://www.statista.com/topics/1729/app-stores/.

OS includes gestures such as swipe, tap, pinch, and reverse pinch, all of which have specific definitions within the context of the iOS operating system and its multitouch interface. Internal accelerometers are used by some applications to respond to shaking the device (one common result is the undo command) or rotating it in three dimensions (one common result is switching from portrait to landscape mode).

iOS shares with OS X (used by Apple laptops and desktops) some frameworks such as Core Foundation and Foundation Kit; however, its UI toolkit is Cocoa Touch rather than OS X's Cocoa, so that it provides the UIKit framework rather than the AppKit framework. It is therefore not compatible with OS X for applications. In addition, while iOS also shares the Darwin foundation with OS X, Unix-like shell access is not available for users and restricted for applications, making iOS not fully Unix-compatible either.

Major versions of iOS are released annually. The current version, iOS 10, was released on September 13, 2016. It is available for the iPhone 5 and later iPhone models, the fourth-generation iPad, the iPad Air and iPad Air 2, the iPad Pro, the iPad mini 2 and later iPad mini models, and the sixth-generation iPod touch.

Native apps must be written in Swift or Objective-C (with some elements optionally in C or C++) and compiled specifically for iOS and the 64-bit ARM architecture or previous 32-bit one (typically using Xcode). Swift is a new language for programming iOS and OS X apps that was first introduced in June 2014. Prior to Swift, most iOS apps were developed with Objective-C. Many existing apps in the App Store are built with it, and it's still possible to build apps with just Objective-C. In iOS, there are four abstraction layers: Core OS, Core Services, Media, and Cocoa Touch. The SDK contents is broken down into the four sets corresponding to the four abstraction layers.

Android

Android (from its former owner Android, Inc.) is a mobile operating system (OS) currently developed by Google, based on the Linux kernel and designed primarily for touchscreen mobile devices such as smartphones and tablets. Android's user interface is mainly based on direct manipulation, using touch gestures that loosely correspond to real-world actions, such as swiping, tapping, and pinching, to manipulate on-screen objects, along with a virtual keyboard for text input. In addition to touchscreen devices, Google has further developed Android TV for televisions, Android Auto for cars, and Android Wear for wrist watches, each with a specialized user interface. Variants of Android are also used on notebooks, game consoles, digital cameras, and other electronics.

Initially developed by Android, Inc., which Google bought in 2005, Android was unveiled in 2007, along with the founding of the Open Handset Alliance – a consortium of hardware, software, and telecommunication companies devoted to advancing open standards for mobile devices. Android applications ("apps") can be downloaded from the Google Play store, which features over 2.8 million apps as of April 2017, among which 2.6 million apps are free apps.[2]

Android's source code is released by Google under open source licenses, although most Android devices ultimately ship with a combination of open source and proprietary software, including proprietary software required for accessing Google services. Android is popular with technology companies that require a ready-made, low-cost and customizable operating system for high-tech devices. Its open nature has encouraged a large community of developers and enthusiasts to use the open-source code as a foundation for community-driven projects, which add new features for advanced users or bring Android to devices originally shipped with other operating systems. The success of Android has made it a target for patent litigation as part of the so-called "smartphone wars" between technology companies.

Android apps are written in Java programming language. The Android SDK tools compile your code along with any data and resource files into an APK, an Android package, which is an archive file with an *.apk* suffix. One APK file contains all the contents of an Android app and is the file that Android-powered devices use to install the app. App components are the essential building blocks of an Android app. Each component is an entry point through which the system or a user can enter your app. There are four different types of app components:

- Activities. An activity is the entry point for interacting with the user. It represents a single screen with a user interface.
- Services. A service is a general-purpose entry point for keeping an app running in the background for all kinds of reasons. It is a component that runs in the background to perform long-running operations or to perform work for remote processes. A service does not provide a user interface.
- Content providers. A content provider manages a shared set of app data that you can store in the file system, in an SQLite database, on the web, or on any other persistent storage location that your app can access. Through the content provider, other apps can query or modify the data if the content provider allows it.
- Broadcast receivers. A broadcast receiver is a component that enables the system to deliver events to the app outside of a regular user flow, allowing the app to respond to system-wide broadcast announcements.

A comparison of Android and iOS features is shown in Table 1.1.

---

[2] http://www.appbrain.com/stats.

Table 1.1: Application Programming Platforms

Features	Android	iOS
Developer	Google	Apple Inc.
Initial release	September 23, 2008	July 29, 2007
Source model	Open source	Closed
App store	Google Play	Apple app store
OS family	Linux	OS X, UNIX
Programmed in	C, C++, Java	C, C++, Objective-C, Swift
Internet browsing	Google Chrome	Mobile Safari
Voice commands	Google Now	Siri
Maps	Google Maps	Apple Maps

1.2.2 Cloud-based Mobile Service Platforms

In this section, we present some of current cloud service platforms that support mobile applications/services, in which a few application examples are presented to help readers get basic ideas of how a mobile cloud application works.

Google Services

- Maps is a Google satellite, which gives an in-depth accurate map of almost every city in the world. Google maps gives directions from how to get from one point to the other, figures out the quickest route possible, and gives an Earth/Satellite/Street view. Maps is available on browsers as well as mobile phones, allowing custom maps as well as saved directions to be saved on Google Accounts and later be accessed from all devices. The map itself is downloaded from the cloud server when the user browses it. If user would like to know the route to some destination, the cloud server calculates the best route and sends it to users' devices.
- Google Translate is an online translating tool, which translates text from one language to the other instantly for a user. The phone does not store all the language mappings. Words or statements are sent to the cloud server to be calculated to the target language, in which processes, the machine learning and natural language processing techniques, are used to enhance the translation accuracy, which cannot be achieved using the limited resources on smartphones.
- Google Docs are online applications, which allow people to create, edit, or view different types of documents. In addition to word documents, Google Docs also support Power-Point slides and Excel spreadsheets. Google Docs can be synchronized across all devices through a user's Google account. This allows the user to access his/her documents on any device as long as he/she can access Google Docs' server using a browser, and edit and share them without time and location restrictions.

The users collaborate on the same document, which requires the cloud to maintain the global document state and synchronize the document state to mobile devices.

Dropbox, cloud storage

Dropbox is a popular cloud-based storage service which supports mobile devices. It can help users store photos, docs, videos, and other files in clouds. Files in Dropbox are tracked with a version control system, each version is backed up, and users can access them using their mobile devices. It provides an easy approach to share a large file by sharing their Dropbox' URL even if a user does not have a Dropbox account. A Drobox client is required to be installed on mobile devices in order to manage files in the cloud. Compared to the desktop Dropbox client, the mobile version only downloads the files to mobile devices as the user instructs it to do so. When some files are added, deleted, or updated, new versions of files are synchronized to the cloud storage and all devices having the same Drobox account will perform an update. In this way, the new version is pushed to every device controlled by the same user and his/her file sharing peers.

The Dropbox API v2[3] is a set of HTTP endpoints that help your app integrate with Dropbox. The officially supported SDKs, which are programming language wrappers of the HTTP API, include .NET, Java, JavaScript, Python, Swift, and Object-C. The Dropbox HTTP API allows developers to work with files in Dropbox, including advanced functionality like fulltext search, thumbnails, and sharing. Dropbox also provides Business API that allows apps to manage the user lifecycle for a Dropbox Business account and perform API actions on all members of a team.

Office365, cloud based collaboration

Microsoft Office365 is made for company employees to work together, sharing similar features with Drobox and Google Docs. Users can share docs with their working partners right from a phone and tablet. Mobile version Office365 along with Microsoft Azure provides:

- Easily sharing documents with the cloud-connected applications;
- Tracking changes, comment and mark-up docs so that everyone knows documents' change history;
- Sharing documents with others by simply e-mailing an URL.

---

[3] https://www.dropbox.com/developers/documentation/http/overview.

Yelp, cloud based virtual augment

Yelp application has a feature called Monocle, which is an *applicationlication* of cloud-based virtual augmentation. When the user points the phone camera to one direction, the shops and restaurants are displayed as an additional layer in front of the background photo. The Monocle *applicationlication* captures the location and direction, fetches the data from the cloud, and organizes shop information on the photo, such as the notes to the real environment.

Internet of things, cloud mirroring

The Internet of Things (IoT) is the network of physical objects—devices, vehicles, buildings, and other items which are embedded with electronics, software, sensors, and network connectivity, which enables these objects collect and exchange data. The Internet of Things allows objects to be sensed and controlled remotely across existing network infrastructure, creating opportunities for more direct integration of the physical world into computer-based systems, and resulting in improved efficiency, accuracy, and economic benefit; when IoT is augmented with sensors and actuators, the technology becomes an instance of the more general class of cyber-physical systems, which also encompasses technologies such as smart grids, smart homes, intelligent transportation, and smart cities. Each thing is uniquely identifiable through its embedded computing system but is able to interoperate within the existing Internet infrastructure. Experts estimate that the IoT will consist of almost 50 billion objects by 2020.

The IoT objects cumulatively build the main sensing capability for mobile cloud computing and they have to be managed well for MCC applications. However, due to the large amount of objects, small systems cannot handle huge data collected through IoT devices. To address this issue, cloud-based storage services come into the picture. IoT objects can be continuously mirrored by using cloud-based monitoring and storage services; while individual or group of IoT device(s) can be virtualized and manipulated in the cloud for MCC applications, and then control or data operation functions can be executed on physical devices.

1.2.3 Mobile Cloud Offloading, Composition and Migration

In a mobile cloud, mobile nodes are usually restricted by their energy supply. Many mobile cloud computing solutions have been recently proposed to describe how to offload applications from mobile devices to surrogates, which usually have high computation capabilities with constant power supplies. One mobile cloud application scenario is when a mobile device offloads one or multiple applications to an Internet cloud. Another scenario is when the Internet cloud is not available, and thus a mobile device can offload its applications to other mobile devices to share the computation overhead. In this scenario, each mobile node in a mobile cloud can be considered a surrogate. Thus, in the rest of this book, we do not differentiate a

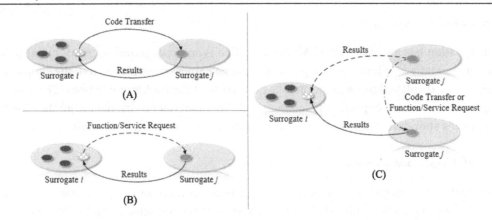

Figure 1.5: Mobile cloud terminologies: (A) Offloading, (B) Composition, and (C) Migration.

service provider's location, i.e., a surrogate can be either a mobile device or an Internet cloud server.

A mobile application can be further partitioned into multiple functions or service components. As a result, an offloading model can be considered a service oriented architecture, where mobile cloud services can be composed of multiple functions or service components provided by multiple surrogates. Thus, it is important to differentiate between offloading and composition. Additionally, another frequently referred to term, migration, is worth clarification from the terms offloading and composition.

In Fig. 1.5, we use several graphs to present the differences among three terminologies: (A) Offloading, (B) Composition, and (C) Migration.

Offloading. An offloading is defined as $e : x_i \Longrightarrow y_j$, where a mapping e is from an application component (or function) $x_i \in X$ to a surrogate $y_j \in Y$, $|X| = n$, $|Y| = m$, function x_i is transferred to surrogate y_j, and $\Longrightarrow$ represents the fact that x_i needs to be transferred to surrogate y_j for processing. After being processed, the surrogate y_j will transfer the results of function x_i back to the offloading requester.

Composition. A composition is defined as $e : x_i \longrightarrow y_j$, where a mapping e is from an application component (or function) $x_i \in X$ to a surrogate $y_j \in Y$, $|X| = n$, $|Y| = m$, function x_i is processed on node y_j, and $\longrightarrow$ represents the fact that surrogate y_j already has the software codes of function x_i. After being processed, the surrogate y_j will transfer the results of function x_i back to the composition requester.

Migration. A migration is a transfer function $T : y_j \xmapsto{x_i} y_k$, where a transfer function T is defined from a surrogate $y_j \in Y$ to a another surrogate $y_k \in Y$, $|X| = n$, $|Y| = m$, function x_i is

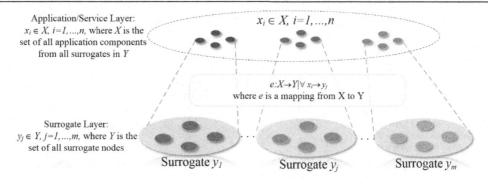

Application/Service Layer:
$x_i \in X$, $i=1,...,n$, where X is the
set of all application components
from all surrogates in Y

$x_i \in X$, $i=1,...,n$

$e:X \rightarrow Y | \forall\ x_i \mapsto y_j$
where e is a mapping from X to Y

Surrogate Layer:
$y_j \in Y$, $j=1,...,m$, where Y is the
set of all surrogate nodes

Surrogate y_1 Surrogate y_j Surrogate y_m

Figure 1.6: Offloading Model: No offloading case.

to be migrated from surrogate y_j to surrogate y_k and $\xmapsto{x_i}$ represents the fact that surrogate y_k may or may not have the software codes of function x_i. After being processed, the surrogate y_k will transfer the results of function x_i back to the application source.

Comparison of different service models

From the above definitions, we can see that composition is a special case of offloading that does not require software code transfer, while migration can be considered a change of surrogates, i.e., from surrogate y_j to surrogate y_k.

In Fig. 1.6, an offloading can be represented by a mapping from a set of application components $X = \{x_i\}_{i=1,...,n}$ to a set of surrogates $Y = \{y_j\}_{j=1,...,m}$. A subset of $S \subseteq X$ comprises a software application (or a service, and here we do not differentiate between an application and a service). Fig. 1.6 shows that there is no offloading present. The application components are processed on their corresponding computation hosts.

Fig. 1.7 shows offloading scenarios, where some of application components are processed on other computation hosts (i.e., surrogates). Thus, we can present offloading as a mapping between application components X to surrogates Y, which can be further classified into three scenarios: one-to-one offloading, one-to-many offloading, and many-to-many offloading.

One-to-one offloading – the offloading mapping $e : x_i \implies y_j$, where $|X| = 1$ and $|Y| = 1$.

One-to-many offloading – the offloading mapping $e : x_i \implies y_j$, where $|X| = 1$, $|Y| = m$, and $m > 1$.

Many-to-many offloading – the offloading mapping $e : x_i \implies y_j$, where $|X| = n$, $|Y| = m$, $n > 1$, and $m > 1$.

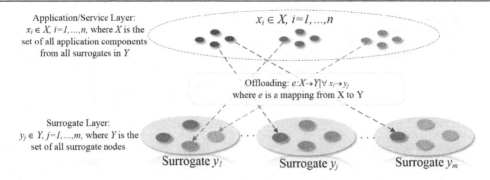

Application/Service Layer:
$x_i \in X$, $i=1,...,n$, where X is the set of all application components from all surrogates in Y

$x_i \in X$, $i=1,...,n$

Offloading: $e: X \to Y | \forall x_i \to y_j$
where e is a mapping from X to Y

Surrogate Layer:
$y_j \in Y$, $j=1,...,m$, where Y is the set of all surrogate nodes

Surrogate y_1 Surrogate y_j Surrogate y_m

Figure 1.7: Offloading Model.

1.2.4 Mobile Cloud Application Partition and Offloading Decision

Three aspects are generally taken into consideration to model the application partition problem:

- Device profiles. The cloud virtual machine computation power is usually several times better than that of the mobile devices, which contributes to execution time modeling. The energy consumption of the CPU and Radio modules on the phone are generally categorized as active and standby parts, which will be discussed in Section 5.1.
- Application profile. Mobile applications are usually modeled as a directed acyclic graph (DAG), where the vertices are the application modules and the edges are module dependencies or data flow. We will discuss the application model in Section 5.1.
- Environment profile. The connection between mobile devices and clouds plays pivotal role in the partition strategy. Especially the wireless connection such as WiFi or cellular connection is not always stable. We will discuss the application partition strategy in an unstable network environment in Section 5.2.2.

After modeling the application partition problem, which is generally an optimization problem, we may adopt deterministic and heuristic approaches to calculate the partition once. For a long time period, we may calculate the optimal solution by a series of partitions, which is discussed in Section 5.3.2.

The objectives of partition and offloading are usually improving performance and/or saving energy. This section collects the recent mobile cloud offloading strategies into Table 1.2.

Partitioning and execution of data stream applications

Yang et al. [285] studied how to optimize the computation partitioning of a data stream application between mobile and cloud to achieve maximum speed/throughput in processing the

Table 1.2:   Mobile Cloud Offloading Strategies

Authors	Deterministic/ Heuristic	Objective	Device profile	Static/ Dynamic
Yang et al. [285]	Heuristic	Maximize throughput	Yes	Dynamic
Abebe et al. [48]	Deterministic	Resource constraint	No	Static
Giurgiu et al. [116]	Heuristic	Minimize time	Yes	Dynamic
Sinha et al. [249]	Heuristic	Minimize assigned cost	No	Static
Kovachev et al. [171]	Deterministic	Minimize memory and time	Yes	Static
Smit et al. [250]	Deterministic	Annotated code	No	Static

streaming data. The authors claimed that it was the first work to study the partitioning problem for mobile data stream applications, where the optimization is placed on achieving high throughput of processing the streaming data rather than minimizing the *makespan*.[4] They proposed a framework to provide runtime support for the dynamic computation partitioning and execution of the application. Different from existing works, the framework not only allows the dynamic partitioning for a single user but also supports the sharing of computation instances among multiple users in the cloud to achieve efficient utilization of the underlying cloud resources.

Distributed abstract class graphs in mobile environments

Abebe et al. [48] presented a distributed approach to application representation in which each device maintains a graph consisting only of components in its memory space, while maintaining abstraction elements for components in remote devices. An extension to an existing application graph partitioning heuristic is proposed to utilize this representation approach.

Dynamic software deployment

Giurgiu et al. [116] developed a system that dynamically adapts the application partition decisions. The system works by continuously profiling an application's performance and dynamically updating its distributed deployment to accommodate changes in the network bandwidth, devices CPU utilization, and data loads.

---

[4]   The makespan is the total length of the schedule, i.e., time for all the jobs to finish processing. In most practical settings, the problem is presented as an online problem (dynamic scheduling), in which the decision of scheduling a job can only be made online, when the job is presented to the algorithm of executions as in other applications.

Fine-grained, multisite computation offloading

Sinha et al. [249] described algorithmic approaches for performing fine-grained, multisite offloading. This allows portions of an application to be offloaded in a data-centric manner, even if that data exists at multiple sites.

Mobile Augmentation Cloud Services (MACS)

Kovachev et al. [171] presented Mobile Augmentation Cloud Services (MACS) middleware which enables adaptive extension of Android application execution from a mobile client into the cloud. MACS uses a dynamic partitioning scheme, and lightweight as extra profiling. Resource monitoring is performed for adaptive partitioning decision during runtime.

Partitioning applications for hybrid and federated clouds

Smit et al. [250] described an approach to partitioning a software application into components that can be run in the public cloud and components that should remain in the private data center. Static code analysis is used to automatically establish a partitioning based on low-effort input from the developer. Public and private versions of the application are created and deployed; at runtime, user navigation proceeds seamlessly with requests routed to the public or private data center as appropriate.

1.2.5 Mobile Cloud Offloading Framework

A mobile cloud offloading framework has to solve two essential problems. First, the offloaded code pieces have to run on the surrogate environment. Second, the offloaded code has to be invoked by the original application. To solve the first problem, the offloaded code is supposed to be compatible in the original and the surrogate environment by synchronizing both environment or code translating. To solve the second problem, there has to be an RPC-like mechanism between the original application and the offloaded code. We will discuss the POEM system in Section 4.2, which implements a mobile cloud offloading framework by OSGi and XMPP based RPC.

Besides POEM, this section collects the recent mobile cloud infrastructure and framework into Table 1.3.

CloneCloud

CloneCloud [80] is a system that automatically transforms mobile applications to benefit from the cloud. The system is a flexible application partitioner and execution runtime that enables unmodified mobile applications running in an application-level virtual machine to seamlessly

Table 1.3: Mobile Cloud Frameworks

Framework	Context Awareness	Latency	Bandwidth	Programming Abstraction
CloneCloud	No	Low	High	No
ThinkAir	Yes	Low	Normal	Yes
MAUI	Yes	Low	Normal	Yes
Cuckoo	No	Normal	High	Yes
Weblet	No	Normal	High	Yes
Cloudlet	No	Low	Normal	Yes

offload part of their execution from mobile devices onto device clones operating in a computational cloud. CloneCloud uses a combination of static analysis and dynamic profiling to partition applications automatically at a fine granularity while optimizing execution time and energy use for a target computation and communication environment. At runtime, the application partitioning is effected by migrating a thread from the mobile device at a chosen point to the clone in the cloud, executing there for the remainder of the partition, and reintegrating the migrated thread back to the mobile device.

The advantage of this model is that when a smartphone is lost or destroyed, the clone can be used as a backup for the recovery of data and applications [162]. Moreover, CloneCloud augments execution of the smartphone applications on the cloud by performing a code analysis for application partitioning, taking into consideration the offloading cost and constraints.

CloneCloud also supports fine-grained thread-level migration that is more beneficial compared to the traditional suspend–migrate–resume mechanisms. Considering the shortcomings, the model is only capable of migrating at points in the execution where no native heap state is collected. Moreover, CloneCloud requires the development of cost model for every application under different partitions, where each partition is executed separately on the mobile device and the cloud. Therefore, the execution of partitions on mobile device for the development of cost model may consume extra energy. Furthermore, to fit all of the proposed augmentation types, basic and fine-grained synchronization is required between the smartphone and the clone that may be resource intensive in terms of bandwidth utilization and energy consumption. Nevertheless, the authors assume that the cloud environment is secure, which is not always the case.

In CloneCloud, the privacy of data and piracy of applications is of high concern from the clones' perspective. For example, if an adversary gets a clone of the smartphone from the cloud, then the clone can be easily installed on the same model of the smartphone. Therefore, the adversary may use the clones' data and installed applications that may lead to data privacy and application piracy issues.

ThinkAir

ThinkAir [169] is a framework that makes it simple for developers to migrate their smartphone applications to the cloud. ThinkAir exploits the concept of smartphone virtualization in the cloud and provides method-level computation offloading. Advancing on previous work, it focuses on the elasticity and scalability of the cloud and enhances the power of mobile cloud computing by parallelizing method execution using multiple VM images.

The main advantage of ThinkAir is that it takes into account the energy consumption when making the offloading decisions, and supports on-demand resource allocation and parallelism to reduce execution delays [162]. The model offloading decisions are based on the profilers, and it uses an energy model to estimate energy consumption. ThinkAir's energy model is inspired by PowerTutor [236] that accounts for all parameters of the supported profilers. Nevertheless, it does not require separate application servers for the distribution of the applications. Considering the shortcomings, ThinkAir does not support unmodified applications and requires programmer support for the demarcation of offloadable methods. Therefore, if any offloadable methods are left unmarked, then ThinkAir will not be able to offload those methods, which may affect the performance of the applications. Nevertheless, the profiling process of the model incurs an overhead on the smartphone because it consumes computation power, memory, and energy.

MAUI

MAUI [89] is a system that enables fine-grained energy-aware offload of mobile code to the infrastructure. Previous approaches to these problems either relied heavily on programmer support to partition an application, or they were coarse-grained requiring full process (or full VM) migration. MAUI uses the benefits of a managed code environment to offer the best of both worlds: it supports fine-grained code offload to maximize energy savings with minimal burden on the programmer. MAUI decides at runtime which methods should be remotely executed, driven by an optimization engine that achieves the best energy savings possible under the mobile device's current connectivity constrains.

Considering the advantages, MAUI provides a programming environment where independent methods can be marked for remote execution [162]. It uses dynamic partitioning of the applications to reduce burden on the programmers. Moreover, MAUI does not only focus on memory constrains of the smartphone but also considers the energy consumption involved in the offloading procedure. Furthermore, MAUI supports fine-grained method level offloading that can offload even single methods instead of offloading the whole software blocks. However, single method offloading is less beneficial compared to combined methods (multiple methods) offloading. Another weakness of MAUI is that if the programmer forgets to mark methods (for remote execution), MAUI will not be able to offload those methods. Also, MAUI saves information about the offloaded methods (for future decisions) and uses online profiling to create an energy consumption model. When new offloading requests are received, MAUI uses history data to predict the execution time of the task. However, the execution time of the task is input size dependent that is not considered by the MAUI. Therefore, the predictions of MAUI might be wrong, resulting in wrong offloading decisions. Nevertheless, the MAUI profilers consume processing power, memory and energy, which is an overhead on the smartphones.

Cuckoo

The Cuckoo [160] framework simplifies the development of smartphone applications that benefit from computation offloading and provides a dynamic runtime system. Cuckoo can, at runtime, decide whether a part of an application will be executed locally or remotely.

The main advantage of Cuckoo is that it supports partial offloading of the applications to the cloud and uses well known tools for application development [162]. Considering the shortcomings, Cuckoo does not support asynchronous callbacks and state transferring from remote resources. Moreover, no states are saved while transferring from local to remote execution or vice versa for which Representational State Transfer (REST) [226] may be required. Another shortcoming of Cuckoo is that it requires programmer support for the modification of applications. Furthermore, it lacks security features to restrict users from installing malfunctioned codes on the server and control illegal access to the resources. Nevertheless, the offloading decisions of Cuckoo are static and context unaware.

Weblet

Zhang et al. proposed an elastic application model that enables seamless and transparent use of cloud resources to augment the capability of resource constrained mobile devices. The salient features of this model include the partition of a single application into multiple components called *weblets* [292], and a dynamic adaptation of weblet execution configuration. While a weblet can be platform independent (e.g., Java or .Net bytecode or Python script) or platform dependent (native code), its execution location is transparent—it can be run on a mobile device or migrated to the cloud, i.e., run on one or more nodes offered by an IaaS provider. Thus, an elastic application can augment the capabilities of a mobile device including computation power, storage, and network bandwidth, with the light of dynamic execution configuration according to device's status including CPU load, memory, battery level, network connection quality, and user preferences.

Among the advantages of Zhang et al.'s model is a wide range of elasticity patterns to optimize the execution of applications according to the users' desired objectives [162]. Consequently, the offloading decisions of the weblets are based on a cost model that accounts for various parameters, such as energy consumption, application performance, and data privacy. Considering the pitfalls, the proposed prototype uses a simple weblet launch scheduling that does not truly reflect the effectiveness of the proposed cost model. The sharing of data and states between the weblets that execute on distributed locations are prone to security issues. Therefore, Zhang et al. [291] critically analyzed elastic applications for various security threats, such as authentication, trustworthiness (of the weblet containers), authorization, communication, and auditing. Nevertheless, the proposed model is also affected by data sharing delays (smartphone–weblet, weblet–weblet) for which data replication solutions may be required. However, the data replication may give rise to data synchronization and integrity issues.

Cloudlet

In this architecture [237], a mobile user exploits VM technology to rapidly instantiate customized service software on a nearby cloudlet and then uses that service over a wireless LAN; the mobile device typically functions as a thin client with respect to the service. A cloudlet is a trusted, resource-rich computer or cluster of computers that's well-connected to the Internet and available for use by nearby mobile devices.

Rather than relying on a distant "cloud", we might be able to address a mobile device's resource poverty via a nearby resource-rich cloudlet. In this way, we could meet the need for real-time interactive response by low latency, one-hop, high-bandwidth wireless access to the cloudlet. The mobile device functions as a thin client, with all significant computation occurring in the nearby cloudlet. This cloudlet's physical proximity is essential: the end-to-end response time of applications executing within it must be fast (a few milliseconds) and predictable. If no cloudlet is available nearby, the mobile device can gracefully degrade to a fallback mode that involves a distant cloud or, in the worst case, solely its own resources. Full functionality and performance can return later, when the device discovers a nearby cloudlet.

The main advantage of Satyanarayanan et al.'s model is that the VM based approach is less fragile compared to the process migration and software virtualization [162]. This approach is also less restrictive in terms of language-based virtualization, where systems are bound to support specific programming languages. Consequently, if the cloudlet is a cluster, then VM parallelism can be achieved by using multiple cores. Among the pitfalls of the model is that the VM synthesis process requires 60 to 90 seconds, which makes the technique unsuitable for real-time tasks. Moreover, the overlay extraction and compression that are performed on the smartphone require computation and consume battery power. Furthermore, if the smart-phone VM overlay is from an old version base VM, then the overlay may not find a compatible cloudlet. Therefore, update patches are required for the old operating systems to make the overlays compatible with all cloudlets. Although the patches may resolve the compatibility issue, the patches increase the size of the overlay. Alternatively, new replacement overlays may be required using update patches. The model also requires trust establishment schemes to keep the users secure from malicious VMs. Lastly, the cloudlets are not available everywhere, which makes the proposed model less scalable.

CHAPTER 2

Virtualization

Great design is a multi-layered relationship between human life and its environment.

Naoto Fukasawa

We have been lately hearing a lot about virtualization whenever there has been a talk about cloud computing. Although most of us may have ourselves used virtual machines (VMs) in the past to solve a very different purpose altogether, most of us are not really sure what virtualization is and why it is so beneficial! Virtualization is a technology that combines or divides computing, storage, or networking resources to present one or many operating environments using methodologies like hardware and software partitioning or aggregation, partial or complete machine simulation, emulation, time-sharing, and others. Virtualization technologies find important applications over a wide range of areas such as server consolidation, secure computing platforms, supporting multiple operating systems (OS), kernel debugging and development, system migration, network management, etc., resulting in widespread usage. Most of them present similar operating environments to the end user; however, they tend to vary widely in the levels of abstraction they operate at and the underlying architecture. In this chapter, we will present the basic concepts of virtualization, and then we will focus on the meanings of virtualization in computer, mobiles, storage, and network.

2.1 The Concept of Virtualization

Generally speaking, virtualization is visible only superficially in cloud computing services. Servers typically take only about a few millionths of a second to service each request to the cloud depending on the communication speed and the computation capacity of cloud servers. Given such a short amount of time for serving the request, the amount of time the server machine is kept up and running relative to the time spent by it servicing the requests is much higher. This clearly demonstrates that a significant amount of energy is wasted per server in the process of keeping the servers up and ever-ready to service requests upon their arrival. Moreover, in addition to energy cost, the equipment cost for single-purpose service for each physical system also contributes to significant investment waste. Additionally, the issue of using one server for a single purpose instead of sharing it for multiple purposes needs to be addressed. So how exactly can cloud computing solutions eliminate this waste and thereby maximize the profits? The answer to this problem lies in *virtualization*.

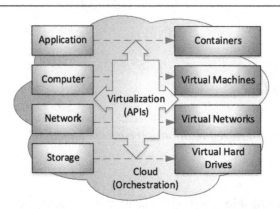

Figure 2.1: Virtualization overview.

Virtualization essentially means creating multiple, logical instances of software or hardware on a single physical hardware resource. The virtualization in a cloud system can be represented as shown in Fig. 2.1, where three main cloud computing resources, i.e., computing, networking, and storage, and applications can be virtualized through virtual machines, virtual networks, virtual hard drives, and containers, respectively. In a cloud system, various APIs are created to build a cloud orchestration layer to manage the virtualized cloud resources. This technique simulates the available hardware and gives every application for a cloud tennet running on top of it the feel that it is the unique holder of the resource. The details of the virtual, simulated environment are kept transparent to the application through various APIs. Organizations may use cloud computing technique to actually do away with many of their physical servers and map their functions onto multiple robust physical servers. The advantage here is the reduced cost of maintenance, reduced energy waste by repurposing multiple single-purpose servers, which had high CPU idle percentage. Virtualization allows IT management use fewer physical servers, making maintenance much easier and cheaper.

2.1.1 What Is Virtualization?

In computing, virtualization refers to the act of creating a virtual (rather than actual) version of something, including virtual computer hardware platforms, storage devices, and computer network resources. Virtualization is similar to abstraction but it does not always hide low layer's details. A real system is transformed so that it appears to be different. Moreover, virtualization can be applied not only to a subsystem, but also to an entire machine, e.g., VM, virtual network. Generally speaking, virtualization is about creating illusions, e.g., in Fig. 2.2, two files appear on separate hard disks, each of which is actually a partition on an actual hard

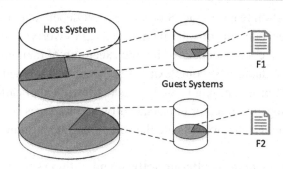

Figure 2.2: From single-node virtualization to cloud computing.

disk. Thus, a virtualized system's interface and resources are mapped onto interface and resources of another ("real") system; and virtualization provides a different interface and/or resources at the same level of abstraction.

Virtualization provides many benefits that are summarized as follows:

- *Resource optimization* – satisfying the real needs of users and applications so that the available computing power, storage space, and network bandwidth can be used much more effectively. Computers no longer need to be idle or perform below their capabilities because there are fewer connected users, or because the hosted application happens to be less demanding than the server can handle.
- *Server consolidation* – providing efficient usage of computer server resources in order to reduce the total number of servers or server locations that an organization requires. For organizations that own hundreds or thousands of servers, consolidation can dramatically reduce the need for floor space, HVAC, power, and colocation resources. This means that the cost of ownership is reduced significantly, since fewer physical servers and less floor and rack space are required, which in turn leads to less heat and lower power consumption, and ultimately a smaller carbon footprint.
- *Application consolidation* – decreasing the number of vendors, licenses, home-built applications can significantly reduce a system's complexity. Moreover, it will help replace legacy applications, and thus make it easier to find technicians with the skills (and desire) to support them.
- *Sandboxing* – separating running programs, which is a security mechanism in computer security. It is often used to execute untested or untrusted programs or code, possibly from unverified or untrusted third parties, suppliers, users or websites, without risking harm to the host machine or operating system (OS).
- *Multiple execution environments* – bringing multifaceted benefits such as isolating application functions for security purpose, providing redundancy for backup, load sharing,

and fail-safe application features, etc. Since a VM is independent and isolated from other servers, programmers can run software without having to worry about affecting other applications, or external components affecting the execution of their codes.

- *Virtual hardware* – reducing the complexity of software development to interact with hardware-dependent programming languages, and allowing application to interact with physical system using simplified or universal software interfaces.
- *Debugging* – making it easier to replicate the software/system running state for debugging purposes.
- *Software migration (mobility)* – offering software migration as several important cloud services are based on it. For example, live migration consists of migrating the memory content of the VM, maintaining access to the existing storage infrastructure containing the VM's stored content while providing continuous network connectivity to the existing network domain. The existing VM transactions can be maintained and any new transaction will be allowed during any stage of live migration, thereby providing continuous data availability.
- *Appliance (software)* – enabling software plug-and-play feature and working as appliances that can be easily enabled and disabled, and applied at any network segment or interfaced to existing services in a cloud-based service platform.
- *Testing/Quality assurance* – offering software developers isolated, constrained, test environments in the form of VMs. Rather than purchasing dedicated physical hardware, VMs can be created on the existing hardware. For testers, they can create unlimited number of user configurations on their physical machines and choose the most suitable configuration at each stage. This gives the possibility to experiment with potentially incompatible applications and perform testing with different user profiles. Moreover, testing will be hardware independent, portable, and backup and replication will be easy.

For computer virtualization, there are typically two types of system involved: the virtualized system is called a guest system, and the "real" system is called a host system. Multiple layers of virtualized host systems is also an option.

The host transformation to a (set of) different virtualized system(s) can be represented as an isomorphic mapping of the guest system to the host system. In Fig. 2.3, the state transition between the host and guest systems is presented, where the S_i, S_j are states in a system, e is an operation sequence modifying S_i to S_j, V is a function mapping guest states to host states S_i', S_j', and e' is an operation sequence corresponding to e. This model can be applied for both virtualization and abstraction, where the same isomorphism can be used to depict both of them; with the main difference being that virtualization does not necessarily hide details.

In essence, virtualization describes a framework that combines or divides "computing" resources to present a transparent view of one or more environments composed by hardware

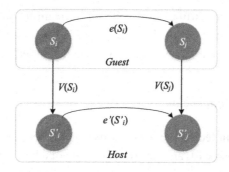

Figure 2.3: State transition mapping between the host and guest systems.

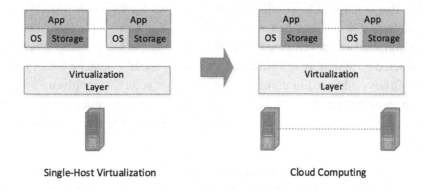

Figure 2.4: From single-node virtualization to cloud computing.

or software partitioning (or aggregation) with partial or complete machine simulation or/and emulation in a time-sharing fashion. In general, a virtualization is constructed by a mapping between the combined or divided "computing" resource that can be an *M-to-N* mapping (i.e., *M* "real" resources and *N* "virtual" resources). For example, VM is an *M-to-N* mapping, grid computing is an *M-to-1* mapping, and network multitasking is a *1-to-N* mapping.

As shown in Fig. 2.4, virtualization is generally realized by a "*Hypervisor*" or "*Virtual Machine Monitor (VMM)*" on a single physical server, which is a piece of computer software, firmware or hardware that creates and runs VMs. A computer on which a hypervisor is running one or more VMs is defined as a host machine. Each VM is called a guest machine. The hypervisor presents the guest OS with a virtual operating platform and manages the execution of the guest OS. Multiple instances of a variety of OS may share the virtualized hardware resources. For a cloud computing system, the virtualization layer is usually implemented through a system of software packages, such as OpenStack [220], which are used to virtualize clusters of physical servers and provision multiple VMs across underlying physical servers interconnected by high-speed networks.

In addition to computer system virtualization, the virtualization concept can also be presented within a host (or computer), on a network (e.g., virtual LAN), or on a networked system (i.e., multiple hosts for setting up cloud IaaS), which will be discussed in Section 2.5.

2.1.2 Abstraction vs. Virtualization

Virtualization is an important technique for establishing modern cloud computing services. However, it is easy to confuse with another overly used concept – *abstraction*. In short, abstraction is about hiding details, and involves constructing interfaces to simplify the use of the underlying resource (e.g., by removing details of the resource's structure). For example, a file on a hard disk that is mapped to a collection of sectors and tracks on the disk. We usually do not directly address disk layout when accessing the file. *Concrete* is the opposite of abstract. For example, software and development goes from concrete, e.g., the actual binary instructions, to abstract, e.g., assembly to C to Java to a framework like Apache Groovy [54] to a customizable Groovy add-on. For computer virtualization solutions, hardware no longer exists for the OS. At some level it does, on the host system, but the host system creates a virtualization layer that maps hardware functions, which allows an OS to run on the software rather than the hardware.

Besides abstraction, two additional concepts are also quite frequently used with the concept of virtualization: *replication* is to create multiple instances of the resource (e.g., to simplify management or allocation); and *isolation* is to separate the uses which clients make of the underlying resources (e.g., to improve security).

2.2 Classifications of Computer/Machine Virtualization

Computer-based virtualization is one of the most popular virtualization techniques. Based on the level of virtualization techniques, in the literature there are a few classification approaches and here we present them in the following sections.

2.2.1 First Classification: Host Internal Process Model

The first virtualization approach is based on a computer's (or machine's) internal process model as shown in Fig. 2.5. From the process perspective, a "machine" is a combination of OS and user level processes involving user-level logical memory address space assigned to the process, user-level registers and instructions for program execution, I/O part of machine visible only through OS, interaction via OS calls, Application Binary Interface (ABI) providing

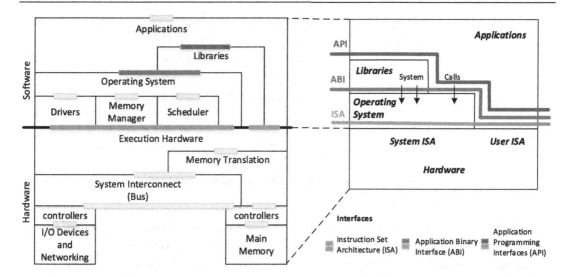

Figure 2.5: Virtualization classification based on host internal process models.

process/machine interface, etc. We can broadly classify virtualization based on three different levels of a machine's internal processes.

ISA (Instruction Set Architecture) based virtualization:

- division between hardware and software;
- subparts – user ISA which describes parts of ISA visible to applications, and system ISA which describes parts of the ISA visible to supervisor software. System ISA can also employ user ISA components;
- software compatibility – software built to a given ISA can run on any hardware that supports that ISA.

Application Binary Interface (ABI) based virtualization:

- provides programs with access to hardware resources and services;
- major components – set of all user instructions;
- system calls – indirect interaction with hardware resources, and OS operations are performed on behalf of user programs, which often includes security checks (w.r.t., access privileges);
- support for portability – binaries compiled to a specific ABI can run unchanged on a system with the same ISA and OS.

API based virtualization:

- abstracts from the details of service implementations;

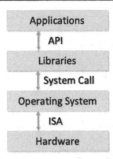

Figure 2.6: The second virtualization classification.

- usually is defined with respect to a High-Level Language (HLL) such as a standard library to invoke OS services, which are typically defined at a source code level;
- support for portability – where software using a given API can be ported to other platforms by recompilation.

2.2.2 Second Classification: ISA, System Calls, and APIs

The second classification broadly covers most of virtualization techniques at different levels of implementation within a computer. Conceptually a VM represents an operating environment for a set of user-level applications, which includes libraries, system call interface/service, system configurations, daemon processes, and file system state. There can be several levels of abstraction where virtualization can take place [79]: instruction set level, hardware abstraction layer (HAL), OS level (system call interface), user-level library interface, or in the application level, as shown in Fig. 2.6. Whatever the level of abstraction may be, the general phenomenon still remains the same; it partitions the lower-level resources using some novel techniques to map to multiple higher level VMs transparently.

Instruction Set Architecture based Virtualization

ISA-based virtualization is implemented in software, and it usually emulates the ISA in software where it interprets and translates guest ISA to native (or host) ISA. It emulates hardware specific IN/OUT instructions to mimic a device, and certain level of device abstractions are provided. A typical ISA based virtualization is QEMU [29]. It supports multiple OS running on top of it and it is mainly used for software debugging and teaching purposes. The drawback of ISA based virtualization is due to its inefficiency in handling exceptions, translating instructions, and thus the performance is not good compared to other types of virtualization solutions. Two examples of ISA-based virtualization are presented as follows:

- *Bochs* [175]. It is an open source x86 emulator which emulates the whole PC environment including x86 processor and most of the hardware (i.e., VGA, disk, keyboard, mouse, etc.). It also provides customizable BIOS, emulates power-up and reboot procedure. Bochs can run on multiple host ISAs such as x86, PowerPC, Alpha, Sun, and MIPS.
- *QEMU* [29]. It is a full implementation of virtualized ISA supporting systems such as x86, ARM, PowerPC, SPARC, etc. It uses *mmap()* as the Memory Management Unit (MMU) function to create a new mapping in the virtual address space of the calling process. QEMU is a very popular ISA-based virtualization solution and can be run as user-space only, which is useful for cross-compilation and cross-debugging.

Hardware Abstraction Layer (HAL)

In computers, a hardware abstraction layer (HAL) is a layer of programming that allows a computer OS to interact with a hardware device at a general or abstract level rather than at a detailed hardware level. HAL can be called from either the OS's kernel or from a device driver. In either case, the calling program can interact with the device in a more general way than it would otherwise.

Virtualization at the HAL exploits the similarity in architectures of the guest and host platforms to cut down the interpretation latency. Virtualization technique helps map the virtual resources to physical resources and use the native hardware for computations in the VM. When the emulated machine needs to talk to critical physical resources, the simulator takes over and multiplexes appropriately. For such a virtualization technology to work correctly, the VM must be able to trap every privileged instruction execution and pass it to the underlying VMM to be taken care of. Hardware-level VMs tend to possess properties like high degree of isolation, i.e., both from other VMs as well as from the underlying physical machine, acceptance of the concept, support for different OSes and applications without requiring to reboot or going through the complicated dual-boot setup procedure, low risk, and easy maintenance. Typical HAL based virtualization solutions include many popular computer virtualization solutions such as VMware [233], Virtual PC [130], Denali [273], Plex86 [174], user model Linux [98], Cooperative Linux [50], etc.

In the third virtualization classification presented in Section 2.2.3, we will present two of the most popular HAL-based virtualization solutions, i.e., parallel virtualization (or bare-metal, or Type-I virtualization) and host-based virtualization (or Type-II virtualization), in detail.

Operating System Level

We present virtualization at a higher level in the machine stack (see Fig. 2.6) to minimize the redundancy of the OS requirement in VMs described above. The VMs at this level share the hardware as well as the OS on the physical machine and use a virtualization layer (similar to the VMMs in VMware) on top of the OS to present multiple independent and isolated machines to the user.

OS virtualization helps create virtualized layer of software on the top of host OS that resides above the hardware layer. Unlike other virtualization, they create an OS interfaces for applications to run, giving the feeling of a complete OS for the applications. Each virtualized environment has its own file system, system libraries, process tables, and network configuration. Since they create a self-contained environment, they are also known as "containers." Therefore, creating the software emulation of an entire OS in a physical server is the essence of OS virtualization. The main disadvantage of OS virtualization is that it supports only one OS as base and guest OS in a single server. A user has to choose a single OS such as Windows or Linux. All the OS in the container should be same version and should have same patch level of the base OS. If the base OS crashes, all virtual containers become unavailable. The main advantage of OS virtualization lies in that it offers highest performance and highest density of virtual environment since OS virtualization provides least overhead among all types of virtualization solutions.

An operating environment for an application consists of the OS, user-level libraries, other applications, some system specific data structures, a file system, and other environmental settings. If all of these are kept intact, an application would find it hard to notice any difference from that of a real environment. This is the key idea behind all the OS-level virtualization techniques, where a virtualization layer above the OS produces a partition per VM on demand that is a replica of the operating environment on the physical machine. With careful partitioning and a multiplexing technique, each VM can export a full operating environment and be fairly isolated from one another and from the underlying physical machine. Typical OS-based virtualization solutions also include many popular computer virtualization solutions such as Jail [154], Ensim [161], OpenVZ [73], Virtuozzo [225], etc.

Library (user-level API) Level

In most computing systems, applications are programmed using a set of APIs exported by a group of user-level library implementations. Such libraries are designed to hide the OS related nitty-gritty details to keep it simpler for normal programmers. However, this gives a new opportunity to the virtualization community. Examples include Wine [39], LxRun [21], etc.

Application (Programming Language) Level

A traditional machine is one that executes a set of instructions as supported by the ISA. Using this approach, OS and user-level programs all execute on a machine-like application for

Table 2.1: Comparison of second classification

	ISA	HAL	OS	Library	PL
Performance	*	****	****	***	**
Flexibility	****	***	**	**	**
Easy of implementation	**	*	***	**	**
Degree of isolation	***	****	**	**	***

the machine. Hardware manipulations are dealt with either by special I/O instructions (I/O mapped), or by mapping a chunk of memory to the I/O and then manipulating the memory. So ultimately, it is a block or sequence of instructions that constitute the application.

The idea is to be able to create a VM at the application-level than can behave like a machine to a set of applications, just like any other machine. Then Java Virtual Machine (JVM) came into the picture, in which it has been widely used in many applications. JVM supports a new self-defined set of instructions (Java byte codes for JVM). Such VMs pose a security threat to the system while letting the user play with it by running applications like he/she would on physical machines. Like a normal machine, it has to be able to provide an operating environment to its applications either by hosting a commercial OS, or by coming up with its own environment. Besides JVM, Microsoft .NET CLI [205] and Parrot [27] also belong to this category. Container-based virtualization such as *Docker* is a similar approach; however, it provides stronger isolation and self-maintained memory and data, which will be discussed in details in Section 2.3.

Comparison and Summary

In Table 2.1, features such as performance, flexibility, ease of implementation, and degree of isolation are presented at a high-level.

A comparative study among presented virtualizations in the second classification is presented in Table 2.2.

2.2.3 Third Classification: Two Types of Hypervisor

As shown in Fig. 2.7A, a process VM is capable of supporting an individual process virtualizing software. For example, the VM can be placed at ABI, on top of OS and hardware. It emulates both user-level instructions and OS calls. As shown in Fig. 2.7B, a system VM provides a complete system environment that can support a "guest OS" with (probably) many user processes. It is placed between underlying hardware and conventional software, and it

Table 2.2: Comparison of second classification II

Type	Description	Advantages	Disadvantages
Emulation	A hypervisor presents a complete VM (of a foreign computing architecture to the host) enabling foreign applications to run in the emulated environment.	Simulates hardware that is not physically available.	Low performance and low density
HAL (Full)	A hypervisor provides a complete VM (of the same computing architecture as the host) enabling unmodified guests to run in isolation.	Flexibility in running different versions of different OS from multiple vendors.	Guest OS does not know that it is being virtualized; can incur a sizable performance hit on commodity hardware, particularly for I/O intensive applications.
HAL (Parallel)	A hypervisor provides a complete but specialized VM (of the same computing architecture as the host) to each guest allowing modified guests to run in isolation.	Lightweight and fast, near native speeds; demonstrated to operate in the 0.5–3.0% overhead range [59]; allows OS to cooperate with a hypervisor – improves IO and resource scheduling; allows virtualizing architectures that do not support full virtualization.	Requires porting quest OS to use *hypercalls* instead of sensitive instructions. The main limitation of parallel virtualization is that the guest OS must be tailored specifically to run on top of the VM monitor (VMM), the host program that supports multiple, identical execution environments. This especially impacts legacy closed-source OSs that have not yet implemented parallel virtualized extensions.
OS level	A single OS is modified in such a way as to allow various user space server processes to be coalesced into functional units, which are executed in isolation from one another while running on a single hardware platform.	Fast, lightweight virtualization layer. It has the best possible (that is, close to native) performance and density, and features dynamic resource and management.	In practice, strong isolation is difficult to implement. Requires the same OS and patch level on all virtualized machines (homogeneous computing infrastructure).

continued on next page

Table 2.2: (*continued*)

Type	Description	Advantages	Disadvantages
Library	Emulates OS or sub-systems via a special software library. Does not provide the illusion of a stand-alone system with a full OS.	Provides missing API for application developers.	Often performs more slowly than a native optimized port of the application.
Application	Applications run in a virtual execution environment that provides a standard API for cross-platform execution and manages the application's consumption of local resources.	Manages resources automatically, which eases programmer learning curve. Increase portability of applications.	Execution is slower than for a native code. Overhead of VM is incurred when compared to native code.

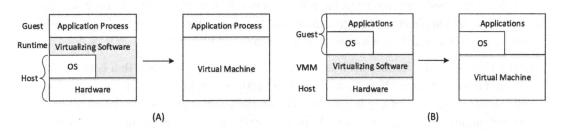

Figure 2.7: **(A) Process Virtual Machine and (B) System Virtual Machine.**

also provides ISA translation. Another alternate approach is using hosted VM, where virtualizing software is built on top of an OS.

A hypervisor (or VMM – Virtual Machine Monitor) is a software layer that allows several VMs to run on a physical machine. A "hypervisor" is the essence of the cloud technology that we all enjoy today. Nowadays, there exist many stable and feature-rich hypervisors: RetHat KVM, VMware, Microsoft Hyper-V, Oracle VirtualBox, and Xen, to name several popular ones. One of the main differences between hypervisor platforms is their classification as "Type 1" or "Type 2" hypervisor, which are presented in Fig. 2.8.

Type 1 hypervisors directly run on the physical hardware. They control the hardware as well as manage the VMs. Type 1 hypervisors are also termed bare metal hypervisors. Type 2 hypervisors run as an application on an existing OS (a.k.a., host OS), which is installed on the bare metal. Here, there is an added complexity of the guest OS calls needing to traverse via the host OS stack before they reach the hardware.

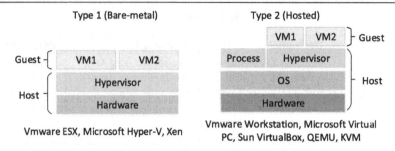

Figure 2.8: The third virtualization classification.

Type 1 Hypervisor

Linux KVM [1]. A KVM (kernel-based VM) is a GNU/Linux based project developed for x86 machines. It operates with a loadable kernel module named *kvm.ko*, which turns the Linux kernel itself into a hypervisor and thus VMs have direct access to the hardware. KVM also contains processor-specific kernel modules such as *kvm-intel.ko* and *kvm-amd.ko*. *Virt-manager* and *virsh* applications are generally used to manage the VMs created using KVM. *Virt-manager* provides a GUI, whereas *virsh* is a command line utility.

A commonly accepted misconception is that KVM is a Type 2 hypervisor that is hosted by the OS, and not a bare metal hypervisor. This is a persistent myth, but the truth is that KVM actually does run directly on x86 hardware. The interface makes it look like KVM is a hosted hypervisor running on the OS, but the VM is running on the bare metal – the host OS provides a launch mechanism for the hypervisor and then engages in a coprocessing relationship with the hypervisor. In a sense, it is taking over part of the machine and sharing it with the Linux kernel.

On x86 hardware, KVM relies on the hardware virtualization instructions. Using these instructions, the hypervisor and each of its guest VMs run directly on the bare metal, and most of the resource translations are performed by the hardware. This fits the traditional definition of a "Type 1," or bare metal hypervisor. KVM also can be packaged as a standalone hypervisor – like VMware ESX.

VMware ESXi [2]. We may think that VMware products are proprietary and not free but that's not always true. VMware's premium hypervisor product, named VMware ESXi, is available for free download. Though it's not open source, some of its components source software is available for download. However, a user can choose to work for 60 days with all advanced features enabled if the free version's serial number is not entered.

Xen [280]. The Xen Project is one of the leading open source virtualization platforms. The Xen hypervisor is licensed under GPLv2 [3]. Like many of its competitors, Xen is also available in a commercial form from Citrix. Oracle VM is another commercial implementation of Xen. The Xen Project platform supports many cloud platforms such as OpenStack [220], CloudStack [84], etc. The Xen hypervisor provides an efficient and secure feature set for virtualization of X86, IA64, ARM, and other CPU architectures, and has been used to virtualize a wide range of guest OS, including Windows, Linux, Solaris, and various versions of the BSD OS.

Microsoft Hyper-V [202]. Microsoft introduced Hyper-V as a competitor for many other virtualization products. It's available for free download from an evaluation point of view [203]. The free standalone Hyper-V server 2012 has all the features which are integrated in the Hyper-V role in Windows Server 2012 such as shared nothing live migration, fail-over clustering, etc.

Type 2 Hypervisor

Xvisor [8]. Xvisor is a Type 2 monolithic open source hypervisor that aims to provide lightweight, portable, and flexible virtualization solutions. It is supported on X86 and ARM CPU architectures. One major difference is that Xvisor is completely monolithic – so it has one common software for hardware access, CPU virtualization, and guest IO emulation. However, other virtualization technologies such as KVM and Xen are partially based on monolithic and micro-kernels, respectively. Partially monolithic hypervisors such as KVM are an extension of general-purpose monolithic OSs (such as Linux), which provide host hardware access and CPU virtualization in the kernel and guest IO emulation from an application running in the user space (such as QEMU). Micro-kernel hypervisors are usually lightweight micro-kernels providing basic host hardware access and CPU virtualization in the kernel, whereas the rest are dependent upon managing guests (such as *Dom0* of Xen).

Oracle VirtualBox [221]. Oracle VirtualBox is a Type 2 hypervisor that can run on Linux, Windows, Macintosh, and Solaris hosts. It is portable as it can run on a large number of 32-bit and 64-bit host OS. It's called a hosted hypervisor as it requires an existing OS to be installed. One good feature of VirtualBox is that VMs can be easily imported and exported using OVF (Open Virtualization Format) [26]. It's even possible to import OVFs that are created by different virtualization software.

VMware Workstation Player [36]. VMware Workstation Player is a Type 2 desktop virtualization application that provides a streamlined user interface for running and evaluating OS and applications in a VM on Windows or Linux machines. Its simple UI makes it the easiest way to deliver a virtual desktop to your employees, contractors, or customers.

Lguest [19]. Lguest is a very lightweight hypervisor built into the Linux kernel. The core of Lguest is the driver module (named *lg*) available from Linux kernel 2.6.23 and above. Lguest provides para-virtualized solutions for Linux. The *lg* driver module, during its initialization, allocates a chunk of memory and maps to the kernel's address space and a small hypervisor is loaded into this memory area. It also provides a virtualized I/O subsystem. It does not provide any of the fancy features other hypervisors do; however, it is a good option when you need to develop and test the kernel boot.

LinuX Containers (LXC)/Docker [5]. LinuX Containers (LXC) is an OS-level visualization method for running multiple isolated Linux systems (containers) on a single control host (LXC host). It does not provide a VM, but a virtual environment that has its own CPU, memory, block I/O, network, etc. It makes use of the Linux kernel's *cgroups* functionality, which provides isolated *namespace(s)* to run isolated applications. One advantage of containers is that they do not require a full-fledged guest OS like VMs. For container's details, see Section 2.3.

Linux-VServer [6]. Linux-VServer is an OS level virtualization solution. It's a soft partitioning concept technology based on security contexts. It basically creates Virtual Private Servers (VPS) that run simultaneously on a single physical server by sharing hardware resources. Each VPS has its own database account and root password so that it's isolated from other virtual servers.

Virtualization for cloud computing

As presented in previous classifications of virtualization approaches, there are several different breeds of virtualization, though all of them share one thing in common – the end result is a virtualized simulation of a device or resource. In other words, virtualization is generally accomplished by dividing a single piece of hardware into two or more "segments." Each segment operates as its own independent environment.

In Cloud Computing, the cloud determines how virtualized resources are allocated, delivered, and presented. Cloud computing is built on virtualization technologies. The relation between cloud and virtualization can be viewed as follows: virtualization can exist without the cloud, but cloud computing cannot exist without virtualization. Virtualization is not necessary to create a cloud environment, but it enables rapid scaling of resources in a way that nonvirtualized environments find hard to achieve.

As shown in Fig. 2.9, it presents the representation between the virtualization of a computer and the virtualization of cloud resources. It shows that both infrastructures are similar in terms of the resource management and control (CTL), and the difference lies in the scale of the management resource. The underpinning for the majority of clouds is a virtualized infrastructure (also called cloud orchestration layer), in which virtualization is used to establish a pool of infrastructure resources, which can also provide the basic building to enhance agility and flexibility. Existing cloud resource management solutions primarily focus on how to virtualize cloud servers' computing, networking, and storage resources.

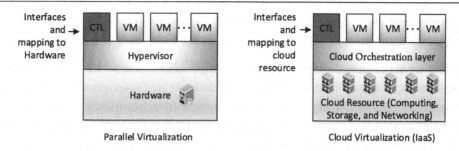

Figure 2.9: Parallel virtualization and cloud virtualization.

2.3 Lightweight Virtualization: Containers

The hypervisor-based virtualization, including emulation, full and parallel virtualization, consumes many resources since the guests have their own OS running, as shown in Table 2.2. What if the guests share the OS to save the guest OS resource consumption? OS level virtualization is a technique, recently gaining popularity, to host more guests on less resources. *Docker* [201] is one typical example of this type of virtualization. Moreover, some software packages provide containers to host client codes, which is library and application level virtualization, and which is much lighter and much more flexible. We will introduce *OSGi* [222] as an example of this type of container. We call the OS, library, and application level virtualization as containers. The key characteristic in all of them is that they share the host OS.

2.3.1 Docker: OS Level Virtualization

OS level virtualization is a server-virtualization method where the kernel of an OS allows for multiple isolated user-space instances, instead of just one. Such instances (sometimes called containers, software containers, Virtualization Engines (VE), Virtual Private Servers (VPS), or jails) may look and feel like a real server from the point of view of its owners and users.

On Unix-like OS, one can see this technology as an advanced implementation of the standard *chroot* [11][1] mechanism. In addition to isolation mechanisms, the kernel often provides resource-management features to limit the impact of one container's activities on other containers.

Operating-system-level virtualization is commonly used in virtual hosting environments, where it is useful for securely allocating finite hardware resources amongst a large number of

---

[1] A *chroot* on Unix OS is an operation that changes the apparent root directory for the current running process and its children. A program that is run in such a modified environment cannot name (and therefore normally cannot access) files outside the designated directory tree.

mutually-distrusting users. System administrators may also use it, to a lesser extent, for consolidating server hardware by moving services on separate hosts into containers on a server.

Other typical scenarios include separating several applications to separate containers for improved security, hardware independence, and added resource management features. The improved security provided by the use of a *chroot* mechanism, however, is nowhere near iron-clad. Operating-system-level virtualization implementations capable of live migration can also be used for dynamic load balancing of containers between nodes in a cluster.

Operating-system-level virtualization usually imposes little to no overhead, because programs in virtual partitions use the OS's normal system call interface and do not need to be subjected to emulation or be run in an intermediate VM, as is the case with whole-system virtualizers (such as VMware ESXi, QEMU, or Hyper-V) and parallel virtualizers (such as Xen or UML). This form of virtualization also does not require support in hardware to perform efficiently.

Operating-system-level virtualization is not as flexible as other virtualization approaches since it cannot host a guest OS different from the host one, or a different guest kernel. For example, with Linux, different distributions are fine, but other OS such as Windows cannot be hosted.

Docker's features

Docker is an open-source engine that automates the deployment of applications into containers. It was written by the team at *Docker*, Inc. (formerly dotCloud Inc., an early player in the Platform-as-a-Service (PAAS) market), and released by them under the Apache 2.0 license.

Docker adds an application deployment engine on top of a virtualized container execution environment. It is designed to provide a lightweight and fast environment in which to run your code as well as an efficient workflow to get that code from your laptop to your test environment and then into production. *Docker* is incredibly simple. Indeed, you can get started with *Docker* on a minimal host running nothing but a compatible Linux kernel and a *Docker* binary.

- *Docker* is fast. Applications can be *Docker*ized in minutes. *Docker* relies on a copy-on-write model so that making changes to your application is also incredibly fast – only what you want to change gets changed. A user can then create containers running your applications. Most *Docker* container take less than a second to launch. Removing the overhead of the hypervisor also means containers are highly performant[2] and a user can pack more of them into his hosts and make the best possible use of his resources.

---

[2] Performant is a word that was made up by software developers to describe software that performs well in whatever way you want to define performance.

- With *Docker*, developers care about their applications running inside containers, and Operators care about managing the containers. *Docker* is designed to enhance consistency by ensuring the environment in which your developers write code matches the environments into which your applications are deployed.
- *Docker* aims to reduce the cycle time between code being written, code being tested, deployed, and used. It aims to make applications portable, easy to build, and easy to collaborate on.

Docker client and server

Docker is a client–server application. The *Docker* client talks to the *Docker* server or daemon, which, in turn, does all the work. *Docker* ships with a command line client binary, *Docker*, as well as an RESTful [86] API. The "docker" command is run in daemon mode, which turns a Linux system into a *Docker* server that can have containers deployed, launched, and torn down via a remote client. The *Docker* command is run in daemon mode to control most of the *Docker* workflow and talk to remote *Docker* servers. You can run the *Docker* daemon and client on the same host or connect your local *Docker* client to a remote daemon running on another host.

Docker image and container

A *Docker* image is a template or a class that has all necessary files to create a container. The difference between an image and a container is like the difference between a class and an object. A class is a manuscript of what should be there without any physical existence; and an image contains what should be there without any actual access to any resources (e.g., CPU time, memory, and storage). A container is the object and it has physical existence on the host with an IP, exposed ports, and real processes.

A *Docker* image is a read-only template. For example, an image can contain an Ubuntu OS with Apache and web applications installed. Images are used to create *Docker* containers. *Docker* provides a simple way to build new images or update existing images, or a user can download *Docker* images that other people have already created. *Docker* images are the build components of the *Docker*.

A container is the physically existing collection of processes that uses the OS resources to implement a functionality. The *Docker* engine takes the image, adds a read–write file system on top, and initializes various settings including network ports, container name, identity, and resource limits. A running container has a currently executing process, and a container can be stopped (or exited to use *Docker*'s terminology). An exited container is not the same as an image, as it can be restarted and will retain its settings and any file system changes.

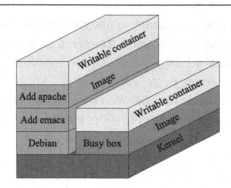

Figure 2.10: Docker *UnionFS* file system. (For interpretation of the colors in this figure, the reader is referred to the web version of this chapter.)

Docker union file system

Union File System (*UnionFS*) is a file system service for Linux, FreeBSD, and NetBSD, which implements a *union mount*[3] for other file systems. *UnionFS* represents file system by grouping directories and files in branches. *Docker* Engine uses *UnionFS* to provide the building blocks for containers.

A *Docker* image is made up of file systems layered over each other. Images can be layered on top of one another. The image below is called the parent image and an application can traverse each layer until reaching the bottom of the image stack where the final image is called the base image. Finally, when a container is launched from an image, *Docker* mounts a read–write file system on top of any layers below. The processes a *Docker* container can run and execute are shown as yellow boxes in Fig. 2.10.

When *Docker* first starts a container, the initial read–write layer is empty. When changes occur, they are applied to this layer. For example, if a user wants to change a file, then that file will be copied from the read-only layer below into the writable layer. The read-only version of the file will still exist, but now be hidden underneath the copy.

This pattern is traditionally called *copy-on-write* and is one of the features that makes *Docker* very attractive for building cloud services. This is because each read-only image layer is read-only and this image never changes; when a container is created, *Docker* builds from the stack of images and then adds the read–write layer on top; and that layer, combined with the knowledge of the image layers below it and some configuration data, forms the container.

---

[3] In computer OS, union mounting is a way of combining multiple directories into one that appears to contain their combined contents.

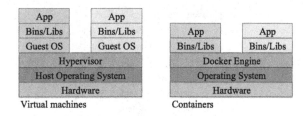

Figure 2.11: Virtual machines vs. Containers.

How is Docker *different from VMs?*

Containers have similar resource isolation and allocation benefits as VMs but use a different architectural approach, allowing them to be more portable and efficient as shown in Fig. 2.11.

Each VM includes applications, necessary binaries and libraries, and an entire guest OS – all of which may be tens of GBs in size. Containers include applications and all of their dependencies, but share the kernel with other containers. They run as an isolated process in *userspace* on the host OS. They are also not tied to any specific infrastructure, i.e., *Docker* containers can run on any computer, on any infrastructure and in any cloud.

2.3.2 OSGi: *Application Level Virtualization Library*

OSGi is another popular virtualized program running environment, which has been widely adopted. It is a framework for Java in which units of resources called bundles can be installed. Bundles can export services or run processes, and have their dependencies managed, such that a bundle can be expected to have its requirements managed by the container. Each bundle can also have its own internal *classpath*,[4] so that it can serve as an independent unit, should that be desirable. All of this is standardized such that any valid *OSGi* bundle can theoretically be installed in any valid *OSGi* container.

OSGi *architecture*

The *OSGi* specification describes a modular system and a service platform for the Java programming language that implements a complete and dynamic component model, something that does not exist in standalone Java/VM environments. Applications or components, coming in the form of bundles for deployment, can be remotely installed, started, stopped, updated, and uninstalled without requiring a reboot; management of Java packages/classes is specified

---

[4] *Classpath* is a parameter in the Java Virtual Machine or the Java compiler that specifies the location of user-defined classes and packages. The parameter may be set either on the command-line, or through an environment variable.

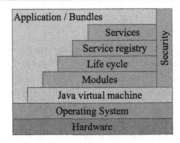

Figure 2.12: *OSGi* **Framework Architecture.**

in great detail. Application life cycle management is implemented via APIs that allow for remote downloading of management policies. The service registry allows bundles to detect the addition of new services, or the removal of services, and adapt accordingly.

Any framework that implements the *OSGi* standard provides an environment for the modularization of applications into smaller bundles. Each bundle is a tightly coupled, dynamically loadable collection of classes, jars, and configuration files that explicitly declare their external dependencies (if any).

The framework is conceptually divided into the following areas, as shown in Fig. 2.12:

- *Bundles* – Bundles are normal jar components with extra manifest headers.
- *Services* – The services layer connects bundles in a dynamic way by offering a publish–find–bind model for Plain Old Java Interfaces (POJI) or Plain Old Java Objects (POJO).
- *Services Registry* – The API for management services.
- *Life-Cycle* – The API for life cycle management (install, start, stop, update, and uninstall) of bundles.
- *Modules* – The layer that defines encapsulation and declaration of dependencies (how a bundle can import and export code).
- *Security* – The layer that handles the security aspects by limiting bundle functionality to predefined capabilities.
- *Execution Environment* – It defines what methods and classes are available in a specific platform.

OSGi *bundles*

An OGSi bundle is a JAR file that has the following features and capabilities [223]:

- It contains the resources necessary to provide some functionality. These resources may be class files for the Java programming language, as well as other data such as HTML files, help files, icons, and so on. A bundle JAR file can also embed additional JAR files that are available as resources and classes. This is, however, not recursive.

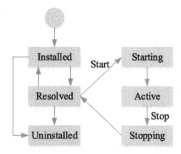

Figure 2.13: *OSGi* **bundle life cycle.**

- It contains a manifest file describing the contents of the JAR file and providing information about the bundle. This file uses headers to specify information that the framework needs to install correctly and activate a bundle. For example, it states dependencies on other resources, such as Java packages, that must be available to the bundle before it can run.
- It can contain optional documentation in the OSGI-OPT directory of the JAR file or one of its subdirectories. Any information in this directory is optional. For example, the OSGI-OPT directory is useful to store the source code of a bundle. Management systems may remove this information to save storage space in the *OSGi* framework.

With the installation of a bundle in the *OSGi* runtime the bundle is persisted in a local bundle cache. The *OSGi* runtime then tries to resolve its dependencies. If all required dependencies are resolved, the bundle is in the RESOLVED status otherwise it stays in the INSTALLED status. In case several bundles exist which can satisfy the dependency, the bundle with the highest valid version is used. If the versions are the same, the bundle with the lowest unique identifier is used. Every bundle gets this identifier assigned by the framework during the installation. When the bundle starts, its status is STARTING. After a successful start, it becomes ACTIVE. This life cycle is depicted in Fig. 2.13.

OSGi *services*

In the *OSGi* framework, bundles are built around a set of cooperating services available from a shared service registry. Such an *OSGi* service is defined semantically by its service interface and implemented as a service object.

The service interface should be specified with as few implementation details as possible. *OSGi* has specified many service interfaces for common needs and will specify more in the future. The service object is owned by, and runs within, a bundle, as shown by the dotted line

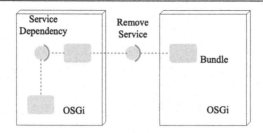

Figure 2.14: *OSGi* **services.**

in Fig. 2.14. This bundle must register the service object with the framework service registry so that the service's functionality is available to other bundles under control of the framework.

Dependencies between the bundle owning the service and the bundles using it are managed by the framework. For example, when a bundle is stopped, all the services registered with the framework by that bundle must be automatically unregistered.

The framework maps services to their underlying service objects, and provides a simple but powerful query mechanism that enables a bundle to request the services it needs. The framework also provides an event mechanism so that bundles can receive events of services that are registered, modified, or unregistered.

2.3.3 Comparison to Hypervisor Virtualization

Compared to hypervisor-based virtualization, the OS level virtualization or containers have the following differences:

- *Fast deployment* – The full VM starts in minutes, whereas the containers starts guests in seconds. The containers avoid initializing the guest OS, which makes the guests start much faster.
- *Less resource requirement* – Since the full virtualization allocates resources for each guest OS, it requires much more resources. On the other hand, guests in the containers either share the OS with the host or even no OS, like *OSGi*, thus, the resource consumption is much less.
- *Flexibility* – Some containers provide start and stop features, which is a lightweight operation to freeze and resume guests and keep the guest state in memory. The full VM freeze and resume function usually saves the guest state in the disk due to the large VM state image, whose cost is much higher than the containers.
- *Forensic* – The container's state is easy to access by the host, since guests share some resources with the host. Full VM state is much harder to get because the host has to interpret a full memory image and get to know the other OS state, which is not that easy.

2.4 Mobile Device Virtualization

Mobile device virtualization has become one hot research area recently and has been widely used. Bring your own device (BYOD) is one of widely used mobile virtualization solutions. In Chapter 8, we present such a solution on ARM-based mobile devices. (See Appendix D for detailed implementation and testing results.)

2.4.1 Bring Your Own Device (BYOD)

The proliferation of devices such as tablets and smart phones, which are now used by many people in their daily lives, has led to a number of companies, such as IBM, to allow employees bring their own devices to work, due to perceived productivity gains and cost savings. In order to achieve increased adoption and sustainability of BYOD schemes within the enterprise, mobile virtualization is rapidly becoming an attractive choice because it provides both employee and enterprise flexibility while addressing the privacy concerns of the user and meeting the organizations security requirements. On the other side of the ecosystem, the device makers and carriers will benefit from mobile virtualization because they will be able to more easily replicate the features found in various devices and also deliver more features at a lower cost. Enterprises that allow employees to use their BYOD devices must also put in place policies that govern how those devices will be used and how they will be managed while maintaining end-user flexibility [152].

BYOD is also called bring your own technology (BYOT), bring your own phone (BYOP), and bring your own PC (BYOPC), and refers to the policy of permitting employees to bring personally owned mobile devices (laptops, tablets, and smart phones) to their workplace, and to use those devices to access privileged company information and applications. BYOD usage is primarily driven by perceived enjoyment. The phenomenon is commonly referred to as IT consumerization.

Mobile separation techniques

A number of technologies for mobile separation have been developed over the last few years, but most of them revolve around two types of technology: hypervisor separation and container-based separation, as shown in Fig. 2.15.

Mobile separation via hypervisors provides the ability to run two or more instances of an OS on the same phone, thereby giving the ability to run personal applications and services on one OS and business services on the more secure OS. In the case of mobile containers, separation is achieved at the application level via the OS by any or all of the following: intercepting specific OS function calls, managing user permissions, enforcing certain security policies, and device management features.

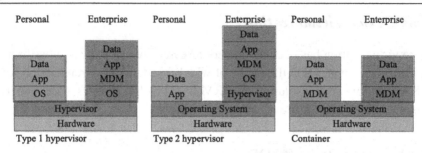

Figure 2.15: Mobile separation techniques [152].

Hypervisor approaches to mobile separation have the advantage of better protection from risks such as rooted phones, because a user rooting his personal OS instance would not put at risk the corporate OS instance. However, such hypervisor approaches will typically have a higher level of performance or battery impact on mobile devices and can also be more expensive to maintain because of the requirement to develop and secure an entire corporate OS image. Container approaches often have the advantage of a more seamless user experience, as some aspects of personal and business use can interact in ways that separate OS instances never could. The trade-off here is typically the need to manage the underlying OS instance to protect the application layer container from attacks at the root of the device.

2.4.2 KVM over ARM

Historically, the ARM architecture is not virtualizable, because there are a number of sensitive instructions which do not trap when they are executed in an unprivileged mode. However, the most recent 32-bit ARM processors, like the Cortex-A15, include hardware support for virtualization as an ARMv7 architectural extension. A number of research projects have attempted to support virtualization on ARM processors without hardware virtualization support, but they require various levels of paravirtualization and have not been stabilized. KVM/ARM is designed specifically to work on ARM processors with the virtualization extensions enabled to run unmodified guest OS.

The ARM hardware extensions differ quite a bit from their x86 counterparts. A simplified view of the ARM CPU modes is that the kernel runs in SVC mode and user space runs in USR mode. ARM introduced a new CPU mode for running hypervisors called HYP mode, which is a more privileged mode than SVC mode. An important characteristic of HYP mode, which is central to the design of KVM/ARM, is that HYP mode is not an extension of SVC mode, but a distinct mode with a separate feature set and a separate virtual memory translation mechanism. For example, if a page fault is taken in HYP mode, the faulting virtual address is stored in a different register in HYP mode than in SVC mode. As another example, for the SVC and USR modes, the hardware has two separate page table base registers, which are used to provide the familiar address space split between user space and kernel. HYP mode only uses a single page table base register and therefore does not allow the address space split between user mode and kernel.

As ARM CPUs become increasingly common in mobile devices and servers, there is a growing demand for providing the benefits of virtualization for ARM-based devices. KVM/ARM [90] introduces split-mode virtualization, allowing a hypervisor to split its execution across CPU modes to take advantage of CPU mode-specific features. This allows KVM/ARM to leverage Linux kernel services and functionality to simplify hypervisor development and maintainability while utilizing recent ARM hardware virtualization extensions to run application workloads in guest OS with comparable performance to native execution. KVM/ARM has been successfully merged into the mainline Linux 3.9 kernel, ensuring that it will gain wide adoption as the virtualization platform of choice for ARM.

2.5 Network Virtualization

Network virtualization (NV) is defined by the ability to create logical, virtual networks that are decoupled from the underlying network hardware to ensure the network can better integrate with and support increasingly virtual environments. NV can be delivered via hardware into a logical virtual network that is decoupled from and runs independently on top of a physical network. Beyond Layer 2 or 3 (L2 or L3) services like switching and routing, NV can also incorporate virtualized L4-7 services. With virtualization, organizations can take advantage of the efficiencies and agility of software-based compute and storage resources. While networks have been moving towards greater virtualization, it is only recently, with the true decoupling of the control and forwarding planes, as advocated by Software-Defined Networking (SDN) [163] and Network Function Virtualization (NFV) [126], that network virtualization has become more of a focus.

2.5.1 From Network Overlay to Virtual Networks

An overlay network is a computer network that is built on top of another network. An example is shown in Fig. 2.16. Nodes in the overlay network can be thought of as being connected by virtual or logical links, each of which corresponds to a path, perhaps through many physical links, in the underlying network. For example, distributed systems such as peer-to-peer networks are overlay networks because their nodes run on top of the Internet. The Internet

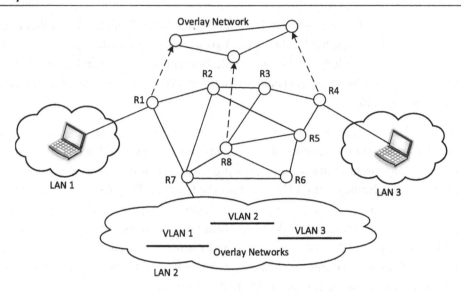

Figure 2.16: An illustrative example of overlay networks.

was originally built as an overlay upon the telephone network, while today (through the advent of Voice over IP (VoIP)), the telephone network is increasingly turning into an overlay network built on top of the Internet.

Overlay networks builds the foundation of virtual networks and they run as independent virtual networks on top of a physical network infrastructure. These virtual network overlays allow resource providers, such as cloud providers, to provision and orchestrate networks alongside other virtual resources. They also offer a new path to converged networks and programmability.

A virtual network is a computer network that consists, at least in part, of virtual network links. A virtual network link is a link that does not consist of a physical (wired or wireless) connection between two computing devices but is implemented using methods of NV.

The two most common forms of NV are protocol-based virtual networks, such as Virtual LANs (VLANs) [7], Virtual Networks (VNs) and Virtual Private Networks (VPNs) [51], Virtual Private LAN Services (VPLS) [173], and virtual networks that are based on virtual devices (such as the networks connecting VMs inside a hypervisor). In practice, both forms can be used in conjunction.

VLANs are logical local area networks (LANs) based on physical LANs as shown in Fig. 2.16. A VLAN can be created by partitioning a physical LAN into multiple logical LANs using a VLAN ID. Alternatively, several physical LANs can function as a single logical LAN.

The partitioned network can be on a single router, or multiple VLANs can be on multiple routers just as multiple physical LANs would be.

A VPN consists of multiple remote end-points (typically routers, VPN gateways of software clients) joined by some sort of tunnel over another network, usually a third-party network. Two such end points constitute a "Point to Point Virtual Private Network" (or a PTP VPN). Connecting more than two end points by putting in place a mesh of tunnels creates a "Multipoint VPN."

A VPLS is a specific type of Multipoint VPN. VPLS are divided into Transparent LAN Services (TLS) and Ethernet Virtual Connection Services. A *TLS* sends what it receives, so it provides geographic separation, but not VLAN subnetting. An Ethernet Virtual Connections (EVCS) adds a VLAN ID, so it provides geographic separation and VLAN subnetting.

A common example of a virtual network that is based on virtual devices is the network inside a hypervisor where traffic between virtual servers are routed using virtual switches (vSwitches) along with virtual routers and virtual firewalls for network segmentation and data isolation. Such networks can use nonvirtual protocols such as Ethernet as well as virtualization protocols such as the VLAN protocol IEEE 802.1Q [146].

2.5.2 Virtual Networks

The two most common forms of network virtualization are protocol-based virtual networks (such as VLANs, VPNs, and VPLSs) and virtual networks that are based on virtual devices (such as the networks connecting VMs inside a hypervisor). Several popular virtual networking protocols are presented as follows:

- *L2TP (Layer 2 Tunneling Protocol)* is a tunneling protocol used to support VPNs or as part of the delivery of services by ISPs. It does not provide any encryption or confidentiality by itself. Rather, it relies on an encryption protocol that it passes within the tunnel to provide privacy. The entire L2TP packet, including payload and L2TP header, is sent within a User Datagram Protocol (UDP) datagram. It is common to carry PPP sessions within an L2TP tunnel. L2TP does not provide confidentiality or strong authentication by itself. IPsec is often used to secure L2TP packets by providing confidentiality, authentication and integrity. The combination of these two protocols is generally known as L2TP/IPsec.
- *PPP (Point-to-Point Protocol)* is a data link (layer 2) protocol used to establish a direct connection between two nodes. It connects two routers directly without any host or any other networking device in between. It can provide connection authentication, transmission encryption, and compression. PPP is used over many types of physical networks

including serial cable, phone line, trunk line, cellular telephone, specialized radio links, and fiber optic links such as SONET. PPP is also used over Internet access connections. Internet service providers (ISPs) have used PPP for customer dial-up access to the Internet, since IP packets cannot be transmitted over a modem line on their own, without some data link protocol.

• *VLAN (Virtual Local Area Networks)* is any broadcast domain that is partitioned and isolated in a computer network at the data link layer. VLANs allow network administrators to group hosts together even if the hosts are not on the same network switch. This can greatly simplify network design and deployment, because VLAN membership can be configured through software. To subdivide a network into virtual LANs, one configures network equipment. Simpler equipment can partition based on physical ports, MAC addresses, or IP addresses. More sophisticated switching devices can mark frames through VLAN tagging, so that a single interconnect (trunk) may be used to transport data for multiple VLANs.

• *VXLAN (Virtual eXtensible LAN)* is a network virtualization technology that attempts to improve the scalability problems associated with large cloud computing deployments. It uses a VLAN-like encapsulation technique to encapsulate layer 2 Ethernet frames within layer 4 UDP packets, using 4789 as the default IANA-assigned destination UDP port number. VXLAN endpoints, which terminate VXLAN tunnels and may be both virtual or physical switch ports, are known as VXLAN tunnel endpoints (VTEPs). It is an alternative of Generic Routing Encapsulation (GRE) protocol in cloud system to build private networks as layer 2 tunnels.

• *Generic Routing Encapsulation (GRE)* is a communication protocol used to establish a direct, point-to-point connection between network nodes. Being a simple and effective method of transporting data over a public network, such as the Internet, GRE lets two peers share data they will not be able to share over the public network itself. GRE encapsulates data packets and redirects them to a device that deencapsulates them and routes them to their final destination. This allows the source and destination switches to operate as if they have a virtual point-to-point connection with each other (because the outer header applied by GRE is transparent to the encapsulated payload packet). For example, GRE tunnels allow routing protocols such as RIP and OSPF to forward data packets from one switch to another switch across the Internet. In addition, GRE tunnels can encapsulate multicast data streams for transmission over the Internet.

• *SSL (Secure Socket Layer)* is a standard security technology for establishing an encrypted link between a server and a client – typically a web server (website) and a browser, or a mail server and a mail client (e.g., Outlook) by encrypting data above the transport layer. The SSL protocol has always been used to encrypt and secure transmitted data. For example, all browsers have the capability to interact with secured web servers using the SSL protocol. However, the browser and the server need what is called an SSL Certificate to be able to establish a secure connection, where SSL Certificates is constructed based on a key pair: a public and a private key, and a certificate that contains a public key digital signed by using a trusted third party's private key. A client can use the server's certificate to establish an encrypted connection.

• *IPSec (IP security)* is a network protocol suite that authenticates and encrypts the packets of data sent over a network at the IP layer. IPsec includes protocols for establishing mutual authentication between agents at the beginning of the session and negotiation of cryptographic keys for use during the session. IPsec can protect data flows between a pair of hosts (host-to-host), between a pair of security gateways (network-to-network), or between a security gateway and a host (network-to-host).

2.5.3 Software Defined Networking

Software-Defined Networking (SDN) is a new computer networking management framework that allows network administrators to manage network services through abstraction of lower-level functionalities. Moreover, it provides programmable APIs allowing computer networking applications to interact with networking functions based on predefined programming logic and network traffic situations. SDN is meant to address the fact that the static architecture of traditional networks does not support the dynamic, scalable computing and storage needs of more modern computing environments such as data centers. This is done by decoupling or disassociating the system that makes decisions about where traffic is sent (the control plane) from the underlying systems that forward traffic to the selected destination (the data plane).

OpenFlow

SDN was commonly associated with the OpenFlow protocol [255] (for remote communication with network plane elements for the purpose of determining the path of network packets across network switches) since the latter's emergence in 2011.

OpenFlow is a Layer 2 communications protocol that gives access to the forwarding plane of a network switch or router over the network, as shown in Fig. 2.17. The OpenFlow pipeline of every OpenFlow switch contains multiple flow tables, each flow table containing multiple flow entries.

OpenFlow-compliant switches come in two types:

• OpenFlow-only – supporting only OpenFlow operation, in those switches all packets are processed by the OpenFlow pipeline, and cannot be processed otherwise.

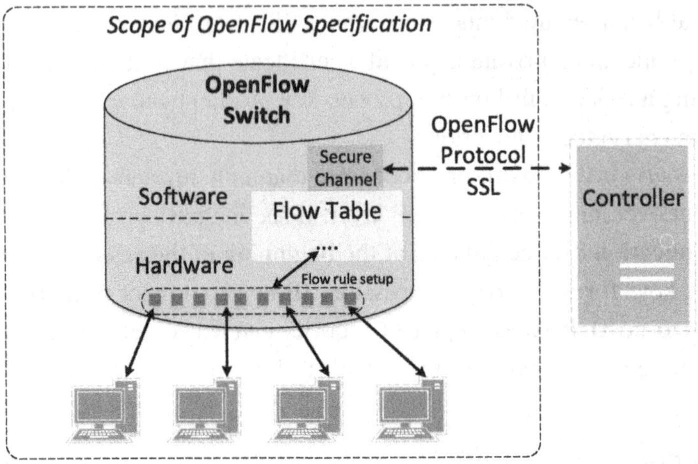

Figure 2.17: OpenFlow Switch.

- OpenFlow-hybrid – supporting both OpenFlow operation and normal Ethernet switching operation, i.e., traditional L2 Ethernet switching, VLAN isolation, L3 routing (IPv4 routing, IPv6 routing, etc.), ACL and QoS processing.

2.5.4 Network Function Virtualization

Network Function Virtualization (NFV) is a network architecture concept that uses the technologies of IT virtualization to virtualize entire classes of network node functions into building blocks that may connect, or chain together, to create communication services.

NFV relies upon, but differs from, traditional server-virtualization techniques, such as those used in enterprise IT. A Virtualized Network Function (VNF) may consist of one or more VMs running different software and processes, on top of standard high-volume servers, switches and storage devices, or even cloud computing infrastructure, instead of having custom hardware appliances for each network function.

The goal of NFV is to decouple network functions from dedicated hardware devices and allow network services that are now being carried out by routers, firewalls, load balancers, and other dedicated hardware devices to be hosted on VMs. Once the network functions are under the control of a hypervisor, the services that once require dedicated hardware can be performed on standard x86 servers.

This capability is important because it means that network administrators will no longer need to purchase dedicated hardware devices in order to build a service chain. Because server capacity will be able to be added through software, there will be no need for network administrators to overprovision their data centers which will reduce both capital expenses (CAPex) and operating expenses (OPex). If an application running on a VM required more bandwidth, for example, the administrator could move the VM to another physical server or provision another VM on the original server to take part of the load. Having this flexibility will allow an IT department to respond in a more agile manner to changing business goals and network service demands.

NFV is different from SDN but is complementary to it. When SDN runs on the NFV infrastructure, the SDN forwards the data packets from one network device to another while the network routing (control) functions run on a VM in, for example, a rack mount server. The NFV concept, which was presented by a group of network service providers at the Software Defined Network and OpenFlow World Congress in October 2012, is being developed by the ETSI Industry Specification Group (ISG) for Network Functions Virtualization.

2.6 Storage Virtualization

When we talk about the storage on the system, we usually categorize storage into two types: the disks and the file system. In a similar way, storage virtualization solutions can be classified into block and file store.

2.6.1 Block Store

The Block Store is virtualized disks. For a computer system, the disks are connected to the south bridge chip on the motherboard, through which the disks can talk to the motherboard BIOS by various protocols. The typical disk protocols are (P)ATA, SATA, and SCSI. The SCSI is widely used to implement the virtualized block storage due to the popular iSCSI protocol. In essence, iSCSI allows two hosts to negotiate and then exchange SCSI commands using Internet Protocol (IP) networks. By doing this, iSCSI takes a popular high-performance local storage bus and emulates it over a wide range of networks, creating a storage area network (SAN).

Examples

- OpenStack Cinder. Cinder is a Block Storage service for OpenStack. It's designed to present storage resources to end users that can be consumed by the OpenStack Compute Project (Nova). This is done through the use of either a reference implementation (LVM) or plug-in drivers for other storage. The short description of Cinder is that it virtualizes the management of block storage devices and provides end users with a self-service API to request and consume those resources without requiring any knowledge of where their storage is actually deployed or on what type of device.

- AWS EBS. Amazon Elastic Block Store (Amazon EBS) provides persistent block storage volumes for use with Amazon EC2 instances in the AWS Cloud. Each Amazon EBS volume is automatically replicated within an availability zone to protect you from component failure, offering high availability and durability. Amazon EBS volumes offer the consistent and low-latency performance needed to run. With Amazon EBS, you can scale your usage up or down within minutes – all while paying a low price for only what you provision.

2.6.2 File Store

The widely used Linux system has a feature to mount a remote file directory to a local file system, which is usually called NFS (network file system). The NFS server is actually a virtualized file store.

Examples

- OpenStack Manila implements the concept and vision for establishing a shared file system service for OpenStack. The File Share Service prototype provides coordinated access to shared or distributed file systems. While the primary consumption of file shares would be across OpenStack Compute instances, the service is also intended to be accessible as an independent capability in line with the modular design established by other OpenStack services. The design and prototype implementation provide extensibility for multiple back-ends (to support vendor or file system specific nuances/capabilities) but is intended to be sufficiently abstract to accommodate any of a variety of shared or distributed file system types. The team's intention is to introduce the capability as an OpenStack incubated project in the Juno time-frame, graduate it, and submit for consideration as a core service as early as the Kilo release.
- NFS is a distributed file system protocol originally developed by Sun Microsystems in 1984, allowing a user on a client computer to access files over a computer network much like local storage is accessed. NFS, like many other protocols, builds on the Open Network Computing Remote Procedure Call (ONC RPC) system. The NFS is an open standard defined in Request for Comments (RFC), allowing anyone to implement the protocol.

CHAPTER 3

Mobile Cloud Service Models

I slept and I dreamed that life is all joy. I woke and I saw that life is all service.
I served and I saw that service is joy.

Kahlil Gibran

Cloud services are usually classified as IaaS, PaaS, and SaaS according to service level the cloud provides. IaaS provides the lower level infrastructure services where the users would like to manipulate the resources directly with the guest operating system. PaaS and SaaS provide the higher-level service, for which users do not work on operating system directly, but instead, on the software platforms or the service products. From a naïve service perspective, where the service operation involves three actors: service provider, service consumer and service broker, the previous cloud service classification focuses on the service provider side. To extend the cloud service model into mobile cloud service model, we will, from the involved service actors' perspective, look into the mobile cloud service models. The addition of mobile devices to the cloud service model introduces additional reaction patterns in the service operation, including service offloading, migration, and composition. After studying the basics of mobile cloud service models, we will discuss some state-of-the-art mobile cloud service models.

This chapter is organized as follows. We review the cloud service models including IaaS, PaaS and Saas in Section 3.1. We will discuss the state-of-the-art on mobile cloud service models in Section 3.2; and then we will focus on the mobile cloud service models in Section 3.3. Finally, we will present Internet of Things and the applied microservice patterns in Section 3.4.

3.1 Review Cloud Service Models

Though service-oriented architecture advocates "everything as a service" (with the acronyms EaaS or XaaS, or simply aaS), cloud-computing providers offer their "services" according to different models, which happen to form a stack: infrastructure-, platform-, and software-as-a-service. IaaS is like a vehicle, where it needs to be maintained and supplied with fuel, but a driver can go pretty much everywhere he/she wants to; PaaS is like a taxi, where a rider chooses where he wants to go, but keeping the car running is up to the driver; finally, SaaS is like a public transport, which is cheap and takes care of everything; however, it may not get as close to where the rider wants to go. The three cloud service models are listed in Fig. 3.1.

Mobile Cloud Computing
DOI: 10.1016/B978-0-12-809641-3.00004-1

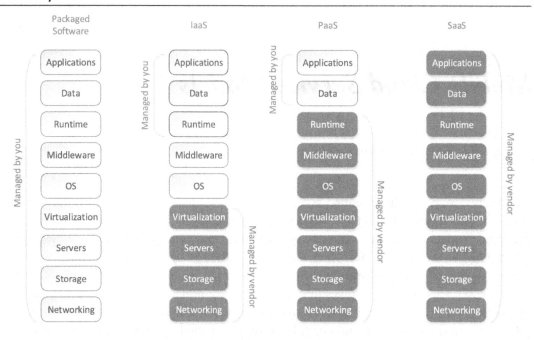

Figure 3.1: Three layers of cloud computing.

3.1.1 Infrastructure as a Service

In the most basic cloud-service model, and according to the Internet Engineering Task Force (IETF), providers of IaaS offer computers – physical or (more often) virtual machines – and other resources. IaaS refers to online services that abstract the user from the details of infrastructure like physical computing resources, location, data partitioning, scaling, security, backup, etc. A hypervisor, such as Xen, Oracle VirtualBox, Oracle VM, KVM, VMware ESX/ESXi, or Hyper-V runs the virtual machines as guests. Pools of hypervisors within the cloud operational system can support large numbers of virtual machines and have the ability to scale services up and down according to customers' varying requirements. IaaS clouds often offer additional resources such as a virtual-machine disk-image library, raw block storage, file or object storage, firewalls, load balancers, IP addresses, VLANs, and software bundles. IaaS-cloud providers supply these resources on-demand from their large pools of equipment installed in data centers. For wide-area connectivity, customers can use either the Internet or carrier clouds (dedicated virtual private networks).

To deploy their applications, cloud users install operating-system images and their application software on the cloud infrastructure. In this model, the cloud user patches and maintains the operating systems and the application software. Cloud providers typically bill IaaS services on a utility computing basis: cost reflects the amount of resources allocated and consumed.

IaaS examples

- *Amazon Web Services EC2 and S3.* Amazon EC2 forms a central part of Amazon's cloud-computing platform, Amazon Web Services (AWS), by allowing users to rent virtual computers on which to run their own computer applications. EC2 encourages scalable deployment of applications by providing a web service through which a user can boot an Amazon Machine Image to configure a virtual machine, which Amazon calls an "instance", containing any software desired. A user can create, launch, and terminate server-instances as needed, paying by the hour for active servers – hence the term "elastic." EC2 provides users with control over the geographical location of instances that allows for latency optimization and high levels of redundancy.
  Amazon S3 (Simple Storage Service) is an online file storage web service offered by Amazon Web Services. Amazon S3 provides storage through web services interfaces (REST, SOAP, and BitTorrent). S3 stores arbitrary objects (computer files) up to 5 terabytes in size, each accompanied by up to 2 kilobytes of metadata. Objects are organized into buckets (each owned by an Amazon Web Services account), and identified within each bucket by a unique, user-assigned key. Amazon Machine Images (AMIs) which are used in the Elastic Compute Cloud (EC2) can be exported to S3 as bundles. Buckets and objects can be created, listed, and retrieved using either an REST-style HTTP interface or a SOAP interface. Additionally, objects can be downloaded using the HTTP GET interface and the BitTorrent protocol. Requests are authorized using an access control list associated with each bucket and object.
- *OpenStack Nova, Swift, and Neutron.* Nova is an OpenStack project designed to provide power massively scalable, on-demand, self-service access to compute resources. Swift is a highly available, distributed, eventually consistent object/blob store. Organizations can use Swift to store lots of data efficiently, safely, and cheaply. Neutron is an OpenStack project to provide "network connectivity as a service" between interface devices (e.g., virtual Network Interface Cards – vNICs) managed by other OpenStack services (e.g., Nova). It implements the Neutron API.

3.1.2 Platform as a Service

PaaS vendors offer a development environment to application developers. The provider typically develops toolkit and standards for development and channels for distribution and payment. In the PaaS models, cloud providers deliver a computing platform, typically including operating system, programming-language execution environment, database, and web server. Application developers can develop and run their software solutions on a cloud platform without the cost and complexity of buying and managing the underlying hardware and software layers. With some PaaS offers like Microsoft Azure and Google App Engine, the underlying computer and storage resources scale automatically to match application demand so that the cloud user does not have to allocate resources manually. The latter has also been proposed by an architecture aiming to facilitate real-time in cloud environments. Even more specific application types can be provided via PaaS, such as media encoding as provided by services like bitmovin or media.io.

Some integration and data management providers have also embraced specialized applications of PaaS as delivery models for data solutions. Examples include iPaaS and dPaaS. Integration Platform as a Service (iPaaS) enables customers to develop, execute, and govern integration flows. Under the iPaaS integration model, customers drive the development and deployment of integrations without installing or managing any hardware or middleware. Data Platform as a Service (dPaaS) delivers integration and data-management products as a fully managed service. Under the dPaaS model, the PaaS provider, not the customer, manages the development and execution of data solutions by building tailored data applications for the customer. dPaaS users retain transparency and control over data through data-visualization tools.

PaaS consumers do not manage or control the underlying cloud infrastructure including network, servers, operating systems, or storage, but have control over the deployed applications and possibly configuration settings for the application-hosting environment.

PaaS examples

*   *Microsoft Azure.* Microsoft lists over 50 Azure services including the following PaaS:
    1. *App services*, PaaS environment letting developers easily publish and manage web sites.
    2. *Websites*, high density hosting of websites allows developers to build sites using ASP.NET, PHP, Node.js, or Python and can be deployed using FTP, Git, Mercurial, or Team Foundation Server. This feature was announced in preview form in June 2012 at the Meet Microsoft Azure event. This comprises one aspect of the PaaS offerings for the Microsoft Azure Platform. It was renamed Web Apps in April 2015.
    3. *WebJobs*, applications which can be deployed to a Web apps to implement background processing that can be invoked on a schedule, on demand or can run continuously. Blob, Table, and Queue services can be used to communicate between Web Apps and Web Jobs and to provide state.
*   *Google App Engine.* Google App Engine (often referred to as GAE or simply App Engine) is a PaaS cloud computing platform for developing and hosting web applications in Google-managed data centers. Applications are sandboxed and run across multiple servers. App Engine offers automatic scaling for web applications – as the number of requests increases for an application, App Engine automatically allocates more resources for the web application to handle the additional demand.

Currently, the supported programming languages are Python, Java (and, by extension, other JVM languages such as Groovy, JRuby, Scala, Clojure), Go, and PHP. *Node.js* is also available in the managed VM environment, and Google App Engine has been written to be language independent.

Python web frameworks that run on Google App Engine include Django, CherryPy, Pyramid, Flask, web2py, and webapp2, as well as a custom Google-written webapp framework and several others designed specifically for the platform that emerged since the release. Any Python framework that supports the WSGI using the CGI adapter can be used to create an application and the framework can be uploaded with the developed application. Third-party libraries written in pure Python may also be uploaded.

Google App Engine supports many Java standards and frameworks. Central to this is the servlet 2.5 technology using the open-source Jetty Web Server, along with accompanying technologies such as JSP. JavaServer Faces operates with some workarounds.

Though the datastore used may be unfamiliar to programmers, it is easily accessed and supported with JPA, JDO, and by the simple low-level API. There are several alternative libraries and frameworks you can use to model and map the data to the datastore such as Objectify, Slim3, and Jello framework. Jello framework is a full-stack Java framework optimized for Google App Engine that includes comprehensive Data Authorization model and a powerful RESTful engine.

The Spring Framework works with GAE; however, the Spring Security module (if used) requires workarounds. Apache Struts 1 is supported, and Struts 2 runs with workarounds. The Django web framework and applications running on it can be used on App Engine with modification. Django-nonrel aims to allow Django to work with nonrelational databases and the project includes support for App Engine.

- *Heroku.* Heroku is a cloud PaaS supporting several programming languages. Heroku was acquired by Salesforce.com in 2010. Heroku, one of the first cloud platforms, has been in development since June 2007, when it supported only the Ruby programming language, but has since added support for Java, Node.js, Scala, Clojure, Python, PHP, and Go.
- *OpenShift.* OpenShift is a Kubernetes and Docker powered cloud PaaS developed by Red Hat.

Online is Red Hat's public cloud application development and hosting platform. Online is currently powered by version 2 of the Origin project source code, which is also available under the Apache License version 2.0. Online supports a variety of languages, frameworks, and databases out of the box. In addition to the built-in languages and services, developers can add other language, database, or middleware components that they need via the OpenShift Cartridge API.

Origin is the upstream community project that powers OpenShift *Online*, OpenShift *Dedicated*, and OpenShift *Enterprise*. Built around a core of Docker container packaging and

Kubernetes container cluster management, Origin is also augmented by application life-cycle management functionality and DevOps tooling. Origin provides a complete open source application container platform. All source code for the Origin project is available under the Apache License (version 2.0) on GitHub.

3.1.3 Software as a Service

In the SaaS model, users gain access to application software and databases. Cloud providers manage the infrastructure and platforms that run the applications. SaaS is sometimes referred to as "on-demand software" and is usually priced on a pay-per-use basis or using a subscription fee.

In the SaaS model, cloud providers install and operate application software in the cloud and cloud users access the software from cloud clients. Cloud users do not manage the cloud infrastructure and platform where the application runs. This eliminates the need to install and run the application on the cloud user's own computers, which simplifies maintenance and support. Cloud applications differ from other applications in their scalability – which can be achieved by cloning tasks onto multiple virtual machines at run-time to meet changing work demand. Load balancers distribute the work over the set of virtual machines. This process is transparent to the cloud user, who sees only a single access-point. To accommodate a large number of cloud users, cloud applications can be multitenant, meaning that any machine may serve more than one cloud-user organization.

The pricing model for SaaS applications is typically a monthly or yearly flat fee per user, so prices become scalable and adjustable if users are added or removed at any point.

Proponents claim that SaaS gives a business the potential to reduce IT operational costs by outsourcing hardware and software maintenance and support to the cloud provider. This enables the business to reallocate IT operations costs away from hardware/software spending and from personnel expenses, towards meeting other goals. In addition, with applications hosted centrally, updates can be released without the need for users to install new software. One drawback of SaaS comes with storing the users' data on the cloud provider's server. As a result, there could be unauthorized access to the data. For this reason, users are increasingly adopting intelligent third-party key-management systems to help secure their data.

SaaS examples

- *Google for Work.* Google for Work is a service from Google that provides customizable enterprise versions of several Google products using a domain name provided by the customer. It features several Web applications with similar functionality to traditional office suites, including Gmail, Hangouts, Google Calendar, Drive, Docs, Sheets, Slides, Groups, News, Play, Sites, and Vault. It was the vision of Rajen Sheth, a Google employee who later developed Chromebooks.

Gmail, a free webmail service provided by Google, was launched as an invitation-only beta program on April 1, 2004, and became available to the public on February 7, 2007. The service was upgraded from beta status on July 7, 2009, at which time it had 146 million users monthly. The service was the first online e-mail service with one gigabyte of storage. It was also the first to keep e-mails from the same conversation together in one thread, similar to an Internet forum. The service offers over 15 GB of free storage, shared with other Google Apps, with additional storage ranging from 20 GB to 16 TB available for $0.25 per 1 GB per year.

- *iCloud.* iCloud is a cloud storage and cloud computing service from Apple Inc. launched on October 12, 2011. As of February 2016, the service had 782 million users.

  The service provides its users with means to store data such as documents, photos, and music on remote servers for download to iOS, Macintosh or Windows devices, to share and send data to other users, and to manage their Apple devices if lost or stolen.

  The service also provides the means to wirelessly back up iOS devices directly to iCloud, instead of being reliant on manual backups to a host Mac or Windows computer using iTunes. Service users are also able to share photos, music, and games instantly by linking accounts via AirDrop wireless.

3.2 Current Mobile Cloud Service Models

Current Internet clouds have been broadly classified in three-type service models: Infrastructure-as-a-service (IaaS), Platform-as-a-Service (PaaS), and Software-as-a-Service (SaaS). They are classified according to the layers of virtualization. However, due to the involvement of both Cyber-Physical Systems (CPS) and Cyber Virtual Systems (CVS), the MCC's service models are more appropriate to be classified according to the roles of computational entities within its service framework, where the classification of MCC service models can use the roles and relations between mobile entities and their invoked cloud-based resource provisioning. Based on this view, existing MCC services can be classified into three major models: Mobile-as-a-Service-Consumer (MaaSC), Mobile-as-a-Service-Provider (MaaSP), and Mobile-as-a-Service-Broker (MaaSB). These MCC service models are illustrated in Fig. 3.2, in which arrows indicate service processing flows from service providers to service recipients.

MaaSC originated from the traditional client–server model by introducing virtualization, fine-grained access control, and other cloud-based technologies at the initial stage. Mobile devices

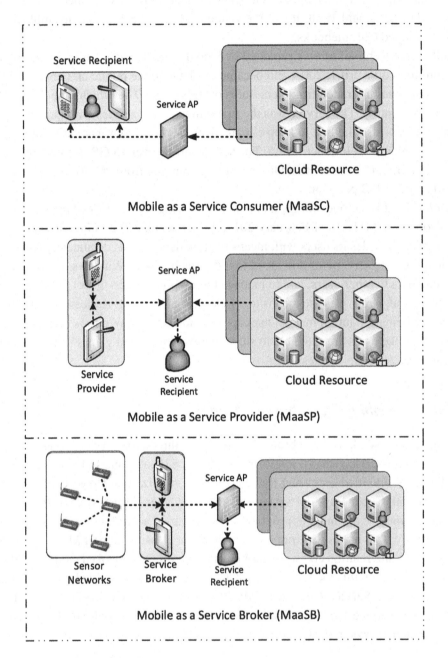

Figure 3.2: Current Service Models of MCC.

can outsource their computation and storage functions onto the cloud in order to achieve better performance and more application capabilities. In this architecture, the service is one-way from the cloud to mobile devices, and mobile devices are service consumers. Most existing MCC services fall into this category.

MaaSP is different from MaaSC in that the role of a mobile device is shifted from a service consumer to a service provider. For example, with on-board sensors, i.e., GPS module, camera, gyroscope, etc., mobile devices are able to sense data from the devices and their neighboring environment, and further provide sensing services to other mobile devices through the cloud. In Fig. 3.2, consumers receive services provided by both the cloud and mobile devices. The types of services provided by mobile devices are diverse based on their sensing and processing capabilities.

MaaSB can be considered an extension of MaaSP, where MaaSB provides networking and data forwarding services for other mobile devices or sensing nodes. MaaSB is desired under some circumstances because mobile devices usually have limited sensing capability compared to sensors that are dedicated to specially designed functionalities and sensing locations. For example, mobile phones can be used to collect users' physical activities from Nike Fuelband [215]. MaaSB extends the cloud edges to mobile devices and wireless sensors. Thus, a mobile device can be configured as a gateway or a proxy, providing networking services through various communication approaches such as 3/4G, Bluetooth, WiFi, etc. Moreover, the proxy mobile device can also provide security and privacy protections to their interfaced sensors.

We summarize existing MCC services and applications in Table 3.1. We discuss four major MCC service types and corresponding representatives. Each service or application can be categorized into one or multiple service models. MaaSC is the most common MCC service model because most of existing mobile devices are still restricted by their computation and energy capacities. For example, CloneCloud [80] provides the computation task offloading service for mobile devices. In this case, the mobile device is the service consumer since it only gets benefit from the service provided by cloud rather than providing services for other users.

3.2.1 Mobile Cloud Computation

Computation task offloading is a demanding feature for mobile devices relying on Internet clouds to perform resources-intensive computation tasks. Partitioning computation tasks and allocating them between mobile devices and clouds can be very inefficient during the application runtime considering various performance metrics such as energy consumption, CPU power, network delay, etc. Efficiently and intelligently offloading the computation tasks onto

Table 3.1: Summary of MCC Services and Applications

MCC Services and Applications		Service Models		
MCC Service Types	*Representative Approaches*	*MaaSC*	*MaaSP*	*MaaSB*
Mobile Cloud Computation	CloneCloud [80]	✓		
	MAUI [89]	✓		
	ThinkAir [168]	✓		
Mobile Cloud Storage	Dropbox, Box, iCloud, GoogleDrive, and Skydrive [87]	✓		
	WhereStore [257]	✓		
	STACEE [213]	✓	✓	
Security and Privacy	CloudAV [218]	✓		
	Secure Web Referral Services for Mobile Cloud Computing [176]	✓		
	Zscaler [300]	✓		
	Google Wallet [119]	✓		
Context Awareness	An Integrated Cloud-based Framework for Mobile Phone Sensing [105]		✓	✓

the cloud is one of the main research issues of MCC. CloneCloud [80] and MAUI [89] are two pioneers in this area. They both can automatically offload computing tasks to the cloud.

CloneCloud serves as an application partitioner as well as an execution runtime environment that allows unmodified mobile applications to seamlessly offload parts of the executions from mobile devices onto a cloud server. The offloading decision is made by optimizing execution time and energy usage for mobile devices. Contrary to CloneCloud, MAUI allows modification of offloading applications at the coding level to maximize the energy saving of mobile devices. Thinkair [168] demands dedicated VMs in clouds as part of a complete smart phone system, and removes the restrictions on applications/inputs/environmental conditions by using an online method-level offloading.

3.2.2 Mobile Cloud Storage

Storage capacity is another constraint of mobile devices. There are many existing storage services for mobile devices, e.g., Dropbox, Box, iCloud, Google Drive, and Skydrive [60][87]. Besides manually uploading the files or data onto the cloud, one desired feature of mobile cloud storage services is the automatic synchronization between mobile devices and the cloud. Multimedia data generated by mobile devices demands a stable and high available storage solution. This is the reason that many smart phone operating systems natively implant the multimedia data synchronization feature, e.g., iCloud for iOS, Skydrive for Windows Phone, Google Drive for Android, etc. Moreover, mobile users' behavior data such as location traces, browsing history, personal contacts, and preference settings need to be kept in a reliable and protected storage space. Most existing commercial cloud storage solutions are built on a centralized data center, which is appropriate for Internet clouds.

Storage mobility has been gradually becoming a recent research focus. WhereStore [257] is a location-based data storage solution for smart phones. It uses filtered replication (a filter expressing the set of data items that are likely to be accessed in the near future) along with each device's location history to distribute data items between smart phones and the cloud. STACEE [213] proposes a peer-to-peer cloud storage where mobile phones, tablets, set-top boxes, modems and networked storage devices can all contribute as storage within these storage clouds. It provides a peer-to-peer (P2P) cloud storage solution and addresses the storage issue for mobile users as a QoS-aware scheduling problem.

3.2.3 Security and Privacy

Security related services aim to provide data security protection through the cloud. Security of mobile devices can be enhanced with the help of cloud security mechanisms including cloud-based secure proxy, remote anti-virus, remote attestation, etc.

CloudAV [218] advocates such a cloud-based security model for malware detection for end hosts by providing antivirus as an in-cloud security service. Secure web referral services [176] enable the antivirus and antiphishing services through the cloud. The referral services depend on a secure search engine to validate URLs accessed by a mobile device to prevent mobile users from accessing phishing websites.

Zscaler [300] is one of the most well-known commercial cloud-based security companies that provide policy-based, secure internet access for mobile devices. It provides a comprehensive cloud-based security solution including three main components: ZEN (proxy), CA (central authority), and Nanologs server (log server). Various cloud-based security services are built based on these components. For example, the *ByteScan* service enables each ZEN to scan every byte of the web request, content, responses and all related data to block malicious actions and data such as viruses, cross site scripting (XSS), botnets, etc. The *PageRisk* service relies on the ZEN to compute a PageRisk index for every page that is loaded and enables the administrator to control content served to their users based on an acceptable risk evaluation. The *NanoLog* service enables administrators to access any transaction log in realtime.

An increasing number of security features can be enabled in the cloud, in which a reliable and secure connection between a mobile device and the cloud is the main challenge for this type of solutions. Google Wallet [119] is developed on a cloud-mobile dual trust root model, where the cloud is in charge of the application level security such as credit card transactions and user credential management, and the Google Wallet mobile device is protected by strong trust computing elements on the board to prevent malicious attacks on the mobile devices.

3.2.4 MCC Context Awareness

Nowadays, a smart mobile device usually serves as an information gateway for mobile users involving various personalized activities such as checking e-mails, making appointments, surfing the web, locating interested spots, analyzing personal behavior data based on data mining and machine learning, etc. For example, in [105], each mobile device has a dedicated Mobile Cloud Engine (MCE) including three modules: decision module, publish subscribe module, and context awareness module. The decision module regulates the transactions among the different parts of the MCE. The publish subscribe module is responsible for establishing the data flow between the mobile application and the MCE. Finally, the context awareness module provides context information to the application. The state-of-the-art solutions lack a unified approach suitable to support diverse applications while reducing the energy consumption and providing intelligent assistance to mobile users.

3.3 Mobile Cloud Service Models and Examples

The Internet cloud service model is categorized by the service content in a layered structure. From the service composition perspective, we can see the cloud usually works as service provider, while users consume the service through web service interfaces. When we extend the Internet cloud to the mobile cloud, we introduce mobile devices into the picture, which can be service provider, service consumer and service broker as well.

3.3.1 Mobile as a Service Consumer

Mobile as a Service Consumer (MaaSC) originated from the traditional client–server model by introducing virtualization, fine-grained access control, and other cloud-based technologies at the initial stage. Mobile devices can outsource their computation and storage functions onto the cloud in order to achieve better performance and more application capabilities. In this architecture, the service is one-way from the cloud to mobile devices and mobile devices are service consumers. Most existing MCC services fall into this category. One typical example of MaaSC is surrogate as a service, which is introduced next.

Mobile devices consume VM resources

The resources in the mobile devices are usually limited due to the device size and weight. Not only are the computation power and storage space bounded, but the battery limits the active lifetime. To offload some tasks from mobile devices to the clouds is one of the promising approaches to reduce the computation and storage requirement on the mobile devices as well as to increase the device battery duration. The cloud which can host the offloaded tasks are providing surrogate as a service.

The mobile device to offload the task usually completes in three steps. First, the mobile device discovers the surrogate service and migrates the task code to the cloud. This piece of code should be compatible with cloud surrogate running environment. The application may contain the cloud version of code which is migrated, or the cloud accepts the mobile code and knows how to run it. Second, the cloud hosts a surrogate container to run the code and provides the interfaces for the mobile device to call. The application on the mobile device call the interface to pass in the input and fetch the task result. This remote function call may happen many times during the application lifetime. Last, when the application on the mobile device decides not to call the offloaded code any more, it tells the cloud surrogate to terminate the hosting and release the resources to finalize the cloud billing for this session.

Surrogate as a service is not good in various situations. Since the communication between mobile device and cloud costs some resource and energy, and causes delay, the tradeoff should be considered seriously to get the offloading benefits. The cost of offloading includes the network delay, energy consumption for the networking, development effort to make code compatible, and the boxing and unboxing data during the remote function call. The impacted aspects include not only the application performance in terms of running time or delay, but also the battery lifetime and development effort. Thus, the offloading decision plays a key role to guarantee the offloading benefits. For the different situations, the offloading decision may be different. Various offloading decision models are discussed in Chapter 5.

Mobile devices consume cloud data

Many systems collect huge amounts of data from the users and store them in the clouds or datacenters. For example, Twitter.com puts all the data in its datacenters; Uber.com collects the cars' and drivers' information and stores it in its clouds. The operations on these huge datasets cannot be done in the mobile devices. If a user would like to search a topic or search the nearby available cab cars, the users' requests are sent to the clouds to calculate on the dataset. In other words, the computation happens where the data is. If the mobile applications would like to compute based on the data that are only available in the clouds or moving the raw data to the mobile devices to compute is too expensive, mobile applications have to consume the data in the clouds, which can be named "data as a service."

A system implementing "Data as a Service" usually evolves from large data store systems. One typical example is Hadoop project. The Hadoop project provides a data store named HDFS (Hadoop Distributed File System) which can host very large amount of data on disks in clouds. Besides data hosting, Hadoop provides the Map-Reduce operations on the data to compute the user queries. Let's discuss an example of a user searching for a topic on tweets implemented using Hadoop. The users' tweets are collected and stored in the HDFS in the clouds, and the tweets are processed to build Inverted Index. Both the tweets content and the indexes are stored in the HDFS. When a user wants to search a key word, the request goes to the cloud and follows the indexes to fetch the query results.

Mobile devices composite cloud services

The cloud provides containers for the mobile application to run the offloaded code. However, if we put common codes or services are available in the clouds already, the mobile applications will not have to transfer the computation code. Moreover, the mobile applications may compose the available services in the cloud to form the specific services they would like. The mobile applications may consume the complex service composed from simple common cloud services in a flexible way.

In summary, MaaSC examples include mobile devices consuming VM resources, cloud data, and composing cloud services. They can be differentiated by the services the cloud provides to mobiles:

1. A mobile consumes VM resources and the cloud provides containers or surrogates;
2. A mobile consumes cloud data and the cloud provides containers and data;
3. A mobile composes cloud services and the cloud provides containers and codes or services.

3.3.2 Mobile as a Service Provider

Mobile as a Service Provider (MaaSP) is different from MaaSC in that the role of a mobile device is shifted from a service consumer to a service provider. For example, with on-board sensors, i.e., GPS module, camera, gyroscope, etc., mobile devices are able to sense data from the devices and their neighboring environment, and further provide sensing services to other mobile devices through the cloud. Consumers receive services provided by both the cloud and mobile devices. The types of services provided by mobile devices are diverse based on their sensing and processing capabilities.

Mobile provides location

Location as a service is one of emerging MaaSP service model. As one of the most typical services in MCC, it highly relies on Location-Based Services (LBS), which make use of the geographical position of a mobile device, have the advantages of both user mobility and cloud resources in MCC. These services gain user's current position by utilizing GPS, and provide various location-related services. However, experiments show that GPS only allows continuously working for 9 hours on smartphones, which indicates that saving energy costs in mobile location sensing is a significant issue [268].

The locating technologies used today mainly include GPS, WiFi, and GSM. Each of these technologies can vary widely in energy consumption and localization accuracy. Experiments have shown that GPS is able to run continuously for 9 hours only, while WiFi and GSM can be sustained for 40 and 60 hours, respectively. At the same time, the corresponding localization accuracies are about 10, 40, and 400 m. Most LBAs prefer GPS for their accuracy although it is perceived as extremely power-hungry. What is worse, phones currently only offer a black box interface to the GPS for the request of location estimates, and the lack of sensor control makes energy consumption even more inefficient. Additionally, many LBAs require continuous localization over reasonably long time scales. Therefore, energy-efficient location sensing methods must be adopted to obtain accurate position information while expending minimal energy.

Dynamic tracking.

The basic idea of dynamic tracking is attempting to minimize the frequency of position updates by only sampling positions (generally with GPS) when the estimated uncertainty in position exceeds the accuracy threshold [268].

This process obtains a GPS position and then uses a certain method to determine the user state (i.e., whether the device is moving or not). If the device is not moving, the logic waits for movement. When it is moving, the speed of the device is determined. Then a scheduling plan of sensors and radio is calculated with some principles included to minimize power consumption. When the estimated uncertainty in position exceeds the accuracy threshold, the process restarts and samples the next GPS position. In this process, the methods of movement detection, velocity estimation, and scheduling principles can be very different.

Trajectory simplification.

Trajectory simplification has been proposed as a means to reduce data size and communication costs caused by sending motion information. It is used for applications which need trajectory information instead of a single position [268].

The basic idea of trajectory simplification is to use a smaller subset of obtained positions, one which is minimal in size while still reflecting the overall motion information. In EnTracked [165], trajectory simplification is viewed as a special case of line simplification (which has been thoroughly discussed in the computational geometry community).

Mobile provides sensor data

Sensor as a service is another emerging MaaSP service model. Present mobile devices such as smart phones carry various sensors such as fingerprint sensor, accelerometer, gyroscope, barometer, proximity sensor, ambient light sensor, and hall sensor. These sensors profile the device environment or the user environment for smart phone. The device environment profile is very important for context-based or user-based applications. Besides, the device environment is also very important for cloud applications. In this model, the mobile devices or smart phones work as service providers, which expose their sensing function to the cloud.

The cloud can build a virtual mirror world by the device environment profile. A virtual mirror world enables a new cloud mobile application scheme, which is a mirror-synchronization scheme. The mirror-synchronization scheme works in three steps as its name indicates. First, the mobile device senses the environment and sends the environment profile to the cloud. The cloud builds the virtual world by the profile. Second, the cloud application aggregates lots of small mirror virtual worlds into one big world, based on which many applications can run. Third, in return for the mobile device sensing profile data, the cloud provides the application for the mobile devices. Due to the aggregation of small mirror virtual worlds in the cloud, the mobile devices actually use the data from other mobile devices and the cloud computation power. Both the mobile device and cloud benefit in the mirror-synchronization scheme.

Mobile Health

There is substantial enthusiasm for the concept of mobile health (mHealth), a broad term typically used to describe the use of mobile telecommunication technologies for the delivery of health care and in support of wellness. In 2011, US Secretary of Health and Human Services Kathleen Sebelius referred to mHealth as *"the biggest technology breakthrough of our time"* and maintained that its use would *"address our greatest national challenge."* This level of exuberance for mHealth is driven by the convergence of three powerful forces. The first is the unsustainability of current health care spending and the recognition of the need for disruptive solutions. The second is the rapid and ongoing growth in wireless connectivity – there now are more than 3.2 billion unique mobile users worldwide – and this brings about a remarkable capability for the bidirectional instantaneous transfer of information. The third is the need for more precise and individualized medicine; a refinement in phenotypes that mandates novel, personal data streams well beyond the occasional vital sign or laboratory data available through intermittent clinic visits [256].

More and more mobile applications are developed to help us monitor our health. A typical mobile health application monitors our body activities through phone sensors, for example, location and speed to estimate the calories burned during exercises, and send the data to the cloud servers for analysis. The mobile provides the monitoring as a service, which helps the doctors diagnose.

3.3.3 Mobile as a Service Broker

Mobile as a Service Broker (MaaSB) can be considered as an extension of MaaSP. MaaSB provides additional networking and data forwarding services for other mobile devices. For example, MaaSB is useful when mobile devices have limited sensing capability compared to sensors that are dedicated for specially designed functionalities and sensing locations. A mobile phone can be used to collect users' physical activities from wearable devices such as Nike Fuelband, in which mobile devices and wireless sensors can be added to the cloud edge through the MaaSB service model. In this way, a mobile device can be configured as a proxy through various communication approaches and the proxy device can also provide security and privacy protections to MaaSB consumers.

Mobile web caching

A mobile ad hoc network enables a mobile device to fetch web information through another mobile device. Since some mobile devices may have better connection to the base station or WiFi hot-spot and have already downloaded the web pages that the other mobile devices are interested, the other mobile devices may directly access the cached web information from this relay node. The mobile devices may communicate through direct communication channel rather than through the far connection to the remote Internet cloud. One copy of cached web pages may benefit all the other mobile devices.

Vehicular cloud

The vehicles on the road may form local small vehicular cloud, which consists of a group of cars, buses, and trucks. The buses and big trucks may carry the network endpoint devices to enable them as network access point such as WiFi hot-spot. The other cars may access the WiFi endpoint on the buses for the Internet information. Since the buses and big trucks can carry lots of devices and they usually keep regular routines, the network coverage and network signal should be predictable and stable, so that the cars nearby can have good connection to them.

A platoon of vehicles may collaborate to provide information for each other. For example, the vehicles at the head of the platoon may provide the road condition information to the vehicles at the end of the platoon. Some vehicle may be elected as relay node for the communication in the platoon, which is also a form of mobile as a service broker.

Relay as a Service

Sometimes the service consumer and service provider are separated due to the communication limitation. The mobile devices can help to broker service binding through communication relay. Ad hoc mobile wireless networks are examples for "*relay as a service.*" Ad hoc networks are deployed in situations where no base station is available and a network has to be built impromptu. Since there is no wired backbone, each host is a router and a packet forwarder. Each node may be mobile, and topology changes frequently and unpredictably. Routing protocol development has received much attention because of mobility management. And efficient bandwidth and power usage are critical in ad hoc networks [178].

3.3.4 Summary of Mobile Cloud Services

The mobile devices, such as smart phones, are more and more popular. These devices are becoming powerful and carrying more sensors, so they become good candidates to collect environment data as well as to be a computation platform. The mobile clouds eventually serve users. As the bridge between users and resources or clouds, the mobile devices can be service providers for clouds to collect data, or be service consumers to delegate the tasks to the cloud, or connect the other service providers and consumers. The flexible role of the mobile devices leads to the various roles in the mobile cloud service model.

3.4 IoT and Microservices

The Internet of Things (IoT) has connected an incredible diversity of devices in novel ways, which has enabled exciting new services and opportunities. As figure in page 1 shows, we are at the age when IoT are booming. Prior success with traditional approaches in no way guarantees that we shall be as successful in using the same techniques to build the future IoT system we desire. Instead of focusing on the things as the atomic elements in systems, we argue it can be beneficial to follow the service-oriented approach and conceive IoT systems as being built out of services. Any IoT node can be abstracted as a smart object providing certain services over the network, and the focus of developers can be raised to the level of data and services rather than on the devices and end-to-end communication.

3.4.1 From Things to Distributed Microservices

The way in which cloud computing and web service applications are engineered – the techniques and technologies used – have changed substantially since the invention of the Web less than three decades ago, and recently one approach known as "microservice architecture" [261] has gained some notable adherents, including Netflix, Linkedin, and Amazon [262].

A microservice is a minimal functional software module which is independently developed and deployed. A microservice architecture is a composition of microservices that are deployed and connected through composition mechanisms. Desirable characteristics of microservice-based systems include: decomposition of larger services into small, focused, self-contained services, loose coupling, and clear execution context boundaries. Due to these characteristics, microservices can often be deployed inside portable lightweight execution environments called containers. Even the services of cloud infrastructure itself can be developed and deployed in this way [156]. Much of the excitement from switching to a microservices approach comes from their promise for improvements to system and process qualities: improved alignment of system structures to teams and business, easier integration of software components using heterogeneous technologies, easier system evolution, simplified continuous delivery, and improved resilience, and scalability [100][214].

3.4.2 Microservices Patterns for IoT

We wish to work towards a vision future in which we are able to efficiently develop IoT systems that are extremely interoperable, flexible, and secure. The structure of the vision consists of a high-level, abstract model of general microservices-based IoT systems, together with patterns of solutions that one might expect to see employed in the design and deployment of any given IoT system following the vision.

Fig. 3.3 shows a visualization of the overall abstract model of IoT systems using microservices patterns. We focus on the two major patterns, microservices and API gateway, in the vision of microservices-focused IoT solutions in the following subsections.

Microservices

We take "microservices"-based IoT systems to be composed of one or more individual self-contained and independent deployable software components, i.e., microservices interacting with each other by messages abstracted as method calls (e.g., web service call, or message RPC), or through publishing/subscribing events.

From the service consumer's point of view, a microservice is nothing but a collection of APIs. To make it easier to discuss the organization of these APIs, we propose an abstract model of

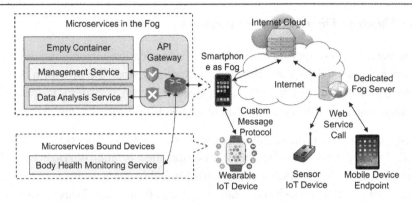

Figure 3.3: Abstract model for IoT systems structured using microservices.

the internal structure of a microservice, which can be mapped onto various protocols such as MQTT [254], CoAP [242], AMQP [253], or REST API. In our model, a microservice contains one or more virtual objects, which we take to be akin to objects in object oriented programming (OOP) languages. A virtual object can have two types of service APIs: methods, or event channels. Methods resemble the methods in OOP languages or services in REST APIs: they provide a remote procedure call (RPC). Event channels implements a publisher–subscriber model such that anyone that subscribes to the event channel will be notified when an event is published by an event producer.

Sensors and devices with sensing capability are examples of what might typically be an event producer. The events they publish might usually be intermittent, and their traffic is normally a push style. Actuators and services in the cloud are examples of event consumers and method providers (callee). They are typically continuously online, and their traffic style is typically that of request-response. It may be that one event or method call might generate a cascade of additional events or method calls. A method that does not return anything can be used as an event consumer as long as the method and the event channel is compatible in data format as well as semantics. Virtual objects, event channels and methods can be dynamically created by a microservice.

API Gateway

An API gateway is an interface that relays calls or requests between two or more microservices. API gateways can aggregate the APIs for multiple microservices into one client interface, and can also distribute or route the calls or requests from one entry point to multiple target microservices. Rather than allowing direct communication among microservices, an API gateway can be placed in-between them, which can have the effect of adjusting interconnectivity through the aggregation and distribution function of the gateway. Microservice connection is then established through registration; when a microservice registers itself to an API gateway, it creates one or more endpoints with unique identity, which can be further bound to an event channel or method through static configuration or dynamic negotiation with the API gateway. Besides the microservices, any user or machine client can also be required to present its identity as a name of identifier to interact with the API gateway to access its associated microservices. The identity management and authentication service might leverage existing systems that managing accounts, such as single-sign-on (SSO) or OAuth [127].

From the API gateway's point of view, each endpoint is uniquely identifiable, where the identity may be represented as a unique name or just an identifier. Such endpoint name or identifier only exist in the model, and the API gateway implementation needs to map it into actual protocol, such as an URL in REST API or CoAP, a queue or exchange in AMQP, or a topic in MQTT. In a cloud-supported body weight management IoT system as described in the example above, the weight management plan virtual object can be mapped to REST resource URL on the cloud server, which runs the weight management and recommendation microservices, and the method as well as parameter format on this virtual object can be mapped to the HTTP methods. In typical uses of this approach, the method name is encoded in the JSON payload to AUGMENT the limited types of HTTP methods. Such mappings impose additional constraints on our model, such as requiring that consecutive method calls in a session must be "nonsticky."

PART 2

Mobile Cloud Computing

MCC is an emerging cloud service model following the trend to extend the cloud to the edge of networks. It includes numerous mobile devices that are closely associated with their users. They will be directly involved in many cloud activities that extend the cloud boundaries into the entire cyber physical system. According to comScore [44], the time spent on mobile devices to access Internet for US adults has exceeded the time spent on PCs in 2014. Thus, mobile devices will become more important and will be involved in almost all aspects of our daily life.

Mobile computing research is to study how mobile devices sense and learn the status of other devices and the context related to their mobility and networking to better access the Internet and/or support mobile applications in an ad hoc communication environment. Cloud computing research mainly focuses on how to manage computing, storage, and communication resources that are shared by multiple users in a virtualized and isolated environment (a more complete definition of cloud computing, as provided by NIST is presented in Chapter 1, Section 1.1.1). Mobile cloud computing cannot be simply illustrated as merging mobile computing and cloud computing technologies.

An illustrative example of mobile cloud computing is how a smart phone can best utilize the cloud resource to reduce its energy consumption. A computing task can be either executed on the mobile device or outsourced to the cloud. Where to compute depends on the overhead tradeoffs between computation and communication while considering the requirements of applications' Quality of Service (QoS) and users' Quality of Experience (QoE) [151]. On the one hand, the dual computing model involving both the cloud and the mobile device should minimize the entire system cost, usually with more focus on reducing resource consumption on mobile devices. On the other hand, a mobile cloud computing service model should improve mobile users' QoE to fulfill their satisfaction when using mobile cloud applications. To address the aforementioned issues, researchers need to have a comprehensive view of mobile cloud computing. If research is limited to within each individual research domain, it will not be enough to address complex problems arising from the new mobile cloud service model.

Existing research tries to cross the disciplines' boundaries by applying cloud computing solutions into mobile applications or incorporating mobile features when constructing new cloud services. However, the immense information involved in mobile cloud applications and the high complexity of designing mobile cloud applications demanded a new transdisciplinary research to better understand the nature and principles of MCC.

One important feature of MCC applications is functional collaboration. For example, mobile social network based data mining requires collaborations among mobile users. To this end, MCC will serve as not only a nexus that interconnects information sources gathered from both cloud computing service domains and mobile computing domains, but also a knowledge center to help mobile users in their daily activities. With these capabilities, MCC can assist a mobile entity in discovering other interested entities to construct self-organized MCC subdomains that may only have a short lifespan. Similar functional collaboration approach is the microservice model presented in Chapter 3, Section 3.4. In Chapter 4, we present a Personal On-demand Execution environment for Mobile cloud applications (POEM) [278] service framework to realize the functional collaboration feature.

In MCC, QoE measures the subjective feeling of mobile users' experiences when using MCC based applications. QoS objectively measures the services such as communication delay, throughput, battery lifespan, etc. QoS usually has a strong impact on QoE. However, a better QoS measurement does not mean improved QoE. For example, running powerful CPU on mobile devices may improve the performance of applications; however, it may also shorten the device's use time due to high power consumption that will decrease users' QoE. If migrating computing tasks to the cloud is a solution to address the high-energy consumption, MCC service model needs to consider the trade-offs caused by migration delay, communication overhead, and power consumption due to the migration. Thus, MCC needs to consider the relationship between QoS and QoE as a measurement to evaluate the performance of the cloud system. We call this measurement as Quality of Service and Experience (QoSE).

To improve QoSE, MCC should adopt a geography-based service model (or geo-based model). This is because mobile users can access the cloud services from any location in the world. The geo-based model can push the cloud computing and storage service nodes to the mobile device as close as possible. In this way, service delay, which is a major QoSE measure, can be greatly reduced. The geo-based model requires MCC server nodes (or clusters) to mirror VMs (or through VM migration) in different geographic locations. The states of the mirrored VMs must be synchronized.

Context awareness between a mobile device and its dedicated VM(s) is another important feature to improve QoSE. Nowadays, a smart mobile device usually serves as an information gateway for the mobile user involving many personalized activities such as checking e-mails, making an appointment, surfing the web, calling a number, locating some interested spots, etc. Context awareness can be at either the device level or the application level. When it is at the device-level, the device's states such as CPU utilization, available memory and storage, and battery levels need to be learned by its VM to decide whether computing operations should be migrated or not. At the application level, mobile devices can be interfaced to various wireless-capable devices such as sensors, RFIDs, and other smart devices. MCC will serve as a knowledge base to instruct mobile devices on how to locate them and interface with (or control) them. Without the support of MCC services, these tasks are difficult to execute for individual mobile devices. Each mobile device can be considered as a sensing service node for the cloud to sense the application running situation and to assist the MCC on the decision where to deploy application functions, i.e., a subapplication function can be deployed on an MCC service node to gain the maximum QoSE for mobile users. In Chapter 5, we provide detailed analysis and decision models on two-party (one-to-one) service offloading and multi-party (one-to-many and many-to-many) service offloading scenarios.

MCC is a cloud service platform supporting many mobile application scenarios. Here, we just name a few: mobile health, smart home, intelligent transportation, etc. These mobile applications scenarios share some common features that we have discussed previously, which are summarized as follows:

- Individual and collective sensing capability. MCC applications can utilize the sensing capabilities from each mobile device to learn the context of a given application situation.
- Personalized functions and features. A mobile device and its associated VM(s) serve as personal information assistants to help mobile users (equipped with several devices) to learn his/her activities and behaviors.
- Strong reliability and fail-over protection. Damage and loss of mobile devices are common due to their small and portable nature. MCC can provide a suite of solutions to protect the mobile users' data and provide service recovery it due to unreliable communication failure, lost (or stolen), and upgrade.
- Easy software development platform, e.g., using virtualization technologies to establish MCC PaaS platform, which enable MCC application developers to develop various applications enjoying all features provided by MCC service entities. Moreover, it is easier to integrate various applications in the MCC system with little compatibility issue.
- Caching capability. MCC can help mobile devices maintain the states of MCC applications. Partially delivered data, lost connections, and half operated functions can be resumed; thus, this will reduce the overhead due to the uncertainty caused by the mobility of mobile users.

In Chapter 6, several MCC application scenarios including remote healthcare, smart home, and autonomous vehicle platooning will be presented on how to realize the described features using MCC service offloading/composition approaches.

CHAPTER 4

Mobile Cloud Computing Service Framework

Mobile cloud technologies enable effective interactions between the physical world and the virtual world.

Dijiang Huang

Today, the Internet web service is the main way that people access information from fixed or mobile terminals. Information is stored in Internet clouds where computing, communication, and storage are common services provided for Internet users. In the near future, many of our queries will be beyond the current Internet scope – they will be about the people, the physical environments that surround us, and the virtual environments that we will be involved in. With the Internet being pervasive, mobile phones have already overtook PCs as the most common web access entities worldwide by 2013 [194]. Current mobile devices have many advanced features such as mobility, communication and sensing capabilities, and can serve as the personal information gateway for mobile users. However, when running complex data mining and storing operations, the computation, energy, and storage limitations of mobile devices demand an integrated solution relying on cloud-based computation and storage support.

In MCC, a mobile entity can be considered either a physical mobile device or a mobile computing/storage software agent within a virtualized cloud resource provisioning system. In the latter view of the cloud system, a software agent's main functionality is the mobility associated with the software code. In other words, mobile cloud applications may migrate or compose software codes in the distributed MCC resource-provisioning environment. Mobile cloud services will account for delay, energy consumption, real-time entity presence, information caching capabilities, networking connectivity, data protection, sharing requirements, and more. By achieving these features, we are actually able to create a new world composed of both physically networked systems and virtualized entities that are mapped to the physical systems, preserving and sometimes extending their functions and capabilities.

MCC distinguishes its research focus on close interaction, construction, and integration of the Physical System (PS) and Cyber Virtual System (CVS). The PS is composed of smart and mobile devices, and the CVS is mainly formed by cloud-based virtualized resources and services. Recent developments of Augmented Reality (AR)[1] have demonstrated some of the application capabilities of MCC.

This chapter first focuses on a comprehensive study in existing mobile cloud computing (MCC) service models, and then a user-centric MCC service framework. The rest of this article is arranged as follows. Section 4.1 describes how the transformation occurs from traditional Internet cloud to mobile cloud and highlights features of MCC. Section 4.2 presents an MCC service offloading and composition framework, called POEM [278].

4.1 Transitions from Internet Clouds to User-centric Mobile Clouds

From the service point of view, current MCC service providers and their services customers (i.e., mobile devices) are clearly defined. Most existing computing models are similar to the traditional "client–server" type of service models. Several issues for the existing MCC services and the expected transition characteristics are explained and discussed below.

Symmetric MCC Service Model. Most current MCC service models are asymmetric. As examples presented in Table 3.1, mobile devices are usually considered clients of cloud services. The service (e.g., computing and storage services) direction is mainly one directional, i.e., from cloud to mobile devices. With the increasing capability of mobile devices, mobile devices can also collaboratively execute the applications' tasks. Moreover, the virtualized environment should provide intelligent feedback to physical devices to adjust their behaviors or actions in order to provide better virtualized services. This virtualization-feedback loop model demands a symmetric MCC service model, i.e., both mobile devices and the virtualized cloud are service providers as well as clients at the same time.

Personalized Situation Awareness. In the current complicated mobile cloud environment, data sources could be diverse, e.g., mobile device, environment, or social network. Sometimes, a single data source is not sufficient for supporting MCC applications in the cloud. Moreover, data collected from heterogeneous network might be unstructured or unclassified. For example, in the physical world, there could be multiple networking interfaces and services that are available to a user's device, e.g., wireless sensor network, social network, vehicular network, personal and body area network, etc. Cloud should be able to get data from different source networks and cluster them together to make the data structural and readable in the future. Thus, more work is expected to construct situation-aware services that can be personalized according to individual users in the virtual environment.

---

[1]   Augmented reality (AR) is a live direct or indirect view of a physical, real-world environment whose elements are augmented (or supplemented) by computer-generated sensory input such as sound, video, graphics, or GPS data.

User-Centric Trust Model. Most of the current cloud trust model is centralized, i.e., all mobile entities need to trust the cloud service provider. Storing private data in the cloud environment is a big hurdle for most mobile cloud applications. It is desirable to establish a distributed or decentralized trust management framework within the virtualized cloud system to address the privacy concerns of mobile users. In the physical world, the virtualized resource could be hosted in either public or private clouds that are tailored according to user preference. This requirement demands to transfer the current centralized cloud to into a distributed or decentralized cloud. For example, including mobile users' computing and storage resources into the mobile cloud infrastructure without requiring (or even allowing) administrative privilege can significantly reduce the privacy concerns of mobile users.

4.1.1 User-centric Mobile Cloud Computing

The next-generation MCC applications demand tight integration of the physical and virtual functions running on the mobile devices and cloud servers, respectively. Moreover, due to the mobility of mobile users and the changes of the application running environment, the MCC application functions are not fixed on their running hosts. As an illustrative vehicle traffic management example shown in Fig. 4.1A, a vehicle may request Video Capture (VC) functions from other vehicles directly (the dashed line) or through a centralized video fusion function to get a holistic view of the entire road intersection. In this example, the VC providers are not fixed and are selected by their location. Moreover, a VC function may not only be used for individual vehicle, but also for road traffic management, accident/hazard detection, traffic monitoring, etc. The resources include mobiles, cloud servers, and corresponding networking that form an ad hoc cloud application running environment that can be customized for each individual user. We refer to such a customizable ad hoc cloud application running system as a user-centric MCC application. The basic functions that are used to form this MCC application (VC, display, and data fusion, etc.) are called Provisioning Functions (*PFs*) and is similar to the microservices described in Chapter 3, Section 3.4.

The user-centric mobile cloud application running environment can be further illustrated in Fig. 4.1B, where mobiles (M_A, M_B, M_C) and their corresponding cloud virtual resources (CVR_A, CVR_B, CVR_C) construct a pairwise resource pool $R_X = (M_X, CVR_X)$ including both physical and virtualized resource. R_X represents the user X to construct MCC applications formed by a set of provisioning functions $\{PF\}_X$ running on local or remote resource pools. In this user-centric mobile cloud application running environment, a *PF* can be highly mobile, and it can be composed and used by multiple applications at the same time.

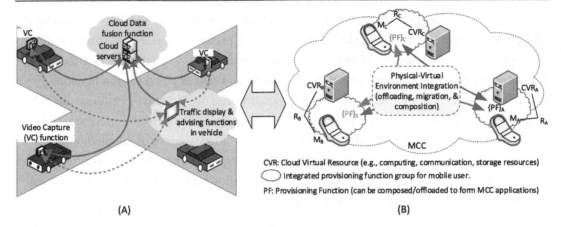

Figure 4.1: An example of mobile cloud applications. (A) MCC application scenario. (B) User-centric MCC application model.

4.1.2 Design Principles of User-centric Mobile Cloud Computing

Future MCC should be reconsidered as a new service model, where mobile agents, i.e., both physical and virtual entities, and related resources collectively operate as mobile clouds that enable computing, storage and networking capabilities, context awareness modeling, content discovery, data collection and dissemination. To build the future user-centric mobile cloud computing based on the described concepts and requirements, mobile clouds should be shifted from the traditional Internet cloud by using the following principles:

- *Principle 1: User-centric.* MCC applications should be designed in a way that the users can control their own data and activities with strong privacy and security protection. Cloud resources should be collected and allocated according to mobile applications customized for each individual user.
- *Principle 2: Service-oriented application platform.* Due to the symmetric service model, every mobile node can potentially serve as an MCC service provider, and thus service-oriented application platform is the natural choice for MCC. With the popularity of IoT devices and services established based on IoT, microservice model has become one of important service frameworks for MCC.
- *Principle 3: Mobility-aware.* MCC resources should be dynamically allocated and managed according to the need of mobile cloud applications. Mobility of MCC should be confined through a set of mobile cloud application constrains to maximize the efficiency using a set of system performance evaluation metrics such as availability, computing power, storage, and their spatiotemporal boundaries.

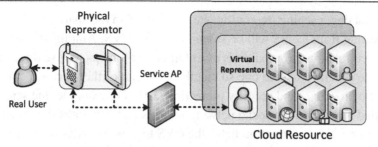

Figure 4.2: Mobile-as-a-Representer (MaaR).

- *Principle 4: Virtual representation.* MCC maintains a trustworthy, reliable, and accessible virtual representation for each user. The virtualized representation can be considered an assistant for mobile users and performs actions such as sensing a user's daily activity to build user's behavior and activity profiles, and delegates the user's activities in the virtual environment. The virtual representation concepts can be extended to any entity that may mirror its functions into the CVS.

4.1.3 Mobile-as-a-Representer: A User-centric Approach

The future mobile cloud service model should be delivered based on the principles illustrated in Section 4.1.2. Besides previously presented service models, i.e., MaaSC, MaaSP, and MaaSB, we present a new user-centric MCC service model called Mobile-as-a-Representer (MaaR). The architecture of MaaR can be found in Fig. 4.2. In MaaR, each user can be represented by a virtualized entity in the cloud through his/her physical entity (i.e., mobile device). User behaviors and attributes can be collected from the real world (people, environment, or mobile devices) in real time and sent to their corresponding virtual entities in the cloud to perform further analysis and processing. Data mining and machine learning algorithms can be used to analyze a mobile user's situation and perform actions proactively. MaaR can be regarded as the next-generation MCC service model in that both physical systems and virtual systems are seamlessly integrated through virtualization technologies to provide services. In MaaR, the mobile devices and clouds are highly interactive, and as a result, the service flow can be presented as bidirectional arrows. In addition to helping mobile entities execute tasks more efficiently, MaaR is able to accomplish some tasks that are impossible with current MCC architecture.

MaaR model is presented to support the next-generation user-centric MCC services and applications. A conceptual architecture of MaaR is presented in Chapter 1, Fig. 1.3, where both PS and CVS are integrated as a whole system. In the PS, heterogeneous networks coexist, and all these networks can be virtualized at the CVS by performing operations including presenting, offloading, abstracting, caching, migration, etc. All data with the spatial, temporal, and correlation information from the PS will be submitted to the CVS. Among all these three types of information, correlation information is essential in that it helps to fuse different types of data together into a well formatted one so that the CVS can further perform context awareness, user-centric proactive, and security protection tasks. For example, the sensor network carries the sensed data while the social network collects and generates the social relationship data. The correlation information helps the CVS to generate sensing data with social attributes (e.g., personal data that is only accessible from a specific social group, like people in the user's friend list).

In MaaR, the CVS has three main types of provisioning resources: computing resource, storage resource, and networking resource. The user's virtual entity is represented by maintaining seamless communication between the PS and the CVS, which also allows for establishing multiple personalized MCC clouds due to different application purposes. An MCC application is able to control integration of PS and CVS through a well-defined API and MCC tools. The traditional Internet cloud is one-way operational as users can only submit data from the PS to the CVS, while it is possible to allow the CVS to further control the PS functions in a highly adaptive and dynamic fashion based on the MaaR model. Besides physical data being virtualized, the CVS can provide feedback and control functions in the PS.

To enable the service-oriented application running environment, MaaR provides POEM (Personal On-demand execution Environment for Mobile cloud computing) framework [278] to achieve the user-centric MCC service running platform, where an illustrative vehicular system example is provided in Fig. 4.1. POEM is a mobile cloud application execution platform that enables mobile devices to easily discover and compose cloud resources for their applications. For mobile resource providers, they may not even know what applications and who may call their provisioned functions beforehand. In this way, the mobile application design should not be application-oriented; instead, it should be functionality-oriented (or service-oriented). To achieve these features, we can consider those *PFs* as the fundamental application components in the MaaR model, which can be composed by mobile cloud service requesters at runtime.

POEM takes a comprehensive approach by incorporating the OSGi-based [222] service-oriented architecture into MCC. OSGi bundles[2] are treated as implementations of *PFs* in MCC conceptual model. It treats the offloading as part of service composition, and as a result, bundles (or computation tasks) are considered services provided by mobile devices and the

---

[2]   OSGi (Open Service Gateway Initiative) is a Java framework for developing and deploying modular software programs and libraries. Each bundle is a tightly coupled, dynamically loadable collection of classes, jars, and configuration files that explicitly declare their external dependencies (if any).

cloud. In this way, offloading and migration operations can be multidirectional (i.e., among mobile devices and the cloud) compared to one-directional (i.e., from a mobile device to the cloud) in previous solutions. Moreover, due to the popular Java-based OSGi framework, POEM can greatly improve the adoption of the Service-Oriented Architecture (SOA)[3]-based code reuse and composition for MCC.

4.1.4 An Application Scenario Based on User-centric MaaR Model

To better understand the proposed MaaR model, we revisit the vehicular video sensing and collaboration example presented in Fig. 4.1A. We assume that MaaR service modules are already equipped on many users' smart phones. When user Alice is driving, her smart phone uses onboard sensors, like camera or GPS, to detect her location, driving speed, and image/video captured on the road. As shown in Fig. 4.1B, the information can be collected and virtualized into the CVS to construct a virtual representation of the mobile device in the cloud for Alice, which is the essence of MaaR in that the virtual representer depicts the real situation of the physical user. Practically, the representer is implemented through a set of software agents (i.e., OSGi bundles) on a dedicated VM allocated for Alice, where Alice has the administrative privilege, to decide what data can be shared and protected (by encryption). The dedicated VM is the application holder for Alice to incorporate various data processing models and functions for security, data mining, and intelligent situation-aware decision making that are personalized for the uses of Alice. In this model, the VM can be hosted in public or private cloud as the choice of Alice.

User Bob may want to know the current traffic status around the bridge 5 miles ahead of where Alice is driving. Users with MaaR services running on their mobile devices near the bridge can provide sensing functions, e.g., GPS, video/camera, which are searchable by Bob so that Bob's display function can call those functions in real-time through either direct P2P connections or a centralized traffic monitoring function provided by a third party. In addition to the presented video capturing usage of the application, MaaR services and applications can also maintain social diagrams for each user. For example, when Bob is driving in the area during the lunchtime, the MaaR service representer of Bob can prepare for suggestions such as good nearby restaurants with high ratings by Bob's trusted friends. Other suggestions may relate to Bob's daily activities and job functions according to his current location, and can be provided promptly when Bob needs them. These personalized suggestions are based on correlating the location and various sensed data by the MaaR service representer.

---

[3] A service-oriented architecture (SOA) is a style of software design where services are provided to the other components by application components, through a communication protocol over a network. The basic principles of service oriented architecture are independent of vendors, products, and technologies.

4.2 Overview of POEM

In mobile clouds, mobile devices and cloud resources compose a distributed mobile application running environment, where a mobile application may consume resources from both local and remote resource providers who provide computing, networking, sensing, and storage resource provisioning. Mobile devices can serve as either service consumers or service providers in the mobile cloud, in which the cloud boundaries are extended into the mobile domain [140]. Mobile applications may require a mobile device to interact with other mobile devices and cloud resource providers to achieve desired computing, storing, collaboration, or sensing features.

An ideal mobile cloud application running system should enable mobile devices to easily discover and compose cloud resources for its applications. From mobile resource providers' perspective, they may not even know what applications are using their resources and who may call their provisioned functions beforehand. In this way, the mobile application design should not be application-oriented; instead, it should be functionality-oriented (or service-oriented). For example, the video function of a mobile device should provide general interfaces that can be called by multiple local or remote functions in the runtime. To achieve this feature, we can consider these *PFs* as the fundamental application components in the mobile cloud, which can be composed by mobile cloud service requesters in the runtime. As a result, the mobile cloud can significantly reduce the mobile application development overhead and greatly improve the agility and flexibility to build a personalized mobile cloud computing system that can be customized for each mobile user.

There are several challenges invoked by the application scenario described above. The first challenge is that knowing the status of mobile devices, e.g., online/offline and runtime information (such as battery, computing power, connectivity, etc.), is difficult due to the mobility of mobile users. The second challenge is that knowing the available *PFs* on each mobile device is not a trivial task. Currently, there is no such common framework allowing mobile devices to exchange the available *PFs* information and run such a system in a distributed environment. The third challenge is to compose *PFs* crossing various hardware and software platforms, which demands a universal programming and application running environment with little compatibility issues.

To address these challenges, we present POEM, a new mobile cloud application running system as shown in Fig. 4.3. POEM treats each mobile device as a *PF* provider. In addition, POEM is designed based on a cloud framework, where a dedicated VM is assigned to each mobile device providing computing and storage support. Moreover, *PFs* can be offloaded/migrated from a mobile device to its assigned VM. Thus, the VM can not only run mobile devices' *PFs* (i.e., as shadows), but also can run extended *PFs* that mobile devices may not have

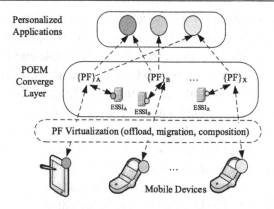

Figure 4.3: Overview of POEM system.

the capacity to execute. Collectively, the *PFs* provided by a mobile device X and its corresponding VM_X are denoted as $\{PF\}_X$. POEM regards both mobile devices and their dedicated VMs as *PF* providers. As a result, the mobile user's applications can be composed by *PFs* from local *PFs* (may be offloaded/migrated to its dedicated VM) and/or remote *PFs* (may run on remote mobile devices or their dedicated VMs).

POEM is an open source project using OSGi [223]. Besides OSGi, it also uses XMPP [282] techniques. In summary, the key features of POEM are highlighted as follows:

- *Social mobile cloud computing.* POEM solution enables the mobile cloud application to utilize social network power, i.e., in addition to the discovered *PFs* through the mobile cloud system, users can establish mobile cloud applications through their trusted social connections. In this way, POEM applications can not only use the resource in cloud by offloading resource intensive components but also can use services provided from their social connections.
- *Versatile and personalized application offloading, migration, and composition.* POEM maintains available mobile cloud resource and allows users choosing a mobile cloud application by using different approaches (offloading, migration, and composition) based on the available system resources and their personalized application requirements.

4.2.1 POEM Application Framework

POEM is implemented based on OSGi framework [223] that is a general purpose, secure, and managed Java framework and supports the deployment of extensible and downloadable applications [223]. Due to the popularity of Java, OSGi framework is compatible with major operating systems for both desktop and mobile device systems. The layered framework is stacked from bottom-up into three layers: module layer, life cycle layer, and service layer. The framework defines a unit of modularization, called a bundle, i.e., "*PF*" in the POEM. In the later descriptions, we do not differentiate the terms bundle and *PF*. In POEM, a *PF* comprises Java classes and other resources, and is deployed as a Java ARchive (JAR) file. *PF* sits on the top of stacked layers and interacts with them through *PF* context. Module layer and life cycle layer handle *PF* installation and activation. *PF* can be installed/uninstalled and started/stopped. The service layer has a service registry and handles service publication and discovery. A service is a normal Java object that is registered under one or more Java interfaces with the service registry. *PFs* can register services, search for them, or receive notifications when services' states change. When *PF* is installed, the framework must cache the *PF* JAR file. A *SERVICE_RANKING* property may be specified when a service is being registered. The service with the highest ranking is returned when the framework receives service query. Before the service is consumed, it may become a stale reference. Service tracker is usually used for service consumer to prevent stale reference by obtaining reference when consumption happens. Besides local service activities, a distribution provider can export service to another framework by creating an end point or import services from another framework by creating a proxy for service composition, and then registering the proxy as an imported service.

POEM models a mobile cloud application as a set of *PFs*. The *PF* may provide class definitions and host services that implements *PFs*. POEM does not differentiate *PFs* on mobile devices and *PFs* on their VMs as the *PFs* may be migrated from mobile side to cloud side or vice versa without any modification. The uniform *PF* format makes *PFs* reusable and reduces develops' workload by avoiding developing separate *PFs* for specific platform. The application may use services provided by local or remote *PFs*. The application can migrate *PFs* between mobile devices and VMs without disrupting the other active *PFs*.

POEM achieves social feature through an implemented the XMPP [282] system within a cloud, e.g., MobiCloud [141]. The availability information of the system resources and mobile devices is maintained through a decentralized client–server architecture, where every mobile cloud entity needs an address called a JabberID (JID). JID is presented in the form of user@domain/resource. Domain represents the XMPP service provider, user represents virtual identity in the domain, and resource identifies connection to an XMPP server. Three basic status services are achieved through XMPP: message, presence, and info/query(or iq). POEM's service discovery protocol provides two discovery methods: one enables discovering information about an entity, and the other enables discovery of items associated with an entity.

In POEM, each entity, i.e., a mobile device or a VM, runs an OSGi framework, which is identified uniquely by its JID. One POEM entity discovers services hosted by his/her friends through XMPP service discovery protocol and XMPP publish–subscribe protocol. Mobile

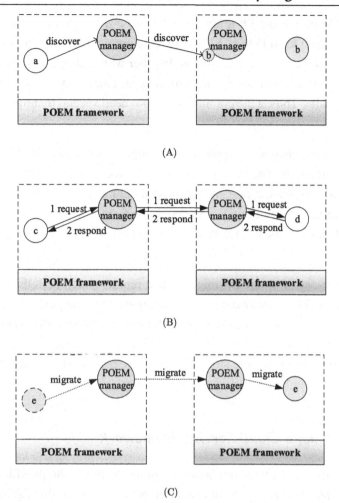

Figure 4.4: Execution patterns in POEM. (A) *PF* **publishing and discovery pattern. (B)** *PF* **composition pattern. (C)** *PF* **offloading pattern.**

applications offload *PFs* to VMs through XMPP file transfer protocol, and the data exchange with remote application in POEM is through XMPP *iq* communication.

4.2.2 Execution Model

According to previous application scenario, there are three fundamental execution patterns in POEM, as shown in Fig. 4.4. The first pattern describes how one *PF* discovers remote available *PFs*, which is shown in Fig. 4.4A. *PF b* hosts a service and it publishes the service through local POEM for remote *PF* to discover. Then *PF a* can discover the published service on remote side with local POEM *PF*'s help. One prerequisite for *a* to discover and use the service of *b* is that they are mutual friends. In other words, they are on each other's contact lists. *PF a* does not know that *PF b* is running on a remote side because POEM pretends that *b* is running locally. Thus, a programmer does not need special treatment in coding when developing *PF a*.

The second pattern presents how an application recruits a service provided by a remote *PF*, which is shown in Fig. 4.4B. The *PF c* sends method invocation parameters, which are transferred by the POEM on the local side and then on the remote side, to the destination *PF d*. Then, the service result returns along the reverse route from *d* back to *c*. *PF c* also believes it is calling a local target *d* due to POEM's transparent transfer, and *d* also thinks a local *c* is calling it.

The third pattern presents how one *PF* migrates to a remote entity. A POEM *PF* initializes the migration process. There are two types of migrations, pull and push. In pull migration, the POEM *PF* on the right side sends request to the left side POEM *PF*, and then the latter fetches and transfers the target *PF e* to the right side. In push migration, the POEM *PF* on the left side transfers *PF e* to the remote side. The source keeps the *PF e* active during transfer to provide the failsafe when the transfer is not successful.

4.3 Design of Mobile Cloud Service Framework

POEM is designed for a distributed application running platform and provides service publish, discovery, and composition as a uniform execution environment. In this environment, transparent and seamless *PF* migration is the key POEM function, i.e., mobile users will not notice the platform level operations when running POEM supported applications.

Fig. 4.5 illustrates the overall design of the POEM system. The POEM Manager monitors local services, tracks service state change, maintains local *PF* repository, and responds to remote service queries. Its networking component also maintains XMPP connections to XMPP peers that provide the communication and signaling infrastructure among mobile devices and their VMs. The POEM composition component creates local proxy for remote service provider that responds to service requests by transferring the request to the remote *PF*, and then getting the result to the local *PFs*. Based on a systematic decision model, POEM initiates the migration operations for *PF* offloading. In the following sections, we describe each component within the POEM framework.

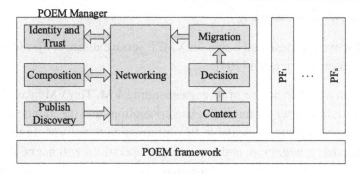

Figure 4.5: POEM components.

4.3.1 Distributed POEM Service Platform

POEM's networking and signaling system is deployed based on XMPP approaches. The communication between POEM entities (i.e., mobile devices and VMs) is a full duplex compared to a half duplex HTTP approach deployed by many web-based service frameworks. In a distributed execution environment, any entity can be both a client and a server at the same time, which is different from web-based service models where clients and servers are explicitly defined. Moreover, POEM inherits the XMPP trust and identity management framework, where every POEM entity is authenticated when joining the system, and the data transferred is also protected through cryptographic approaches. As a result, the *PF* offloading and *PF* compositions can utilize the XMPP trust management framework with fine-grained access control capabilities. Furthermore, POEM entities need to provide their presence information to indicate their availability information in real-time, which is also used to indicate their service status.

Identity and Trust Management

In the POEM framework, each POEM entity has a POEM manager that manages the local/remote *PFs* and it is uniquely identified by a unique JID when the user registered in the system. A user's JID can be shared among POEM entities, and it must be included in messages to identify the source/destination of the messages. The security features such as data privacy, integrity, user authentications, etc., can be easily incorporated by establishing a centralized trust authority, e.g., certificate authority or Kerberos-based key management, authentication, and authorization. Trust management related research including focus on how to establish trust among POEM entities is scheduled for future work. We must note that using XMPP the social network-based trust can be easily established through friend lists (a.k.a., contact list). Using this feature, POEM entities can first request desired *PF*(s) to their friends before sending the discovery message to all other POEM users.

POEM Service Discovery and Publishing

POEM service discovery is designed based on XMPP service discovery protocol [129] and XMPP publish–subscribe extension [204].

A *PF* may reside on a mobile device or its corresponding VM. The VM takes the responsibility to represent the mobile user for any *PF* related operations and the mobile device POEM Manager can frequently update its available *PFs* information to the VM. In this way, the main POEM service discovery, migration, and composition operations will not be flooded to end mobile devices. The VM POEM Manager also maintains the mobile device availability information and provides its reachability information to its trusted POEM peers. When the VM POEM Manager receives the service discovery message, it replies with its available *PFs* with the available remote service interfaces.

POEM Manager also monitors local service changes and notifies its friends. This is done through a publishing procedure. POEM Manager first registers a publish node (i.e., a virtual node in the XMPP server) under its JID. Thus, when local service status changes, POEM Manager can post the notice on its publish node and its friends get notified and update their *PFs* availability database. We note that this concept can be extended to the scenario for POEM users that are not on each other's friend list. POEM can create interest groups for those who have registered and receive notices published in the corresponding interest group.

POEM Service Composition

When POEM discovers service provided by remote POEM entities, it tries to create a proxy so that remote *PF* can be used locally. POEM uses Java dynamic proxy technique to create proxy. Dynamic proxy requires that the target interface's Class instance must exist. To have remote service interface's Class instance in a local OSGi framework instance, POEM fetches *PF* JAR file corresponding to the target service from a remote POEM framework. POEM Manager installs the *PF*, and then the target Class instance is available and proxy generation is done.

PF *Offloading*

When the application decides to offload a service provider object and migrate it to the cloud, POEM Manager chooses to send the object's byte code to the cloud and start the object from byte code. How to choose POEM *PFs* to be migrated is based on several conditions described as follows. First, thread migration solution is not adopted because some objects that exist in the same thread have to run on mobile devices, such as user interfaces and sensors. Second, an application usually wants to migrate only the compute intensive operations rather than the whole thread. Third, object state is not maintained because insight into private details of the object to be migrated cannot be fetched due to Java security management. Our recent practice suggests that service implementation should be stateless, so that the object states will not bother POEM like REST does [108].

When the *PF* offloading starts, the POEM Manager sends the corresponding *PF* JAR file that contains the target service provider object byte codes. Instead of dedicating object byte codes, POEM sends the whole *PF* JAR file because the object starts in the *PF* context and it depends on the *PF* context to be executed. If object serialization is chosen to migrate the target object, all the objects in that *PF* have to be serialized and transferred. However, not all objects in that *PF* can be accessed due to OSGi modularization. So the entire *PF* should be transferred rather than only the target object.

POEM needs a *PF* repository that stores all the candidate *PF* JAR files that have possibility to be migrated. When *PF* is plugged into the POEM framework, a copy of *PF* JAR file is stored in the *PF* repository.

Migration

The service provider object offloading process follows a three-step approach: First, the target *PF* JAR file is transferred to VM and started. Then, a proxy object is created to intercept and capture service request to a remote target service. Finally, the *PF* containing target service provider object is stopped.

The first step prepares for the service request sent by the proxy object that is created by Java dynamic proxy technique. The proxy object registers to POEM framework with a higher-ranking number than the target service provider object. The POEM framework treats the proxy object as the service provider according to its ranking order. The request to the service interface is sent to the proxy object. Up to now, the service composition works fine and the last step stops original *PF*.

The migration happens according to the migration decision module command. POEM constructs the migration decision module as a plug-in framework. A user can develop the migration decision strategy plug-ins and install the strategy bundle into POEM, which not only provides the flexibility for the user customized migration strategy but also scales the POEM intelligence.

PF *Isolation*

The migrated *PFs* are running in the surrogate POEM framework to provide service for its origination. These *PFs* may interact with the POEM framework and interrupt the *PFs* that belong to surrogate host. The *PF* isolation is required to protect the surrogate POEM framework and cease the potential attack from the migrated *PF*.

The POEM Manager initializes a separate *PF* container for each friend who wants to offload his/her *PF*. The *PF* container is a duplication of the surrogate host POEM framework. The only difference is that this nested *PF* container is empty and dedicated for the corresponding friend. The friend's identity is stored and managed by the identity manager. The surrogate host defines the accepted *PF* policies that are enforced by the policy manager.

Connection Failsafe

The connection between mobile device and cloud is usually not stable as the mobile device moves. When the connection is lost, POEM Manager restarts the *PF* that has been stopped in offloading process. The recovery process has the following two steps. First, the target *PF* is started. Then, the proxy service is unregistered and the proxy object is destroyed. The first step prepares for receiving a service request. The second step destroys the proxy, which makes the target service provider object, which is the first in the ranking order, to receive the service request.

4.3.2 POEM Implementation

POEM Manager consists of several objects as shown in Fig. 4.6. They are categorized as three sets – XMPP connection and related listeners, *PF* context and related listeners, and proxy and migration management. The three object sets represent three POEM functional sets: XMPP connection set represents remote POEM framework; *PF* context set represents local POEM framework; proxy and migration management represent core POEM logic and operation that connect the other two parts.

XMPP connection object maintains three XMPP managers that manage service discovery, publish–subscribe, and file transfer separately. Besides, it also maintains a *roster* that publishes local presence and a *publish node* that local service change notification is posted on. There is a set of listeners registered with XMPP connection. They are noticed when corresponding events occur. *Roster listener* tracks friends' presence and updates proxy pool accordingly. *Item event listeners*, one listener for each friend, waits for friends' service change notice and updates proxy pool accordingly. *Connection listener* monitors connection status and executes robustness strategy. *File transfer listener* handles file transferring. *Packet listeners* handle *iq* packets defined in POEM name space between POEM *PFs*. *Service discovery provider* responds to remote service discovery by querying *PF* context.

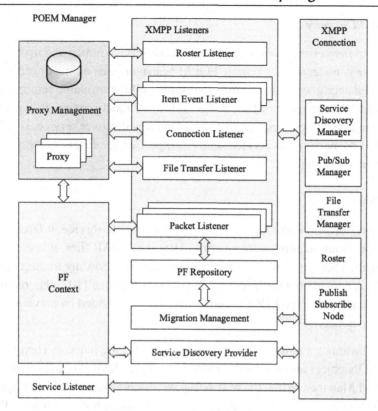

Figure 4.6: POEM Manager details.

Other POEM components are as follows: PF *context* handles interaction to POEM framework. *Service listener* monitors local service change and publishes change to a publish node maintained by XMPP connection. *Proxy management* contains a database and a *proxy* pool. It memorizes remote service status and local proxy status in database, and provides proxy generation and recycling methods. *Migration management* implements migration service registered by POEM Manager. PF *repository* provides JAR file source for file transfer request.

POEM on Android

For the mobile device side, POEM is implemented on Android devices. Android uses a different byte code format from normal Java byte code. Normal Java JAR file can be recognized by Android after DEX and AAPT operations [53] [76]. Android SDK provides the necessary tools. DEX tool collects class information and generates *classes.dex* file. AAPT tool injects *classes.dex* file into the original JAR file. After these two steps, the JAR file can be recognized by Android.

Service Publish and Discovery

Roster listener and *item event listener* monitors remote service notice and updates local proxies. *Roster listener* is noticed when remote POEM Manager goes online or offline. If the
remote POEM Manager goes online, it tries to discover all the available remote services. If
the remote POEM Manager goes offline, it tries to recycle local proxies. *Item event listener*,
instead of being noticed by presence and trying to actively discover service, is noticed when
the remote POEM Manager posts service status change. *Service listener* is responsible for
publishing the service change.

Service Composition

After *roster listener* or *item event listener* discovers the remote service, it fetches the corresponding JAR files from the remote framework. After it gets JAR files, it installs them but
does not start them. Then *proxy management* create proxies according to discovered service
name. The *proxy* is constructed by Java dynamic proxy technique [102] that requires class information provided by installed JAR file and service name provided by service discovery or
publish–subscribe notice.

When local *PF* consumes a remote service, *proxy* intercepts the request. Then *proxy* wraps the
request into a JSON object and inserts the JSON object into XMPP *iq* packet which is sent to
the remote POEM Manager. When the remote *packet listener* receives the *iq* request packet,
it parses the JSON object and calls the local service and replies to the requestor POEM Manager in the same way. The requestor *proxy* collects the *iq* response, parses it, and returns to the
local requestor.

4.3.3 Seamless Offloading

POEM Manager registers a service with a Java interface that contains a method to do service
migration. Service migration involves two framework instances that are the source and destination frameworks. The offloading process can be illustrated using the following application
scenario. The source is device 1 and the destination is a VM. The migration method is called
on device 1. Service name and destination XMPP identity are passed to the migration method.
The migration process consists of five steps as follows. First, a migration notice is sent by device 1 to the VM. Along with the migration notice, the *PF* JAR file that owns the indicated
service is transferred from device 1 to the VM. Second, POEM Manager in the VM starts
the *PF*. When *PF* is running, services including the indicated service are registered. Third,
POEM Manager in the VM is notified with service changes in last step. It unregisters the existing proxy under the same service name. Then it publishes the new services to the VM's
publish node. At this point, both sides have the running *PF* that provides services to local

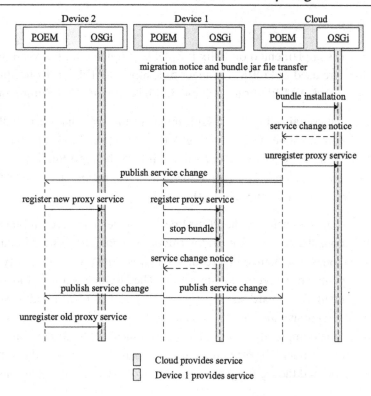

Figure 4.7: POEM migration sequence.

PFs. Fourth, POEM Manager on device 1 is notified due to the publishing in the last step. It creates the proxy for the published services with a higher ranking. Then it stops the local *PF*. At this point, the *PFs* on device 1 are consuming services provided by the VM. The sequence diagram of migration process is shown in Fig. 4.7.

Besides device 1 and the VM, a third framework instance on device 2 is using the service being migrated. When POEM Manager in the VM signals the new service, POEM Manager on device 2 creates a proxy for the new service with a higher ranking than device 1 does. When POEM Manager in the VM signals the service recycling, POEM Manager on device 2 recycles the proxy for that service. Other *PFs* on device 2 are not disturbed during the process.

4.4 Performance Considerations of Mobile Cloud Service Platform

This section describes POEM performance evaluation through both macro- and micro-benchmarks. Then migration evaluation is followed.

4.4.1 Methodology

The POEM Manager is implemented on Felix [52] OSGi implementation version 4.0.3. Felix cached *PF* JAR files are used as POEM Manager repository. XMPP *PF* from SpringSource [252], which wraps smack XMPP library version 3.1.0, is used as XMPP implementation.

Mobile application that contains a Felix OSGi framework instance that hosts POEM Manager runs on Android Motorola phone A855, running Android version 2.2.3. The phone's parameters are 600 MHz CPU and 256 MB memory. One Felix OSGi Gogo Shell runs in one Ubuntu virtual machine hosted by a cloud. The virtual machine's parameters are 1 GHZ CPU and 512 MB memory. The Ubuntu version is 11.10.

Four applications are used to evaluate the POEM performance. They are Fibonacci sequence generator, N-Queens puzzle, nested loop, and permutation generator. The Fibonacci application generates the Fibonacci sequence in a recursive manner. Its time complexity is $O(2^n)$ and its stack usage is high due to the recursive algorithm. The N-Queens application calculates all solutions for the input chessboard size. Its time complexity is $O(n^2)$ and its stack usage is also high due to the recursive algorithm. The nested loop application contains a six layer loop which leads to time complexity $O(n^6)$. The permutation application's time complexity is $O(n!)$ and it uses little memory. Experiment result is obtained by running the application 50 times for every scenario and then averaging. Between two consecutive executions there is a pause of 1 second.

The experiments are run under two scenarios:

•   Phone – the applications are run only in phone.
•   WiFi – the phone is connected to the VM through WiFi.

The WiFi connection has average latency of 70 ms, download bandwidth of 7 Mbps, and upload bandwidth of 0.9 Mbps. Ping is used to report the average latency from the phone to the VM, and Xtremelabs Speedtest [42], downloaded from Android market, is used to measure download and upload bandwidth.

4.4.2 Macro-benchmarks

For typical input parameter values, four applications are run on the phone and in the VM separately. The application running time is recorded in Table 4.1. By subtracting time on the phone and in the VM, the max speedup is put in the last column of the table. However, the max speedup is seldom achieved due to cost of communication and proxy. This cost changes a little while offloading, but the benefit changes a lot, so there should be some point when the benefit of offloading surpasses its cost, giving application net gain.

Table 4.1: Max speedup

Case	Input	Phone (ms)	Cloud (ms)	Max speedup (ms)
Fibonacci	26	59.25	2	57.25
	27	99.5	3.05	96.45
	28	156.75	5	151.75
	29	251	7.65	243.35
	30	408.25	12	396.25
N-Queens	8	11	1.1	9.9
	9	39.75	3.05	36.7
	10	222.75	12.2	210.55
	11	1593.5	64.4	1529.1
	12	9630.25	377.2	9253.05
Nested loop	14	157	15.05	141.95
	15	332	21.55	310.45
	16	276.75	28.6	248.15
	17	392.5	39.85	352.65
	18	560.25	54.35	505.9
Permutation	5	1.25	0.25	1
	6	1	0.25	0.75
	7	6.5	0.4	6.1
	8	49.25	2.05	47.2
	9	1124.75	12.1	1114.65

Table 4.2: Boundary input value

Application	BIV	Time complexity	Storage usage
Fibonacci	29	$O(2^n)$	high
N-Queens	11	$O(n^2)$	high
Nested loop	9	$O(n^6)$	low
Permutation	17	$O(n!)$	low

Boundary input value (BIV) [169] is measured to show the offloading benefit starting point. The BIV values are shown in Table 4.2. The result shows that BIV is higher for an application that is of high time complexity and space complexity. High time and space complexity application component tends to be offloaded and migrated to the VM. So BIV provides an indicator for application optimizer to decide which service should be offloaded and migrated to the VM. By comparing BIV and expected value range, the application can decide whether to move to the VM. For example, if one application often calculates Fibonacci numbers greater than 50, the Fibonacci component should be put into the VM. On the contrary, if the Fibonacci component is usually called with input less than 10, it is not necessary to be moved out of the mobile device.

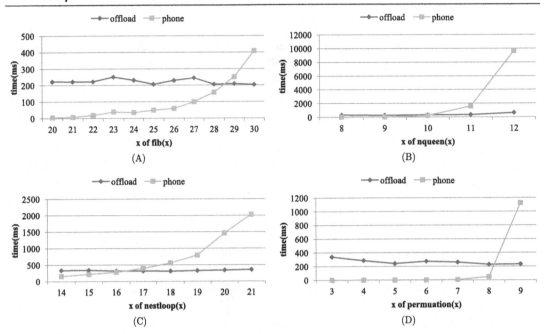

Figure 4.8: Execution time showing macro-benchmarks. (A) Execution time of Fibonacci application. (B) Execution time of N-Queens application. (C) Execution time of nested loop application. (D) Execution time of permutation application.

The macro-service execution time evaluation results are presented in Fig. 4.8. Fibonacci application takes a sequence index number and calculates the corresponding number in the Fibonacci sequence. Fig. 4.8A shows the execution time of Fibonacci application. The intersection of execution time on the phone and WiFi offloading is the BIV value. N-Queens application takes a chess board size and calculates all solutions and returns solution number. Fig. 4.8B shows execution time of N-Queens application. The execution time on the phone rises dramatically as the chessboard size increases one scale step. Offloading offers benefit as soon as the chess board size is larger than 10. Nested loop application takes loop times and executes a loop without memory operation. The execution time on the phone is convex, which means it is less than an exponential increase compared to the above two applications that require both computing and storage. The execution time of offloading increases slowly. Permutation application takes a max number N and returns count of prime number within the range $(1, N)$. The prime number searching algorithm used is Permutation algorithm. The execution time increases on the phone; however, the execution time for offloading approach remains almost the same.

The offloading line of the four applications is increasing slowly compared to the phone line. As the phone line starts from a low point, which indicates the application runs fast when input

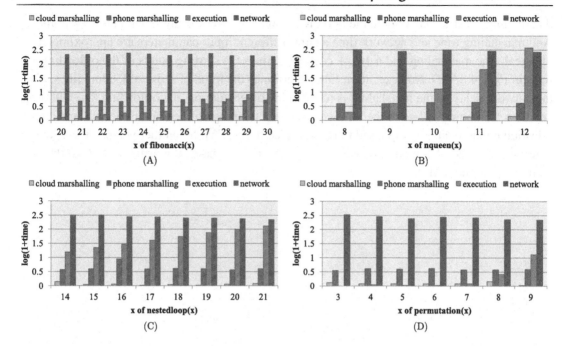

Figure 4.9: Service invocation times. (A) Invocation time of Fibonacci application. (B) Invocation time of N-Queens application. (C) Invocation time of nested loop application. (D) Invocation time of permutation application.

is small, the offloading and phone lines intersect finally. Comparing the offloading line and the VM execution time column in Table 4.1, the slow increase is reasonable due to the execution time increase, which is slowing in the VM as well. Besides, the starting point of the offloading line is higher than that of the phone line, so there must be a cost for the remote method invocation.

4.4.3 Micro-benchmarks

This experiment measures service invocation time. The time is measured on the phone where there is service on the consumer side. The remote service consuming time consists of three parts: marshaling time of both consumer and provider sides, network transfer time, and actual execution time. The result is shown in Fig. 4.9.

Fig. 4.9 shows time against different input parameters. The actual execution time is similar to the execution in the VM; see the VM time column in Table 4.1. At the beginning, execution time is nearly zero. The execution time increases as input parameter increases. Fig. 4.9 shows that marshaling time is relatively small compared to network delay. Fig. 4.9 also shows that the main cost for the remote method invocation is network delay around the BIV point. And marshaling time and network time against different input parameters are approximately identical. The marshaling and network cost determines the starting points of the offloading lines in Figs. 4.8A–D. And execution time determines the trend of those offloading lines. If the network delay or the marshaling is reduced in some situation, the offloading line will drop and then BIV point will go to the left, which means the range of benefit will increase and application components are supposed to be offloaded to the VM. In another perspective, if the component's ratio of computation cost to network cost increases, it is better to offload that component to the VM.

CHAPTER 5

Mobile Cloud Offloading Models

A true capitalist does not have a job, because other people and other people's money work for them.

Robert Kiyosaki

Chapter 4 describes the mobile cloud service systems. Based on the mobile cloud system, many computation offloading strategies are developed. Yang et al. [285] studied the partitioning problem for mobile data stream applications, where the optimization focus is placed on achieving high throughput of processing the streaming data rather than minimizing the makespan (i.e., the total length of the schedule, that is when all the jobs have finished processing) of executions as in other applications. They designed a genetic algorithm for optimal computation partition. Abebe et al. [47] proposed a type of adaptation granularity which combines the efficiency of coarse level approaches with the efficacy of fine-grained adaptation. An approach for achieving this level of granularity through the dynamic decomposition of runtime class graphs was presented. Abebe et al. [48] presented a distributed approach to application representation in which each device maintains a graph consisting only of components in its memory space, while maintaining abstraction elements for components in remote devices. An extension to an existing application graph partitioning heuristic is proposed to utilize this representation approach. Giurgiu et al. [116] developed a system that dynamically adapts the application partition decisions. The system works by continuously profiling an applications performance and dynamically updating its distributed deployment to accommodate changes in the network bandwidth, devices CPU utilization, and data loads. Sinha et al. [249] and Mtibaa et al. [208] described algorithmic approaches for performing fine-grained, multisite offloading. This allows portions of an application to be offloaded in a data-centric manner, even if that data exists at multiple sites. Kovachev [170] presented Mobile Augmentation Cloud Services (MACS) middleware which enables adaptive extension of Android application execution from a mobile client into the cloud. MACS uses a dynamic partitioning scheme, and lightweight as extra profiling. Resource monitoring is performed for adaptive partitioning decision during runtime. Ra et al. [231] experimentally and analytically investigated the design considerations – which segments of the application are most efficient to be hosted on the low power processor, and how to select an appropriate low power processor using linear programming. Smit et al. [250] described an approach to partitioning a software application into components that can be run in the public cloud and components that should remain in the private data center. Static code analysis was used to automatically establish a partitioning based on low-effort input from the developer. Niu et al. [217] took the bandwidth as a variable to improve static partitioning and avoid high costs of dynamic partitioning. They proposed the Branch-and-Bound based Application Partitioning (BBAP) algorithm and Min-Cut based Greedy Application Partitioning (MCGAP) algorithm based on application Object Relation Graphs (ORGs) by combining static analysis and dynamic profiling. Verbelen et al. [266] designed graph partitioning algorithms that allocate software components to machines in the cloud while minimizing the required bandwidth. Their algorithms are not restricted to balanced partitions and take into account infrastructure heterogeneity. Besides the above work, [72][75][85][114][131][209][243][244] discussed the mobile cloud systems in specific areas.

This chapter first describes the general mobile cloud offloading setup in Section 5.1, then presents the offloading models including one-to-one case in Section 5.2 and many-to-many case in Section 5.3. Section 5.4 finally discusses the research challenges.

5.1 Mobile Cloud Offloading Setup

In mobile clouds, mobile devices and cloud resources compose a distributed mobile application running environment, where a mobile application may consume resources from both local and remote resource providers who provide computing, networking, sensing, and storage resource provisioning. Mobile devices can serve as either service consumers or service providers in the mobile cloud, in which the cloud boundaries are extended into the mobile domain [140]. Mobile applications may require a mobile device to interact with other mobile devices and cloud resource providers to achieve desired computing, storing, collaborating, or sensing features.

An ideal mobile cloud application running system should enable mobile devices to easily discover and compose cloud resources for its applications. From mobile resource providers' perspective, they may not even know what applications are using their resources and who may call their provisioned functions beforehand. In this way, the mobile application design should not be application-oriented; instead, it should be functionality-oriented (or service-oriented). For example, the video function of a mobile device should provide general interfaces that can be called by multiple local or remote functions in the runtime. To achieve this feature, we can consider these *PFs* as the fundamental application components in the mobile cloud, which can be composed by mobile cloud service requesters in the runtime. As a result, mobile cloud can significantly reduce the mobile application development overhead and greatly improve the agility and flexibility to build a personalized mobile cloud computing system that can be customized for each mobile user.

A simple vehicular video sensing example is used to illustrate the above described mobile cloud features. Alice is driving on the road and her smart phone, which is mounted on the front dashboard for navigation, has the basic video capture *PF*. Bob is driving next to Alice and is running an image processing *PF* on his phone and wants to utilize more video clips from the neighboring vehicles in order to reconstruct the road situations around his vicinity. Then, Bob can consume Alice's video *PF* to reconstruct the view of the entire road segment captured by their video cameras. Moreover, Bob wants to share his captured video clips to his friend Carol who is managing a traffic monitoring website that posts videos from smart phone users for the public to access the real-time road traffic information. As a result, Bob can share his augmented traffic view with Alice, i.e., through Carol's website. In this mobile application scenario, all participants have the basic *PFs*: (a) Alice, video capture; (b) Bob, video augmentation; and (c) Carol, video display. Note that a *PF* can be called by multiple other *PFs* for different application purposes, and they altogether can build several mobile cloud applications.

There are several challenges invoked by the application scenario described above. The first challenge is that knowing the status of mobile devices, e.g., online/offline and runtime information (such as battery, computing power, connectivity, etc.), is difficult due to the mobility of mobile users. The second challenge is that knowing the available *PFs* on each mobile device is not a trivial task. Currently, there is no such common framework allowing mobile devices for exchanging the available *PFs* information and running such a system in a distributed environment. The third challenge is to compose *PFs* crossing various hardware and software platforms, which demands a universal programming and application running environment with little compatibility issues.

5.1.1 Application-Surrogate Offloading Mapping

The mobile cloud offloading solves the partition problem to map the application components to the surrogate sites. The modular mobile applications are composed by a group of small components between which the data exchange happens. Some of the application components that can be moved to other places to run are the offloading subjects. The devices or the machines that can host these movable application components are surrogates. The offloading partition problem maps the application components to the surrogate sites as shown in Fig. 5.1.

The offloading mapping or the offloading topology decides code or task space distribution. Moreover, the offloading topology can change for the long time horizon. Based on the space and time attributes, we can categorize the mobile cloud offloading problem into 8 types as shown in Fig. 5.2. We will discuss the most simple category in Section 5.2 and the most complex category in Section 5.3. This section discusses the general offloading topology and offloading series.

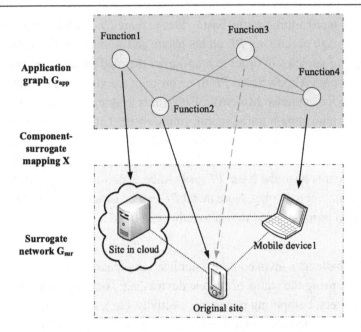

Figure 5.1: Application components – surrogate sites mapping.

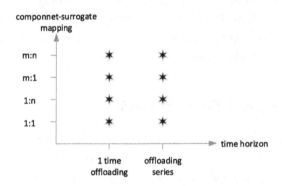

Figure 5.2: Mobile cloud offloading categories.

Offloading Topology

Application components and the surrogate sites are the two sides of the offloading topology. While there can be one or multiple application components and there can be one or multiple surrogate sites, there are four total combinations. They are $1:1$, $1:n$, $m:1$, and $m:n$ topologies.

If a Boolean matrix named E is used to describe the mapping and the rows corresponding to application components and the columns are corresponding to surrogate sites, the four topologies are $E_{1\times 1}$, $E_{1\times m}$, $E_{m\times 1}$, and $E_{m\times n}$. For each row, there are at least one 1 since that application component has to find a surrogate to run. If there is more than one surrogate running an application component, that application component gets duplicate copies to be resistant to device or network failures.

Offloading Series

The execution environment changes with time, thus the impact of one time offloading may diminish. In this scenario, the subsequent offloading may be applied to adjust the offloading topology and maintain the offloading benefit. Multiple offloading forms the offloading series. For each offloading topology above, there could be a series as shown in Fig. 5.2.

5.1.2 Offloading Objectives

In our framework, a mobile application is programmed based on component-based design, where components provide functionality via interfaces and may, conversely, consume functionality provided by other components via their interfaces [125]. The application can be presented as a graph $G_{app} = (X, A)$ where each vertex is a component $x \in X$ and an edge $a \in A$ represents the interaction between components [275].

In a multisite offloading scenario, some computation workload is offloaded from an original mobile device and distributed onto candidate surrogate sites. The original site and its candidate surrogate sites form an egocentric network $G_{sur} = (Y, B)$, where a node is a site $y \in Y$ and a link $b \in B$ represents a network connection between two sites.

The multisite offloading problem can be modeled to find a mapping from the application graph G_{app} to the candidate network G_{sur} to achieve a given optimization objective function. Let matrix E present this mapping, whose element e_{ij} is set to either 1 when component i is assigned to site j or 0 otherwise. Matrix E has the following properties:

1. Let n be the order of all components $n = |X|$ and m be the order of all candidate sites $m = |Y|$. Therefore, E is a matrix $E_{n\times m}$. The relation of n and m is not strict, thus $n > m$, $n < m$, and $n = m$ are all valid.
2. Each component in the offloading application is assigned to exact one site, which means there is one and only one 1 in each row of E. As a result, $\sum_{j=1}^{m} e_{ij} = 1$ for every row i.
3. In a mobile application, some components must be assigned to particular sites due to application requirements. For example, the human–machine interaction component must be

put on the local mobile site. This requirement enforces that positions of some 1's in E are predefined and cannot be moved.

Based on E, four more mappings can be defined. Mapping $f_{X \to Y}$ implements a similar function as E, which maps component i to site j: $f_{X \to Y}(i) = j, \forall e_{ij} = 1, e_{ij} \in E$. Mapping $f_{Y \to X}$ is the reverse mapping of $f_{X \to Y}$, which given site j outputs a set of components $\{i_1, i_2, \ldots, i_k\}$ coded as a vector $\mathbf{i}$. Besides, mappings can also be defined between W and U. Mapping $f_{A \to B}$ maps edge $a = (i_1, i_2)$ to link $b = (f_{X \to Y}(i_1), f_{X \to Y}(i_2))$; and similar to $f_{Y \to X}$, $f_{B \to A}$ maps a link to a vector of edges. These four mappings can easily be expended to accept vectors as well.

Execution Time

According to [269], at any time, the computation load for every component and the volume of data exchange for every edge in application graph is known based on a given task, or is predictable based on the application and user historical behavior. The workload is distributed on the application graph, which makes G_{app} into a weighted graph. The computation load is presented as a weight value on each vertex: the component x is labeled with computation load w_x and vector $\mathbf{w}$ is computation load of all vertexes. The data exchange amount is presented as a weight value on an edge: the edge $a = (x_1, x_2)$ from x_1 to x_2 is labeled with data transfer load $f_{x_1 x_2}$ and matrix $F_{n \times n}$ is data exchange load of all edges. The diagonal of F are all 0's because the component's interaction with itself does not count for intercomponent data exchange load; and $f_a = 0$ if $a \in A$ is false.

Meanwhile, the surrogates' capability is measurable, so the egocentric network G_{sur} is transformed into a weighted graph as well. The available computation capability on a candidate site s is labeled as a vertex weight u_s and vector $\mathbf{u}$ is the weights of all the sites. The network throughput on link $b = (y_1, y_2)$ from y_1 to y_2 is labeled as link weight $d_{y_1 y_2}$ and matrix $D_{m \times m}$ is the weights of all the links. The diagonal of D are large values because data exchange in the same site can be considered negligible.

In this article, we define the operator $.*$ as array inner multiplication that multiplies arrays or matrices in an element-by-element way, which is different from matrix multiplication. Let $\tilde{\mathbf{u}}$ be the vector that satisfies $\mathbf{u}.*\tilde{\mathbf{u}} = \mathbf{1}$ where $\mathbf{1}$ is the vector whose elements are all 1's. Then the upper bound of total time spent for computation load is the sum of workload on every site over its processing capability:

$$t_c = \mathbf{w}^T X \tilde{\mathbf{u}}. \tag{5.1}$$

Similarly, let $\tilde{D}_{n \times n}$ be the matrix that satisfies $D.*\tilde{D} = \mathbf{1}_{m \times m}$ where $\mathbf{1}_{m \times m}$ is the matrix whose elements are all 1's. The transformation $E^T F E$ redistributes the communication load of $F_{n \times n}$ into an $m \times m$ matrix where element positions are corresponding to $\tilde{D}_{m \times m}$. The upper bound of total time spent on networks for data exchange load is the sum of workload on every link over its throughput:

$$t_n = tr(E^T F E \tilde{D}^T), \tag{5.2}$$

where the $tr(\cdot)$ function calculates matrix trace $tr(H_{n \times n}) = \sum_{i=1}^{n} h_{ii}$. So the upper bound of total time is the sum of the computation and communication times:

$$t = t_c + t_n. \tag{5.3}$$

Energy Consumption

Energy consumption on mobile devices can be categorized according to hardware modules. The major categories are CPU, radio module (including WiFi and Cellular), display, audio device, GPS module, and vibration motor [153][245][286][289]. The components that involve modules, except CPU and radio, are hardware dependent components that have to run on the original mobile device and are not considered for offloading. Both CPU and radio power can be modeled as a linear model that consists of two parts: base consumption and dynamic consumption when hardware module is active [196][269]. The dynamic part of CPU power is proportional to the utilized processing capability according to [153][206][245][289]:

$$P^{CPU} = \mathbf{1}^T E(\mathbf{u} .* \mathbf{c}^{CPU}), \tag{5.4}$$

where $\mathbf{c}^{CPU}$ is the coefficient vector for all sites, and the coefficients of nonmobile sites in $\mathbf{c}^{CPU}$ are 0's. Let's code E as $\mathbf{e}$, then the dynamic part of radio module power is proportional to the outgoing packet rate [153][289]:

$$D' = D.*(\mathbf{1}_{n \times n} - I).*(\mathbf{c}^{radio} \mathbf{1}^T), \tag{5.5}$$

$$P^{radio} = \sum_{\forall l \in f_{E \to L}(\mathbf{e})} d'_l, \tag{5.6}$$

where $\mathbf{c}^{radio}$ is the coefficient vector for all sites, I is the identity matrix, and d'_l is the element of D' corresponding to link l. The coefficients of nonmobile sites in $\mathbf{c}^{radio}$ are 0's. Let P^{CPU}_{idle} be the static part of CPU power and P^{radio}_{base} be the static power of radio module. Then the total power is the sum of the above four parts:

$$P = P^{CPU} + P^{CPU}_{idle} + P^{radio} + P^{radio}_{base}. \tag{5.7}$$

Table 5.1: Notation

Terms	Meaning	Terms	Meaning
B	bundle set	b_i	a bundle
e_{ij}	service dependency from b_i to b_j	B_{phone}, B_{cloud}	bundle set for smart phone and cloud separately
t_i	execution time of b_i	c	partition configuration
t_{phone}	application execution time in non-offloading mode	$p(c)$	offloading rate
q	how faster cloud is than smart phone	d_{ij}	size of data transferred over e_{ij}
w	bandwidth	$t(c)$	total execution time
$t'(c)$	total execution time in unstable network	ξ, η	*on* state duration, *off* state duration
χ	cycle duration, $\chi = \xi + \eta$	ρ	network availability, $\rho = \xi/\chi$
$P_{CPU}(c)$, $P_{RF}(c)$	energy consumption for CPU and RF separately	$P'_{CPU}(c)$, $P'_{RF}(c)$	energy consumption in unstable network
$P(c)$	total energy consumption on mobile device	$P'(c)$	total energy consumption in unstable network
P_{phone}	energy consumption in nonoffloading mode	$\rho'_{time}(c)$, $\rho'_{energy}(c)$	critical value for time and energy benefit
$\rho'(c)$	circuital value for both time and energy benefit	$\Delta t(c)$, $\Delta P(c)$	time benefit, energy benefit
K_{CPU}^{sta}, K_{CPU}^{dyn}, K_{RF}^{sta}, K_{RF}^{dyn}	power of CPU and RF on smart phone		

5.2 One-to-One Offloading Case

A mobile cloud consists of mobile devices and cloud. There is usually one-to-one mapping between mobile devices and virtual machines in the cloud [138]. A mobile cloud application is constructed as a set of components or bundles. Some components can run on either mobile devices or virtual machines, while the other components, such as user interface and sensors, have to run on mobile devices. The major offloading objectives are saving application execution time and energy consumption on mobile devices. Notation in the following discussion is summarized in Table 5.1 for convenience.

5.2.1 Application Model and Ideal Network Model

The application is presented as a directed acyclic graph $G = \{X, A\}$ where every vertex is a bundle and every edge is the data exchange between bundles [117]. Each bundle has an attribute indicating whether it can be offloaded. The unmovable bundles are marked as *local*, which means these bundles cannot be offloaded due to application requirements. Let n'

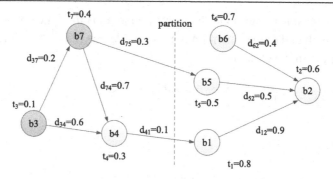

Figure 5.3: Application graph example.

be the total count of bundles in the application, then the initial bundle set is $X = \{x_i \mid i \in [1, 2, \ldots, n']\}$ and the edge set is $A = \{a_{ij} \mid i, j \in [1, 2, \ldots, n]\}$ where e_{ij} represents directed data transfer from x_i to x_j. Let n be the count of movable bundles and $n \leq n'$. A configuration c [117] is defined as a tuple of partitions from the initial bundle set, $< X_{phone}, X_{cloud} >$, where $X_{phone} = \{x_i \mid i \in [1, 2, \ldots, k]\}$ has k bundles and $X_{cloud} = \{x_i \mid i \in [1, 2, \ldots, s]\}$ has s bundles. And they satisfy $X_{phone} \cap X_{cloud} = \emptyset$ and $X_{phone} \cup X_{cloud} = X$. The bundles that are marked as *local* are initially put in the set B_{phone} and cannot be moved. An example is shown in Fig. 5.3 where unmovable bundles are marked as gray and dotted line indicates configuration. The bundles on the left side are X_{phone} and the bundles on the right side are X_{cloud}.

Execution Time

For a given task, bundle x_i has an attribute t_i indicating its computation time on smart phone. And edge a_{ij} is associated with an attribute d_{ij} indicating the transferred date size from bundle i to bundle j. These values can be measured or estimated from collected application and device data. Total time of running the task only on the smart phone is

$$t_{phone} = \sum_{x_i \in X} t_i \tag{5.8}$$

where data exchanges between bundles are not counted as they happen locally and cost little time compared to time of data exchange over the network. For a particular configuration c, offloading rate p [224] is defined as the proportion of offloaded task to all tasks in terms of computation time. The proportion of the task is the same as time proportion due to the same processing capability on the same mobile device $p(c) = (\sum_{x_i \in X_{cloud}} t_i)/t_{phone}$, and $p(c)$ satisfies $0 \leq p(c) \leq 1$. Then, the computation time on the smart phone is

$$t_{computation}^{phone}(c) = \sum_{x_i \in X_{phone}} t_i = (\sum_{x_i \in X} - \sum_{x_i \in X_{cloud}})t_i = (1 - p(c))t_{phone}. \tag{5.9}$$

Assume the cloud is q times faster than the smart phone, thus the time consumption in the cloud is q times less than the time spent on the mobile device [281], which is $t_i^{cloud} = t_i/q$. The computation time in the cloud is

$$t_{computation}^{cloud}(c) = \sum_{x_i \in X_{cloud}} t_i^{cloud} = \frac{1}{q} \sum_{x_i \in X_{cloud}} t_i = \frac{p(c)}{q} t_{phone}. \tag{5.10}$$

Thus the total computation time is

$$t_{computation}(c) = t_{computation}^{phone}(c) + t_{computation}^{cloud}(c) = (1 - (1 - \frac{1}{q}) p(c)) t_{phone}. \tag{5.11}$$

A typical offloading process works as follows: Initially, the application starts on the smart phone and all components run locally. Then, the application may offload some components to a remote virtual machine. These offloaded bundles run in the cloud remotely. However, they need to communicate with the bundles resident on the smart phone. Thus, they have to exchange data through the network. Assume that the network bandwidth is w, then the network delay is the sum of delays in both data transfer directions, namely

$$t_{network}(c) = \sum_{\substack{x_i \in X_{phone} \\ x_j \in X_{cloud}}} \frac{d_{ij}}{w} + \sum_{\substack{x_i \in X_{cloud} \\ x_j \in X_{phone}}} \frac{d_{ij}}{w}. \tag{5.12}$$

In an ideal network environment, the total execution time for a given configuration c is the sum of computation time and network delay, that is,

$$t(c) = t_{computation}(c) + t_{network}(c). \tag{5.13}$$

The offloading benefit of execution time comes from the trade of $t_{computation}$ and $t_{network}$. The computation part saves execution time because the cloud processing capability is greater than that of the mobile device. However, the offloading has to pay for network delay, which counteracts the computation time saving. For computation-intensive applications whose computation time saving is much larger than the network delay, the offloading benefit is obviously seen.

Energy Consumption

Two hardware modules of the mobile device are involved in the energy consumption estimation: CPU and radio frequency (RF) module. Other modules like display, audio, GPS etc., are not considered because the components that interact with these modules have to run on the mobile device locally. The energy consumption on both CPU and RF modules can be further separated into the dynamic and static parts [269]. When the hardware module is in the idle state, the energy consumption is corresponding to the static part. When the hardware module is in the active state, more energy is consumed, which is corresponding to the dynamic part. Assume that the power of CPU in the idle state is K_{CPU}^{sta} and the power of CPU in the active state is $K_{CPU}^{sta} + K_{CPU}^{dyn}$. The energy consumption of CPU is then

$$P_{CPU}(c) = K_{CPU}^{sta} t(c) + K_{CPU}^{dyn} t_{computation}^{phone}(c). \qquad (5.14)$$

Similarly, let K_{RF}^{sta} and K_{RF}^{dyn} be the power of RF module in the idle and active states separately. The energy consumption on radio frequency module is

$$P_{RF}(c) = K_{RF}^{sta} t(c) + K_{RF}^{dyn} t_{network}(c). \qquad (5.15)$$

Thus, the total energy consumption is

$$P(c) = P_{CPU}(c) + P_{RF}(c). \qquad (5.16)$$

If offloading is not applied, only CPU consumes energy and its active period is the whole execution time. The total energy consumption of running tasks only on the smart phone is

$$P_{phone} = (K_{CPU}^{sta} + K_{CPU}^{dyn}) t_{phone}. \qquad (5.17)$$

The offloading influences energy consumption of the mobile device in two aspects. First, the mobile device may save energy because the mobile device does not pay for the energy consumption corresponding to the tasks that are offloaded and completed in the cloud. Second, the data exchanges between application components are now fulfilled by networking instead of local procedure invocation, which leads to energy cost for sending and receiving packets. Similar to the time benefit of offloading, the computation-intensive application may obtain an obvious energy benefit when computation tasks are offloaded as large CPU energy consumption is spared and network energy consumption is small.

5.2.2 Model and Impact of Network Unavailability

Connection between the mobile device and the cloud is usually not stable due to mobility of devices. When the mobile device moves out of wireless coverage, it loses connection to the cloud. The mobile device continues to make attempts to reconnect to the cloud when the network is unavailable. When it moves into coverage again, the connection resumes. As the mobile device moves, the connection state changes as *on, off, on, off, . . .*, which can be modeled as an alternating renewal process.

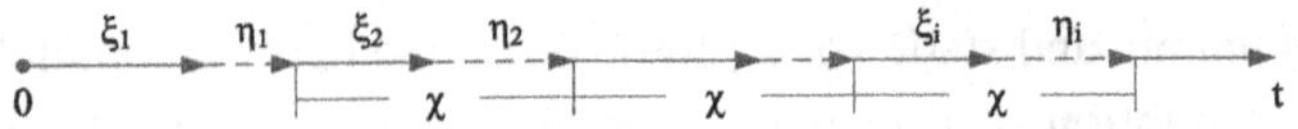

Figure 5.4: Networking model under unavailability of communication links.

Fig. 5.4 shows how network availability changes along with time. The solid line represents that the network is available, while the dashed line represents that the network is unavailable. Two network states alternate with each other. One *on* duration and one *off* duration form a cycle. The *on* state duration is denoted as ξ and the *off* state duration is denoted as η. The variables $\{\xi_i, i = 1, 2, \ldots\}$ are independent and identically distributed (i.i.d.), and so are $\{\eta_i, i = 1, 2, \ldots\}$. And ξ_i and η_j are independent for any $i \neq j$, but ξ_i and η_i can be dependent [228]. The cycle duration is denoted as χ, and $\chi_i = \xi_i + \eta_i$ where $i = 1, 2, \ldots$. The proportion of *on* duration in any individual cycle is a random variable denoted as $\rho = \xi/\chi$.

Execution Time

When the network is unavailable, the application has to wait because the phone cannot send input to the cloud and cannot retrieve output from the cloud either. The application resumes the execution after the network becomes available again. The total execution time is prolonged according to the proportion of ρ, namely

$$t'(c) = \frac{t(c)}{\rho}. \tag{5.18}$$

The offloading gives time benefit when $t'(c) < t_{phone}(c)$. In an ideal network environment, $\rho = 1$ and $t'(c) = t(c)$. $t'(c)$ rises to infinity when ρ decreases from 1 to 0. At some point, the benefit finally disappears. We define this point as a critical value of ρ for the time benefit,

$$\rho'_{time}(c) = \frac{t(c)}{t_{phone}}. \tag{5.19}$$

And the time benefit is

$$\Delta t(c) = t_{phone}(c) - t'(c) \tag{5.20}$$

when $\rho > \rho'_{time}(c)$.

Energy Consumption

During the time $t'(c)$, the computation time $t'_{computation}(c)$ and network time $t'_{network}(c)$ are the same as $t_{computation}(c)$ and $t_{network}(c)$, respectively, in an ideal network environment because computation and data transfer only work properly when an ideal network is available.

The CPU active time period is the same as that in an ideal network model because the given task is the same. However, the CPU idle time period is the whole execution time that is different from that in an ideal network model. Thus, the energy consumption for CPU is

$$P'_{CPU}(c) = K^{sta}_{CPU} t'(c) + K^{dyn}_{CPU} t^{phone}_{computation}(c). \tag{5.21}$$

The RF module is active even when the network is unavailable because it continues scanning for the available network to resume connection. Thus, the active time period for the RF module is $t'(c) - t_{computation}(c)$. The energy consumption for RF is

$$P'_{RF}(c) = K^{sta}_{RF} t'(c) + K^{dyn}_{RF}(t'(c) - t_{computation}(c)). \tag{5.22}$$

Thus, the total energy consumption is

$$P'(c) = P'_{CPU}(c) + P'_{RF}(c). \tag{5.23}$$

The offloading gives energy benefit if $P'(c) < P_{phone}$. As ρ decreases, both $P'_{CPU}(c)$ and $P'_{RF}(c)$ increase. Similarly, the critical value of ρ for energy is defined as the point where the energy benefit disappears, i.e.,

$$\rho'_{energy}(c)$$
$$= (K^{sta}_{CPU} + K^{sta}_{RF} + K^{dyn}_{RF}) t(c) / (P_{phone} - K^{dyn}_{CPU} t^{phone}_{computation}(c) + K^{dyn}_{RF} t_{computation}(c)). \tag{5.24}$$

And the offloading energy benefit is

$$\Delta P(c) = P_{phone}(c) - P'(c) \tag{5.25}$$

when $\rho > \rho'_{energy}(c)$.

Problem Formulation

When network availability ρ is greater than the larger of the $\rho'_{time}(c)$ and $\rho'_{energy}(c)$, both time and energy benefits are obtained. We define the critical value of ρ as

$$\rho'(c) = \max\{\rho'_{time}(c), \rho'_{energy}(c)\}. \tag{5.26}$$

The offloading problem with possible network unavailability is finding the application partition c to minimize $\rho'(c)$:

$$\min \ \rho'(c) \tag{5.27}$$

while both time and energy benefits exist, i.e., when

$$\rho > \rho'(c), \tag{5.28}$$

where ρ is the current network availability estimated based on observations. The c satisfying (5.28) may not exist when ρ is too low. In this situation, the application should not offload any components to the cloud. The solution to (5.27) is the best partition that tolerates network unavailability, and it may give benefit when current network availability ρ gets worse.

5.2.3 Optimization Solution and Simulation Analysis

Bundle computation times t_i form a vector $\mathbf{t}$ of dimension m. Data sizes d_{ij} form a square matrix $\mathbf{D}_{m \times m}$. If there is no edge from b_i to b_j, then d_{ij} is set to 0.

The configuration c can be represented as a vector $\mathbf{x}$ of dimension m where x_i indicates whether b_i should be offloaded. $x_i = 1$ means that b_i should be offloaded to a remote cloud, and $x_i = 0$ means b_i should be kept on the smart phone locally. For b_i that cannot be offloaded, x_i is set to 0 initially and does not change. Vector $\mathbf{x}$ has m elements in which n elements are variables and the others are 0. For simplicity, all 0s are put at the end of $\mathbf{x}$.

Let $\mathbf{1}$ be a column vector whose elements are all 1s, then $t_{phone} = \mathbf{t}^T \mathbf{1}$. Offloading rate $p(c)$ is now $p(\mathbf{x}) = \mathbf{t}^T \mathbf{x} / \mathbf{t}^T \mathbf{1}$. And $t_{network}(c)$ is $t_{network}(\mathbf{x}) = ((\mathbf{1} - \mathbf{x})^T \mathbf{D} \mathbf{x} + \mathbf{x}^T \mathbf{D}(\mathbf{1} - \mathbf{x}))/w$. Thus $t(c)$ is finally a function of $\mathbf{x}$, which is $t(\mathbf{x})$.

The objective of the offloading decision is to find a configuration $\mathbf{x}$ satisfying (5.27). This is a 0–1 Integer Programming (IP) problem.

Optimization Solution

The solution space for configuration $\mathbf{x}$ is 2^n, which means it costs a lot of time to search for the optimal solution. To find a proper $\mathbf{x}$ within acceptable time, we propose an Artificial Bee Colony (ABC) [157] based algorithm. The colony consists of three types of bees: employed bees, onlooker bees, and scout bees. A bee that goes to a food source visited by it before is named an employed bee. A bee that waits in the dance area to make a selection of the food source is called an onlooker bee. And a bee that carries a random search to discover a new food source is named a scout bee. The food source is a possible solution $\mathbf{x}$, and every bee can memorize one food source. It is assumed that there is only one employed bee for each food source. The memory of employed bees is considered as the consensus of the whole colony, and the food sources found by onlooker or scout bees merge into employed bees' memory in the algorithm. Assume that the number of employed bees is N and the number of onlooker

---

Algorithm 5.1 Application partition algorithm overview.

1: Initialize employed bees
2: $cycle \leftarrow 1$
3: **repeat**
4:     Produce new solution for employed bees
5:     Apply greedy selection process for employed bees
6:     Determine probabilities, and assign M onlooker bees to N employed bees accordingly
7:     Produce new solution for onlooker bees
8:     Apply greedy selection process for onlooker bees
9:     Determine abandon solution, if it exists, and replace it with a scout bee
10:     Memorize the best solution so far
11:     $cycle \leftarrow cycle + 1$
12: **until** $cycle = MCN$

---

bees is M ($M > N$). And let MCN be the Maximum Cycle Number. The algorithm overview is shown in Algorithm 5.1.

In the first step, the algorithm generates a random initial population X ($cycle = 0$) of N solutions where the population size is the same as the number of employed bees. Based on this initial generation, the algorithm starts to evolve the generation in cycles. The evolution repeats until the cycle number reaches the limit MCN. The algorithm outputs the best solution, denoted as $\mathbf{x}_{best}$, ever found in all cycles.

In the cycle, three types of bees work in sequence. The details of various bees' actions are shown in Algorithm 5.2. Employed bees produce new solutions by two local search methods:

Flip   when an employed bee randomly flips one element in the vector $\mathbf{x}$.
Swap   when an employed bee randomly flips two elements of different values in the vector $\mathbf{x}$, which is equivalent to swapping two different elements in that vector.

Each employed bee evaluates the fitness of its original solution $\mathbf{x}$, newly found $\mathbf{x}_{flip}$, and $\mathbf{x}_{swap}$ by (5.26). Then, each employed bee memorizes the best one of these three food sources and forgets the others.

Onlooker bees watch employed bees dancing, and plan the preferred food source. Onlooker bees record critical values of all food sources and calculate the probability for the ith food source as follows:

$$p_i = \frac{1/\rho'(\mathbf{x}_i)}{\sum_{j=1}^{N}(1/\rho'(\mathbf{x}_j))}. \tag{5.29}$$

Algorithm 5.2 Application partition algorithm details.

 1: Initialize employed bees randomly
 2:    $\mathbf{x}_i$: the ith employed bee
 3: $cycle \leftarrow 1$
 4: **repeat**
 5:        **for** each employed bee $\mathbf{x}_i$ **do**
 6:                Apply $Flip$ local search and find $\mathbf{x}_{flip}$
 7:                Apply $Swap$ local search and find $\mathbf{x}_{swap}$
 8:                **if** $\rho'(\mathbf{x}_i) > \min\{\rho'(\mathbf{x}_i), \rho'(\mathbf{x}_{flip}), \rho'(\mathbf{x}_{swap})\}$ **then**
 9:                        $\mathbf{x}_i \leftarrow \arg\min\{\rho'(\mathbf{x}_i), \rho'(\mathbf{x}_{flip}), \rho'(\mathbf{x}_{swap})\}$
10:                **end if**
11:        **end for**
12:        Determine probabilities (p_i) by (5.29)
13:        $M_i \leftarrow p_i M$: number of onlooker bees sent to
14:    the ith food source
15:        $\mathbf{y}_{ij} \leftarrow \mathbf{x}_i$ $(j = 1, 2, \dots, M_i)$: the jth onlooker bee
16:    of the ith food source
17:        **for** each onlooker bee $\mathbf{y}_{ij}$ **do**
18:                Apply $Flip$ local search and find $\mathbf{y}_{flip}$
19:                Apply $Swap$ local search and find $\mathbf{y}_{swap}$
20:                **if** $\rho'(\mathbf{y}_{ij}) > \min\{\rho'(\mathbf{y}_{ij}), \rho'(\mathbf{y}_{flip}), \rho'(\mathbf{y}_{swap})\}$ **then**
21:                        $\mathbf{y}_{ij} \leftarrow \arg\min\{\rho'(\mathbf{y}_{ij}), \rho'(\mathbf{y}_{flip}), \rho'(\mathbf{y}_{swap})\}$
22:                **end if**
23:        **end for**
24:        **for** each employed bee $\mathbf{x}_i$ **do**
25:                **if** $\rho'(\mathbf{x}_i) > \min\limits_{j=1,2,\dots,M_i}\{\rho'(\mathbf{y}_{ij})\}$ **then**
26:                        $\mathbf{x}_i \leftarrow \arg\min\limits_{j=1,2,\dots,M_i}\{\rho'(\mathbf{y}_{ij})\}$
27:                **end if**
28:        **end for**
29:        Generate scout bee $\mathbf{z}$ randomly
30:        **if** $\max\limits_{i=1,2,\dots,N}\{\rho'(\mathbf{x}_i)\} > \rho'(\mathbf{z})$ **then**
31:                $\arg\max\limits_{i=1,2,\dots,N}\{\rho'(\mathbf{x}_i)\} \leftarrow \mathbf{z}$
32:        **end if**
33:        **if** $\rho'(\mathbf{x}_{best}) > \min\limits_{i=1,2,\dots,N}\{\rho'(\mathbf{x}_i)\}$ **then**
34:                $\mathbf{x}_{best} \leftarrow \arg\min\limits_{i=1,2,\dots,N}\{\rho'(\mathbf{x}_i)\}$
35:        **end if**
36:        $cycle \leftarrow cycle + 1$
37: **until** $cycle = MCN$

Table 5.2: Default parameter setting

Parameter		Default value
Application	m	10
	n	8
Cloud [274][281]	q	30
Phone [269]	K_{CPU}^{sta}	2.5
	K_{CPU}^{dyn}	5
	K_{RF}^{sta}	1.25
	K_{RF}^{dyn}	1.25
Algorithm	N	3
	M	5

Intentionally, the lower the food source's critical value, the more likely the onlooker bee would like to go. The onlooker bees choose the food source **y** randomly according to its probability. Since $M > N$, several onlooker bees may follow the same employed bee and choose the same food source. Then each onlooker bee applies the same local search methods used by employed bees previously to explore new neighbor solutions, and picks the best one of the three. After all onlooker bees update their solution, each employed bee compares its solution with its followers' solutions, and picks the best one as its new solution.

In our algorithm, only one scout bee is used. This scout bee randomly generates a vector **z** and compares **z** to the worst solution of employed bees. If this randomly generated **z** is better than the worst solution of employed bees, the corresponding employed bee memorizes this new solution and forgets the old one.

Evaluation and Tuning

In this section, we evaluate ABC based partition algorithm, including algorithm tuning and impact of different mobile applications and the cloud. We evaluate our model and algorithms in MATLAB.

We generate 200 random application graphs as a base evaluation data set. The default parameter settings are shown in Table 5.2. We use a set of typical energy parameters K for a phone according to [269]. The cloud–phone processing ability ratio q varies in a large range from previous work [274][281]. We pick a medium value from the possible range as the default value and evaluate its impact to algorithm in Section 5.2.3. We evaluate the algorithm based on three aspects: bee colony, different applications, and cloud–phone relation.

Bee Colony and Algorithm Tuning

This experiment is based on 200 random application graphs (**t** and **D**). These application graphs are randomly generated, and at least one configuration of each graph is guaranteed to obtain both time and energy benefit in an ideal network environment. We evaluate the proposed algorithm performance with respect to different bee colony size. The results are shown in Fig. 5.5. The x-axis represents how many iterations the algorithm needs to reach x_{best}, and the y-axis represents how many cases are needed to reach the solution of corresponding iterations. From the figure, we may draw the following guidelines for algorithm tuning:

- By increasing the onlooker bee number, the algorithm shows better convergence rate. For the same employed bee number (N), the more onlooker bees there are, the fewer iterations are obviously required to reach the optimal solution in all three situations ($N = 2, 3, 4$).
- While increasing the employed bee number improves convergence rate, the improvement is not as obvious compared to increasing the onlooker bee number. For the same onlooker bees of $M = 3$ (Fig. 5.5B, Fig. 5.5D), $M = 4$ (Fig. 5.5C, Fig. 5.5G), and $M = 7$ (Fig. 5.5F, Fig. 5.5H), the cases that have more employed bees have slightly better performance improvement, which is not as obvious as the improvement given by increasing onlooker bees. For $M = 4$ figures, more than 0.05 cases reach the optimal solution in 7 iterations in Fig. 5.5C while there are only 0.05 cases that reach a solution in 7 iterations, which means more cases reach a solution in less than 7 iterations, in Fig. 5.5G. Similar phenomenon is found for $M = 3$ and $M = 7$ figures.
- For the same total numbers of employed and onlooker bees, the algorithm prefers more onlooker bees slightly. For the same total bees of $N + M = 6$ (Fig. 5.5C, Fig. 5.5D) and $N + M = 8$ (Fig. 5.5E, Fig. 5.5G), we can see that the overall performance is almost the same. But the iterations needed to get optimal solutions in the cases that have more onlooker bees are slightly concentrated on some iteration numbers. For $N + M = 6$, the iterations in Fig. 5.5C are concentrated demonstrated by a higher summit at iteration 4, while they are diversely distributed from 1 to 8 in Fig. 5.5D. A similar situation occurs for $N + M = 8$.

Application Impact

To evaluate the algorithm performance for different applications, three experiments are done for varying component number, unmovable component proportion, and computation–communication ratio separately. The experiment result for different component number is shown in Fig. 5.6. For the same bee colony, the iterations to find the solution increase along with the component number. For the large applications that have many components, the algorithm may use a large bee colony to assure small number of iterations.

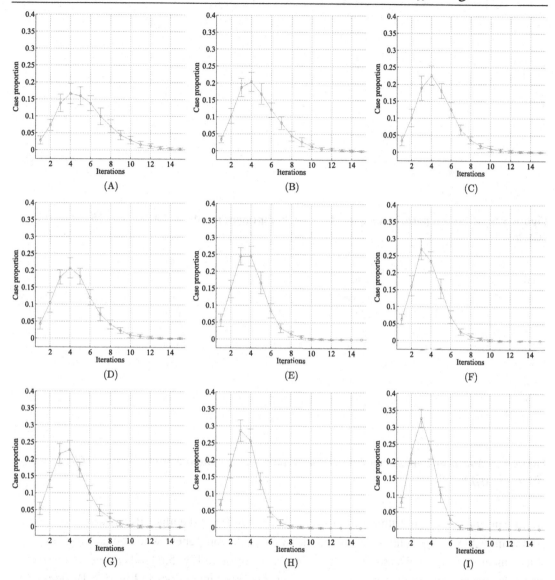

Figure 5.5: Partition performance of difference bee colonies. (A) $N = 2$, $M = 2$. (B) $N = 2$, $M = 3$. (C) $N = 2$, $M = 4$. (D) $N = 3$, $M = 3$. (E) $N = 3$, $M = 5$. (F) $N = 3$, $M = 7$. (G) $N = 4$, $M = 4$. (H) $N = 4$, $M = 7$. (I) $N = 4$, $M = 10$.

We evaluate the impact of unmovable component proportion of application in the second experiment, and the result is shown in Fig. 5.7. From the figure, we find that more iterations are required to get the solution when the movable component number increases. The trend is very like that in Fig. 5.6, which implies that the unmovable component number does not play a

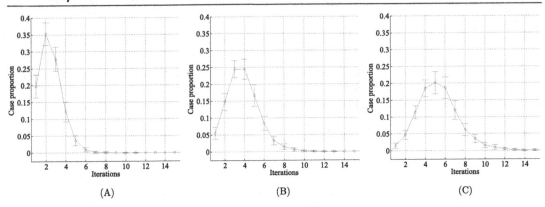

Figure 5.6: Partition performance for different component numbers. **(A)** $m = 8$. **(B)** $m = 10$.
(C) $m = 12$.

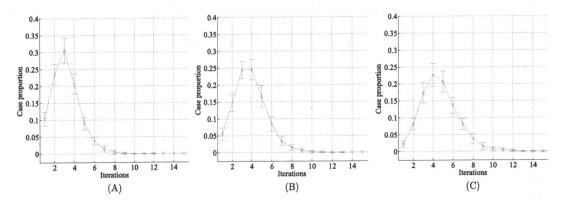

Figure 5.7: Partition performance for different unmovable component proportions. **(A)** $n = 7$.
(B) $n = 8$. **(C)** $n = 9$.

significant role in the algorithm performance. This is because the algorithm always considers the movable components and ignores the unmovable component when generating new solutions in each cycle. The total component size increase in Fig. 5.6 leads to the increase of movable component number, which is like what this experiment does in Fig. 5.7. Besides, we also found in this experiment that a higher movable proportion results in the robust solution that can work under low network availability $\rho'(c)$ situations. This is because the high movable proportion provides more candidate partition options so that a more robust solution may be achieved.

We generate another two sets of application graph data for different computation load. The data sets used in previous experiments are used as the reference data set. Then we adjust the computation task to half and double of the reference data set in the application graph gen-

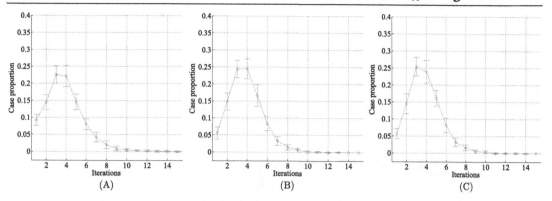

Figure 5.8: Partition performance for different computation tasks. (A) Half computation task. (B) Reference computation task. (C) Double computation task.

eration process. The network task remains the same, thus the computation–communication ratio is adjusted to half and double in the new data sets. The experiment results for these three data sets are shown in Fig. 5.8. From the figure, we can see that the iterations, distributed at 2, 3, 4, 5, and 6, are almost the same, which implies the computation proportion of the given task does not influence the algorithm performance. This is because the computation proportion in the task influences the time and energy benefits in the same direction. In the experiment, we also find that the computation proportion impacts the $\rho'(c)$, because a larger computation proportion leads to a larger offloading benefit and the possible solution is more resistant to network unavailability.

Cloud Impact

We evaluate the algorithm performance under different cloud speedup ratios shown in Fig. 5.9. The figure shows that the iteration number does not depend on the cloud processing capability. The cloud processing capability influences the execution time considered in the algorithm, which is similar to the computation proportion impact. And similarly, the higher cloud processing capability results in a more robust partition configuration.

5.3 Many-to-Many Offloading Case

Nowadays, many mobile cloud applications adopt a multisite service model [189][249]. To maximize the benefits from multiple service providers, the research focuses on how to compose services that have been already implemented on multiple service providers. Here, we do not differentiate between application functions and services since our model can be applied to both. A simple example can be used to highlight the application scenario: a mobile device

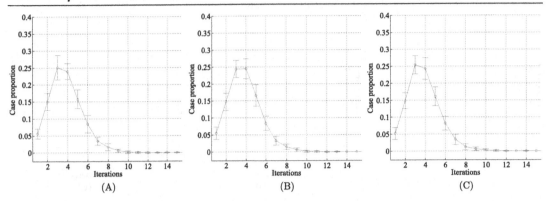

Figure 5.9: Partition performance for different cloud speedup ratios. (A) $q = 5$. **(B)** $q = 10$. **(C)** $q = 20$.

calls a video capturing function from multiple remote mobile devices at a congested road segment, an image processing function uses this to recognize vehicles on the road segment from the cloud, and then the requesting mobile device uses its local UI to display the road traffic with identified lanes and vehicles. Compared to the traditional approach where users upload captured videos to the cloud and the requester downloads the processed videos from the cloud, the presented application scenario does not require a presetup application scenario to each function. This approach is very flexible in terms of ad hoc application composition, and it can maximally improve the resource utilization. For example, the video capturing function of mobile devices can be shared by multiple users for different purposes, e.g., congestion monitoring, road events detection, vehicle identification and tracking, etc.

Besides the flexibility of the service/function composition using multisite service composition, it also introduces benefits in reducing execution time and energy consumption of mobile devices; however, at the same time, it brings more management issues as well. The multisite service composition paradigm involves multiple surrogate sites in the service composition process, and the application running environment changes demand a decision model in the service composition decision processes to consider the application running environment changes related to network connectivity, delay, device resource consumption, energy usage, etc. Moreover, due to the mobility, the benefits of service composition may not be consistent during the entire application execution time period. To adapt to the application running environment changes, we need to study the service reconfiguration strategy by modeling the service composition as a service-topology mapping (or reconfiguration) problem that is illustrated in Fig. 5.10. Relying on a cloud service framework, once the mobile application running environment state changes, a new service-topology reconfiguration is decided, and then the application components are redistributed to the surrogate sites through the cloud. In

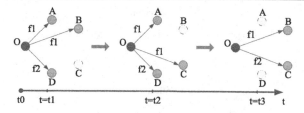

Figure 5.10: Service composition topology reconfiguration motivation.

this way, the service composition is adaptive to gain the maximum service benefits during the entire execution time period [276].

To address the above mobile cloud service composition problem, many existing approaches (e.g., [117] [160] [274]) only focus on solving the one-time service composition topology configuration without considering a sequence of service composition due to the application running environment changes (e.g., due to the mobility of nodes). When considering multiple service composition decisions, one decision may impact other service mapping decisions at an upcoming service mapping. This demands that the topology reconfiguration decision must not only consider the current environment state but also predict future environment changes, and thus, the service-topology reconfiguration issue can be modeled as a decision process issue. To address the above described issues, we model the service composition topology re-configuration as a five-element tuple system and we present three algorithms to solve these decision process problems for three mobile cloud application scenarios: (1) finite horizon process where the application execution time is restricted by a certain time period, (2) infinite horizon process where there is no clear boundary of the application execution time, and (3) large-state situation where the large numbers of many-to-many service mappings demand a parallel computing framework to compute the service mapping decision.

The offloading as a service and service composition in mobile cloud computing achieve three essential tasks: *First*, the mobile application components, which can be offloaded, are partitioned into several groups. *Second*, the surrogate sites are picked from candidate sites that are usually virtual machines in cloud. *Third*, the component groups in the first task are mapped to surrogate sites in the second task, and then computation is offloaded. The service composition is not a one-time process. Instead, the mapping in the third task should be dynamically changed to adapt to the system and environment changes, especially in mobile cloud computing where mobility adds to the environment variation.

This section first describes the normal service composition system, and then models the players in the system including mobile application and surrogate network, and finally formulates the service composition topology reconfiguration process.

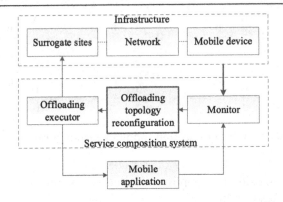

Figure 5.11: Continuous service composition system.

5.3.1 Service Composition System

The *Service composition system* consists of three parts shown in Fig. 5.11, which can be emulated as human decision processes. The *Monitor* represents the human's eyes watching both the mobile applications and infrastructure, and notifying the *Service composition topology reconfiguration* about their states' changes. The *Service composition topology reconfiguration* is the human's brain thinking about how to put application components onto which surrogate sites. The *Service composition executor* represents the human's hands that enforce the component–surrogate mapping and make sure a mobile device and its surrogates work together properly. These three interdependent modules can be deployed in a cloud computation platform to provide offloading-as-a-service, which exposes http REST API for mobile applications and the infrastructure to interact with. The infrastructure registers itself to the service and pushes the state information to the *Monitor*. The mobile application as well registers itself to the service and receives the execution command from the *Service composition executor*.

Besides the *Service composition system*, the *Mobile application* and *Infrastructure* are involved in the service composition process, and they form a loop where the *Mobile application* and the *Infrastructure* share a part of the loop in parallel. The *Service composition system* initiates the service composition operations that stimulate the *Mobile application* and the *Infrastructure*. The *Mobile application* and the *Infrastructure* integrate the service composition impacts and the variances form the outside, such as user inputs to the application and the device load variance, and feedback to the *Service composition system*. Then, the *Service composition system* based on the feedback makes the service composition operation.

The *Mobile application* is the objective of the *Service composition system*. The *Infrastructure* consists of the three players that are involved in the service composition process: the *Mobile device*, the *Surrogate sites,* and the *Network* between them; they are modeled in the following subsections.

Application Graph

A modern mobile application is usually guided by component oriented design. Components provide functionality via interfaces and may, conversely, consume functionality provided by other components [277]. The application can be presented as a graph $G_{app} = (C, E)$ where the vertexes are the components and the edges show the interaction between components.

To be extensible, the application graph is not limited to present only one application. The application graph can be extended to contain several applications and even the connections between applications.

Surrogate Network

In a multisite service composition scenario, some computation workload is offloaded from the original mobile device and distributed onto the chosen surrogate sites from candidate sites. The original site and its candidate sites form an egocentric network $G_{sur} = (S, L)$, where the node is the site and the link is the network connection between sites.

Component–Surrogate Mapping

The service composition mapping is a mapping from the application graph G_{app} to a surrogate network G_{sur}, where vertexes are mapped to nodes and the edges are mapped to links correspondingly. Let matrix X present this mapping, whose element x_{ij} is set to either 1 when component i is assigned to site j or 0, otherwise. Matrix X has the following properties:

1. Let n be the component number, $n = |X|$, and m be the candidate site number, $m = |Y|$. Then, E is $E_{n \times m}$. The relation of m and n is not strict, which means $m > n$, $m < n$, and $m = n$ are all valid.
2. The mapping is also not strict, which means several components may be mapped to the same surrogate site and some surrogate site may not host any components. However, each component in the application is assigned to exactly one site, thus, there is one and only one 1 in each row of E, i.e., $\sum_{j=1}^{n} e_{ij} = 1$ for every row i.
3. In a mobile application, some components have to be assigned to particular sites due to application requirements. For example, human–machine interaction components and sensor components have to be put on the original mobile device because they use mobile device hardware that is not available on surrogate sites. This requirement enforces the positions of some 1's in some rows of E to be predefined and not to be moved. These rows are put at the bottom of E. Except for these rows, the rest of E is the effective matrix $E_{\tilde{n} \times m}$, which corresponds to the movable components.

Based on E, four more mappings can be defined for easy expression in the following sections. Mapping $f_{C \to S}$ implements a similar function as E, which maps component i to site j: $f_{X \to Y}(i) = j$, $\forall e_{ij} = 1$, $e_{ij} \in E$. Mapping $f_{Y \to X}$ is the reverse mapping of $f_{X \to Y}$, which given site j outputs a set of components $\{i_1, i_2, \ldots, i_k\}$ coded as a vector $\mathbf{i}$. Besides, mappings can also be defined between A and B. Mapping $f_{A \to B}$ maps edge $a = (i_1, i_2)$ to link $b = (f_{X \to Y}(i_1), f_{X \to Y}(i_2))$. And similarly to $f_{Y \to X}$, mapping $f_{B \to A}$ maps a link to a vector of edges.

5.3.2 Model Statement

This subsection models several factors involved in the service composition topology reconfiguration, followed by model formulation in the end.

Decision Points

Decision points are the moments when the service composition topology reconfiguration decisions are made. At these moments in Fig. 5.11, the *Monitor* triggers the *Service composition topology reconfiguration* to generate a service composition topology. The moments are decided by the *Monitor* that is always observing the *Infrastructure* and the *Mobile application* states. The *Monitor* can trigger decisions periodically according to a predefined period Δt.

The decision points are a sequence that starts from the time when the application starts to the time when the application ends, $T = \{0, 1, 2, \ldots, N - 1\}$. In some scenarios, the application termination time is not expected and the sequence is an infinite sequence, $T = \{0, 1, 2, \ldots\}$.

Measures

The *Monitor* measures the *Infrastructure* states. The node computation capability and link throughput are labeled on the surrogate network, which transforms G_{sur} into a weighted graph. The available computation capability on a candidate site s is labeled as a node weight u_s and vector $\mathbf{u}$ collects weights of all sites. The network throughput on link $l = (s_1, s_2)$ from s_1 to s_2 is labeled as link weight $d_{s_1 s_2}$ and matrix $D_{n \times n}$ contains weights of all links. The diagonal of D has large values because the delay in the same site can be considered negligible.

The above measures may be continuous variables. They are manipulated by normalization and quantization to make them into discrete states. A relatively large value is picked and the observation is scaled to be in $[0, 1]$. Quantization precision determines the size of state space. The evaluation shows the results of different state space. The state space is denoted as S.

Service Composition Topology

The service composition topology is the effective component surrogate mapping $X_{\tilde{m} \times n}$. Each mapping corresponds to an action that enforces the mapping. The size of service composition topology space is $n^{\tilde{m}}$ since each component has n choices and there are $\tilde{m}$ components that make their choices independently. Let A be the corresponding action space from which the *Service composition system* in Fig. 5.11 acts – picking and enforcing the mappings. The output of the *Service composition topology reconfiguration* is a service composition topology. If the outputted service composition topology is different from the old one, reconfiguration is needed. "Reconfiguration" means that the components in the old service composition topology should be moved properly to satisfy the new service composition topology, which is fulfilled by the *Service composition executor*.

Observation Learning

The *Service composition topology reconfiguration* in Fig. 5.11 counts the historical states and actions, and estimates the state transition probability $p(j \mid i, a)$ where $i, j \in S$ and $a \in A$. The transition probability satisfies $\sum_{j \in S} p(j \mid i, a) = 1$. This probability is updated at decision points. The *Service composition topology reconfiguration* maintains a buffer that keeps the count for valid observed states and the count of historical actions. At each decision point, it gets the current state j from the *Monitor* and, the last state i and the last topology decision a from its buffer. Then it calculates the state transition probability for every pair of states with every action. This transition probability that comes from the recent history is used to predict the probability of transition for the near future Δt period assuming the transition probability stays steady in a short time period.

Service Composition Objective

One major service composition goal in mobile cloud computing is to save mobile device energy. Following the same procedures of equations from (5.4) to (5.7), the total power is calculated through the following equations:

$$P^{CPU}(i, a) = \mathbf{1}^T E(\mathbf{u}.*\mathbf{c}^{CPU}), \tag{5.30}$$

$$D'(i) = D.*(\mathbf{1}_{n \times n} - I).*(\mathbf{c}^{radio}\mathbf{1}^T), \tag{5.31}$$

$$P^{radio}(i, a) = \sum_{\forall l \in f_{A \to B}(\mathbf{e})} d'_l, \tag{5.32}$$

$$P(i, a) = P^{CPU} + P^{CPU}_{idle} + P^{radio} + P^{radio}_{base}. \tag{5.33}$$

When a topology is picked at a decision point, a reward value is calculated to indicate how good the decision is. The reward of choosing action a at state i depends on not only state i and action a but also the next state j. The reward is

$$r(i, a) = \sum_{j \in S} r(i, a, j) p(j \mid i, a), \tag{5.34}$$

where the reward of transition from state i to state j with action a is the expected delta power between two states i and j with the same action a, and

$$r(i, a, j) = P(j, a) - P(i, a). \tag{5.35}$$

Model Formulation

The service composition topology reconfiguration process is modeled as a five element tuple:

$$\{T, S, A, p(\cdot \mid i, a), r(i, a)\}. \tag{5.36}$$

This is a Markov decision process [188].

5.3.3 Optimization Solution

Based on the proposed service composition topology reconfiguration system and model, this section formulates the topology reconfiguration policy problem in both finite horizon scenario and infinite horizon scenario. The solutions in both scenarios are presented. Besides, the MapReduce based algorithms are discussed for large state count situations that are common in real world.

Topology Reconfiguration Policy

The service composition reconfiguration policy is a function π that maps states to actions $\pi : S \rightarrow A$. The function π can be stored in memory as an array whose index is the state and whose content of each element is the corresponding action.

Let Y_t and Δ_t be the system state and the picked action at decision point t, $\Delta_t = \pi(Y_t)$. The sequence $L(\pi) = \{Y_0, \Delta_0, Y_1, \Delta_1, \ldots\}$ is a stochastic process depending on π. Let $R_t(\pi) = r(Y_t, \Delta_t)$, then the sequence $\{R_0(\pi), R_1(\pi), \ldots\}$ is a reward process depending on π.

Finite Decision Points

At any decision point, the current period reward could be used as a decision goal, which, however, is shortsighted because the maximum current period reward does not guarantee that the sum of rewards in all periods is maximum. To make a proper decision on service composition topology, the total rewards of N periods should be considered as the goal:

$$V_N(Y_0, \pi) = \sum_{t=0}^{N-1} \beta^t R_t(\pi) = \sum_{t=0}^{N-1} \beta^t r(Y_t, \Delta_t) \tag{5.37}$$

where β is the confidence index. As the N periods' rewards are estimated future rewards, the degree of confidence on the reward sequence $R_t(\pi)$ decreases with t. The confidence index presents this decreasing confidence trend. The service composition topology reconfiguration problem is to find the policy π that maximizes $V_N(Y_0, \pi)$.

Let u_t be the reward sum from decision point t to N. There is backward recursive relation between $t + 1$ and t:

$$u_t(i_t, a_t) = r(i_t, a_t) + \beta \sum_{j \in S} p(j \mid i_t, a_t) u_{t+1}(j) \tag{5.38}$$

$$= \sum_{j \in S} p(j \mid i_t, a_t)(r(i_t, a_t, j) + \beta u_{t+1}(j)) \tag{5.39}$$

where $i_t \in S$ is the state at time t. Equation (5.38) shows the reward sum from time t to N consists of the current period reward and the β scaled reward sum from time $t + 1$ to N.

Let the superscript notation * represent the maximum value of the corresponding variable. To get the maximum rewards, the backward recursive relation formulation is

$$u_t^*(i_t) =$$

$$\max_{a_t \in A} \left\{ r(i_t, a_t) + \beta \sum_{j \in S} p(j \mid i_t, a_t) u_{t+1}^*(j) \right\} \tag{5.40}$$

Algorithm 5.3 shows the algorithm to calculate the policy π. The main body of the algorithm repeats equation (5.40) N times. In the algorithm, line 5 and line 6 could share the intermediate result of equation (5.38), which means $r(i_t, a) + \sum_{j \in S} p(j \mid i_t, a) u_{t+1}^*(j), \forall i_t \in S$ is calculated only once but used in both operations.

Algorithm 5.3 Finite horizon backward induction.

1: $t \leftarrow N$

2: $u_t^*(i_t) \leftarrow 0, \forall i_t \in S$

3: **while** $t > 0$ **do**

4:     $t \leftarrow t - 1$

5:     $u_t^*(i_t) \leftarrow$

$$\max_{a \in A} \left\{ r(i_t, a) + \beta \sum_{j \in S} p(j \mid i_t, a) u_{t+1}^*(j) \right\}, \forall i_t \in S$$

6:     $\pi_t^*(i_t) \leftarrow$

$$\arg \max_{a \in A} \left\{ r(i_t, a) + \beta \sum_{j \in S} p(j \mid i_t, a) u_{t+1}^*(j) \right\}, \forall i_t \in S$$

7: **end while**

The algorithm requires storage for two arrays indexed by state, $\mathbf{v}$ and $\mathbf{f}$. The ith element of the array $\mathbf{v}$ is $u^*(i)$ where $i \in S$. The ith element of the array $\mathbf{f}$ is an action $\pi^*(i) \in A$ that is the optimal action corresponding to state $i \in S$. The array $\mathbf{f}$ hosts one instance of π. The length of both $\mathbf{v}$ and $\mathbf{f}$ is $|S|$.

At the end of the algorithm, $\mathbf{v}$ contains the discounted sum of the rewards to be earned on average from the corresponding initial state i: $V_N^*(i) = \mathbf{v}(i) = u_0^*(i)$ where $i \in S$. The policy is $\pi = \{\pi_0^*, \pi_1^*, \ldots, \pi_{N-1}^*\}$ for N decision points. The array $\mathbf{f}$ contains π_0^* when the algorithm ends. The action $\pi_0^*(Y_0) = \mathbf{f}(Y_0)$ is the action that should be performed at the current decision point.

Infinite Decision Points

The previous discussion of the finite horizon scenario can be extended to the infinite horizon scenario. The objective function for the infinite horizon scenario can be achieved by pushing N to ∞ in equation (5.37), i.e.,

$$V(Y_0, \pi) = \lim_{N \to \infty} V_N(Y_0, \pi). \tag{5.41}$$

Similarly, the problem is to find the policy π that maximizes the total rewards $V(Y_0, \pi)$. In the infinite horizon scenario, the recursive relation (5.38) is generalized by removing iteration subscript:

$$u(i, a) = r(i, a) + \beta \sum_{j \in S} p(j \mid i, a) u(j). \tag{5.42}$$

Similarly, the recursive relation (5.40) changes to

$$u^*(i) = \max_{a \in A} \left\{ r(i, a) + \beta \sum_{j \in S} p(j \mid i, a) u^*(j) \right\} \tag{5.43}$$

which means the $u^*(i)$ achieves to the maximum total rewards.

Algorithm 5.4 shows the algorithm to calculate the policy π. Compared to Algorithm 5.3, the iteration termination condition is changed to comparing the vector norm and tolerance. ε indicates the tolerance for the converging state. In line 6, $\|\cdot\|$ is a vector norm that could be any type of L_p: L_1, L_2, or L_∞ norm. In addition, a local improvement loop is added inside the main iteration. The sequence $\{m\}$ consists of nonnegative integers that are used in each iteration as improvement depth; $\{m\}$ could be generated in many ways. For example, it may be constant, i.e., $m_n = m$, or it may get more precise along with the iteration sequence number, i.e., $m_n = n$. When the algorithm ends, the policy is π_{n+1} that is stored in the array $\mathbf{f}$.

The column vector $\mathbf{r}(\pi)$ and matrix $P(\pi)$ are defined to simplify expressions in the algorithm. The ith element of vector $\mathbf{r}(\pi)$ is $r(i, \pi(i))$ where $i \in S$. The size of $\mathbf{r}(\pi)$ is $|S|$. The (i, j)th element of matrix $P(\pi)$ is $p(j \mid i, \pi(i))$ where $i, j \in S$. The size of $P(\pi)$ is $|S| \times |S|$. In the algorithm, lines 13 through 15 repeat the same operations as lines 3 to 5. Line 8 is the vector version of equation (5.42). Lines 5 and 15 are the vector version of equation (5.43). Lines 3 and 5 share the intermediate computation result. Similarly, lines 13 and 15 also share the intermediate computation result.

Large State Space

To make a more accurate and agile decision, the real world measures usually lead to a large state space in Section 5.3.2. The large state space size results in a long responding time. To mitigate the response time in a large state space situation, MapReduce could be used. This section discusses the conversion from Algorithm 5.3 and Algorithm 5.4 to MapReduce algorithms.

Algorithm 5.5 and Algorithm 5.6 show the MapReduce algorithms for the finite horizon scenario. The input to the mapper function, which is also the output of the reducer function, is the state id i and an object Q that encapsulates the state information defined in Section 5.3.2. Besides encoded state information, two components $Q.v$ and $Q.f$ corresponding to the arrays $\mathbf{v}$ and $\mathbf{f}$ are also included in the state object. Moreover, a component $Q.p$ corresponding to the state transition probability obtained in Section 5.3.2 is included in the state object as well. The state object is passed from the mapper to the reducer for calculating Equation (5.39). This

---

Algorithm 5.4 Infinite horizon induction.

1: $n \leftarrow 0$
2: $\mathbf{v}^n \leftarrow \mathbf{0}$
3: $\pi_{n+1} \leftarrow \arg\max_{\pi \in \Pi} \{\mathbf{r}(\pi) + \beta P(\pi)\mathbf{v}^n\}$
4: $k \leftarrow 0$
5: $\mathbf{u}_n^k \leftarrow \max_{\pi \in \Pi} \{\mathbf{r}(\pi) + \beta P(\pi)\mathbf{v}^n\}$ ▷ Equation (5.43)
6: **while** $\|\mathbf{u}_n^k - \mathbf{v}^n\| < \varepsilon$ **do**
7:       **while** $k < m_n$ **do**   ▷ Equation (5.42)
8:             $\mathbf{u}_n^{k+1} \leftarrow \mathbf{r}(\pi_{n+1}) + \beta P(\pi_{n+1})\mathbf{u}_n^k$
9:             $k \leftarrow k + 1$
10:     **end while**
11:     $\mathbf{v}^{n+1} \leftarrow \mathbf{u}_n^{m_n}$
12:     $n \leftarrow n + 1$
13:     $\pi_{n+1} \leftarrow \arg\max_{\pi \in \Pi} \{\mathbf{r}(\pi) + \beta P(\pi)\mathbf{v}^n\}$
14:     $k \leftarrow 0$
15:     $\mathbf{u}_n^k \leftarrow \max_{\pi \in \Pi} \{\mathbf{r}(\pi) + \beta P(\pi)\mathbf{v}^n\}$ ▷ Equation (5.43)
16: **end while**

---

is accomplished by emitting the state data structure itself, with the state id as a key in line 2 of the mapper. In the reducer line 3, the node data structure is distinguished from other values.

Algorithm 5.5 Finite horizon Mapper.

1: **function** MAP(i, Q)
2:     Emit (i, Q) ▷ Pass state i
3:     **for all** $j \in S$ **do**
4:           **for all** $a \in A$ **do**
5:                 Emit $(j, < i, Q, a >)$
6:           **end for**
7:     **end for**
8: **end function**

The mapper function associates the current state with all backward states. The reducer function aggregates the reward sum of all forward states according to Equation (5.39), which is categorized by action. Then it picks the maximum reward sum and the corresponding action as the current reward sum and action according to Equation (5.40).

Algorithm 5.6 Finite horizon Reducer.

1: **function** REDUCE(i, [$< j, Q, a >$])
2:     **for all** $x \in [< j, Q, a >]$ **do**
3:         **if** Is(x) **then**   ▷ Recover state i
4:             $Q \leftarrow x$
5:         **end if**
6:     **end for**
7:     $set \leftarrow$ new HashSet
8:     **for all** $x \in [< j, Q, a >]$ **do**
9:         **if** IsNot(x) **then**   ▷ Equation (5.39)
10:             $set(a) \leftarrow set(a)+$

$$Q.p(j, a)(r(Q, a, x.Q) + \beta x.Q.v)$$

11:         **end if**
12:     **end for**
13:     **for all** $x \in set$ **do**
14:         **if** $Q.v < set(a)$ **then**   ▷ Equation (5.40)
15:             $Q.v \leftarrow set(a)$
16:             $Q.f \leftarrow a$
17:         **end if**
18:     **end for**
19:     Emit (i, Q)
20: **end function**

It is apparent that Algorithm 5.3 is an iterative algorithm, where each iteration corresponds to a MapReduce job. The actual checking of the termination condition must occur outside of MapReduce. Typically, execution of an iterative MapReduce algorithm requires a non-MapReduce "driver" program, which submits a MapReduce job to iterate the algorithm, checks to see if a termination condition has been met, and if not, repeats [187].

As presented in Section 5.3.3, just as the infinite horizon algorithm is obtained by extending the finite algorithm, the MapReduce based algorithm for the infinite horizon scenario can be obtained by extending the MapReduce based finite horizon algorithms. The mapper function could be used without modification in the infinite horizon algorithms. The improvement loop in the infinite horizon algorithm can be achieved by repeating lines 8 through 12 $m + n$ times. Besides the modification on the reduce function, a modification on the driver is required. The iteration termination condition in the driver is changed from a fixed number to a comparison of norm and coverage tolerance.

Table 5.3: Default parameter setting

Parameter		Default value
application and cloud	$\tilde{m}$	8
	n	5
	$|S|$	100
finite horizon	N	3
	β	0.7
infinite horizon	L_p	L_2
	m_n	n
	ε	1
large state space	$|S|$	1000

5.3.4 Evaluation

This section discusses the proposed models and presents the evaluations of the proposed algorithms including finite horizon, infinite horizon, and MapReduce based algorithms.

Evaluation Cases and Default Parameter Setting

We generate 200 test cases of the proposed model in Section 5.3.2. To make the mobile device profile based on solid ground, we pick up the mobile device profiling parameters obtained in a previous work [289]. The maximum dynamic power consumption values in each mobile CPU and RF components, c^{CPU} and c^{radio}, are normally distributed with mean of 4.34 and 710, and variance of 1.46 and 48, respectively. The static power consumption values in each mobile CPU and RF components, P_{idle}^{CPU} and P_{base}^{radio}, are normally distributed with mean of 121.46 and 20, and variance of 9.20 and 4.86, respectively. To estimate the surrogate infrastructure, we pick up the cloud profiling parameters obtained in a previous experience report [81]. The CPU utility is uniformly distributed from 40% to 90%. The network throughput is uniformly distributed from 10% to 40% after normalization.

Besides the mobile device and cloud profiling, we use the default algorithm parameter values (see Table 5.3). These values may be changed in the experiments to show their impact on the algorithms.

Experiments on Finite Horizon

We first evaluate the norm of the reward sum trend along with the variance of forecast decision point number N for different confidence index β. Since the reward sum range of test cases vary, we normalize the reward sum against the maximum reward sum in the evaluation. The experiment result is shown in Fig. 5.12. The trend in the figure shows that the reward sum

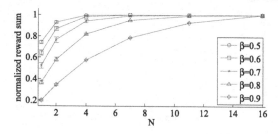

Figure 5.12: N and β correlation in the finite horizon scenario.

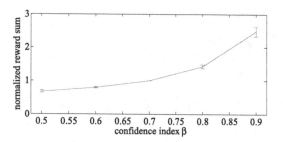

Figure 5.13: Reward sum vs. β in the finite horizon scenario.

approaches the maximum reward sum as N increases. The approach follows a monotonically increasing trend. When the reward sum approximates a stable value (e.g., N is greater than 8 for $\beta = 0.7$), we can claim that N is large enough to be considered as an infinite horizon scenario.

In Fig. 5.12, when the confidence index is small ($\beta = 0.5$), the reward sum converges after a short period ($N = 4$). When $\beta = 0.7$, the value for the reward sum to converge ($N = 8$) is twice as that for $\beta = 0.5$. The higher the confidence index, the larger the decision point number to make the expected reward sum converge. Since the N values for convergence are related to the iteration times in the infinite scenario, we can infer that the smaller the confidence index, the fewer iterations are required in the infinite horizon scenario.

We then evaluate the norm of the reward sum trend along with the variance of confidence index β. The experiment result is shown in Fig. 5.13. In the figure, the reward sum is normalized against the values of the default confidence index. The reward sum increases monotonically along with the confidence index. The higher the confidence index, the more reward values are added to the total considered reward, which leads to the higher norm value of the reward norm. The reward sum increases sharply when the confidence index approaches 1, which leads to a linear proportional relation between the reward sum and the forecast period N or an infinite horizon reward sum calculation failure. When the confidence index is small,

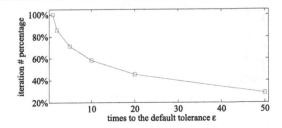

Figure 5.14: Reward sum vs. N in the finite horizon scenario.

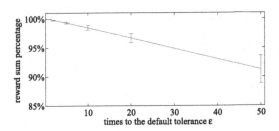

Figure 5.15: Reward sum for different ε.

the reward sum is steady because the reward sum mainly consists of rewards in several near future forecast periods.

Experiments on Infinite Horizon

In the infinite horizon algorithm, the main loop of the infinite horizon algorithm terminates using a condition controlled by the reward sum tolerance. We experiment with different toler-ance and their corresponding main loop iteration cycles and show the results in Fig. 5.14. In the figure, the x-axis ranges from 1 times ε to 50 times ε, and the y-axis is the iteration cycle number that is normalized against the cycle number of the default ε situation. Obviously, the higher the tolerance, the sooner the iteration ends. A large tolerance means that larger reward sum values fall into the area of considered converged values, so fewer iterations may let the reward sum trend go into that area and terminate the iteration cycle. We also illustrate the re-ward sum of different ε in Fig. 5.15. Here, similar to Fig. 5.14, the x-axis ranges from 1 times ε to 50 times ε, and the y-axis is the reward sum that is normalized against the cycle number of the default ε situation. We can see that the reward sum decreases when the tolerance in-creases, which demonstrates the that the coverage area is enlarged by the large tolerance. In addition, the reward sum decreases proportionally to the tolerance variance, which is expected because the convergence area is enlarged by turbulence proportionally.

5.4 Evolving Mobile Cloud Computing

In the previous and this chapter, we saw how a mobile cloud system works. The world changes fast, as does the mobile cloud. In this section, we discuss several promising research areas of mobile cloud computing, hoping to inspire users explore future research ideas.

Semantic Compute Offloading

Information-centric networking (ICN) is initially conceptualized as a general form of communication architecture to achieve efficient content distribution on the Internet. ICN focuses on what (content) instead of where (host). This is to fulfill the primary demands that consumers are only interested in content itself, not its provenance, and publishers strive to efficiently distribute contents to consumers. To this end, ICN uses node or data attributes (e.g., content name, geo-location, or context) for routing rather than a specific node address (i.e., IP address). This decouples the content from the publishers. In this sense, content-based routing, geo-routing, and context-based routing can be classified into types of ICN [177].

Service discovery plays a key role in the computation offloading and service composition. The current mobile cloud offloading systems and strategies work based on the addresses. Thus, a system-wide central service registry or service broker is necessary to route the offloading request or to answer the service searching. When ICN is introduced to fulfill the service discovery of the mobile cloud offloading, the offloading architecture may be simplified and the service composition can be more flexible.

MicroService

A microservice [100] [179] [261] [214] is a minimal functional service module which is independently developed and deployed, and microservice architecture is an architecture of distributed software modules composed by a microservice which is rather an evolved software engineering pattern from successful field practice as opposed to an invented principle. The major characteristics of microservice include small, focused, self-contained service for componentization, loosely coupled architecture, clear boundary by contexts, autonomous and software architecture aligned development team, decentralized governance, design for failure, etc. These architectural characteristics bring many benefits such as capability of integration of heterogeneous technology, continuous delivery, resilience, scalability, and eventually a fast-evolutionary architecture.

Microservice patterns are mainly discussed in the context of large web based applications, while less focus has been on the IoT system. It is interesting to see that they actually share many similar characteristics [70] [172]. First, they have a similar loosely coupled architecture. A typical IoT system will integrate many devices and software components from different vendors, where each of them has its own life cycle. Second, most IoT systems need to integrate heterogeneous software components implemented on different hardware devices. To cope with the fast-evolving technology, some of them might be changed or updated without the influence of the other parts of the system. Third, communications among different software modules in an IoT system are usually based on well-defined message oriented interfaces, or REST API, which is similar to calling a service. Fourth, they both try to maintain minimum deployment and management effort in the field. The smaller the services, the easier it is to offload. Especially on the IOT devices, which are more resource constrained than smart phones, offloading the tasks to other devices might be necessary. Besides, the number of IOT devices may be much larger than that of phones, which leads to offloading scalability research topic.

Multistage Offloading

The present offloading model regards the mobile device and cloud as the only two layers in the model. However, more devices are involved in the mobile cloud system, such as IOT devices, vehicles, road site units, and mobile stations. These devices are equipped with computation and storage capability, which can host offloaded computation. The advantage of these devices compared to the Internet cloud is that they are closer to the user. Naturally, they can be candidate surrogates. A typical example is the vehicle cloud. When a smart phone connects to a vehicle, the computation can be offloaded from the phone to the vehicle, which is supposed to be faster than that offloaded to the Internet cloud due to network length. However, the computation and storage on the vehicle are still limited compared to the cloud. In some application scenarios, the vehicle cannot provide all the required resources and the vehicle may choose to offload the overload compute request to the road site unit or further Internet cloud. The cascading offloading for multistage offloading is more suitable in the present world where everything gets smart.

CHAPTER 6

Edge Clouds – Pushing the Boundary of Mobile Clouds

The Edge... there is no honest way to explain it because the only people who really know where it is are the ones who have gone over.

Hunter S. Thompson

In cloud and mobile computing communities, there is no consensus on the taxonomic relations between edge and mobile clouds. If the definition of "mobiles" is extended to various embedded devices, sensors, and we relax the computing bounding between Internet clouds and mobile devices, then edge cloud can be considered as a special case of mobile cloud. The offloading targets in mobile cloud computing can be extended to mobile devices, sensors, and many nontraditional computers. As shown in Fig. 6.1, if the code transfer procedure is not required in the offloading models, then we can use composing approach to build a more flexible mobile cloud application scenario to maximally reuse the mobile edge devices' functions.

Edge cloud is pushing the frontier of computing applications, data, and services away from centralized nodes to the logical extremes of a network. It enables analytics and knowledge generation to occur at the source of the data, especially mobile devices. This approach requires leveraging resources that may not be continuously connected to a network such as laptops, smartphones, tablets, and sensors. Edge computing covers a wide range of technologies including wireless sensor networks, mobile data acquisition, mobile signature analysis, cooperative distributed peer-to-peer ad hoc networking and processing also classifiable as local cloud/fog computing and grid/mesh computing, dew computing, mobile edge computing, cloudlet, distributed data storage and retrieval, autonomic self-healing networks, remote cloud services, augmented reality, and more.

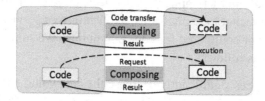

Figure 6.1: From offloading to composing.

This chapter describes edge cloud concept in Section 6.1, followed by the comparisons of edge cloud vs Internet cloud in Section 6.1.1. The edge cloud examples and applications are presented in Section 6.1.2. Finally, the microservices and several case studies are presented.

6.1 Edge Cloud

Security cameras, phones, machine sensors, thermostats, cars, and televisions are just a few of the items in daily use that create data which can be mined and analyzed. Add to it the data created at retail stores, manufacturing plants, financial institutions, oil and gas drilling platforms, pipelines and processing plants, and it is not hard to understand that the deluge of streaming and IoT sensor data can — and will — very quickly overwhelm today's traditional data analytics tools.

Organizations are beginning to look at edge cloud computing (or simply edge computing) as the answer. Edge computing consists of putting micro data centers or even small, purpose-built high-performance data analytics machines in remote offices and locations in order to gain real-time insights from the data collected, or to promote data thinning at the edge, by dramatically reducing the amount of data that needs to be transmitted to a central data center. Without having to move unnecessary data to a central data center, analytics at the edge can simplify and drastically speed analysis while also cutting costs.

Edge computing pushes applications, data, and computing power (services) away from centralized points to the logical extremes of a network. Edge computing replicates fragments of information across distributed networks of web servers, which may be vast. As a topological paradigm, edge computing is also referred to as mesh computing, peer-to-peer computing, autonomic (self-healing) computing, grid computing, and using other names implying non-centralized, nodeless availability.

To ensure acceptable performance of widely dispersed distributed services, large organizations typically implement edge computing by deploying Web server farms with clustering. Previously available only to very large corporate and government organizations, technology advancement and cost reduction for large-scale implementations have made the technology available to small and medium-sized businesses. The target end-user is any Internet client making use of commercial Internet application services. Edge computing imposes certain limitations on the choices of technology platforms, applications or services, all of which need to be specifically developed or configured for edge computing. We summarize the main advantages of edge computing as follows:

1. Edge application services significantly decrease the data volume that must be moved, the consequent traffic, and the distance the data must go, thereby reducing transmission costs, shrinking latency, and improving quality of service (QoS).

2. Edge computing eliminates, or at least deemphasizes, the core computing environment, limiting or removing a major bottleneck and a potential point of failure.
3. Security is also improved as encrypted data moves further in, toward the network core. As it approaches the enterprise, the data is checked as it passes through protected firewalls and other security points, where viruses, compromised data, and active hackers can be caught early on.
4. Finally, the ability to "virtualize" (i.e., logically group CPU capabilities on an as-needed, real-time basis) extends scalability. The edge computing market is generally based on a "charge for network services" model, and it could be argued that typical customers for edge services are organizations desiring linear scale of business application performance to the growth of, e.g., a subscriber base.

6.1.1 Edge Cloud vs Internet Cloud

Edge cloud is fundamentally different from Internet clouds. First, resource organization and location are different. Edge computing refers to data processing power at the edge of a network instead of holding that processing power in a cloud or a central data warehouse. There are several examples where it's advantageous to do so. For example, in industrial IoT applications such as power production, smart traffic lights, or manufacturing, the edge devices capture streaming data that can be used to prevent a part from failing, reroute traffic, optimize production, and prevent product defects.

Edge computing relates to mobile networks application and data stream acceleration through caching and/or compressing of relevant (mainly localized) data at the edge of the mobile network, as near as possible to the end user location. In this sense edge computing is a method of accelerating and improving the performance of cloud computing for mobile users.

An edge device could also be an ATM (the bank wants to stop fraudulent financial transactions); a retail store that is using a beacon to push in-store incentives to a mobile application; a smartphone; a gateway device that collects data from other endpoints before sending it to the cloud, etc.

Second, data value and processing model are different. Much like the time value of money, the time value of data means that the data you have in this second will not mean as much a week, day or even hour from now. This coupled with the proliferation of IoT sensor, social, and other streaming data is driving organizations to use edge computing to provide the real-time analytics that impact the bottom line, or in some cases, stop a disaster from happening before it starts.

Organizations are currently reliant on large and complex clusters for data analytics, and these clusters are rife with bottlenecks including data transport, indexing and extract, as well as transform and load processes. While centralized infrastructures work for analyses that rely on static or historical data, it is critical for many of today's organizations to have fast and actionable insight by correlating newly obtained information with legacy information in order to gain and maintain a strong competitive advantage.

An increasing amount of data is priceless in the seconds after it's collected – consider the instance of a fraudster or hacker accessing accounts – but it loses all value during the time it takes to move it to the centralized data center infrastructure or upload it to the cloud. Losing value from that data due to slow decisions is not acceptable, especially when an edge-computing platform that eliminates moving data provides the near-instant intelligence needed. Organizations cannot afford to wait days, weeks or even months for insights from data. With data analytics at the edge, they do not have to. When data analysis is done at the edge of a network, that's known as "edge analytics."

For example, recently Facebook announced Caffe2 [12] to help developers and researchers train large machine learning models and deliver AI on mobile devices. This release provides access to many of the same tools, allowing you to run large-scale distributed training scenarios and build machine learning applications for mobile. Caffe2 comes with native Python and C++ APIs that work interchangeably so a developer can prototype quickly now, easily optimize later. Caffe2 also integrates with Android Studio, Microsoft Visual Studio, or Apple XCode for mobile development.

Finally, edge computing does not replace cloud computing. In reality, an analytic model or rules might be created in a cloud then pushed out to edge devices. Some edge devices are also incapable of doing analysis. Edge computing is also closely related to "fog computing", which also entails data processing from the edge to the cloud.

6.1.2 Edge Cloud Platforms

In this section, we provide an overview of two edge-cloud computing platforms, fog computing and Nebula.

Fog Computing

Fog computing or fog networking, also known as fogging, is an architecture that uses one or more collaborative multitude of end-user clients or near-user edge devices to carry out a substantial amount of storage (rather than stored primarily in cloud data centers), communication (rather than routed over the Internet backbone), control, configuration, measurement, and management (rather than controlled primarily by network gateways such as those in the

LTE core network). On November 19, 2015, Cisco Systems, ARM Holdings, Dell, Intel, Microsoft, and Princeton University founded the OpenFog Consortium [25] to promote interests and development in fog computing.

Fog computing can be perceived both in large cloud systems and big data structures, making reference to the growing difficulties in accessing information objectively. This results in a lack of quality of the obtained content. The effects of fog computing on cloud computing and big data systems may vary; yet, a common aspect that can be extracted is a limitation in accurate content distribution, an issue that has been tackled with the creation of metrics that attempt to improve accuracy.

Fog networking consists of a control plane and a data plane. For example, on the data plane, fog computing enables computing services to reside at the edge of the network as opposed to servers in a data-center. Compared to cloud computing, fog computing emphasizes proximity to end-users and client objectives, dense geographical distribution and local resource pooling, latency reduction for QoS and edge analytics/stream mining, resulting in superior user-experience and redundancy in case of failure.

Fog networking supports the Internet of Everything (IoE) concept, in which most of the devices used by humans on a daily basis will be connected to each other. Examples include phones, wearable health monitoring devices, connected vehicle and augmented reality using devices such as the Google Glass. ISO/IEC 20248 [18] is an ISO standard describing automatic identification and data capture techniques – data structures – digital signature meta structure. It is an international standard specification provides a method whereby the data of objects identified by edge computing using Automated Identification Data Carriers (AIDC), a bar-code and/or RFID tag, can be read, interpreted, verified and made available into the "Fog" and on the "Edge" even when the AIDC tag has moved on.

Nebula

Nebula [234] is a dispersed cloud infrastructure that uses voluntary edge resources for both computation and data storage, which is developed by University of Minnesota. The design goals of Nebula include the following features:

- *Support for distributed data-intensive computing.* Nebula is designed to support data-intensive applications that require efficient movement and availability of large quantities of data to compute resources. As a result, in addition to an efficient computational platform, Nebula must also support a scalable data storage platform. Further, Nebula is designed to support applications where data may originate in a geographically distributed manner, and is not necessarily preloaded to a central location.

- *Location-aware resource management.* To enable efficient execution of distributed data-intensive applications, Nebula considers network bandwidth along with computation capabilities of resources in the volunteer platform. As a result, resource management decisions must optimize on computation time as well as data movement costs. In particular, compute resources may be selected based on their locality and proximity to their input data, while data may be staged closer to efficient computational resources.
- *Sandboxed execution environment.* To ensure that volunteer nodes are completely safe and isolated from malicious code that might be executed as part of a Nebula-based application, volunteer nodes must be able to execute all user-injected application code within a protected sandbox.
- *Fault tolerance.* Nebula ensures fault tolerant execution of applications in the presence of node churn and transient network failures that are typical in a volunteer environment.

Nebula consists of volunteer nodes that donate their computation and storage resources, along with a set of global and application-specific services that are hosted on dedicated, stable nodes. These resources and services together constitute four major components in Nebula: *Nebula Central, DataStore, ComputePool,* and *Nebula Monitor.*

These components work with each other to enable the execution of data-intensive applications on the Nebula platform. Each volunteer node can choose to participate as a data node or a compute node depending on whether it donates its storage, compute resources, or both. The volunteer nodes are multiplexed among different applications, so each compute (or data) node can be part of multiple *ComputePools* (or *DataStores*). The centralized components only provide control and monitoring information, and all data flow and work flow happens directly between the volunteer nodes in the system. As a result, these components do not become bottlenecks in the execution path.

FemtoClouds

A collection of colocated devices can be orchestrated to provide a cloud service at the edge. Scenarios with colocated devices include, but are not limited to, passengers with mobile devices using public transit services, students in classrooms and groups of people sitting in a coffee shop. The FemtoCloud system [124] which provides a dynamic, self-configuring and multidevice mobile cloud out of a cluster of mobile devices. The FemtoCloud system architecture designed to enable multiple mobile devices to be configured into a coordinated cloud computing service despite churn in mobile device participation.

The FemtoCloud computing service executes a variety of tasks that arrive at the control device. The FemtoCloud client service, running on the mobile devices, estimates the computational capability of the mobile device, and uses it along with user input to determine the computational capacity available for sharing. This client leverages device sensors, user input, and utilization history, to build and maintain a user profile. Afterwards, the service shares the available information with the control device, which is then responsible for estimating the user presence time and configuring the participating mobile devices as a cloud offering compute as a service.

6.2 Microservices for Mobile Cloud Computing

6.2.1 Microservices

"Microservices" became a hot term in 2014 [179], attracting lots of attention as a new way to think about structuring applications. In short, the microservice architectural style is an approach to developing a single application as a suite of small services, each running in its own process and communicating with lightweight mechanisms, often an HTTP resource API. These services are built around business capabilities and independently deployable by fully automated deployment machinery. There is a bare minimum of centralized management of these services, which may be written in different programming languages and use different data storage technologies.

6.2.1.1 Microservices vs. SOA

Some advocates believe that the microservice style is very similar to that of Service Oriented Architecture (SOA) [264]. However, SOA usually means too many different things, and the differences are usually due to the SOA's focus on Enterprise Service Buses (ESBs)[1] used to integrate monolithic applications.

Microservice architecture is an agile software architecture. While microservices and SOA are different on many levels – architectural style, implementation examples, associated technologies – they have played strikingly similar roles in the technology landscape. Both promised to be transformational, and they succeeded in attracting adherents who attracted still more adherents. In short, while both microservices and SOA began as architectures, they ultimately became movements.

The distributed nature of cloud infrastructure challenged the placement of the centralized ESB topology. Organizationally and culturally, the agile movement was driving decentralization and team autonomy. The combination of factors among others took the SOA movement out of

---

[1] An enterprise service bus (ESB) implements a communication system between mutually interacting software applications in a service-oriented architecture (SOA).

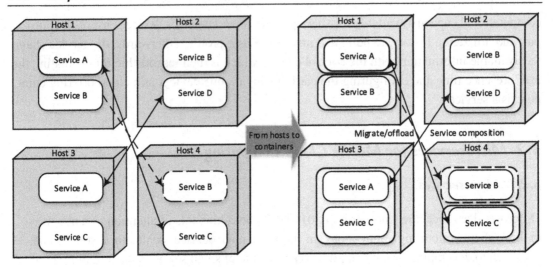

Figure 6.2: Microservices and containers.

the mainstream. By 2009, people were not merely questioning the SOA approach but marking its death. RESTful Web APIs – a style of interconnecting applications that had evolved organically on the Web – arose as a lighter-weight alternative to SOAP services.

Matt McLarty provided a detailed discussion [198] on explaining the history of SOA, contrasting SOA and Microservices as movements rather than technology, and pointing out the lessons the microservices movement needs to learn from the fate of SOA. In short, the design of a successful service model should be rooted in the business need and not in a conceptual design.

6.2.1.2 Microservices Architectural Style

The microservices relations are highlighted in Fig. 6.2. The architectural styles of microservices are described below.

Monolithic style – a monolithic application built as a single unit. For example, enterprise applications are often built in three main parts: a client-side user interface (consisting of HTML pages and JavaScript running in a browser on the user's machine), a database (consisting of many tables inserted into a common, and usually relational, database management system), and a server-side application. The server-side application will handle HTTP requests, execute domain logic, retrieve and update data from the database, and select and populate HTML views to be sent to the browser. This server-side application is a monolith – a single logical executable. Any changes to the system involve building and deploying a new version of the server-side application.

Many of web-based applications use JSON via REST endpoints applied a monolithic architecture. The application is deployed as a single file (e.g., Java) or a collection of files rooted at the same directory (e.g., Rails [31]). All the application code runs in the same process. Scaling requires deploying multiple copies of the exact same application code to multiple servers. As shown in Fig. 6.2, the services defined in the monolithic application architecture are decomposed into individual services, and deployed separately from one another on separate hosts.

Each microservice is aligned with a specific business function, and only defines the operations necessary to that business function. This may sound exactly like SOA, and indeed, microservices architecture and SOA share some common characteristics. Both architectures organize code into services, and both define clear boundaries representing the points at which a service should be decoupled from another. However, SOA arose from the need to integrate monolithic applications that exposed an API (usually SOAP-based[2]) with one another. In SOA, integration relies heavily on middleware, in particular Enterprise Service Bus (ESB). Microservices architecture may often make use of a message bus, but there is no logic in the messaging layer whatsoever – it is purely used as a transport for messages from one service to another. This differs dramatically from ESB, which contains substantial logic for message routing, schema validation, message translation, and business rules. As a result, microservices architectures are substantially less cumbersome than traditional SOA, and do not require the same level of governance and canonical data modeling to define the interface between services. With microservices, development is rapid and services evolve alongside the needs of the business.

Monolithic applications can be successful, but increasingly people are feeling frustrations with them – especially as more applications are being deployed to the cloud. Change cycles are tied together – a change made to a small part of the application requires the entire monolith to be rebuilt and deployed. Over time it is often hard to keep a good modular structure, making it harder to keep changes that ought to only affect one module within that module. Scaling requires scaling of the entire application rather than parts of it that require greater resource. This leads to the second architectural style.

Independently deployable services are independently deployable and scalable, each service also provides a firm module boundary, even allowing for different services to be written in different programming languages. They can also be managed by different teams. This is a key advantage of the microservices architecture, in which a service can be individually scaled

---

[2] SOAP (originally Simple Object Access Protocol) is a protocol specification for exchanging structured information in the implementation of web services in computer networks. Its purpose is to induce extensibility, neutrality, and independence. It uses XML Information Set for its message format, and relies on application layer protocols, most often Hypertext Transfer Protocol (HTTP) or Simple Mail Transfer Protocol (SMTP), for message negotiation and transmission.

based on its resource requirements. Rather than having to run large servers with lots of CPU and RAM, microservices can be deployed on smaller hosts containing only those resources required by that service. In addition, each service can be implemented in the language most suitable for the operations that service performs. An image processing service can be implemented using a high-performance language like C++. A service performing math or statistical operations may be implemented in Python. Services performing basic CRUD operations[3] for resources might be best implemented in Ruby. The microservices architecture does not require the "one size fits all" model of the monolithic architecture, which will generally use a single application framework and a single programming language.

Decentralized Governance – one of the consequences of centralized governance is the tendency to standardize on single technology platforms, and make it incompatible with other platforms' components.

The above three described architectural styles fit perfectly into mobile cloud application scenarios, where mobile devices may request services from other nodes. Since microservices inherit some features of SOA, the POEM approach presented in Chapter 4 and Appendix A can be used as a foundation to implement the microservices architectural styles, and this will lead to a future development.

6.2.1.3 Using Container for Microservices

But there are some disadvantages to microservices as well. Because services will be spread across multiple hosts, it can be difficult to keep track of which hosts are running certain services. Also, even though each host may not be as powerful as the host running the monolithic application, as the microservices architecture scales out, the number of hosts will grow faster than it will with a monolithic architecture. In the AWS environment, there may even be microservices that do not require all the resources of even the smallest EC2 instance type. This results in over-provisioning and increased costs. If services are implemented in different programming languages, this means the deployment of each service will require a completely different set of libraries and frameworks, making deployment to a server complex.

Linux containers can help mitigate many of these challenges with the microservices architecture as shown in Fig. 6.2. Linux containers make use of kernel interfaces such as *cnames* and *namespaces*, which allow multiple containers to share the same kernel while running in complete isolation from one another. The Docker execution environment uses a module called *libcontainer*, which standardizes these interfaces. Docker also provided a *GitHub*-like repository for container images called *DockerHub*, making it easy to share and distribute containers. It is this isolation between containers running on the same host that makes deploying

---
[3] In computer programming, create, read, update, and delete (as an acronym CRUD).

microservice code developed using different languages and frameworks very easy. Using Docker, we could create a *DockerFile* describing all the language, framework, and library dependencies for that service.

The container execution environment isolates each container running on the host from one another, so there is no risk that the language, library, or framework dependencies used by one container will collide with that of another. The portability of containers also makes deployment of microservices easily. To push out a new version of a service running on a given host, the running container can simply be stopped and a new container started that is based on a Docker image using the latest version of the service code. All the other containers running on the host will be unaffected by this change.

Containers also help with the efficient utilization of resources on a host. If a given service is not using all the resources on an Amazon EC2 instance, additional services can be launched in containers on that instance that make use of the idle resources. Of course, deploying services in containers, managing which services are running on which hosts, and tracking the capacity utilization of all hosts that are running containers will quickly become unmanageable if done manually.

6.3 Microservices Patterns for IoT

Microservices patterns, like all patterns, are meant not to define a single solution, API, standard, or framework, but rather to identify common patterns found in systems that successfully manage important forces [179]. It is important to keep in mind, therefore, that a given IoT system might simultaneously involve multiple technical implementations of key elements like containers and event notification protocols – some of these legacies and difficult to change – but these particulars should not stop us from recognizing the pattern in use.

We wish to work towards a vision future in which we are able to efficiently develop IoT systems that are extremely interoperable, flexible, and secure. The structure of the vision consists of a high-level, abstract model of general microservices-based IoT systems, together with patterns of solutions that one might expect to see employed in the design and deployment of any given IoT system following the vision. We must note that some of the key requirements and forces within IoT systems are exhibited differently than within typical cloud-only, web-centric microservices solutions. Therefore, one should reasonably expect that the sorts of patterns that one might find in use in successful IoT systems will contain common elements to cloud systems, but nevertheless can be instantiated and combined in different ways.

Though undoubtedly many patterns will be used in IoT systems in the future, we focus our vision on the combination of six patterns that we expect to combine constructively to build solutions well. These are listed in Table 6.1 which, for each pattern, provides a name to the type

Table 6.1: Key patterns in the vision of microservices-focused IoT solutions

Name	Type	Solution of	Qualities
Microservices	Structural	Decomposition	Team structure alignment (Conway's law); independent development and testing; enabling microservices marketplaces
API Gateway	Structural	Aggregation and distribution	Service API aggregation; event distribution; policy enforcement; network bridging
Distribution	Structural	Locality decomposition	Performance; resilience; scaling
Service discovery	Action	System coupling	Dynamic reconfiguration; extensibility
Containers	Structural	Deployment	Deployment simplicity; security; scaling
Access Control	Structural	Data sharing	Interoperability; scaling; flexibility; security

of the pattern, what kinds of IoT problems it may be applied to, and some of the desirable system qualities that may be enabled more easily through using the pattern.

6.3.1 IoT-Based Microservices

We take "microservices"-based IoT systems to be composed of one or more individual self-contained and independent deployable software components, i.e., microservices interacting with each other by messages abstracted as method calls (e.g., web service call, or message RPC), or through publishing–subscribing events.

For example, consider a hypothetical body weight management IoT system that provides a service to help a user manage his/her body weight. The system consists of 3 components: a wristband with sensors that measures how many calories the user is burning, an application on his/her smartphone that asks to input what he/she eats and calculates the calorie intake, and a cloud-based software component that offers recommendations for meals and sport activities. Following a microservices pattern, the overall functionality could be separated into a collection of independent microservices, which communicate with each other through well-defined message interface. For example, the wristband may connect to the smartphone through Bluetooth and send body activity intensity information to the app, and the application can connect to the recommendation service through platform-level inter-application messaging, or perhaps through an REST API in the case of a recommender service in the cloud. It is completely possible these three microservices are developed by different teams, or even different companies, as long as their interfaces are well maintained.

From the service consumer's point of view, a microservice is nothing but a collection of APIs. To make it easier to discuss the organization of these APIs, we propose an abstract model of the internal structure of a microservice, which can be mapped onto various protocols such

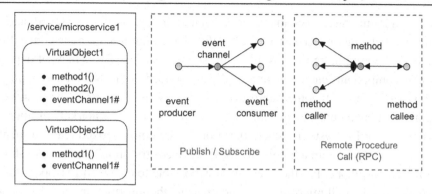

Figure 6.3: Virtual object, event channel, and method.

as MQTT, CoAP, AMQP, or REST API. In our model, a microservice contains one or more virtual objects, which we take to be akin to objects in object oriented programming (OOP) languages. A virtual object can have two types of service APIs, methods and event channels. Methods resemble the methods in OOP languages or services in REST APIs: they provide a remote procedure call (RPC). Event channels implements a publisher–subscriber model such that anyone that subscribes to the event channel will be notified when an event is published by an event producer.

Sensors and devices with sensing capability are examples of what might typically be an event producer. The events they publish might usually be intermittent, and their traffic is normally a push style. Actuators and services in the cloud are examples of event consumers and method providers (callee). They are typically continuously online, and their traffic style is typically that of request-response. It may be that one event or method call might generate a cascade of additional events or method calls. A method that does not return anything can be used as an event consumer as long as the method and the event channel are compatible in data format as well as semantics. Virtual objects, event channels and methods can also be dynamically created by a microservice. Fig. 6.3 shows the relationship of virtual object, method, event channel, and the binding with service endpoints.

A common claim of microservice patterns is that they can ease development in several ways [179]. For example, for the developers, it is easy to create simulators and sandbox environments for a real world IoT systems since devices can be abstracted to microservices with well-specified message interface. Additionally, sensor events can be logged and replayed in the sandbox environment to help debugging, testing, and troubleshooting of the microservices under development. Since a self-contained microservice usually does not have external dependencies, the development of a large IoT system can be broken into many small, semiindependent and focused teams.

For the system administrator, each microservice can be independently deployed, and if the method and event channel interfaces are well-defined and common then the connections may be as simple as plugging in light bulbs into standard receptacles. These facts of deployment mean that new components can be incrementally introduced to the system and deployed side-by-side with existing ones. If some microservices are broken or obsolete, they can be simply unplugged and switched out. We envision that there will be a "supermarket" of microservices as well as devices for IoT systems, where the "goods" are containerized ready-to-deploy microservices, such that a system administrator merely needs to "shop" online, like shopping the App Store for a smartphone. For the operator, it is possible to create an IoT operations center that collects the status of all microservices and presents the information on a dashboard. The IoT operations center functionality itself can be implemented as a microservice with required privileges so that it can access the entire system service registry, call any methods, and listen to any events. In this way, the operator is similar to a commander in the NASA mission control center, sitting in her office and manipulating smart devices and microservices as required.

API Gateway

An API gateway is an interface that relays calls or requests between two or more microservices. API gateways can aggregate the APIs for multiple microservices into one client interface, and can also distribute or route the calls or requests from one entry point to multiple target microservices. Rather than allowing direct communication among microservices, therefore, an API gateway can be placed in-between them, which can have the effect of adjusting interconnectivity through the aggregation and distribution function of the gateway. Microservice connection is then through registration; when a microservice registers itself to an API gateway. It creates one or more endpoints with unique identity, which can be further bound to an event channel or method through static configuration or dynamic negotiation with the API gateway. Besides the microservices, any user or machine client can also be required to present its identity as a name of identifier to interact with the API gateway to access its associated microservices. The identity management and authentication service might leverage existing systems that managing accounts, such as single-sign-on (SSO) or OAuth [24].

From the API gateway's point of view, each endpoint is uniquely identifiable, where the identity may be represented as a unique name or just an identifier. Such endpoint name or identifier only exist in the model, and the API gateway implementation needs to map it into actual protocol, such as an URL in REST API or CoAP, a queue or exchange in AMQP, or a topic in MQTT. In a cloud-supported body weight management IoT system as described in the example above, the weight management plan virtual object can be mapped to REST resource URL on the cloud server, which runs the weight management and recommendation microservices, and the method as well as parameter format on this virtual object can be mapped to the

HTTP methods. In typical uses of this approach, the method name is encoded in the JSON payload to augment the limited types of HTTP methods. Such mappings impose additional constraints on our model, such as requiring that consecutive method calls in a session must be "nonsticky."

For addressing across heterogeneous IoT devices and networks, virtual objects, methods, and event channels have site-scope unique hierarchical names like URNs. In some cases it may be feasible to create unique IDs using URN style approaches that encodes the device unique identifier (e.g., `snac.asu.edu/device/edb15825-92e2-e7b1-7c97-ddd102258a70` which uses the Bluetooth MAC address for uniqueness). Taking our body weight management IoT system as an example, imagine the API gateway is in the cloud with domain name `snac.asu.edu`; then there can be a virtual object `snac.asu.edu/WeightManagement-Plan` with `createPlan` method. After a plan with user profile and weight management goal is created, a virtual object `snac.asu.edu/WeightManagementPlan/plan1` is created with `checkGoal` and `getRecommendation` methods.

Our model is compatible with many message queue protocols as well as REST or CoAP API used in real world IoT systems. For example, the role of our API gateway is similar as a load balancing proxy for web services, or a message broker of MQTT protocol. The virtual object can be mapped to the resource using an RESTful URL, and the method can be mapped to the combination of HTTP methods on that URL and JSON payload. This allows us to apply a microservices pattern on a broader scope than just web based applications. However, some protocols may not be able to provide both method type and event channel type of service APIs. For example, MQTT can only provide publish–subscribe interface and, while CoAP can provide service call natively, publish–subscribe through CoAP will probably be difficult and unnatural to implement. In such scenarios, it is important for the API gateway to support multiple protocols to connect those "IoT islands" to the rest of the system.

In many cases microservices on the devices do not possess publicly reachable IP address, a trait which prevents them being accessed over the Internet outside the domain intranet. Multiprotocol API gateways can bridge the gap. In our model, we call the subsystem made of an API gateway and its associated microservices an IoT site (like website in traditional Internet). The API gateway works as a hub that translating messages from one protocol to another, making microservices in different domain accessible to each other. Meanwhile, the gateway also accepts API calls from user or machine clients outside the site and translates them to corresponding messages to intranet API calls. Sometimes an API gateway is able to deliver messages or initiate service call to another API gateway to fulfill complex services spanning over multiple sites.

The existence of API gateway as well as the binding of endpoint to method or event channel makes a natural place to enforce policies. We borrowed the approach of policy enforcement from SDN and, in our model, there are three types of policies: rules to allow or deny the creation or destruction of a certain named service APIs, rules to allow or deny a binding of service API to an endpoint, and constraints on the binding. The first two resemble file system permissions in operating system, and the last one resembles flow policies in SDN, in which the flow is a binding. We explain three examples of policy based on the usage, which are name resolution policy and QoS policy (in this subsection), and access control policy (in a later subsection).

A name resolution policy is a static binding between a service API and an endpoint. This type of policy is useful for integrating microservices of different versions, or for load balancing. Consider again our body weight management IoT system: the developers may construct a new version of the recommendation microservice and deploy it to the cloud. In response, the system administrator needs only change a few policies to bind the methods on the API gateway to the endpoints of new version of the microservice. The replacement is easy if the new version is backward-compatible in syntax and semantics. If it is incompatible, the system administrator can instead create new virtual objects and methods, bind them to the microservice of the new version, and run both versions in parallel until all clients that use the old microservice shift to the new version. For load balancing, the administrator has the option of running multiple instances of the same microservice and to bind them to the same set of virtual objects and methods. Similarly, balance can also be facilitated by binding multiple event consumers to the same event channel so that events are dispatched among them instead of duplicated to all of them. Name resolution policies and API gateways can combine to decouple the event producer from the consumer (or caller from callee). In an IoT system, microservices might not have fixed location on the network. For example, services on mobile IoT devices might need to attach to different API gateways at different times. Name resolution policies might be used also to redirect requests to other sites if they can work together with service registry mechanism.

A QoS policy is primarily concerned with traffic restriction on a binding (if we regard a binding as a traffic flow). Restrictions could include limiting the number of messages per second or traffic amount in bytes per second. Such policies can help protect the microservice from DoS attacks, or prevent launching DoS from some device or external client. Additionally it provides more flexibility needed to fulfill service level agreements and accounting processes. As with access control policies, QoS policies can also be dynamically generated by a policy controller. Another usage of a QoS policy is to implement so-called "circuit breaker" [207] in which, if the running status of the microservice shows it is exhausting its capability, a QoS policy can be dynamically generated to restrict further requests to prevent cascading failures.

Distribution

Traditionally, microservices are all located in the cloud. In IoT systems, we expect that microservices can additionally be associated with a device, edge cloud or gateway component, or deployed in the larger Internet cloud. Because of the distribution, API gateways also may be distributed on the edge, including within a personal area network or on a smartphone. These gateways may have various forms, which can be an independent physical machine, or a software component deployed on a router or server.

One of the advantages of distributing microservices and gateways among the cloud is better performance, due to the locality and the data stream management. In many IoT scenarios, the cost of carrying all the device generated data to the centralized remote cloud for processing and decision making outweigh the benefit. For example, some IoT applications may be latency sensitive, or the sheer amount of data generated by the device exceeds available network bandwidth, which requires us to run microservices close to the devices. An API gateway within a smartphone can aggregate data from a connected wearable that provides event data at high data rates, but it might relay only summarized, aggregated, or otherwise "rolled-up" data back to a cloud microservice. Edge cloud and fog computing extends the traditional cloud computing paradigm to the rim of IoT, which enables new types of applications [67,78]. In our architecture, edge cloud or fog is a virtualized platform serving as an on-demand execution environment of microservices close to the devices or the data source, which is different from running the microservices on the device itself. Providing an edge cloud or fog platform can also provide better architectural flexibility. For example, microservices can be off-loaded or migrated to the edge cloud or fog from devices to meet changing requirements of service performance.

Service Description and Discovery

In an IoT system, integrating microservices requires description of the service APIs in both syntactic and semantic level. Such description will also serve as an important way to search existing services and compose new services by the machine. We propose using ontology for service description and discovery. Our ontology is made of three parts: the IoT system domain ontology, the service profile, and ontology of microservices in the IoT system, shown in Fig. 6.4. The first part is the domain ontology, which contains the domain knowledge of entities and relations. For example, in a smart building IoT system domain ontology may describe the structure of the building, real world entities such gate, room, and the IoT devices attached to the entity. This part of ontology should follow IoT-Lite ontology [17], or SSN ontology [33], or other domain standards. The second part is service profile, which contains the description of service interface of a domain, including the category, process, parameter, result, condition of a method or an event channel. Additionally, service level agreement (SLA)

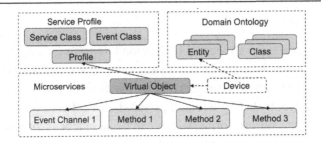

Figure 6.4: Ontology for service description and discovery.

should also be specified as part of the profile. This part of ontology should partially follow WSMO [37], or OWL-S [32], and the service grounding should support commonly used protocols in IoT system other than only web service. The third part is the ontology describing the microservice structure in the IoT system, including the virtual objects, methods, event channels, and their enclosing microservice. This part may also include deployment related entities, such where is the microservice deployed, on a device or in the cloud, in the fog/edge cloud or remote cloud. The three parts of ontology can be managed by an individual ontology database microservice associated with the API gateway. When new services are registered, corresponding ontology segments are added to this ontology database. Other microservice may query the ontology or run reasoning procedure through this ontology management microservice.

Besides ontology, each microservice should provide a human readable service manifest document for developers. We recommend that each microservice should provide a virtual object of the microservice's name, and the virtual object should have a method called "introspect", which returns a manifest detailing all the virtual objects and service interfaces (with the mapping to various protocols) of the microservice. Such manifest may just contain a plaintext document for human developers, or an annotated XML/HTML to be rendered on browser, or even an annotated document in OWL/RDF to be readable for both human developers and machine programs. In addition, since microservices can be dynamically added to an IoT system, ontology is subject to change. It is helpful to provide a global service registry microservice (possibly colocated with the API gateway) which manages the ontology and manifest to allow service registration and discovery among multiple sites. Each individual microservice can talk to the registry in order to publish its structures and interfaces so that other microservices can make SPARQL query to locate it.

Containers

Containers are used frequently in cloud computing for ease of deploy and to provide secure containment between different tenants. We treat containers generally here as an infrastructure that provides a local context for execution that can be instantiated multiply and separately, and hold something that can be recognized as a microservice. By this we mean to include not only OS-level container solutions like Docker [201], but also typical application-level or platform-level "sandbox" containers like Chromium containers [229] or Android for Work [121].

Containers in IoT systems can serve functions similar in cloud computing in terms of ease of deployment, replication, and scaling. They permit convenient and efficient deployment of a microservice by packing the microservice along with its dependencies into a single image deployed to the container. From the system administrator's point of view, the deployed container with the microservice is a black box with a few interfaces that can be easily "plugged into" the API gateway. The containerized microservice maintains its own states and stores its data, so that some of the complexity is encapsulated inside the black box. In addition, virtualized execution environments provide isolation and control of the microservices, such as by forcing all traffic to follow the policies enforced on the API gateway. This can ease troubleshooting, online A/B tests, and roll back, and it can simplify overall management. However, when the containers are used on smartphones or other smart devices, the security and isolation of each microservice is the more compelling need.

The use of containers for security, as a pattern, can succeed because of the way that essential security functions of isolation and encryption can be performed comprehensively according to enforced policy rather than requiring the microservice developers to implement them – and relying on them to unfailingly and correctly implement them too. For example, some containers can force all traffic out of the container to be passed through a VPN all data stored locally be encrypted with a container-specific key stored securely in trusted memory. As such, they can establish a level of security for the data-in-transit and data-at-rest. Wrapping microservices and API gateways in containers with known, tested levels of security can greatly simplify the problem of certifying or verifying some facts of the system's overall security. As the security of containers improve, the security of the IoT solutions can improve without changing the microservices, and the container solutions are patched to close holes from newly-discovered vulnerabilities, every part of the IoT system can rise with the tide without any changes to the code whatsoever. While this containment may not help stop device manufacturers from shipping devices with other weaknesses (e.g., default passwords in the manual), using containers as a pattern for pervasive security meshes well with a comprehensive microservices approach to service decomposition.

6.3.2 Case Study: Personal Health Management

We show an example of the aforementioned weight management IoT system with microservice architecture using simulated wearable sensors and cloud resources. In this system, there are 5 microservices (Fig. 6.5). First, an activity intensity tracking microservice on a wristband reports calorie consumption of the user (simulated using recorded heart rate data and an

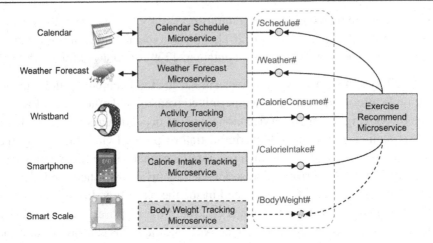

Figure 6.5: Microservice architecture of example body weight management application.

algorithm calculating metabolism rate and further calorie consumption based on heart rate). Second, a smartphone application allows the user to input what he/she eats to calculate calorie intake (simulated using a dialog panel on a PC). Third, a program running in the cloud obtains online hourly weather forecast and translates it to our defined record format. Fourth, a program running in the cloud retrieves the user's Google calendar and translate his/her daily schedule to our defined record format.

All these 4 microservices are considered as sensors bonded to their own event channels, and they connect to the API gateway (in the cloud) through a custom message protocol. Microservice connection is then through registration; when a microservice registers itself to an API gateway, it creates one or more endpoints with unique identity, which can be further bound to an event channel or method through static configuration or dynamic negotiation with the API gateway. Besides the microservices, any user or machine client can also be required to present its identity as a name of identifier to interact with the API gateway to access its associated microservices. The identity management and authentication service might leverage existing systems that managing accounts, such as Single-Sign-On (SSO)[4] or OAuth [24].

The last part is a microservice that makes exercise recommendations according to the user's weight management goal, and schedules a time slot for each of the recommended exercise instances in some type of sport with a certain duration. Then the user can be notified and decide which is preferred and add it to his/her calendar. The exercise recommendation microservice will consider both weather and user schedule constraints.

---

[4] Single sign-on (SSO) is a session and user authentication service that permits a user to use one set of login
credentials (e.g., name and password) to access multiple applications.

For example, if it is raining, we should not recommend outdoor sports; it will not recommend any activity after a meal or before bedtime. The weight management goal is set by the user, in a format of expected body weight loss or gain within a certain period of time, e.g., losing 10 kg in 6 months. Together with a user profile and preference of the intensity of sports, the recommendation microservice decides which sport type and for how long the exercise activity should be recommended. The wearable sensors and smartphone App track daily calorie input and consumption so as to tell the user whether the weight management plan is effectively executed. Optionally, a smart body weight scale can be included in this system to further improve the accuracy of the weight management process.

The API gateway delivers sensor events to the exercise recommendation microservice through HTTP, and they are stored in a Resource Description Framework (RDF)[5] database (Apache Jena Fuseki [10]) managed by the microservice itself. We choose to use RDF database instead of SQL database because the core part of the recommendation microservice is written in a reasoning language (Potassco [28]), so it is easy to translate RDF triples to predicates of parameters. A sensor data record can also be easily converted to RDF triples by creating a record object and attaching each field with a data relation (through Apache Jena RDF API [10]), e.g., *hasType(record1, BodyWeight)* and *hasValue(record1, 85)*, which means a body weight measurement record of 85 kg. The exercise recommendation microservice exposes a few REST API to allow for user input and interaction with the other parts of the system.

The loosely coupled microservice architecture shows its benefits in our prototype system, especially, enhanced interoperability among different software components implemented with different technology. If we want add a smart body scale (e.g., Withings Body [41]) to track weight besides the wearable sensors and smartphone Apps that only track calories, we just need to write an adapter program to retrieve weight measurement through their API (e.g., Withings API [40]) and feed to our system.

6.3.3 Case Study: Smart Building

In this section, we show an example of a smart building system with microservice architecture. A smart building may be equipped with many networked devices as well as software services which are gradually installed with a period of many years or even decades. Microservice architecture provides a graceful solution to cope with the diversity and evolution of the system, since each individual microservice can be independently developed and deployed.

---

[5] The Resource Description Framework (RDF) is a family of World Wide Web Consortium (W3C) specifications originally designed as a metadata model.

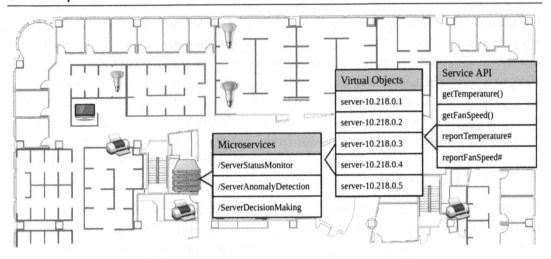

Figure 6.6: Image view of the IoT operation center of a smart building system.

The presented example consists of 3 microservices that monitor the status of a few public desktop computers, printers, smart light bulbs, and a server room with physical server machines that support many virtual machines. An imagined view of the IoT operation center of the smart building system will be like that in Fig. 6.6. Each physical server machine in the server room is equipped with a software sensor that can monitor a CPU temperature and chassis fan speed in real-time (using Linux lm-sensors [22]). Sensor data is streamed through Advanced Message Queue Protocol (AMQP, we use RabbitMQ implementation [30]). The whole server status monitoring software is a self-contained microservice. We developed a microservice to detect an anomalous server status, using a machine learning algorithm (we trained a decision tree using WEKA library [38] with collected data from normal and abnormal server running conditions, as well as simulated data when the server machines are injected with an error, like CPU fan power loss).

The anomaly detection microservice listens to server status sensor, and sends out server status data. Then, a decision making microservice listens to such an event, and if an unhealthy physical server is detected, it quickly migrates all virtual machines on that server to other physical servers in a way that the load is evenly distributed. In real applications, the decision making microservice may have many available actions, and different actions can be taken for a different server status event. All these microservices are independently deployed (anomaly detection and decision making microservices are deployed in their own virtual machines), and they are connected to the API gateway (in the example, it is the RabbitMQ broker) through a messaging protocol. If new machines are added, we just need to deploy status monitoring microservices on them. If a new version of the decision making microservice is available, we can simply deploy it in a newly created virtual machine and turn off the old version, as long as they follow the same sensor data format. This example demonstrates the flexibility of the microservice architecture in an IoT system.

6.3.4 Case Study: Autonomous Vehicle

We built a prototype demonstration system to explore the use of microservice architectures in the context of exploring so-called "platooning" algorithms for autonomous vehicles. Longitudinal platooning means that several vehicles form a physically-local chain that maintains close proximity while traveling down a road [241]. The system employed six VC-trucks within our VC-mobile test bed [190]. Each mobile robot vehicle is an independent IoT subsystem both offering event services to other vehicles and connecting to other services. The event services include both data and control APIs. For example, the vehicles have an event stream `reportState()` to provide vehicle state, and may provide `join()` and `leave()` so that a lead vehicle can check safety constraints to decide whether to approve vehicles to join.

Platooning requires continuous intercommunication of vehicle motion and location data, including speed and acceleration, and frequent adjustment of motion as needed to maintain a tight platoon. Motion data comes from the cruise control, and location data are collected from ultrasonic range finders. The data are exchanged through vehicle-to-vehicle (V2V) communication over WiFi. Our platooning algorithm uses a platoon leader vehicle, which broadcasts its motion data to the entire cluster, while each different leader vehicle in the chain interchanges motion information with its neighbors behind. Platooning calculation uses a PID controller to calculate desired speeds based on predecessor states, as well as the separation distance to the predecessor, and also uses the leader's states to make adjustments in order to maintain string stability of the whole platoon, and thereby prevent speed oscillation. The platooning gathers sensor readings and also adjusts target driving speed 10 times per second. At a lower level, the vehicle motion controller drives the cruise control to adjust or maintain the vehicle's speed. In our demo, we operate 6 VC-trucks to form a platoon. Starting from zero speed, when the leader starts to move, the platoon successfully achieves a stable state of constant velocity (0.2 m/s) and a preset separation distance (0.7 m), as illustrated in Fig. 6.7.

Microservices architecture. We built the system according to a distributed microservices architecture, as illustrated in Fig. 6.7. The services offered by the vehicles are decomposed into microservices that collect coherent but loosely coupled parts of the service in the form of separate platoon and status reporting microservices. In real-world contexts, future automated vehicles might have a variety of other microservices offered by third parties in addition to these platooning services offered by the manufacturer, and each can be deployed in a different microservice.

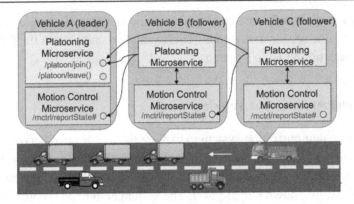

Figure 6.7: Communication among microservices for vehicle platooning.

API gateways. Each vehicle has its own API gateway that aggregates the services making it simpler to deploy the microservices differently or manage independent protocol evolution for the microservices. In addition, the API gateway can provide a flexible and fine-grained location for configuring and enforcing access control policies. Since the platooning microservice can control critical safety features like vehicle speed, and since the appropriateness of access may depend upon context not "owned" by the platooning microservice itself, the gateway can be the most suitable location to implement the enforcement.

Containers. Robot vehicles are outfitted with computers running a Hypervisor (KVM [164]), which lets us deploy microservices flexibly. It also provides a security boundary for isolation of the microservices, which is important perhaps particularly for the speed-controlling platooning microservice.

From this example, we showed that microservice architecture is also suitable for mobile IoT system. In this example, each vehicle is an independent IoT subsystem with its own API gateway and microservices, and other vehicles can connect to this vehicle and call its service. For example, vehicle A may provide an event channel called "vehicleA.asu.edu/sensors/LIDAR/scan" to expose its LIDAR point cloud frame so that other vehicles can share its vision. In this scenario, access control on the service APIs are crucial to the safety of the vehicle. For example, trusted applications like the platooning microservice is allowed to control the motion of the vehicle, while other applications or external requests are denied. This can be achieved through the access control policy enforced by the API gateway on each vehicle, and such policy can be generated when the platooning microservice is deployed.

PART 3

Mobile Cloud Computing Security

Security is one of the most critical challenges for mobile cloud computing. Mobile cloud computing endures a number of security issues, for instance, data access control, data distribution over a distributed infrastructure, data integrity, service availability, secure communication, and application security. In addition, the mobility adds more challenging security issues.

In general, mobile cloud computing can consider security problems from two perspectives: the mobiles (or lightweight embedded devices) and the virtualized resource provisioning system (e.g., Internet clouds or dedicated computing resources closely located to mobiles). The mobiles must be clean from the malicious codes, such as viruses, Trojan horses, and worms. The malicious codes are security threats and can change an application's behavior, which may cause privacy leakage or data corruption. Therefore, to keep mobiles clean from the malicious codes, security monitoring and scanning must be used continuously and regularly. However, secure monitoring and scanning processes of mobile cloud applications is a resource-intensive task, which usually incurs real-time requirements that cannot be easily fulfilled in a mobile and resource-restricted environment.

In [107], seven security risks are outlined for users to consider in the general cloud computing areas:

1. *Privileged user access*. Offloading sensitive data to the cloud would mean the loss of direct physical, logical and personnel control over the data.
2. *Regulatory compliance*. The cloud service providers should be willing to undergo external audits and security certifications.
3. *Data location*. The exact physical location of user's data is not transparent, which may lead to confusion on specific jurisdictions and commitments on local privacy requirements.
4. *Data segregation*. Since cloud data is usually stored in a shared space, it is important that each user's data is separated from others with efficient encryption schemes.
5. *Recovery*. It is imperative that cloud providers provide proper recovery mechanisms for data and services in case of technological failure or other disaster.
6. *Investigative support*. Since logging and data for multiple customers may be colocated, inappropriate or illegal activity, should it occur, may be very hard to investigate.

7. *Long-term viability*. Assurance that users' data would be safe and accessible even if the cloud company itself goes out of business.

In mobile cloud computing, all these security risks still exist; however, some of their important points are not prominent compared to Internet clouds. Risks such as recovery, investigative support, and long-term viability become less important due to mobility and real-time requirements of mobile cloud computing applications. These properties of mobile cloud computing require that proactive and preventive security solutions are more appealing than detecting and reactive approaches.

In a mobile cloud, data is mobile, where it can be transferred and cached from one device to another. The traditional data access control models such as Role-Based Access Control (RBAC)[1] are not scalable, where the data storage infrastructure provides access control. RBAC is widely adopted by various information systems (such as Windows/Active Directory) and requires associating capabilities directly to users or their roles, which is often cumbersome to manage and insufficient for capturing real-world access control policies. For example, RBAC usually needs cumbersome management and identity, groups and roles, which are not sufficient in expressing the access control policies in the real world. For example, in a personal health information system, since data is collected from multiple sources with different health care providers, whether a data access request is granted or not is usually decided by the attributes of the requester, selected attributes of the object, and environment conditions that can be globally recognized. At times, access control policy enforcement is performed even without prior knowledge of the specific subjects.

Another significant drawback of RBAC is the lack of mobility when data is moved between different storage services under separated administrative control domains. It is extremely difficult to translate the data access policies from one domain to another. In an ideal situation, access control can be incorporated into the protected data, e.g., using encrypted data with access policy enforcement. In this way, data can be freely moved from one device to another without the need to transfer the access control polices from one service provider to another.

To address the above mentioned drawbacks, here we present a Policy-Based Access Control (PBAC), sometimes referred to as Attribute-Based Access Control (ABAC), which defines an access control paradigm whereby access rights are granted to users through the use of policies which combine attributes together, and we use PBAC and ABAC interchangeably in this book. The policies can use any type of attributes (user attributes, resource attributes, object, environment attributes etc.), unlike RBAC, which employs predefined roles that carry a

---

[1] Role-based access control (RBAC) is a method of regulating access to computer or network resources based on the roles of individual users within an enterprise. In this context, access is the ability of an individual user to perform a specific task, such as view, create, or modify a file.

specific set of privileges associated with them and to which subjects are assigned. The key difference with ABAC is the concept of policies that express a complex Boolean rule set that can evaluate many different attributes without predefined roles. In Chapter 7, we present the foundation of ABAC, particularly, the presentation will focus on using Attribute-Based Encryption (ABE) as the building block to establish ABAC for mobile cloud computing.

The increasing usage of low power consuming and high performance devices in mobile cloud computing environment has brought about a unique set of challenges and opportunities. ARM architecture [239] in particular has evolved to a point where it supports implementations across a wide spectrum of performance points. The enhancements to basic Reduced Instruction Set Computer (RISC) architecture [155] allow ARM to have high performance, small code size, low power consumption, and small silicon area. Because of these enhancements to ARM architecture, mobile phones are exclusively based on ARM, and there is a surge in popularity of ARM based smartphones, tablets, and laptops. Users want their devices to perform many tasks such as read e-mail, play games, and run other online applications also on the fly.

The key factors that contributed to a shift of working mode to mobile working style are mobility, consumerization, and advent of mobile cloud computing. This new work style demands for any device anywhere a kind of setup so that people can do work and personal activities on the same device, and for this they are also willing to pay (e.g., Cisco employees on average pay $600 annually to use such devices [58]). The term Bring Your Own Device (BYOD) [115] has come into being from the demand of such a work setup. This indeed calls for a new research and development direction to create an application running environment through resource and execution isolation approaches on mobile devices. In Chapter 8, we present a resource isolation approach based on ARM architecture-based mobile devices. The prototype is presented in Appendix D.

CHAPTER 7

Mobile Cloud Security: Attribute-Based Access Control

At the end of the day, the goals are simple: safety and security.

Jodi Rell

Attribute-Based Encryption (ABE) [271] and its supported data access models have made big strides in the access control and cryptography areas. There are, however, important research questions that need to be investigated to make ABE more suitable and applicable in real data access control scenarios.

Recent Attribute-Based Access Control (ABAC) reference model developed by NIST [135] provides a flexible access control framework to handle various access management scenarios based on scrutinized attributes assigned to both subjects and objects. ABAC is an advanced method for managing access rights for people and systems connecting to networks and assets. Its dynamic capabilities offer greater efficiency, flexibility, scalability and security than traditional access control methods, without burdening administrators or users.

In fact, Gartner recently predicted that by 2020, 70% of enterprises will use ABAC as the dominant mechanism to protect critical assets, up from less than 5% since 2014 [113]. ABE approaches have the capability to realize various access control features demanded by ABAC; and as a result, they have become good candidates as the fundamental building blocks to enable ABAC. Thus, determining how to use ABE approaches to realize ABAC becomes an active and promising research area.

In this chapter, we first present the foundation of ABAC and ABE in Section 7.1, and then present a few case studies using ABAC/ABE in mobile cloud application scenarios, including Information Centric Networking (ICN) naming scheme in Section 7.2, ontology-based attribute management in Section 7.3, and mobile cloud computing storage solution using security offloading in Section 7.4.

7.1 Attribute-Based Access Control

Attribute-Based Encryption (ABE) and its supported data access models have made big strides in the access control and cryptography areas. There are, however, important research questions that need to be investigated to make ABE more suitable and applicable in mobile cloud application scenarios. ABE approaches have the capability to realize various access control features demanded by ABAC; and as a result, they have become good candidates as the fundamental building blocks to enable ABAC. Thus, how to use ABE approaches to realize ABAC becomes an active and promising research area.

User Group and Application Scenarios

The confidentiality and integrity of data distributed in mobile clouds are of the utmost importance. For example, in an enterprise environment, one critical data sharing feature should assist organizations in ensuring that sensitive documents can be shared and accessed securely from any mobile device. A secure data sharing solution must be a document-centric security platform that allows users to easily and effectively access, share and control all their important documents across the extended enterprise on any tablet, smartphone, or PC – even those outside the corporate firewall. ABE-based ABAC model fits in such a secure data sharing application scenario really well. A secure data sharing solution can be deployed in multiple ways, as a cloud-based solution, as a dedicated private cloud, or as an on-premises virtual appliance, where data sharing is focused on security policies and theres is a lack of a trusted third party to build a secure communication group during the application runtime. The secure data sharing service can be applied to many organizations worldwide in various industries including financial services, pharmaceutical and biotechnology, legal, energy, healthcare, manufacturing, insurance, real estate, technology and government agencies.

In December 2011, the FICAM Roadmap and Implementation Plan v2.0 [122] called ABAC a recommended access control model for promoting information sharing between diverse and disparate organizations. ABAC is a logical access control model that is distinguishable because it controls access to objects by evaluating rules against the attributes of the entities (subject and object) actions and the environment relevant to a request. Attributes may be considered characteristics of anything that may be defined and to which a value may be assigned. In its most basic form, ABAC relies upon the evaluation of attributes of the subject, attributes of the object, environment conditions, and a formal relationship or access control rule defining the allowable operations for subject–object attribute and environment condition combinations. All ABAC solutions contain these basic core capabilities to evaluate attributes and environment conditions, and enforce rules or relationships between those attributes and environment conditions.

For example, in an ABE-enabled ABAC application scenario, a trusted authority is required to predistribute private keys (SK, as shown in Fig. 7.1) corresponding to each attribute assigned to individual users. An object's (e.g., a document's) attributes are usually not used directly

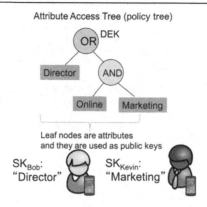

Figure 7.1: **Example of ABE access control policy.**

to design the data access policy. Instead, they are maintained at an information level for data owner to specify what policies for data receivers to comply with, i.e., attributes assigned to receivers. In the presented example, Bob has an attribute *director* and Kevin has an attribute *marketing*. Based on the logic gates (i.e., internal nodes of the policy tree), Bob can access the root, where the Data Encrypting Key (*DEK*) resides; however, Kevin cannot. This policy tree was generated by the data owner, and the data owner does not even need to know who can access the data, just specifying the data access policy and using ABE to encrypt the DEK suffice. Once Bob has derived the DEK, he can access the data encrypted by this crypto key.

Access Control for Data Sharing Applications

In the presented ABAC reference model, document owners (or data owner) can maintain control over their documents at all times – even after they have been sent and downloaded to a recipient's PC, smartphone, or tablet. Data access control allows applying granular permissions to documents, enabling or restricting recipients from viewing a document based on recipients' access privileges, which is decided by attributes assigned to a recipient. Further, additional controls can be applied according to document's expiration time and location constraints, etc. Additional software running framework is needed to enforce the attributes-based policy and environment (location and time) controls.

7.1.1 ABAC Reference Model

FICAM Roadmap and Implementation Plan v2.0 [122] called ABAC a recommended access control model for promoting information sharing between diverse and disparate organizations. In 2014, NIST proposed an ABAC reference model [135], which includes subjects (such as

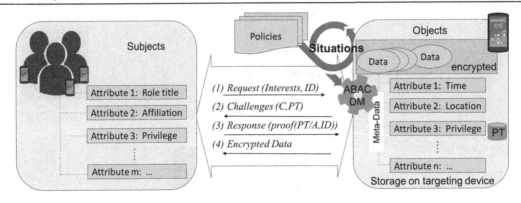

Figure 7.2: An example of using attribute-based access control for objective storage services.

human) and objects (such as data) having their associated attributes to describe their access properties. In addition, security and privacy policies are predefined according to nonchangeable features associated with subjects and objects, which include standardized regulations such as FISMA Compliance [14], HIPPA Compliance [15], FERPA Compliance [13], etc., and any organizational level of security policies. The situations of access control can be changed according to dynamic impact factors, such as time, location, ad hoc decisions, etc. When a subject tries to access the data, the ABAC Decision Module (DM) needs to process the request by considering attributes owned by subjects and objects, security and privacy policies, and situations to make a decision if access is or is not granted.

ABAC Data Access Model

To realize ABAC reference model [135], in this section, we present an ABAC solution for objective storage service, which is presented in Fig. 7.2. ABAC is a logical access control model that is distinguishable because it controls access to objects by evaluating rules against the attributes of the entities (subject and object) actions and the environment relevant to a request. Attributes may be considered characteristics of anything that may be defined and to which a value may be assigned. In its most basic form, ABAC relies upon the evaluation of attributes of the subject, attributes of the object, environment conditions, and a formal relationship or access control rule defining the allowable operations for subject–object attribute and environment condition combinations. All ABAC solutions contain these basic core capabilities to evaluate attributes and environment conditions, and enforce rules or relationships between them.

The presented ABAC reference model includes a typical 4-step data access protocol, which is illustrated as follows:

(1) *Request (interests,ID)* – The requester describes data of interest to access with his unique ID, e.g., interests can be medical records, X-ray picture, blood test results, etc., and the user's ID can be a user's e-mail address, etc.

(2) *Challenges (C,PT)* – The storage server sends a randomly selected challenge C, and a policy tree (PT) that had been used to secure the data according to the requester's interests. A $PT = [PT_s, PT_d]$ is an attribute-tree where internal nodes are logical gates and leave nodes are descriptive attributes including static attributes PT_s such as *Doctor, Nurse, Nutritionist*, etc., and dynamic attributes PT_d such as time duration, ranking range, etc. Usually, the PT is given by the data owner or originator when he/she stores the data in the storage service.

(3) *Response (proof(PT/A, ID))* – Based on the challenge C, the requester generates proofs to validate his/her attributes (A) that can satisfy the required static policy tree portion (PT_s). The requester also needs to prove own ID for the strong auditing purpose. The proof of dynamic attributes PT_d is optional. It can be simply done by sending the challenge C: the storage server can send it in an encrypted form by using PT_d as the public key. In step 3, the requester needs to use his/her dynamic attributes, e.g., a date range attribute, and can successfully decrypt the challenge and then reply to the storage server.

(4) *Encrypted Data* – If the verification of message (3) passes, the storage service sends a block of ciphertext to the requester by encrypting the data using PT (in practice, PT is the public key, and it is used to encrypt an AES Data Encrypting Key (DEK); and the AES key is the actual key to encrypt the data). Then, the requester can decrypt the data by using corresponding private keys for both PT_s and PT_d.

ABAC Building Blocks

In order to establish the ABAC model presented in Fig. 7.2, we need to investigate a few cryptography and protocol design approaches that can be used to realize the functions/features related to the transmitted messages (1)–(4) and corresponding processing and verification procedures:

(i) *ID and Attribute-Based Signature (ABS)* can be used to verify users' privilege, i.e., to validate both user's ID and his/her owned attributes that can fulfill a given PT. This feature will provide a strong auditing feature in the system to know who had accessed the system with what access privileges. Messages (2) and (3) are used for this purpose.

(ii) *Comparable Attribute-Based Encryption* [270] will be used to realize message (4). After verifying users' credentials, the system will encrypt the data by using PT, which will include both static and dynamic attributes. The comparable ABE is used to have an effective attribute-based encryption system that can easily handle a comparison ranging as an attribute.

(iii) *Multiauthority Attribute Management* is required to make sure that the users' attributes can be used in a different administrative domain. Moreover, we should be able to interface the presented ABAC to existing well-developed federated ID management system, such as InCommon [16].

7.1.2 Federated IDM and ABAC

Federation profiles define the syntax and semantics of the data being federated. These technologies leverage widely accepted, open web communication languages, like the Security Assertion Markup Language (SAML) standard [144], which utilizes Extensible Markup Language (XML) [69], or the OpenID [232] and InCommon [16]. Connect standard is built upon JavaScript Object Notation (JSON) [88]. Federation profiles allow identity and attribute information to be sent over HTTP in a manner that can be understood and used by the receiving organization (hereafter referred to as the Relying Party (RP)) to make access control decisions.

Using such profiles, identity information can be federated from a trusted third-party entity that has issued subject credentials known as an Identity Provider (IdP). Attributes associated with a specific identity may be federated by an IdP, but can also be obtained from a trustworthy or authoritative external source known as an Attribute Provider (AP). Often, an AP's authority applies only to its domain.

Institutions looking to participate in federation must have a degree of trust with the organization from which they are receiving identity and attribute information. To facilitate these trust relationships, nonprofit organizations such as the Kantara Initiative [148] and the Open Identity Exchange (OIX) [191] have proposed trust framework specifications that provide a complete set of contracts, regulations, and commitments that enable parties of a trust relationship to rely on identity and attribute assertions from external entities.

To date, few demonstrations of ABAC utilizing federated identity and attribute information exist, which is still an open research issue.

7.1.3 Using Attribute-Based Cryptography to Build ABAC

Traditionally, access control is based on the identity of a user, either directly or through predefined attributes types, e.g., roles or groups assigned to that user. However, practitioners have noted that this access control approach usually needs cumbersome management and identity, groups, as well as roles, which are not sufficient in expressing the access control policies in the real world. Therefore, a new approach which is referred to as Attribute-Based Access Control (ABAC) was proposed [134]. With ABAC, whether a user's request is granted or not is decided by the attributes of the user, selected attributes of the object, and environment conditions that can be globally recognized. Compared with role-based access control, ABAC provides the following nice properties. First, ABAC is more expressive. Second, ABAC enables access control policy enforcement without prior knowledge of the specific subjects. Because of its flexibility, ABAC is nowadays the fastest-growing access control model [133, 136,135]. ABAC considers attributes as users' credentials for composing access control policies, and as a result using ABE as the foundation to realize ABAC is a promising approach.

Current State-of-the-Art of ABE

The research on Attribute-Based Encryption (ABE) originated from Identity-Based Encryption (IBE) in [66], in which an identity can be considered as an attribute in ABE. In IBE, an identity or an ID is a descriptive term used as the user's public key. The user can acquire a private key corresponding this ID from a trusted authority, a.k.a., the private key generator. ABE extends the IBE scheme by enabling expressive logics, such as AND, OR, k out of n, etc., among multiple attributes (i.e., descriptive terms) for data access control [142].

The ABE scheme was originally proposed by Sahai and Waters [235] in 2005, as a fuzzy version of identity-based encryption with a single threshold gate, whereby an identity is represented by a set of descriptive attributes. Since then ABE has received much attention in cryptographic access control, with plenty of research works of ABE derivation as presented in [63,77,112,120,158,216,294]. Goyal et al. [120] first defined two complimentary forms of ABE, namely Key Policy ABE (KP-ABE) and Ciphertext-Policy ABE (CP-ABE), and provided the first construction for KP-ABE. Bethencourt et al. [63] then gave the first construction for a CP-ABE scheme in the generic group model. Comparatively, CP-ABE is more compelling than KP-ABE in that CP-ABE is compliant with role-based access control model. In addition, there have been numerous solutions proposed to improve the efficiency of CP-ABE in [49,97,99,104,128,271].

CP-ABE is more suitable for enforcing data access control over data stored on the cloud servers. CP-ABE allows data owners to define an access structure on attributes and upload the data encrypted under this access structure to the cloud servers. Therefore, CP-ABE enables users to define the attributes a data user needs to possess in order to access the data. Based on ABE, various security protocols have been proposed. For example, Yu et al. [288] proposed a new design to integrate CP-ABE and centralized flat table together for secure group management. Nabeel et al. [210] proposed a new attribute-based group key management construction based on an optimized version of the Access Control Vector Broadcast Group Key Management [240]. Lewko et al. [181] proposed a new multiauthority ABE system wherein any party can become an authority, without any requirement for global coordination other than the creation of an initial set of common reference parameters.

As promising as it is, CP-ABE suffers from user revocation problem. This issue was first addressed in [287] as a rough idea. There were also several researches [145,184,284,288] that are not suitable for user revocation. Boldyreva et al. [65] proposed an identity-based scheme with efficient user revocation capability. It applies key updates with significantly reduced computational cost based on a binary tree data structure, which is also applicable to KP-ABE and fuzzy IBE user revocation. However, its applicability to CP-ABE is not clear. Libert et al. [185] proposed an IBE scheme with stronger adaptive-ID sense to address the selective security issue of [65]. Lewko et al. [180] proposed two novel broadcast encryption schemes with effective user revocation capability. EASiER [150] architecture is described to support fine-grained access control policies and dynamic group membership based on attribute-based encryption. It relies on a proxy to participate in the decryption and to enforce revocation, such that the user can be revoked without reencrypting ciphertexts or issuing new keys to other users. Chen et al. [74] presented an IBE scheme based on lattices to realize efficient key revocation. In the literature, a few important ABE solutions can be summarized as follows:

Efficient Group Communication: Comparable ABE. In [283], the authors presented a dual comparative expression of integer ranges to extend the power of attribute expression for implementing various temporal constraints. This work presented a comparative ABE scheme with high flexibility and improved over the bitwise-comparison method in BSW scheme [63]. To demonstrate how to use the comparable ABE scheme, a Location-Based Service (LBS) [299] was presented, where according to users' comparable location attributes (e.g., GPS location range information), the users' access could be granted or denied.

Performance Enhancement of ABE. In [294], a privacy preserving ABE scheme was presented, such that the lightweight devices can securely outsource heavy encryption and decryption operations to cloud service providers. In [296], we presented an efficient CP-ABE scheme that provides the following features: (1) the ciphertext is constant regardless of the number of involved attributes; (2) it provides a unique bit-assignment approach to achieve efficient secure group communication. In this scheme, a bit-assignment is a position in a user's ID representing three possible states, A, A^-, and A^* (i.e., Yes, No, and Don't Care) of an attribute. Using the bit-assignment and corresponding attributes, we can establish secure group communication groups efficiently.

ABE-based Policy Management. To address the conversion from RBAC to ABAC, in [298], the authors introduced an attribute lattice approach for ABE to define a seniority relation among all values of an attribute. This scheme implements an efficient comparison operation between attribute values on a poset derived from attribute lattice with high flexibility. In [143,295], the policies were discovered layer by layer in a skewed policy tree structure. In this way, a user can reveal the security policies by decrypting the policy-tree level by level to protect the policy information. To enable multiple trust authorities issue private keys for users, in [184], a distributed ABE-based trust authority framework was presented to relax the reliance on a centralized trust authority to manage attributes. In this approach, trust authority's functions are delegated and distributed amongst network entities. To manage the attributes managed by multiple authorities, an ontology-based approach [183] was presented to address the inconsistency of using attributes among multiple administrative domains.

Privacy for ABE. To anonymize users' ID, in [137], a variant of IBE wherein the PKG (Private Key Generator) was removed and the anonymous users could derive their own private keys based on public parameters and pseudonyms. In [293,296], a new construction of CP-ABE, named Privacy Preserving Constant CP-ABE was presented, which leveraged a hidden policy construction. To provide privacy protection of attributes in the attribute policy tree, in [143,295], an attribute graduate exposure approach was constructed. Based on the available attributes, users could reveal attributes one by one from the attribute policy tree structure. A powerful user, who owns more privileged attributes, can reveal all the attributes in a secure policy tree for ABE.

Besides the above mentioned research, various application scenarios using ABE solutions, such as secure mobile cloud data storage [294], vehicular networking [139], healthcare [270], etc., have been studied. They significantly reduced the ciphertext to constant size with any given number of attributes.

7.1.4 ABE-Based ABAC Example

Role-Based Access Control (RBAC) is widely adopted by various information systems (such as Windows/Active Directory) and requires associating capabilities directly to users or their roles, which is often cumbersome to manage and insufficient for capturing real-world access control policies. For example, RBAC usually needs cumbersome management and identity, groups, as well as roles, which are not sufficient in expressing the access control policies in the real world. In a personal health information system, since data is collected from multiple sources with different health care providers, whether a data access request is granted or not is usually decided by the attributes of the requester, selected attributes of the object, and environment conditions that can be globally recognized. At times, access control policy enforcement is performed even without prior knowledge of the specific subjects, where ABAC perfectly fits these desired requirements.

Trust and Threat Model

Trust model. A Trusted Authority (TA) is required to predistribute private keys (SK, as shown in Fig. 7.3) corresponding to each attribute assigned to individual users. There may be multiple TAs such as TA_{Mayo} and TA_{TGEN}, and Bob (e.g., a cardiologist doctor working

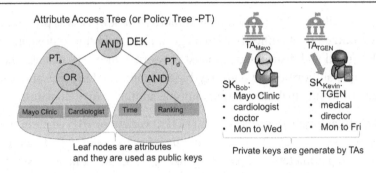

Attribute Access Tree (or Policy Tree -PT)

Leaf nodes are attributes
and they are used as public keys

Private keys are generate by TAs

Figure 7.3: Example of ABE access control policy and trust model.

at Mayo Clinic [23] from Monday to Wednesday) and Kevin (e.g., a medical director working for TGEN [34] from Monday to Friday) derived their private keys from them, respectively. An object's (e.g., a document's) attributes are usually not used directly to design the data access policy. Instead, they are maintained at an information level for the data owner to specify the policies for data receivers to comply with, i.e., attributes assigned to receivers. In the presented example, Bob has four attributes: $TA_s = \{Mayo\ Clinic,\ Cardiologist\}$ and $TA_d = \{Doctor,\ Mon\ to\ Wed\}$. In this example, Bob can satisfy the logical gates based on his PT_s to the root of PT_s. In order to get to the root level of the PT, he also needs to satisfy the dynamic PT_d. Suppose $PT_d = \{Mon\ to\ Tuesday,\ <nurse,\ doctor,\ director>\}$, then Bob can access the root of the PT, and thus he can access the data.

Using the ABAC framework presented in Fig. 7.2, a subject (or user) may have been assigned a set of attributes, and they are assigned by a TA. The object (or data, such as a file or a document) may also have a number of attributes, which can be assigned by the data's owner. Thus, data owners can maintain control over their data and they decide how and where to store the data, and what attributes are assigned to it.

Threat Model. We assume attackers can be system users and their goal is to access the data that they should not have the privilege to access, which means that they cannot fulfill the required data access policy – a PT specified for the data. A storage service provider is generally trusted. However, it can be "honest but curious" and it tries to learn data content stored in objective storage servers. The honest but curious scenario will address data owners' concern when they store their data on an external storage service provider. An attacker can also try to hide his/her data access activities, thus auditing is a desired function of the access control model.

7.2 Using Information Centric Networking and ABAC to Support Mobile Cloud Computing

There is a clear trend showing that the number of wireless connected devices is growing steadily, with IoT devices and users' personal devices representing the biggest share. By 2020 the total number of wireless connected devices will increase beyond 10 billion worldwide, with smartphones and IoT devices collectively accounting for 66% of this number [83]. Interestingly, IoT devices show the largest percentage increase across all devices types, from 8% in 2015 up to 26% by 2020. This results in an emerging scenario recently called immersed human [68], which is represented in Fig. 7.4. In this view, there is a tight and continuous interaction between the human users, their personal devices, and the "things" embedded in the physical environment (sensory swarm). These interactions are primarily information-centric, with IoT and personal devices constantly generating data that is transferred between sources (things and users' devices), places where it can be stored and elaborated, and sent back to the users. Mobile applications that will be more and more data intensive, also in the IoT domain (e.g., IoT multimedia applications).

To fully exploit the potential of the data available in such an environment, cloud computing and Information-Centric Networking (ICN) are currently considered cornerstone technologies. Cloud computing provides a scalable approach to store data generated by things and users devices, and, most importantly, to extract information and knowledge from raw data, providing value-added services to the users. Moreover, ICN is one promising approach to turn the Internet into an information-centric network that natively supports access to data, irrespective of where it is stored or generated, also overcoming possible disconnections of data providers.

ICN technology has changed the requirements for relatively static hosts in network communications. It is designed to provide better support to large scale multicast services. Traditional host-based architecture works well in end-to-end communications between a pair of users. However, in multicast scenarios, where one source is sending the same data to multiple recipients, performance can be further improved. According to [82], most of the current network traffic is video sharing, from 64% in 2014 up to 80% by 2019. To further improve the overall network performance, several different ICN network architectures are proposed.

In a typical ICN network, data is represented as contents. Different contents have different identifiers/names. They are transmitted through the network in the publisher–subscriber model. When a network party publishes a content, it registers the content name to a naming service. Through this naming service, a subscriber who is interested in such content will be notified with the name of the content. Here, names are unique identifiers to contents in the network. Once a subscriber gets the name of the content, he/she is able to retrieve a copy of

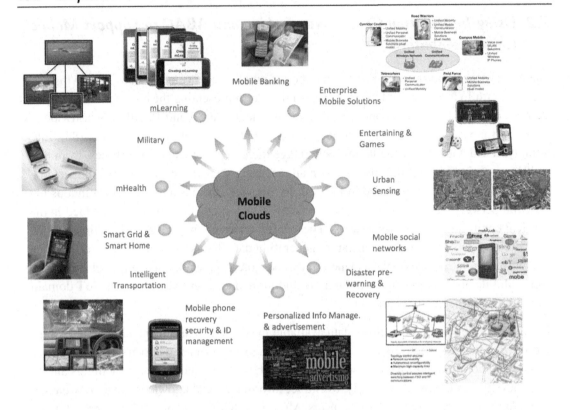

Figure 7.4: Mobile cloud application scenarios.

the content using the name through a name-based routing scheme. Copies of the same content may be scattered all over the network, existing in network caches for a certain period of time, depending on what caching algorithm they are running. Typically, if a copy of a certain content is transmitted from one entity to another, all the network caches along the path will keep a copy of it. In this way, the next time when another entity requests the same content, the network is able to locate a nearby network cache, which maintains a copy of the content, but has a shorter distance from the user.

The name based routing scheme uses content names as identifiers to route a copy of content to its consumers. In traditional session based networking environment, each network party is tagged with a unique identifier, for example, IP address. Network traffic is routed based on the entity's identifier. In ICN network, it is the content that is tagged with a unique identifier. Routers along the network path use the content identifiers to forward traffic. In other words, in a traditional network, a routing decision is made based on the destination address of the traffic, while in ICN network, it is based on the content identifier to make such decisions. In the following subsections, the presented ABE scheme to support ICN naming scheme is based on the research article [182]. For detailed cryptographic constructive of ABE scheme, please refer to Appendix C.1.

7.2.1 Attribute-Based Access Control for ICN Naming Scheme

In traditional networking schemes, if a network entity wants to access some information content, it has to locate and connect to the server that provides such service following network routing protocols. As a result, the information is tightly associated with the location of the server. The entire network is centered around the connections between content consumers and content providers, making connection status an important factor to the network.

Witnessed by the fact that most of the network traffic is file sharing, especially video sharing [82], various ICN architectures [71,167,95,111,290] have been proposed. In ICN architecture, the focus is shifted from consumer–server to consumer–content connections. Thus, instead of identifying the content owner's address, the network changes to identify authentic content copies. In this way, the consumers do not need to know where the content is located, i.e., the IP address of the content owner. The content name is sufficient to direct the consumer to a content copy. Content owners publish the content, which can be copied and stored in the network using network caches [230,258]. This design enables contents being efficiently delivered to consumers.

Though the design is efficient in retrieving content, it brings great challenges to security issues during content caching and retrieving. One of them is that traditional RBAC access control mechanisms cannot be easily enforced. This is because, in ICN, content owners and consumers are not directly connected. Content owners have no control over the distributed network caches. To enforce access control to the content, several frameworks have been proposed [110,248]. Most of them require additional authorities or secure communication channels in network to authenticate each content consumer. These schemes are sound but have too much reliance on traditional control schemes, making them inefficient in practice.

Using ABE, we present an attribute-based access control for ICN naming scheme [182]. The scheme can be divided into two levels. At the upper-level, to address the attribute management problem, we present an ontology-based attribute management solution to manage the distributed attributes in ICN network. In this scheme, attributes defined by different authorities can be synchronized more efficiently than traditional approaches. Content consumers do not need to negotiate their attribute keys when they request contents from other authorities.

At the lower-level, we propose an ABE-based naming scheme. This approach is inspired by Attribute Based Encryption (ABE) schemes [63,287,181]. In this approach, each network

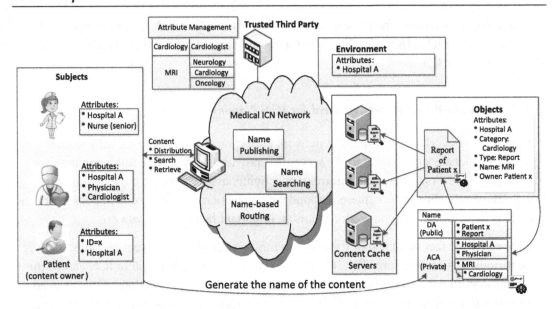

Figure 7.5: Basic ICN system model based on medical application scenarios.

entity is assigned with a set of attributes with the help of a Trusted Third Party (TTP) according to their real identities. The access control policy is enforced according to the content names instead of the contents. Moreover, privacy-preservation is provided for the content access policies. This feature can greatly improve the privacy protection on ICN data when it is distributed in the public domain. In this way, a user is able to identify its eligibility of the accessed contents through the encrypted names before actually accessing the data content.

An Illustrative Example

In the example of Fig. 7.5, there are three subjects: a Nurse, a Physician, and a Patient. Their attributes are as shown in the figure. The patient publishes his MRI report in the network as the content. He, as the content owner, specifies an access policy as shown in Fig. 7.6 for the MRI report. Its object attributes are listed in Fig. 7.5.

The content name is created following the procedure in Fig. 7.7, which will be further illustrated in Section 7.2.2. When the nurse tries to access this content, she can successfully use her {*Hospital A*} attribute to decrypt the first node but will get stuck at {*Physician*}, meaning this content is not intended for her. When the Physician accesses the content, he/she can successfully decrypt the entire decryption process from the leaf to the root level-by-level to reveal the random data encrypting key. Here, {*MRI*} is substituted with {*Cardiology*} since

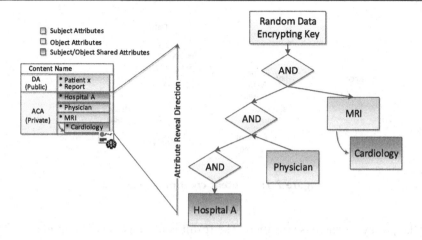

Figure 7.6: Content name creation based on ABE access tree structure.

$\{Cardiology\}$ is a subattribute. This is shown with the arrow in Fig. 7.6. Also, $\{Cardiology\}$ equals to $\{Cardiologist\}$ in this case. Then, the Physician uses the NR system to get the nearest copy of the content and uses the random data encrypting key derived from the name to decrypt the MRI report.

7.2.2 Creating a Content

Initially, the TTP sets up global parameters for the entire network. Then, any entity in the network can create attributes and assign them to other entities. The detailed process on how attributes are distributed is out of the scope of this work. An interested reader can refer to allocation problem solutions such as [64]. Once the attributes are assigned, entities are able to create contents. As shown in Fig. 7.7, when an entity publishes a file, as the content owner, it creates an access policy for the content. The policy is represented as a combination of related attributes with AND and OR gates. For example, if a content owner wants to create a record accessible only to physicians and nurses working at hospital A, the policy can be $\{A\}\,AND\,\{\{Physician\}\,OR\,\{Nurse\}\}$. In this way, the owner does not need to know explicitly who should access the content. All he needs is to identify the attributes and the combination so that as long as a consumer satisfies the policy, he/she is able to access the content. Any entity who does not satisfy the policy will not be able to access the file with this content.

After creating the policy, the owner generates a random data encrypting key and uses it to encrypt the file. The encryption result is set as the data part of the content item. The metadata includes public parameters to decrypt the data and data integrity related information. Then the owner creates a name for the content. He/she uses the proposed scheme to encrypt the random

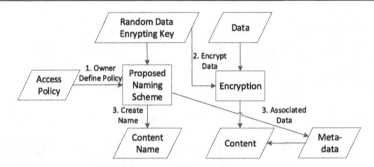

Figure 7.7: Content creation procedure.

key under the policy he/she has specified. The result is used as the content name. Here we need to emphasize that the generated name hides the content access policies so that no one can get the entire policy from the name.

A consumer who needs this file can get the content by its name. Before he/she gets the content, he/she uses his/her assigned attributes to decrypt the name. If his/her attributes satisfy the hidden policy in the name, he/she can get the random data-encrypting key protected in the name. The data of the content then can be decrypted using the random key to get the original file. If a consumer cannot successfully decrypt the content name, it implies the consumer is not allowed to access the original file. Thus, even if he/she downloads the content, he/she still does not have the random data encrypting key to decrypt the content.

7.3 Ontology-Based Attribute Management

In this section, we describe the ontology-based attribute management scheme in details. This scheme is suitable for managing attribute names and values for both ACAs and DAs in a distributed manner, which is very suitable for ICN architecture.

Ontology defines various classes of users, data and object properties that are part of the attribute schema. Data properties are the attributes of the users, and object properties are attributes of user classes that relate a user object to objects of another class. We can query Web Ontology Language (OWL) [61] ontologies using the SPARQL language [43] that takes into account the ontology structure while executing. Information about different attributes can be merged and integrated. This aggregation is useful to determine facts which cannot be acquired from any individual parties in decentralized environment.

In the ICN example presented in Fig. 7.5, we need a scheme for negotiating the attributes to be used by the users to encrypt and decrypt data, so that these processes can occur coherently.

The same attribute can have different names while having the same meaning in real life like synonyms. Sometimes we also need to restrict the possible values for a particular attribute to a realistic range.

In our design, the TTP specifies an Attribute Ontology that defines the set of attributes that the users can use. Users composite the access policies with these attributes for the content they publish over the network. Our design uses the following approach that distinguishes it from the current systems.

7.3.1 Attribute Equivalence

The main advantage of using ontologies to define attributes is that they allow us to declare equivalent attributes. For example, if we declare attributes (or properties) A and A' as equivalent, some users can use the property name A for defining their policy and others can use A' for their policy. The ontology ensures that both properties map to the same attribute, i.e., the same mathematical elements in ABE algorithm. A formal definition for such a equivalence is:

$$A \equiv A' \text{ iff } I_A = I_{A'}, k_A = k_{A'}, \text{and } h_A = h_{A'} \in Z_{n'}^*.$$

Here, I, k, h are mathematical elements used in the proposed naming scheme as in Section 7.2.

Equivalent properties can be specified in an OWL document using the *owl:equivalentProperty* element. We can define two attributes *attribute1* and *attribute2* as data type properties. In any one of these attributes we can declare the equivalence by adding the *owl:equivalentProperty* element in the property definition [61]. Once the equivalent set of attributes is defined, the users can use either of the attributes from the set for sharing as well as accessing data since all of them map to the same attribute. For example, if we have equivalent attributes $Faculty \equiv Teacher$ and they map to a unique triplet of $\{I, k, h\}$, then this unique triplet can be used to encrypt the data using the ABE based naming scheme.

7.3.2 Attribute Hierarchy

Another advantage of using ontologies for defining attributes is that we can define a hierarchy of attributes. One attribute can be defined as a subattribute of another. For example, in a hospital, a user can have the attribute *Employee*. We can define an attribute *Nurse* as a sub-attribute of *Employee*. This means that a "Nurse" is also an "Employee" and he/she can have more properties than other "Employees." This is done by using the *rdfs:subPropertyOf* element in the OWL specification [61]. The advantage is that if the access policies specify that all users having attribute *Employee* can access a particular data, the attribute hierarchy specified in the ontology will also allow a *Nurse* to get it, but any other "Employee" cannot access the data that requires the user to be a "Nurse" to access it. In Appendix C.1.4, an attribute ranking capacity is enabled through the proposed naming scheme. The connection and difference between this example and the one in Section C.1.4 is that:

- In this example, *Nurse* and *Physician* are two values in the category of *Employee*, or *Nurse/Physician* ∈ *Employee*;
- In Appendix C.1.4, *Nurse* has fewer privileges than *Physician*, or *Nurse* < *Physician*.

Here we can treat *Employee* as a set of some ordinal attributes.

In fact, with the attribute hierarchy, a user is able to define the set relationship between attributes. In Appendix C.1.4, the users can further define the ordinal relationship among all the attributes within a set.

7.3.3 Distributed Policy Specification

Since our design assumes multiple trusted attribute authorities, we need an initial negotiation between these authorities to decide the structure of attributes and properties to be specified in the attribute ontology. This can be achieved with the help of the TTP. Once this agreement is established, the users can access this ontology from any of the attribute authorities and design the access policy for their shared data. This policy can then be translated to an equivalent ABE compatible form to be used for encrypting the contents. This approach allows the access policies to be generated in a distributed manner by the users themselves. As long as these access policies satisfy the established ontology, they can be used over the entire network.

7.3.4 Apply ABE-Based Naming Scheme in ICN

With the above naming scheme, we can achieve the following capabilities:

- Specification of the access control policy without knowing the consumers' keys;
- Full preservation of the policy confidentiality from leaking to adversaries;
- Step-by-step attribute exposure for consumers to determine their eligibility efficiently in computation;
- Flexible attribute management.

Using this scheme, any entity that wants to publish data needs to create the content following the process in Fig. 7.7.

The owner firstly creates a random symmetric key K. Then the data to be published is encrypted using K. The resulting ciphertext C is then used to generate metadata of C. Both the metadata and C are parts of the final content. Then the owner needs to specify an access policy P of attributes to define what an authentic consumer should satisfy. Then the owner uses this policy to encrypt K following **Encrypt** algorithm. The result is used as the content name.

In this way, the owner does not need to know individual public keys of all the potential consumers in advance, which is required in traditional methods.

7.3.5 Performance Analysis and Evaluation

In this section, we firstly evaluate the performance of the attribute management scheme. Then, the computation and communication performance for the privacy-preserving naming scheme is analyzed. The security strength of the proposed naming scheme is evaluated in the last part.

7.3.5.1 Evaluation and Analysis on the Attribute Management

In this section we create an application scenario to demonstrate the effectiveness of ontology-based attribute management. Evaluation in this section is carried out in NDN environment [290]. We implemented ndn-cxx v0.3.1 library [211] together with NDF 0.3.1 [212] on Ubuntu 12.04 systems. As mentioned in Section 7.2, users are able to define their own name structure in NDN network, which makes it quite suitable for evaluating the proposed naming scheme in this chapter.

In an ICN healthcare network, there are hospitals, clinics, and medical institutions that share information and data. Each institution defines its own users and attributes. A trusted Attribute Authority (AA) is set for each institution to generate attributes for users and assign them correctly when new users join the system. It also generates the private keys to be used for ABE operations by the users and securely transfers them to intended user(s). An institution defines its own setup like the various departments, employees, patients, etc. We assume that each institution will use its own nomenclature so that the same department can have a different name in different institutions. The users can have a hierarchy among themselves, for example, Nurse < Resident < Consultant < Surgeon < Head of Department < Chief Medical Officer.

Medical Records Transfer

When a patient is being transferred from one hospital to another for better treatment, his/her medical records need to be transferred as well. Since these are highly sensitive data, they are stored in encrypted form (in our case the encryption is ABE-based) and only medical personnel having the required privileges can access and decrypt this data. Let T_E be the time taken to encrypt data and T_D be the time to decrypt it.

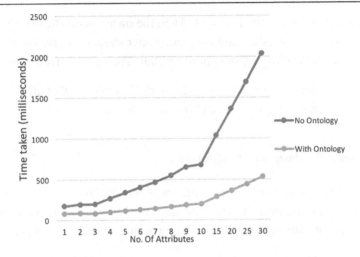

Figure 7.8: Time consumption for medical records transfer.

If no ontology has been specified by the two hospitals and no attributes are shared among them, the attributes used to encrypt the data by the first hospital would be invalid in the second hospital. Therefore, the data has to be decrypted first, and then encrypted using the attributes defined in the second hospital. If we also consider the initial encryption of the data, it accounts for two encryptions and one decryption: $T_{total} = 2 * T_E + T_D$.

Now we consider using an ontology that maps the attributes of one hospital to its equivalent attributes in another hospital over the ICN network. Since the attributes are already mapped, we don't need to encrypt/decrypt the data again. Only the initial encryption is required to be performed in this case: $T_{total} = T_E$.

A comparison of the two cases is illustrated in Fig. 7.8. As shown in the figure, using ontology based management can save about 75% in time when the number of attributes is more than 6, which is significant in real life.

Applying User Hierarchy to Access Policy

When certain data is to be shared with all doctors, irrespective of their rankings, without ontology, the person who issues the policy will need to know all the possible "ranks" of the doctors and then specify a DNF of all these ranks as the access policy specification. If we have an ontology where the hierarchy is specified, i.e., all the various ranks of doctors (Resident, Surgeon, etc.) are structured as subtypes of a parent type *Doctor*, the policy specifier only specifies *Doctor* as the access privilege and the ontology ensures that all the subtypes also satisfy this access requirement. In this way, if we are able to provide a proper parent type for the cases where a large combination of roles are included in the access policy, the size of the policy as well as the corresponding computation, communication, and storage cost will be greatly reduced. For such a gain, the cost is merely one additional level in the attribute hierarchy.

Storage Overhead and Its Effect on Network Throughput

When N institutions are sharing data without using an ICN network, it results in N copies of the data, one for each institution and encrypted using its own set of attributes. Using ICN networking without the attribute management scheme can help improve the network efficiency in file sharing and content distribution, but no benefits will be provided in terms of storage overhead. With the use of ICN network in our design along with ontology-based management to specify relation between the attribute sets of all the different institutions, we reduce the storage overhead to a single copy of the encrypted data. Any eligible user from the various institutions can decrypt the encrypted data, thereby removing the need for multiple copies.

Due to the large differences in caching strategies and hardware capacities, we cannot provide a concrete network performance improvement from the reduced storage overhead. Instead, we calculate the numerical network throughput improvement using a demonstration scenario. Here, we assume that there are m domains with n entities in each domain. A file of k bits is to be shared from one single source to all the entities. The caching capacity for each network cache is m, meaning all the m copies of one single file can be cached at the same time. We also assume that the entities of each domain are evenly distributed in the network. The time needed for distributing one single copy is t seconds. When no inter-domain attribute management scheme is involved, the throughput of the network is $\dfrac{\dfrac{m \times k}{m}}{t} = \dfrac{k}{t}$ bps. However, when the ontology-based management scheme is applied, the throughput is increased to $\dfrac{mk}{t}$ bps. Such an increase is due to the reduced amount of copies need to be transferred in the network.

7.3.5.2 Evaluation of the Naming Scheme

In this section, the ABE-based naming scheme is evaluated from the performance aspect. We analyze its computation and communication (storage) overhead.

From the computation perspective, we tested the time consumption for key generation, encryption and decryption processes. In a real application, we are more concerned with the time consumption for a consumer to decrypt the content's name. This is because each content is encrypted once but decrypted by multiple users. Therefore, we also compare the decryption overhead with existing ABE solutions: CP-ABE [63], CN scheme [77], NYO scheme (the 2nd

Table 7.1: Time-consumption of different operations (in milliseconds)

	Pairing	Exponentiation	Multiplication	Inversion
Time	7.675	0.491	0.029	0.024

construction in [216]), YRL scheme [287], and GIE scheme [142]. The idea is to compare the number of most time-consuming operations needed in each scheme.

We use a machine with a four-core 2.80 GHz processor and 4 GB memory running Ubuntu 10.04 for the experiment. PBC Library [192] is used to handle the pairing computations. We generated a type-A1 curve [193] using the parameter generating tools included in this library for the following tests. It randomly generates the prime numbers used for the curve, with a length of 512 bits for each of them. We run each operation ten times for key generation, encryption and decryption (Fig. 7.9). Here the policies are set to be a conjunctive clause of different number (shown on the x-axis) of attributes. This is because given a number of attributes, this form requires the most time for computation. The reason why encryption consumes more time when attributes are fewer is that the cost for computing C in Algorithm C.5 requires an additional pairing computation which is independent of the number of attributes. When few attributes are involved, this additional pairing takes a high portion of the time consumption. This portion reduces as the attribute numbers grow.

In theory, the time consumption should be linear in the number of attributes involved. The curve in Fig. 7.9 is not perfectly linear, but it meets our expectation. There are several reasons why it is not strictly linear. Before decrypting attribute by attribute, in our program, there are some necessary steps to initialize global parameters, read files, and allocate memory space. Similarly, at the end of the algorithm, we have some clean-up work, such as writing files and releasing memory space. Such time consumption is related to the number of attributes involved but not strictly proportional. Also, at step 4 of Decryption algorithm, there is one additional pairing operation. Thus, when the number of attributes is small, this additional operation takes a larger portion of the total time than when the number of attributes is large. If we further consider the possible variance introduced by system level factors, for instance, the resource consumption from other processes, the variance in the figures is reasonable in practice.

For comparison purpose, we test every operation for 50 times and choose the average value as basics for our comparison. Results of our experiment (Table 7.1) show that pairing operation takes longer than any other operations. Therefore, our comparison metric is set to be the number of pairing operations in the decryption process.

Following the above-mentioned idea, we use N_{attr} to denote the number of attributes a consumer has, N_{all}, as the total number of attributes defined in the network ($N_{all} \gg N_{attr}$). The

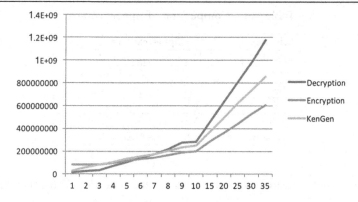

Figure 7.9: Computation performance.

Table 7.2: Comparison of computation cost in decryption

Scheme	Hidden Policy	Number of Pairings
CP-ABE	No	$2N_{invo} + 1$ or 0
CN	No	$N_{all} + 1$ or 0
NYO	Yes	$2N_{attr} + 1$
YRL	Yes	$2N_{attr} + 2$
GIE	Yes	$3N_{invo}$ or $3N_{part}$
ICN-ABE	Yes	$2N_{invo} + 1$ or $2N_{part}$

proposed naming scheme is denoted as ICN-ABE in the rest of this paper. Since the policy is publicly known in CP-ABE and CN, decrypters are able to decide what attributes to use in decryption. Therefore, for those who satisfy the policy, the time taken for decryption is proportional to the number of attributes involved, which is denoted as N_{invo}, $N_{invo} \leqslant N_{attr}$. It is obvious that inauthentic decrypters would not bother to try decryption, which is why it takes no time. An inauthentic decrypter in GIE and ICN-ABE is not able to proceed with the decryption process if it cannot meet the next attribute. In this situation, we use N_{part} to denote the number of attributes that the consumer has already decrypted, where $N_{part} \leqslant N_{invo}$. The result of our test is shown in Table 7.2.

To evaluate the communication costs, we compare the size of the name in various schemes, which are sumarized in Table 7.3. In PBC library [192], a data structure element_t with size of 8 bytes is used to represent an element. For our scheme, we need 24 bytes to store the network name. Compared with this name size, a content in CBCB [71] is identified by a set of attributes determined by the content owners. Thus, we can model the names as a human-readable string of an undetermined size. NDN [290] shares a similar problem with the name size. As mentioned before, DONA [167], NetInf [95], and PURSUIT [111] share the same naming scheme. Therefore, we only use the size of DONA's name for comparison. In [167],

Table 7.3: Comparison of ciphertext size

Scheme	Ciphertext Size
CP-ABE	$1\mathbb{G}_1 + (2N_{ciph} + 1)\mathbb{G}_0$
CN	$1\mathbb{G}_1 + (N_{all} + 1)\mathbb{G}_0$
NYO	$\geqslant 1\mathbb{G}_1 + (2N_{all} + 1)\mathbb{G}_0$
YRL	$1\mathbb{G}_1 + (3N_{all} + 3)\mathbb{G}_0$
GIE	$N_{ciph}\mathbb{G}_1 + 3N_{ciph}\mathbb{G}_0$
ICN-ABE	$1\mathbb{G}_1 + (2N_{ciph} + 4)\mathbb{G}_0 + N_{ciph}\mathbb{Z}_p$

the size of the name is confined to 40 bytes in its protocol header. Thus, the network name size in our scheme is small enough to fit in existing ICN solutions.

7.3.5.3 Security Analysis

From the security perspective of the proposed solution, we analyze the performance based on the attack model presented in below.

> *Attack Model.* We assume that the attackers have two goals in compromising the ICN access control scheme: (1) acquiring unauthorized privilege to the data; (2) retrieving constitutional information of access policies to gain more information about the content, the owner, and the consumers. The information includes but is not limited to the identity of the owner or consumers, the sensitivity of the content and the potential value of data in the content. For the first goal, the attackers have to break the confidentiality mechanism of the protected data. Possible methods include collusion attacks and vulnerability exploitation. For the second goal, attackers need to analyze the proposed ABE-based scheme to identify possible ways to reveal the policy.

Theorem 1. *Let G_0 and G_1 defined as in Section 7.2. For any adversary A, the advantage it can gain from the interaction with the security game defined in Appendix C.1.2 is negligible.*

The proof for this theorem is provided in Appendix C.1.5. In the proof, it is verified that the attacker cannot break the encryption algorithm to get any data exposed. Furthermore, it is also proved that attackers cannot conduct collusion attacks onto the system.

For the second attack goal, the attacker will stop at the first attribute, A_k, that he/she doesn't own in the decryption process. If he/she can get to know this additional attribute, he/she must get it from step 3 in Algorithm C.6. This means that the attacker possesses the secret key $Z_{i,UID}$ of the attribute A_k, which contradicts to the assumption that he/she does not possess this attribute.

7.4 Secure Computation Offloading

With the fast development of wireless technology, mobile cloud computing has become an emerging cloud service model [80,138], where mobile devices and sensors are used as the information collecting and processing nodes for the cloud infrastructure. This new trend demands researchers and practitioners to construct a trustworthy architecture for mobile cloud computing that includes a large numbers of lightweight, resource-constrained mobile devices. In such a mobile cloud sensing environment, cloud users may inquiry the data from sensing devices. A simple solution to protect the data is to encrypt the sensing data with a group key and broadcast the encrypted data; only legitimate users can reveal the data content with the predistributed group key. However, this approach demands high key management overhead and it is vulnerable to single point failure problems.

In this chapter, we present the basis of CP-ABE schemes [63,77,158] to facilitate key management and cryptographic access control in an expressive and efficient way, and then, we present it how to use ABE scheme to establish an ABAC access control model. Particularly, we presented an example using ABE to support ICN naming scheme that supports edge cloud mobile networking and data distribution services.

To illustrate the application scenario, we consider a mobile remote health sensing scenario, where a doctor using a mobile device (e.g., smart phone) to inquire the sensing data collected from a set of body sensors attached on a patient at home. It is convenient to encrypt the data and enforce data access policies that only eligible users can decrypt it. To this end, the sensed data can be encrypted using the following policy:

$$\langle 12/08/2016 \textbf{ AND } Doctor \textbf{ AND } Saint\ Luke\ Hospital \rangle.$$

In this example, doctors who are working at Saint Luke hospital on 12/8/2016 can decrypt the data. Using CP-ABE scheme, the sensor can use the above described policies to encrypt the data, and the data inquirers must satisfy the given policies in order to decrypt the data.

To establish the highlighted mobile cloud data inquiry services, several research challenges need to be addressed:

- With the CP-ABE enabled mobile cloud data inquiry services, the main challenge originates from the fact that CP-ABE schemes always require intensive computing resources for sensors or mobile devices to run the encryption and decryption algorithms.
- Given the sensitivity of data and multitenancy nature of the public cloud, critical customer secrets should not be exposed to the cloud.
- Another major challenge is how to upload/download and update encrypted data stored in the mobile cloud system. Frequent upload/download operations will cause tremendous overhead for resource constrained wireless devices.

To address the above described research challenges, users may securely offload computation intensive CP-ABE encryption and decryption operations to the cloud without revealing data content and secret keys. In this way, lightweight and resource constrained devices can access and manage data stored in the cloud data store. This approach requires users' attributes to be organized in a carefully constructed hierarchy so that the cost of membership revocation can be minimized; and it is suitable for mobile computing to balance communication and storage overhead, thus reducing the cost of data management operations (such as upload, updates, etc.) for both the mobile cloud nodes and storage service providers.

7.4.1 Overview of Secure Computation Offloading

In this section, we denote the data owner as DO. A DO can be a mobile wireless device such as a smart phone or an environmental sensor that can request and/or store encrypted information from/in the cloud storage. The data are encrypted using the presented Partitioning CP-ABE (P-CP-ABE). Other than DO, there are many DRs (Data Requesters or Receivers) who can inquire the information from the storage services of the mobile cloud. For example, a user may want to inquire current pollution map of a particular city area. Since the data provided by DOs can be proprietary, it should be encrypted and only pollution map service subscribers can retrieve the data. In this case, the mobile cloud system only provides a service platform and it should not be able to access the data content from the DOs. Here, the focus is on the encryption and decryption model to support the described application scenario; thus, due to the space limit, we do not describe how exactly the application is established in details. The presented system model should provide the following properties:

1. The data must be encrypted before sending to a Storage Service Provider (SSP);
2. The Encryption Service Provider (ESP) provides encryption service to the data owner without knowing the actual Data Encryption Key (DEK);
3. The Decryption Service Provider (DSP) provides decryption service to data inquirers without knowing the data content;
4. Even if ESP, DSP, and SSP collude, the data content cannot be revealed;

As shown in Fig. 7.10, the SSP, ESP, and DSP form the core components of the proposed system. A DR inquires the data provided by a DO. ESP and DSP provide P-CP-ABE services and SSP, e.g., Amazon S3, provides storage services. The cloud is semitrusted, in which the cloud only provides computing and storage services with the assistance on data security; however, the data is blinded to the cloud. In particular, more powerful PCs and mobile phones can work as communication proxy for sensors that collect information.

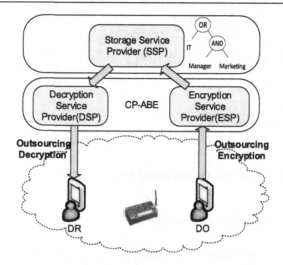

Figure 7.10: System architecture of our proposed framework.

Essentially, the basic idea of P-CP-ABE to outsource intensive but noncritical part of the encryption and decryption algorithm to the service providers while retaining critical secrets. As we can prove later in this chapter, the outsourcing of computation does not reduce the security level compared with original CP-ABE schemes, where all computations are performed locally.

The encryption complexity of CP-ABE grows linearly in the size of access policy. During the encryption, a master secret is embedded into ciphertext according to the access policy tree in a recursive procedure, where, at each level of the access policy, the secret is split to all the subtrees of the current root. However, the security level is independent on the access policy tree. In other words, even if the ESP possesses secrets of most but not all parts of the access policy tree, the master secret is still information theoretically secure given there is at least one secret that is unknown to ESP. Thus, we can safely outsource the majority of encryption complexity to ESP by just retaining a small amount of secret information, which is processed locally.

As for the decryption, the CP-ABE decryption algorithm is computationally expensive since bilinear pairing operations over ciphertext and private key are computationally intensive operations. P-CP-ABE addresses this computation issue by securely blinding the private key and outsourcing the expensive pairing operations to the DSP. Again, the outsourcing will not expose the data content of the ciphertext to the DSP. This is because the final step of decryption is performed by the decryptors.

The mathematical construction of P-CP-ABE is presented in Appendix C.2.

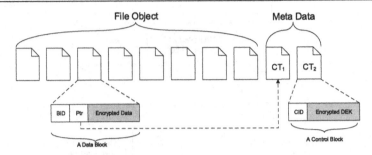

Figure 7.11: Illustration of a file organized into blocks with multiple control blocks.

7.4.2 Use Case: Attribute Based Data Storage

In this section, we present an Attribute Based Data Storage (ABDS) scheme for mobile cloud computing that is based on P-CP-ABE to enable efficient, scalable data management and sharing.

The frequent data updates will cause additional expense for file management, for example, to update existing files, e.g., change certain data fields of an encrypted database, in which the encrypted data need to be downloaded from SSP to DSP for decryption. Upon finishing the updates, the ESP needs to reencrypt and upload the data to the SSP. Thus, the reencryption process requires downloading and uploading the data, which may incur high communication and computation overhead, and as a result, will cost more for DOs.

To address the described cost issue, it is reasonable to divide a file into independent blocks that are encrypted independently. To update files, the DO can simply download the particular blocks to be updated. In this way, we can avoid reencrypting the entire data. Moreover, data access control can be enforced on individual blocks using "lazy" reencryption strategy. For example, when the data access memberships to a particular file are changed (i.e., the access tree is changed), this event can be recorded but no file changes are invoked. If the data content needs to be updated, the reencryption is performed using the proposed P-CP-ABE scheme.

Partitioning the data into multiple small blocks also introduces addition overhead. This is because the extra control information needs to be attached for each data block for data management. For example, the control message should include a block ID and a pointer to its corresponding data access tree T. In Fig. 7.11, we depicted a sample file stored in SSP. Each file is divided into blocks. A block is a tuple {BID, Ptr, Encrypted Data}, where BID is the unique identification of the block; Ptr is the pointer to the control block CT; and data is encrypted with a DEK. A control block {CID, Encrypted DEK} has a control block ID, i.e., CID and DEK encrypted by using P-CP-ABE scheme.

The ABDS system should determine what the appropriate data block size is to be partitioned with a known file size. In this work, our goal is to minimize the storage and communication overhead with the considerations of the following simple assumptions:

1. Every data update should only affect a small amount of data, e.g., updating certain data fields in the database;
2. In each unit time period, the number of blocks to be updated is known;
3. Each data block has the same probability to be updated;

Based on the above discussions, we can model the total cost C in a unit time period as follows:

$$C = 2n S_b C_c + \frac{F}{S_b} S_c C_s, \tag{7.1}$$

where n is the number of updated blocks in a unit time period and $2n$ stands for an update includes one encryption and one decryption that require two transmissions; S_b is the size of block; C_c is the cost rate of data transmission that is charged by both cloud storage providers and wireless communication service providers; F is the size of file; S_c is the size of control data for each data block, and C_s is the charging rate of storage. To minimize cost C, DO can minimize (7.1) and derive the optimal block size:

$$S_b \geq 2\sqrt{2n C_c F S_c C_s}.$$

7.4.3 Setup

P-CP-ABE enables expressive policy with descriptive attributes to enforce data access control on the stored data. For example, if Alice wants to share a file to all CS students, she can specify the policy "CS *AND* Student." All the users whose attributes satisfy this policy can decrypt the data.

Besides the set of descriptive attributes enabled in the system, each user is assigned a unique binary ID: $b_0 b_1 \ldots b_{n-2} b_{n-1}$. We can define the term "*bit-assignment* attribute" that is represented as "B_i" or "$\overline{B_i}$" to indicate the binary value at position i in the ID. B_i indicates that the ith bit of an ID is 1; $\overline{B_i}$ indicates that the ith bit of an ID is 0. If the length of an ID is n, then the total number of bit-assignment attributes is $2n$. This means that two binary values are mapped to one bit position (one for value 0 and one for value 1). Thus, a DO with ID u is uniquely identified by the set of bit-assignments S_u. Also, multiple DOs may have a common subset of bit-assignments. For example, a DO u_1's ID is 000 and a DO u_2's ID is 001, $S_{u_1} = \{\overline{B_0}, \overline{B_1}, \overline{B_2}\}$ and $S_{u_2} = \{\overline{B_0}, \overline{B_1}, B_2\}$ and $S_{u_1} \cap S_{u_2} = \{\overline{B_0}, \overline{B_1}\}$. Bit-assignment attributes can be used when the DO wants to share data to any arbitrary set of DOs. In this case, it may be hard to describe the set of DOs efficiently using descriptive attributes.

7.4.4 Uploading New Files

Before uploading new files to the SSP, both ESP and DO are required determining the encryption parameters such as the block size. DO then invokes ESP with an access policy $\mathcal{T}_{ESP}$, which is the access policy to be enforced on the uploaded files. Here, we define some terms used in the following presentation:

- *Literal* – A variable or its complement, e.g., b_1, $\overline{b_1}$, etc.
- *Product Term* – Literals connected by AND, e.g., $\overline{b_2}b_1\overline{b_0}$.
- *Sum-of-Product Expression (SOPE)* – Product terms connected by OR, e.g., $\overline{b_2}b_1b_0 + b_2$.

Given the set of shared data receivers S, the membership function $f_S()$, which is in the form of SOPE, specifies the list of receivers:

$$f_S(b_1^u, b_2^u, \ldots, b_n^u) = \begin{cases} 0 & \text{iff } u \in S, \\ 1 & \text{iff } u \notin S. \end{cases}$$

For example, if the subgroup $S = \{000, 001, 011, 111\}$ is considered, then $f_S = \overline{b_0}\overline{b_1}\overline{b_2} + \overline{b_0}\overline{b_1}b_2 + \overline{b_0}b_1b_2 + b_0b_1b_2$.

Then, the DO runs the Quine–McCluskey algorithm [195] to reduce f_S to minimal SOPE f_S^{min}. The reduction can consider *do not care* values $*$ on those IDs that are not currently assigned to any DO to further reduce the number of product terms in the membership function. For example, if $S = \{000, 001, 011, 111\}$, then $f_S^{min} = \overline{b_0}\overline{b_1} + b_1b_2$.

Finally, DO uploads the data blocks and the control block to SSP, where each data block is encrypted by the DEK, and DEK is protected by the access policy in the control block.

7.4.5 Data Updates

Now, we investigate how to efficiently handle the data updates, i.e., how to modify encrypted data with or without changing data access control policy.

Data Updates with Access Policy Change

At the beginning of Section 7.4.2, we described the "lazy" reencryption strategy adopted by DOs. Using the "lazy" reencryption scheme, the DO continuously records the revoked data receivers. When there is a need to modify the data, the DO will choose a new data access tree that can revoke all previously recorded data receivers.

When DO updates a data block with access policy change, we need to consider the following cases:

- If there is no control block associated with the latest access policy, i.e., no data updates occurred after the latest access policy change event, the DO encrypts a new random DEK associated with the latest access policy with P-CP-ABE and attaches a new control block to the end of the file, see Fig. 7.11.
- If there exists a control block associated with the latest access policy, i.e., at least one data block was encrypted with the newest access policy, the DO can simply redirect the control block pointer, see Fig. 7.11, to the control block associated with the latest access policy.
- If a control block is not pointed by any data block, this control block should be deleted.

Updates without Access Policy Change

If no change is required to the access policy, DO can simply perform the P-CP-ABE scheme and upload the updated data block in the SSP. The block ID and the pointer to control the block are not changed.

CHAPTER 8

Mobile Cloud Security: Virtualization and Isolation on Mobiles

Isolation doesn't bother me at all. It gives me a sense of security.

Jimmy Page

Organizations no longer desire to provision and maintain an individual's IT equipment. Some employers have strict policies banning or limiting the use of the company-owned device for personal calls, so users ended up in a position where they have to carry both devices around, and in security conservative organizations like government departments, this is still frequently the case.

Using virtualization technologies such as isolating users' own personal applications from organizations' applications potentially resolves that issue and enables employees to consolidate both personal and business calls and mobile data access on a single device. It brings many opportunities such as increased productivity and reduced costs as well as challenges such as secured data access, data leakage, and amount of control by the organization. The solution to be presented in this chapter is to address challenges faced in an enterprise environment to implement a Bring Your Own Device (BYOD) solution on mobiles located at the edge cloud.

The fundamental problem to be investigated is the application delivery issue on multiple mobile platforms. For instance, having purchased many applications from one proprietary application store, individuals may want to move them to a different platform/device but currently this is not possible. To address this issue, in this chapter, we present a KVM-based[1] virtualization solution [92] for ARM devices that will be able to run Virtual Machines (VMs) with nearly unmodified guest OS.

Several security issues in providing such a solution also need to be addressed and they are:

- Unauthorized access to data and applications;
- Attacks from the devices within and outside the network; and
- Data protection issues, which include data exfiltration, tampering, and unavailability.

---

[1] Kernel-based Virtual Machine (KVM) is a virtualization infrastructure for the Linux kernel that turns it into a hypervisor. It was merged into the Linux kernel mainline in kernel version 2.6.20, which was released on February 5, 2007. KVM requires a processor with hardware virtualization extensions.

Mobile Cloud Computing
DOI: 10.1016/B978-0-12-809641-3.00011-9

To address this problem, we will be introducing an SDN-based framework in mobile devices where a host runs the controller and monitor states of guest OS, and makes important control and traffic flow decisions based on security situations. This work would be valuable for dealing with application delivery and security issues in enterprise edge cloud and networking environment and would help in providing a secured BYOD solution to employers.

8.1 Virtualization and Isolation Approaches on Mobiles

BYOD has been coined to describe the *consumerization*[2] of the IT. IT organizations are no longer interested in providing and provisioning the IT equipment for the individuals. Most of the companies in the past had a separate department for maintaining individual IT equipment so the approach of offloading the task of hardware/device to the individual can significantly benefit the organizations in terms of cost cutting, delays in providing IT services due to communication gaps between various departments, etc. [260].

IT organizations can simply provide cash incentive to individuals to bring their own device for work, and use organization approved Operating System (OS), device image, secured emulation environment, and antivirus software when working for the company using the device. The second aspect of BYOD is the advent of high-performance mobiles such as smartphones and tablets devices. In addition, the dramatic growth in computing services and mobility trends, e.g., 3G/4G on smartphones, enable consumers/workers to use their devices on the go as well as during normal work hours. This would come across both as an opportunity as well as a challenge for the organizations. The opportunity is present in the sense that it would lead to productivity increase and significant cost reductions. However, this also brings forth a lot of challenges especially from the security perspective for organizations.

The organizations have to make sure that the devices are secured from external threats and at the same time prevent data exfiltration and unauthorized access to the resources [251]. To address this issue, we need to design a new application running platform on mobiles at the edge of cloud infrastructure, which can serve as a proof of concept for implementation on a large scale.

In this chapter, we select the ARM architecture to serve as the base model. The reason for selecting the ARM platform is performance and ubiquity provided by the ARM devices. The solution would be a KVM/ARM virtualization solution. The other benefit of using KVM is that it is an in-built kernel module, so we can keep KVM/ARM in lines with new kernel releases without the additional maintenance costs. The solution will have host operating system

---

[2]   Consumerization is the specific impact that consumer-originated technologies can have on enterprises. It reflects how enterprises will be affected by, and can take advantage of, new technologies and models that originate and develop in the consumer space, rather than in the enterprise IT sector.

running KVM environment and unmodified guest OS would be running in the emulation environment provided by the host OS [92]. Virtualization can in the future be extended to provide other features such as high availability, load balancing features, etc.

The presented work will make use of a software switch solution – Open vSwitch (OVS)[3] [227] – to establish a networking framework between the host OS and guest OS. This will bring in the scope of introducing programmability into the network using Software Defined Networking (SDN)[4] solution [246]. Programmability in the network will help us build a flexible OpenFlow [197] based framework for our system. OpenFlow is a protocol that allows a server to tell network switches where to send packets. OpenFlow is an implementation to realize the SDN concept. In a conventional switch, packet forwarding (the data path) and high-level routing (the control path) occur on the same device. An OpenFlow switch separates the data path from the control path. The control plane of SDN will have direct control over the Data Plane elements [219]. This will help deal with issues in traditional networks like devices from different vendors and two separate devices from same vendors. In this way, individuals can bring any smart phone/tablets of their choice as long as they have the virtualization feature support. The network of emulated virtual machines would be easily managed by the organization.

We will compare our solution with other mechanism of introducing BYOD security in IT enterprises and see why this solution will be significantly better than other proposed solutions such as Prioritized Defense Deployment for BYOD; feedback based strategic sampling for BYOD security, application Sandbox,[5] etc. The novel aspect of this solution is that using OVS we can introduce the SDN framework and correspondingly programmability in a edge cloud network. It will make the solution vendor agnostic. In this way, we can virtualize and manage the devices from different vendors as long as they support virtualization feature. Since ARM CPUs are common in many smartphone devices, e.g., Samsung Galaxy S5 uses ARM Exynos 5250, the proof of concept can then easily be deployed in real world scenarios, and tested for performance and security aspects. Other important contributions of the work are that it will have significant cost savings, secured environment for managing the VMs, and better scalability as compared to some of the existing BYOD solutions.

---

3   Open vSwitch, sometimes abbreviated as OVS, is an open-source implementation of a distributed virtual multilayer switch. The main purpose of Open vSwitch is to provide a switching stack for hardware virtualization environments, while supporting multiple protocols and standards used in computer networks.

4   Software-defined networking (SDN) is an umbrella term encompassing several kinds of network technology aimed at making the network as agile and flexible as the virtualized server and storage infrastructure of the modern data center.

5   In computer security, a sandbox is a security mechanism for separating running programs. It is often used to execute untested or untrusted programs or code, possibly from unverified or untrusted third parties, suppliers, users or websites, without risking harm to the host machine or operating system.

The presented solution is a base model/prototype serving as experimental platform for BYOD framework. The ARM CPU provides hardware virtualization extensions so we make use of KVM virtualization on base ARM Development board for booting up the host OS and make use of KVM and emulation software QEMU [62] to boot up the guest OS on top of host OS in hypervisor mode. The OVS feature will be installed on top of Host system so that we can introduce SDN framework on host OS and manage guest OS. The details of prototyping and implementation are presented in Appendix D.

8.2 System Design and Architecture

This section introduces the design methodology and approach used for setting up a BYOD framework. Virtual Open System [35] and Linaro Networking Group [20] have focused their efforts on virtualization of ARM. KVM/ARM project [91] started as a research project at Columbia University and is also supported by Virtual Open Systems. Linux kernel 3.9 and beyond provide KVM support for ARM architecture [93].

Since ARM CPU have become common in mobile devices, tablets, servers, so there is a growing demand of utilizing the virtualization benefits for ARM devices. Split mode CPU virtualization offered by ARM/KVM solution allows hypervisor to split execution across CPU modes. The architecture introduces three modes – the normal *user mode USR*, the *kernel mode SVC* for running privileged instructions, and a new *HYP mode* that is more privileged than SVC mode. There are several changes in terms of OS architecture, for instance, HYP mode only maintains a single page table base register, and there is no address space split between the user and kernel modes.

The kernel is by default booted in HYP mode. This makes the architecture backward compatible with the legacy systems since the kernel always boots in SVC mode in legacy systems. Preboot stub known as "decompressor" decompresses kernel image into memory. On detecting that it booted in HYP mode, a temporary stub must be installed which would allow the kernel to fall back to SVC mode and run the decompressor code.

Other architectural details of KVM/ARM such as hardware trap, Virtual Generic Interrupt Controller (GIC) and timers have been discussed in [93]. Various development boards have been used as base models by the organization Virtual Open Systems [259] such as TI – OMAP 5432 [45] based on ARMv7 architecture, Samsung Exynos 5250 [46] based on ARMv7. Fast Models based simulation platform, which could be a good potential solution for KVM/ARM on Juno development board by ARM [147].

The presented model is based on the same KVM/ARM architecture, where VMs can be booted on top of ARM based development boards. Moreover, we use OVS to create a bridged

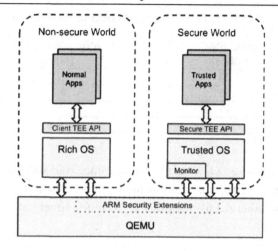

Figure 8.1: ARMv7 security extensions.

network of guest VMs on top of Host VM. This allows us to implement network wide policies, firewall rules, load balancing solutions on guest VMs using a smart OpenFlow controllers, such as POX [159], OpenDayLight [199], etc.

8.2.1 System Components

The goal is to build a BYOD framework that allows easy implementation of corporate policies and data capture for analysis. Two essential components of this framework are hardware assisted virtualization and Open vSwitch.

Hardware Assisted Virtualization

The base model for experimentation and evaluation are ARMv7 based development boards, hence the discussion focuses on the hardware assisted virtualization that ARM offers as part of ARMv7 and ARMv8 releases [109]. The RISC architecture of ARM helps achieve good balance of high performance, small code size, low power consumption, and reduced silicon area [56]. In addition, many smartphones and handheld devices have ARM based processors-with multiple cores. ARM architecture virtualization extensions and Large Physical Address Extension (LPAE) [118] enable efficient implementation of VM hypervisors for ARM architecture compliant processors.

To illustrate how ARM-based security framework works, i.e., TrustZone, Fig. 8.1 highlights the system architecture. TrustZone splits the mode into two worlds – secure and nonsecure. A special mode – monitor mode is used to switch between secure and nonsecure worlds.

Table 8.1: Open vSwitch Performance Analysis

Application	pNIC–pNIC [Mbps]	pNIC–vNIC [Mbps]	pNIC–vNIC–pNIC [Mbps]	pNIC–vNIC–vNIC [Mbps]
Open vSwitch	1.88	0.85	0.3	0.27
IP Forwarding	1.58	0.78	0.19	0.16
Linux bridge	1.11	0.74	0.2	0.19
DPDK vSwitch [149]	11.31	–	10.5*	6.5*

Although secure mode does not work in HYP mode, since trap and emulate support is not present, still we can run sensitive applications in the secure world. In [94], the authors discussed secure world and other details about CPU, memory, timer, and interrupt virtualization of ARM.

Open vSwitch

Virtual switches connect the interfaces of VMs and establish connection to outer network with the help of Physical Network Interface Card (pNIC). Open vSwitch (OVS) is used extensively in OpenStack and OpenNebula. We can explore broad range of OpenFlow features via software switches that cannot be provided by hardware switches. Two important parts of OvS are *ovs-vswitchd* daemon that controls switch and is responsible for implementing OpenFlow protocol, and *datapath* kernel module to implement the packet forwarding [103].

The performance comparison of various forwarding techniques as shown in Table 8.1 with a single CPU core per VM and a switch is discussed in [103], which suggests that Open vSwitch proves to be the fastest Linux kernel packet forwarding application.

Also rule-based system used by Open vSwitch would make it easier to configure a generic OpenFlow controller for VMs connected to Open vSwitch and implement access control based on the flows, e.g., blocking packets from a compromised VM or redirecting packets to a different destination. The SDN model thus formed can be made more scalable by configuring a controller that is logically centralized but physically distributed, e.g., HyperFlow [263]. Open vSwitch across two host systems can also communicate via a Generic Routing Encapsulation (GRE) [106] tunnel.

8.2.2 System Architecture

The system architecture for BYOD framework uses Samsung Exynos 5250 as base platform for demonstration purposes. The board was first introduced in 2012 and features two Cortex-A15 cores clocked at 1.7 GHz [132]. It offers 50% higher per MHz performance compared to commonly used Cortex A9 architecture. It is lightweight (150 g) and is common in

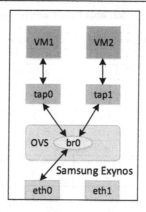

Figure 8.2: BYOD system architecture based on Samsung Exynos.

many handheld devices such as Google Nexus Tablet. It is also very cost effective at about $150/board. The goal is to develop the framework on this platform so it can later be used for deployment in a larger testing environment or code base from this platform to be deployed on other tablets or mobile devices compatible with ARM architecture.

The architecture consists of three basic features:

- As shown in the Fig. 8.2, the host OS should have hardware assisted virtualization enabled and should boot in *HYP mode* enabled. Ubuntu Precise (12.04) is used as the host OS. The host operating system needs a Device Tree Blob (DTB)[6] *exynos5250-arndale.dtb*, which contains description of hardware. It is specific to the development board. Another component required is the kernel *uImage*. Details of generating both are discussed in Appendix D.
- Open vSwitch is run on top of a host platform. This allows us to make use of OpenFlow APIs along with other advantages of Open vSwitch. An important consideration for this prototyping is compatibility of Open vSwitch with the Linux kernel. Table 8.2 shows the compatibility of Linux kernel with Open vSwitch versions. Therefore, we are choosing Linux kernel 3.14.32 and Open vSwitch version "*openvswitch-2.3.1*".
- A guest OS can be booted using the bridged network provided by Open vSwitch. Additionally, the guest OS requires the kernel image to boot the guest OS *zImage,*[7] the *DTB*

---

[6] One of the more challenging aspects of porting Linux (and U-Boot) to a device board is the requirement for a device tree blob (DTB). It is also referred to as a flat device tree, device tree binary, or simply device tree.

[7] zImage is a compressed version of the Linux kernel image that is self-extracting. uImage is an image file that has a U-Boot wrapper (installed by the mkimage utility) that includes the OS type and loader information. A very common practice (e.g., in the typical Linux kernel Makefile) is to use a zImage file.

Table 8.2: Open vSwitch and Linux kernel version compatibility

Open vSwitch	Linux kernel
1.4.x	2.6.18 to 3.2
1.5.x	2.6.18 to 3.2
1.6.x	2.6.18 to 3.2
1.7.x	2.6.18 to 3.3
1.8.x	2.6.18 to 3.4
1.9.x	2.6.18 to 3.8
1.10.x	2.6.18 to 3.8
1.11.x	2.6.18 to 3.8
2.0.x	2.6.32 to 3.10
2.1.x	2.6.32 to 3.11
2.3.x	2.6.32 to 3.14
2.4.x	2.6.32 to 4.0

file, file system image to boot guest, a modified version of QEMU to emulate, and drive KVM from the *userspace*.

8.3 Communication with Remote OpenDayLight Controller

An SDN remote controller can be used for managing and monitoring the network traffic flow, and achieving the functionality of an SDN network. As shown in Fig. 8.3, the controller used is OpenDayLight (ODL) [199], where the modular approach provided by OpenDay-Light project helps provide SDN functionality and achieve solid platform for other important features such as NFV (Network Function Virtualization)[8] [126]. The ODL controller can remotely set up the traffic flow policies on mobiles through OpenFlow protocols [255] and interact with Open vSwitch (OVS) that assumes each guest is an isolated VM on a mobile device (i.e., a VM host). For information about network virtualization and OpenFlow protocols, please refer to Chapter 2, Section 2.5, where an introduction to SDN and OpenFlow protocols is presented.

Using OpenFlow protocols, the Northbound APIs of the OpenDayLight controller can be used for providing the application development functionality through an abstraction layer. The southbound API will connect to the Open vSwitch presented on Samsung Exynos 5250. The controller is very useful for managing the VM in a BYOD scenario. In case of network events such as DoS attacks targeting a particular mobile device, the controller can have an intrusion

---

[8] Network functions' virtualization (NFV) is an initiative to virtualize the network services that are now being carried out by proprietary, dedicated hardware. If successful, NFV will decrease the amount of proprietary hardware that's needed to launch and operate network services.

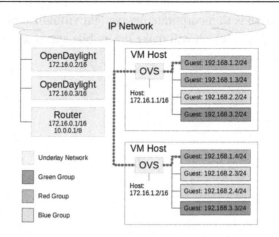

Figure 8.3: Communication between SDN controller and OVS.

detection mechanism configured to monitor application protocols and traffic, and then detect breaches or DoS attack patterns.

For detailed implementation and testing, please refer to Appendix D.

8.4 What Is the Next Step?

Mobile devices such as smartphones and tablets will certainly play a role in a future work setting of each organization. BYOD using an SDN framework can prove very efficient, scalable, and secure solution for organizations in the future. The model in this work uses ARMv7 as a proof-of-concept that ARM is a cost-effective, fast, and stable platform for serving as a base model for such devices.

ARMv7 is a good prospective platform for BYOD implementation. Future work should focus on the implementation of the model in a real application scenario. For example, we have been working on a mobile testbed consisting of 4 Unmanned Ground Vehicles (UGVs) and 6 Unmanned Aerial Vehicles (UAVs). This board being lightweight can be a suitable candidate to be deployed on UAVs. The robotic control functionality for UGVs would be provided by Arduino Uno Development board [55], which is standard for common robotic projects, and UAVs would make use of Ardu Pilot Board [101] with a compatible camera. Since Arduino platforms do not come with sufficient computing capability and the signal and network traffic analysis for testbed would require a platform with good computing capability, Samsung Exynos 5250 can be integrated with Ardu Pilot to provide computing capability.

Another important direction is to incorporate lightweight virtualization solutions, such as using containers (Docker [265]), which will make the mobile spend less overhead to manage heavy VM-based virtualization solutions.

Mobile Cloud Resource Management

This appendix will firstly provide an overview on cloud resource management frameworks and requirements, and then several existing mobile cloud resource management platforms will be discussed.

A.1 Overview of Cloud Resource Management

The tasks of cloud resource management include resource allocation, recycling, scheduling, and monitoring. The resources to be managed include computation resources, such as CPU and GPU time, storage resources, such as memory and disks, and network resources, such as connection between virtual machines and devices. This section presents four major cloud resource management systems: OpenStack, CloudStack, Euclyptus, and OpenNebula.

A.1.1 OpenStack

OpenStack [220] is a free and open-source software platform for cloud computing, mostly deployed as an IaaS. A high-level view of OpenStack framework is presented in Fig. A.1. The software platform consists of interrelated components that control hardware pools of processing, storage, and networking resources throughout a data center. Users either manage it through a web-based dashboard, command-line tools, or a RESTful API. OpenStack.org released it under the terms of the Apache License. OpenStack began in 2010 as a joint project of Rackspace Hosting and NASA. As of 2016, it is managed by the OpenStack Foundation, a nonprofit corporate entity established in September 2012 to promote OpenStack software and its community. More than 500 companies have joined the project.

The OpenStack community collaborates around a six-month, time-based release cycle with frequent development milestones. Its software release history is presented in Table A.1. During the planning phase of each release, the community gathers for an OpenStack Design Summit to facilitate developer working sessions and to assemble plans.

A.1.1.1 OpenStack Software Architecture

Fig. A.2 shows the relationships among the OpenStack services. OpenStack consists of several independent parts, named OpenStack services. All services authenticate through a com-

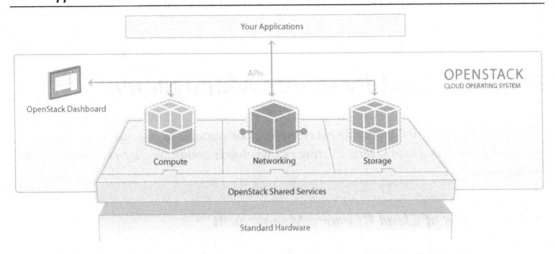

Figure A.1: OpenStack.
Picture source: https://www.openstack.org/software/

Table A.1: History of OpenStack Releases

Series	Status	Initial Release Date	Next Phase	EOL Date
Queens	*Future*	TBD		TBD
Pike	Under Development	TBD		TBD
Ocata	Phase I – Latest release	2017-02-22	Phase II – Maintained release on 2017-08-28	2018-02-26
Newton	Phase II – Maintained release	2016-10-06	Phase III – Legacy release on 2017-08-28	2017-10-11
Mitaka	Phase III – Legacy release	2016-04-07	End of Life	2017-04-10
Liberty	EOL	2015-10-15		2016-11-17
Kilo	EOL	2015-04-30		2016-05-02
Juno	EOL	2014-10-16		2015-12-07
Icehouse	EOL	2014-04-17		2015-07-02
Havana	EOL	2013-10-17		2014-09-30
Grizzly	EOL	2013-04-04		2014-03-29
Folsom	EOL	2012-09-27		2013-11-19
Essex	EOL	2012-04-05		2013-05-06
Diablo	EOL	2011-09-22		2013-05-06
Cactus	Deprecated	2011-04-15		
Bexar	Deprecated	2011-02-03		
Austin	Deprecated	2010-10-21		

OpenStack Release History, source (as of April 2017): https://releases.openstack.org/

mon Identity service. Individual services interact with each other through public APIs, except where privileged administrator commands are necessary.

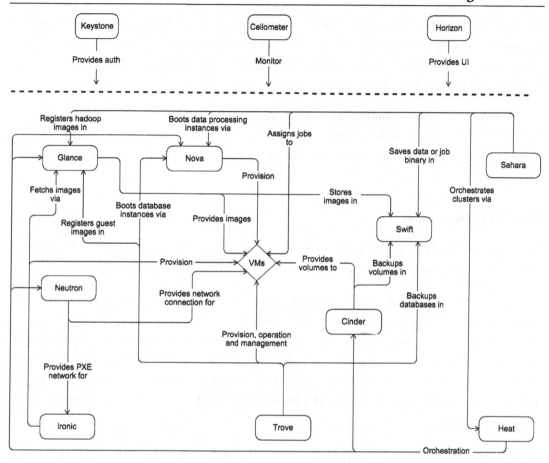

Figure A.2: Conceptual Architecture of OpenStack.
*OpenStack Conceptual architecture, source: https://docs.openstack.org/admin-guide/common/
get-started-conceptual-architecture.html#get-started-conceptual-architecture*

Internally OpenStack services are composed of several processes. All services have at least one API process, which listens for API requests, preprocesses and passes them on to other parts of the service. With the exception of the Identity service, the actual work is done by distinct processes.

For communication between the processes of one service, an *AMQP* message broker is used. The service's state is stored in a database. When deploying and configuring the OpenStack cloud, there are several message broker and database solutions that can be used, such as *RabbitMQ, Qpid, MySQL, MariaDB*, and *SQLite*.

Users can access OpenStack via the web-based user interface implemented by the OpenStack dashboard, via command-line clients, and by issuing API requests through tools like browser plug-ins or curl. For applications, several SDKs are available. Ultimately, all these access methods issue REST API calls to the various OpenStack services.

Fig. A.3 shows the most common, but not the only possible, architecture for an OpenStack cloud. OpenStack has a modular architecture with various code names for its components. The following subsections discuss the core services within the OpenStack service architecture.

A.1.1.2 Compute – Nova

Nova manages the life-cycle of compute instances in an OpenStack environment. Responsibilities include spawning, scheduling, and decommissioning of machines on demand.

Nova is the instance management component. An authenticated user who has access to a Glance image and has created a network for an instance to live on is almost ready to tie all of this together and launch an instance. The last resources that are required are a key pair and a security group. A key pair is simply an SSH key pair. OpenStack will allow a user to import his/her own key pair or generate one to use. When the instance is launched, the public key is placed in the authorized keys file so that a password-less SSH connection can be made to the running instance.

Before that SSH connection can be made, the security groups have to be opened to allow the connection to be made. A security group is a firewall at the cloud infrastructure layer. The OpenStack distribution will have a default security group with rules to allow instances to communicate with each other within the same security group, but rules will have to be added for Internet Control Message Protocol (ICMP), SSH, and other connections to be made from outside the security group.

Once there are an image, network, key pair, and security group available, an instance can be launched. The resource's identifiers are provided to Nova, and Nova looks at what resources are being used on which hypervisors, and schedules the instance to spawn on a compute node. The compute node gets the Glance image, creates the virtual network devices, and boots the instance. During the boot, cloud-init should run and connect to the metadata service. The metadata service provides the SSH public key needed for SSH login to the instance and, if provided, any post-boot configuration that needs to happen. This could be anything from a simple shell script to an invocation of a configuration management engine.

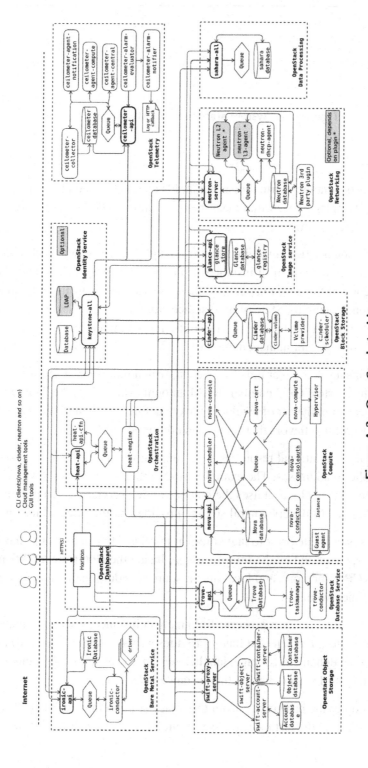

Figure A.3: OpenStack Architecture.

OpenStack Architecture, source: https://docs.openstack.org/admin-guide/common/get-started-logical-architecture.html

Image Store (glance)   Compute Node (nova)   Volume Store (cinder)

Figure A.4: System state before VM creation.

Images and instances

Virtual machine images contain a virtual disk that holds a bootable operating system on it. Disk images provide templates for virtual machine file systems. The Image service controls image storage and management.

Instances are the individual virtual machines that run on physical compute nodes inside the cloud. Users can launch any number of instances from the same image. Each launched instance runs from a copy of the base image. Any changes made to the instance do not affect the base image. Snapshots capture the state of an instances running disk. Users can create a snapshot, and build a new image based on these snapshots. The Compute service controls instance, image, and snapshot storage and management.

When launching an instance, a flavor must be chosen, which represents a set of virtual resources. Flavors define virtual CPU number, RAM amount available, and ephemeral disks size. Users must select from the set of available flavors defined on their cloud. OpenStack provides a number of predefined flavors that a user can edit or add to.

You can add and remove additional resources from running instances, such as persistent volume storage, or public IP addresses. The example used in this chapter is of a typical virtual system within an OpenStack cloud. It uses the cinder-volume service, which provides persistent block storage, instead of the ephemeral storage provided by the selected instance flavor.

Fig. A.4 shows the system state prior to launching an instance. The image store has a number of predefined images, supported by the Image service. Inside the cloud, a compute node contains the available vCPU, memory, and local disk resources. Additionally, the cinder-volume service stores predefined volumes.

Fig. A.5 shows the instance creation process. To launch an instance, select an image, flavor, and any optional attributes. The selected flavor provides a root volume, labeled *vda* in this diagram, and additional ephemeral storage, labeled *vdb*. In this example, the cinder-volume store is mapped to the third virtual disk on this instance, *vdc*.

The Image service copies the base image from the image store to the local disk. The local disk is the first disk that the instance accesses, which is the root volume labeled *vda*.

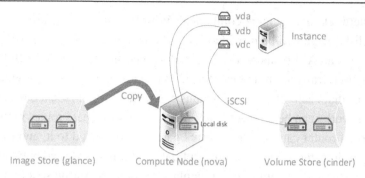

Figure A.5: System state when VM is running. (For interpretation of the colors in this figure, the reader is referred to the web version of this chapter.)

Figure A.6: System state after VM termination.

Smaller instances start faster. Less data needs to be copied across the network. The new empty ephemeral disk is also created, labeled *vdb*. This disk is deleted when the instance is deleted.

The compute node connects to the attached cinder-volume using *iSCSI*. The cinder-volume is mapped to the third disk, labeled *vdc* in this diagram. After the compute node provisions the *vCPU* and memory resources, the instance boots up from root volume *vda*. The instance runs and changes data on the disks (highlighted in red on the diagram). If the volume store is located on a separate network, the *my_block_storage_ip* option specified in the storage node configuration file directs image traffic to the compute node.

Fig. A.6 shows the system state after the instance exits. When deleting an instance, the state is reclaimed with the exception of the persistent volume. The ephemeral storage is purged. Memory and *vCPU* resources are released. The image remains unchanged throughout this process.

A.1.1.3 Networking – Neutron

Neutron enables network connectivity as a service for other OpenStack services, such as OpenStack Compute, provides an API for users to define networks and the attachments into them, and has a pluggable architecture that supports many popular networking vendors and technologies.

Neutron is the network management component. With Keystone, users are authenticated, and from Glance a disk image will be provided. The next resource required for launch is a virtual network. Neutron is an API frontend (and a set of agents) that manages the Software Defined Networking (SDN) infrastructure in OpenStack. When an OpenStack deployment is using Neutron, it means that each of the cloud tenants can create virtual isolated networks. Each of these isolated networks can be connected to virtual routers to create routes between the virtual networks. A virtual router can have an external gateway connected to it, and external access can be given to each instance by associating a floating IP on an external network with an instance. Neutron then puts all configuration in place to route the traffic sent to the floating IP address through these virtual network resources into a launched instance. This is also called Networking as a Service (NaaS). NaaS is the capability to provide networks and network resources on demand via software.

By default, the OpenStack distribution will install Open vSwitch to orchestrate the underlying virtualized networking infrastructure. Open vSwitch is a virtual managed switch. As long as the nodes in the cluster have simple connectivity to each other, Open vSwitch can be the infrastructure configured to isolate the virtual networks for the tenants in OpenStack. There are also many vendor plug-ins that would allow replacing Open vSwitch with a physical managed switch to handle the virtual networks. Neutron even has the capability to use multiple plug-ins to manage multiple network appliances. As an example, Open vSwitch and a vendor's appliance could be used in parallel to manage virtual networks in an OpenStack deployment. This is a great example of how OpenStack is built to provide flexibility and choice to its users.

Networking is the most complex component of OpenStack to configure and maintain. This is because Neutron is built around core networking concepts. To successfully deploy Neutron, a user needs to understand these core concepts and how they interact with one another. In Chapter 5, Network Management, we have spent time covering these concepts while building the Neutron infrastructure for an OpenStack deployment.

A standard OpenStack Networking setup has up to four distinct physical data center networks as shown in Fig. A.7:

Management network is used for internal communication between OpenStack Components. The IP addresses on this network should be reachable only within the data center and it is considered the Management Security Domain.
Guest network is used for VM data communication within the cloud deployment. The IP addressing requirements of this network depend on the OpenStack Networking plug-in in use and the network configuration choices of the virtual networks made by the tenant. This network is considered the Guest Security Domain.

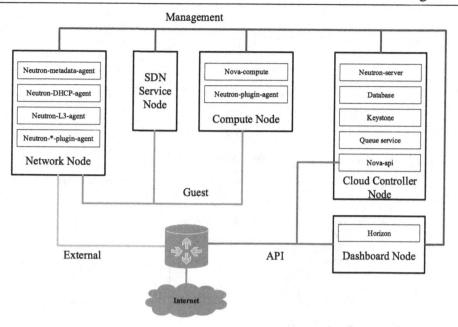

Figure A.7: OpenStack Networking service placement on physical servers.

External network   is used to provide VMs with Internet access in some deployment scenarios. The IP addresses on this network should be reachable by anyone on the Internet. This network is considered to be in the Public Security Domain.

API network   exposes all OpenStack APIs, including the OpenStack Networking API, to tenants. The IP addresses on this network should be reachable by anyone on the Internet. This may be the same network as the external network, as it is possible to create a subnet for the external network that uses IP allocation ranges to use only less than the full range of IP addresses in an IP block. This network is considered the Public Security Domain.

Fig. A.8 shows the flow of ingress and egress traffic for the VM2 instance.

A.1.1.4 Object Storage – Swift

Swift [57] stores and retrieves arbitrary unstructured data objects via a RESTful, HTTP based API. It is highly fault tolerant with its data replication and scaled out architecture. Its implementation is not like a file server with mountable directories.

Swift is the object storage management component. Object storage is a simple content-only storage system. Files are stored without the metadata that a block file system has. These are

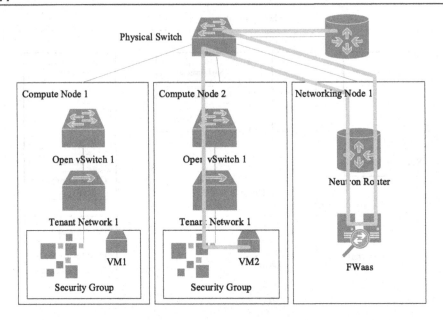

Figure A.8: The flow of ingress and egress traffic for the VM2 instance.

simply containers and files. The files are simply content. Swift has two layers as part of its deployment: the proxy and the storage engine. The proxy is the API layer. It's the service that the end user communicates with. The proxy is configured to talk to the storage engine on the user's behalf. By default, the storage engine is the Swift storage engine. It's able to do software-based storage distribution and replication. GlusterFS [96] and CEPH [272] are also popular storage backends for Swift. They have similar distribution and replication capabilities to those of Swift storage.

Fig. A.9 shows the Swift cluster architecture. Large-scale deployments segment off an access tier, which is considered the Object Storage system's central hub. The access tier fields the incoming API requests from clients and moves data in and out of the system. This tier consists of frontend load balancers, ssl-terminators, and authentication services. It runs the (distributed) brain of the Object Storage system, the proxy server processes. In most configurations, each of the five zones should have an equal amount of storage capacity. Storage nodes use a reasonable amount of memory and CPU. Metadata needs to be readily available to return objects quickly. The object stores run services not only to field incoming requests from the access tier, but to also run replicators, auditors, and reapers. You can provision object stores provisioned with single gigabit or 10 gigabit network interface depending on the expected workload and desired performance.

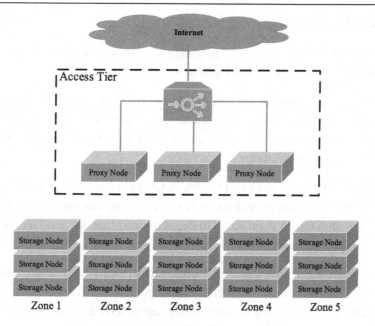

Figure A.9: OpenStack object storage architecture.

A.1.1.5 Block Storage – Cinder

Cinder provides persistent block storage to running instances. Its pluggable driver architecture facilitates the creation and management of block storage devices.

Cinder is the block storage management component. Volumes can be created and attached to instances. Then, they are used on the instances as any other block device would be used. On the instance, the block device can be partitioned and a file system can be created and mounted. Cinder also handles snapshots. Snapshots can be taken of the block volumes or of instances. Instances can also use these snapshots as a boot source.

There is an extensive collection of storage backends that can be configured as the backing store for Cinder volumes and snapshots. By default, Logical Volume Manager (LVM)[1] is configured. GlusterFS and CEPH are two popular software-based storage solutions. There are also many plug-ins for hardware appliances.

---

[1] LVM is a tool for logical volume management which includes allocating disks, striping, mirroring, and resizing logical volumes. With LVM, a hard drive or set of hard drives is allocated to one or more physical volumes. LVM physical volumes can be placed on other block devices which might span two or more disks.

A.1.1.6 Identity – Keystone

Keystone provides an authentication and authorization service for other OpenStack services. It provides a catalog of endpoints for all OpenStack services.

Keystone is the identity management component. The first thing that needs to happen while connecting to an OpenStack deployment is authentication. In its most basic installation, Keystone will manage tenants, users, and roles, and be a catalog of services and endpoints for all the components in the running cluster.

Everything in OpenStack must exist in a tenant. A tenant is simply a grouping of objects. Users, instances, and networks are examples of objects. They cannot exist outside of a tenant. Another name for a tenant is project. On the command line, the term tenant is used. In the web interface, the term project is used.

Users must be granted a role in a tenant. It's important to understand this relationship between the user and a tenant via a role. Identity Management (IDM) is in charge of creating the user and tenant and associating the user with a role in a tenant. For now, it is important to understand that users cannot login to the cluster unless they are members of a tenant. Even the administrator has a tenant. Even the users that the OpenStack components use to communicate with each other have to be members of a tenant to be able to authenticate.

Keystone also keeps a catalog of services and endpoints of each of the OpenStack components in the cluster. This is advantageous because all of the components have different API endpoints. By registering them all with Keystone, an end user only needs to know the address of the Keystone server to interact with the cluster. When a call is made to connect to a component other than Keystone, the call will first have to be authenticated, so Keystone will be contacted regardless.

Within the communication to Keystone, the client also asks Keystone for the address of the component, the user intended to connect to. This makes managing the endpoints easier. If all the endpoints were distributed to the end users, then it would be a complex process to distribute a change in one of the endpoints to all of the end users. By keeping the catalog of services and endpoints in Keystone, a change is easily distributed to end users as new requests are made to connect to the components.

By default, Keystone uses username/password authentication to request a token and Public Key Infrastructure (PKI) tokens for subsequent requests. The token has a user's roles and tenants encoded into it. All the components in the cluster can use the information in the token to verify the user and the user's access. Keystone can also be integrated into other common authentication systems instead of relying on the username and password authentication provided by Keystone. In Chapter 3, Identity Management, each of these resources has been explored. There we have walked through creating a user and a tenant and looked at the service catalog.

Terminologies defined by Keystone:

Token is an alpha-numeric text string that enables access to OpenStack APIs and resources. A token may be revoked at any time and it is valid for a finite time. While OpenStack Identity supports token-based authentication in this release, it intends to support additional protocols in the future. OpenStack Identity is an integration service that does not aspire to be a full-fledged identity store and management solution.

Service is an OpenStack service, such as Compute (nova), Object Storage (swift), or Image service (glance), that provides one or more endpoints through which users can access resources and perform operations.

Project is a container that groups or isolates resources or identity objects. Depending on the service operator, a project might map to a customer, account, organization, or tenant.

User is a digital representation of a person, system, or service that uses OpenStack cloud services. The Identity service validates that incoming requests are made by the user who claims to be making the call. Users have a login and can access resources by using assigned tokens. Users can be directly assigned to a particular project and behave as if they are contained in that project.

Role is a personality with a defined set of user rights and privileges to perform a specific set of operations. The Identity service issues a token that includes a list of roles to a user. When a user calls a service, that service interprets the set of user roles and determines to which operations or resources each role grants access.

Domain is an Identity service API v3 entity. It represents a collection of projects and users that defines administrative boundaries for the management of Identity entities. A domain, which can represent an individual, company, or operator-owned space, exposes administrative activities directly to system users. Users can be granted the administrator role for a domain. A domain administrator can create projects, users, and groups in a domain and assign roles to users and groups in a domain.

Region is an Identity service API v3 entity. It represents a general division in an OpenStack deployment. You can associate zero or more subregions with a region to make a tree-like structured hierarchy. Although a region does not have a geographical connotation, a deployment can use a geographical name for a region, such as US-East.

Group is an Identity service API v3 entity. It represents a collection of users that are owned by a domain. A group role granted to a domain or project applies to all users in the group. Adding users to or removing them from a group respectively grants or revokes their role and authentication to the associated domain or project.

A.1.1.7 Image Service – Glance

Glance stores and retrieves virtual machine disk images. OpenStack Compute makes use of this during instance provisioning.

Glance is the image management component. Once we're authenticated, there are a few resources that need to be available for an instance to launch. The first resource we'll look at is the disk image to launch from. Before a server is useful, it needs to have an operating system installed on it. This is a boilerplate task that cloud computing has streamlined by creating a registry of preinstalled disk images to boot from. Glance serves as this registry within an OpenStack deployment. In preparation for an instance to launch, a copy of a selected Glance image is first cached to the compute node where the instance is being launched. Then, a copy is made to the ephemeral disk location of the new instance. Subsequent instances launched on the same compute node using the same disk image will use the cached copy of the Glance image.

The images stored in Glance are sometimes called sealed-disk images. These images are disk images that have had the operating system installed but have had things such as Secure Shell (SSH) host key and network device MAC addresses removed. This makes the disk images generic, so they can be reused and launched repeatedly without the running copies conflicting with each other. To do this, the host-specific information is provided or generated at boot. The provided information is passed in through a post-boot configuration facility called cloud-init.

The images can also be customized for special purposes beyond a base operating system install. If there was a specific purpose for which an instance would be launched many times, then some of the repetitive configuration tasks could be performed ahead of time and built into the disk image. For example, if a disk image was intended to be used to build a cluster of web servers, it would make sense to install a web server package on the disk image before it was used to launch an instance. It would save time and bandwidth to do it once before it is registered with Glance instead of doing this package installation and configuration over and over each time a web server instance is booted.

There are quite a few ways to build these disk images. The simplest way is to do a virtual machine install manually, make sure that the host-specific information is removed, and include *cloud-init* in the built image. Cloud-init is packaged in most major distributions; a user should be able to simply add it to a package list. There are also tools to make this happen in a more autonomous fashion. Some of the more popular tools are *virt-install*, *Oz*, and *appliance-creator*. The most important thing about building a cloud image for OpenStack is to make sure that cloud-init is installed. Cloud-init is a script that should run post boot to connect back to the metadata service.

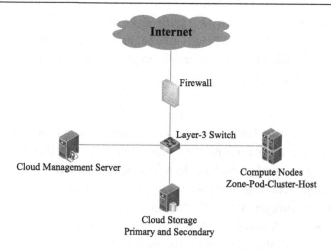

Figure A.10: CloudStack basic deployment.

A.1.2 CloudStack

CloudStack is an open source cloud computing software for creating, managing, and deploying infrastructure cloud services. It uses existing hypervisors such as KVM, VMware vSphere, and XenServer/XCP for virtualization. In addition to its own API, CloudStack also supports the Amazon Web Services (AWS) API and the Open Cloud Computing Interface from the Open Grid Forum.

Architecture

Generally speaking, most CloudStack deployments consist of the management server and the resources to be managed. During deployment, a management server is in charge of the resource allocation, such as IP address blocks, storage devices, hypervisors, and VLANs.

As shown in Fig. A.10, the minimum installation consists of one machine running the Cloud-Stack Management Server and another machine to act as the cloud infrastructure (in this case, a very simple infrastructure consisting of one host running hypervisor software). In its smallest deployment, a single machine can act as both the Management Server and the hypervisor host (using the KVM hypervisor).

A more full-featured installation consists of a highly-available multinode Management Server installation and up to tens of thousands of hosts using any of several networking technologies.

Management Server

The management server orchestrates and allocates the resources in the cloud deployment.

The management server typically runs on a dedicated machine or as a virtual machine. It controls allocation of virtual machines to hosts and assigns storage and IP addresses to the virtual machine instances. The Management Server runs in an Apache Tomcat container and requires a MySQL database for persistence.

The management server:

- Provides the web interface for both the administrator and end user;
- Provides the API interfaces for both the CloudStack API as well as the EC2 interface;
- Manages the assignment of guest VMs to a specific compute resource;
- Manages the assignment of public and private IP addresses;
- Allocates storage during the VM instantiation process;
- Manages snapshots, disk images (templates), and ISO images;
- Provides a single point of configuration for the cloud.

Cloud Infrastructure

Resources within the cloud are managed as follows:

- Regions. A region is a collection of one or more geographically proximate zones managed by one or more management servers.
- Zones. Typically, a zone is equivalent to a single data-center. A zone consists of one or more pods and secondary storage.
- Pods. A pod is usually a rack or row of racks that include a layer-2 switch and one or more clusters.
- Clusters. A cluster consists of one or more homogeneous hosts and primary storage.
- Host. A host is a single compute node within a cluster, often a hypervisor.
- Primary Storage. A storage resource typically provided to a single cluster for the actual running of instance disk images. (Zone-wide primary storage is an option, though not typically used.)
- Secondary Storage. It is a zone-wide resource which stores disk templates, ISO images, and snapshots.

Networking

A basic CloudStack networking setup is illustrated in Fig. A.11.

A.1.3 Eucalyptus

Eucalyptus is free and open-source computer software for building Amazon Web Services (AWS)-compatible private and hybrid cloud computing environments marketed by the com-

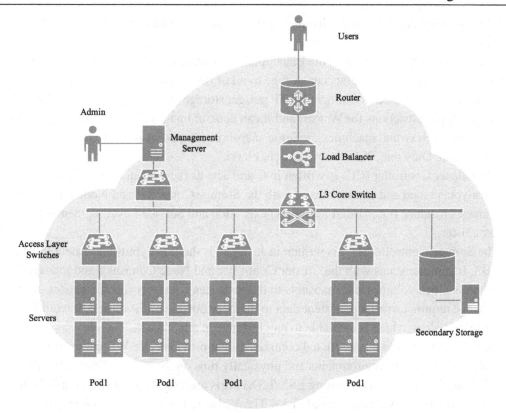

Figure A.11: CloudStack basic networking configuration.

pany Eucalyptus Systems. Eucalyptus is the acronym for *Elastic Utility Computing Architecture for Linking Your Programs To Useful Systems*. Eucalyptus enables pooling compute, storage, and network resources that can be dynamically scaled up or down as application workloads change. Eucalyptus Systems announced a formal agreement with AWS in March 2012 to maintain compatibility. Mårten Mickos is the CEO of Eucalyptus. In September 2014, Eucalyptus was acquired by Hewlett-Packard.

Eucalyptus has six components:

- The Cloud Controller (CLC) is a Java program that offers EC2-compatible interfaces, as well as a web interface to the outside world. In addition to handling incoming requests, the CLC acts as the administrative interface for cloud management and performs high-level resource scheduling and system accounting. The CLC accepts user API requests from command-line interfaces like euca2ools or GUI-based tools like the Eucalyptus User Console and manages the underlying compute, storage, and network resources. Only one

CLC can exist per cloud and it handles authentication, accounting, reporting, and quota management.

- Walrus, also written in Java, is the Eucalyptus equivalent to AWS Simple Storage Service (S3). Walrus offers persistent storage to all of the virtual machines in the Eucalyptus cloud and can be used as a simple HTTP put/get storage as a service solution. There are no data type restrictions for Walrus, and it can contain images (i.e., the building blocks used to launch virtual machines), volume snapshots (i.e., point-in-time copies), and application data. Only one Walrus can exist per cloud.

- The Cluster Controller (CC) is written in C and acts as the frontend for a cluster within a Eucalyptus cloud and communicates with the Storage Controller and Node Controller. It manages instance (i.e., virtual machines) execution and Service Level Agreements (SLAs) per cluster.

- The Storage Controller (SC) is written in Java and is the Eucalyptus equivalent to AWS EBS. It communicates with the Cluster Controller and Node Controller and manages Eucalyptus block volumes and snapshots to the instances within its specific cluster. If an instance requires writing persistent data to memory outside of the cluster, it would need to write to Walrus, which is available to any instance in any cluster.

- The VMware Broker is an optional component that provides an AWS-compatible interface for VMware environments and physically runs on the Cluster Controller. The VMware Broker overlays existing ESX/ESXi hosts and transforms Eucalyptus Machine Images (EMIs) to VMware virtual disks. The VMware Broker mediates interactions between the Cluster Controller and VMware and can connect directly to either ESX/ESXi hosts or to vCenter Server.

- The Node Controller (NC) is written in C and hosts the virtual machine instances and manages the virtual network endpoints. It downloads and caches images from Walrus as well as creates and caches instances. While there is no theoretical limit to the number of Node Controllers per cluster, performance limits do exist.

A.1.4 OpenNebula

OpenNebula is a cloud computing platform for managing heterogeneous distributed data center infrastructures. The OpenNebula platform manages a data center's virtual infrastructure to build private, public and hybrid implementations of infrastructure as a service. OpenNebula is free and open-source software, subject to the requirements of the Apache License version 2 [4].

OpenNebula is used by hosting providers, telecom operators, IT services providers, supercomputing centers, research labs, and international research projects. Some other cloud solutions use OpenNebula as the cloud engine or kernel service. OpenNebula orchestrates storage, network, virtualization, monitoring, and security technologies to deploy multitier services (e.g., compute clusters) as virtual machines on distributed infrastructures, combining both data center resources and remote cloud resources, according to allocation policies. According to the European Commission's 2010 report, "...only few cloud dedicated research projects in the widest sense have been initiated – most prominent amongst them probably OpenNebula ..."

The toolkit includes features for integration, management, scalability, security and accounting. It also claims standardization, interoperability and portability, providing cloud users and administrators with a choice of several cloud interfaces (Amazon EC2 Query, OGF Open Cloud Computing Interface and vCloud) and hypervisors (Xen, KVM and VMware), and can accommodate multiple hardware and software combinations in a data center.

A.2 Mobile Cloud Resource Management

The mobile cloud resource management include more resources into the resource pool besides what the previous cloud management covers. The mobile devices, such as smart phones and sensors, are typical resources in the mobile cloud resource pool. This section presents several mobile cloud resource management systems.

A.2.1 Cloudlet

A cloudlet is a trusted, resource-rich computer or cluster of computers that's well-connected to the Internet and available for use by nearby mobile devices [237]. Cloudlet represents the middle tier of a 3-tier hierarchy: mobile device–cloudlet–cloud. A cloudlet can be viewed as a "data center in a box" whose goal is to "bring the cloud closer." A cloudlet has four key attributes [238]:

- only soft state. It does not have any hard state, but may contain cached state from the cloud. It may also buffer data originating from a mobile device (such as video or photographs) en route to safety in the cloud. Avoiding hard state means that each cloudlet adds close to zero management burden after installation – it is entirely self-managing.
- powerful, well-connected and safe. It possesses sufficient compute power (i.e., CPU, RAM, etc.) to offload resource-intensive computations from one or more mobile devices. It has excellent connectivity to the cloud (typically a wired Internet connection) and is not limited by finite battery life (i.e., it is plugged into a power outlet). Its integrity as a computing platform is assumed; in a production-quality implementation this will have to be enforced through some combination of tamper-resistance, surveillance, and run-time attestation.

- close at hand. It is logically proximate to the associated mobile devices. "Logical proximity" is defined as low end-to-end latency and high bandwidth (e.g., one-hop WiFi). Often, logical proximity implies physical proximity. However, because of "last mile" effects, the inverse may not be true: physical proximity may not imply logical proximity. Building on standard cloud technology, it encapsulates offload code from mobile devices in virtual machines (VMs), and thus resembles classic cloud infrastructure such as Amazon EC2 and OpenStack. In addition, each cloudlet has functionality that is specific to its cloudlet role.
- builds on standard cloud technology. It encapsulates offload code from mobile devices in virtual machines (VMs), and thus resembles classic cloud infrastructure such as Amazon EC2 and OpenStack. In addition, each cloudlet has functionality that is specific to its cloudlet role.

OpenStack++

OpenStack++ provides extensions of OpenStack so that any individual or any vendor who uses OpenStack for his/her cloud computing can easily use cloudlets [123].

OpenStack provides an extension mechanism to add new features to support innovative approaches. This allows developers to experiment and develop new features without worrying about the implications to the standard APIs. Since the extension is queryable, a user can first send a query to a particular OpenStack cluster to check the availability of the cloudlet features. APIs for extensions are provided to the users by implementing an Extension class. An API request from the user will arrive at the extension class and a set of internal APIs will be called to accomplish desired functionality. Some of the internal API calls will be passed to a corresponding compute node via the messaging layer if necessary. Then, the API manager at the compute node will receive the message and handle it by sending commands to the hypervisor via a driver. Finally, the driver class will return the result and pass it to the user following the reverse call sequence.

The cloudlet extensions follow the same call hierarchy. Once a user sends a request via a RESTful interface, the message will be propagated to the matching compute node. Then the hypervisor driver performs the given task. Here's an example command flow for creating a VM overlay. The command is applied to a running virtual machine and generates a VM overlay which extracts the difference between the running VM and the base VM. To define a new action for creating a VM overlay, a cloudlet extension class is declared following the OpenStack extension rule. The user-issued API request first arrives at the extension class, and then is passed to a corresponding compute node via API and message layer. At the compute node, the message is then handled by a cloudlet hypervisor driver, which interacts with a target virtual machine. Finally, the cloudlet hypervisor driver will create a VM overlay using the VM snapshot.

A.2.2 POEM

POEM is short for Personal On-demand execution Environment for Mobile cloud computing. It is a service oriented system or middleware that connects the mobile devices and virtual machines in the cloud to provide a uniform interface for the application developers. Developers build mobile applications running on top of the POEM system which helps partition the applications and offload some computation tasks from mobile devices to the virtual machines or the other mobile devices.

Based on the POEM system, the partition and offloading strategies can be applied for various scenarios. POEM models a mobile application as a graph where a vertex is a computation task or application component and an edge is the data transfer between components or the dependency between computation tasks. Besides the application graph, POEM models the mobile devices and virtual machines in the cloud as the site graph where the devices and virtual machines are the nodes and the network provides the links. The POEM system maps the application graph to the site graph to achieve two objectives: (i) to save energy consumption on the mobile devices and (ii) to decrease the execution time for particular tasks.

A.2.3 Fog Computing

Fog computing or fog networking, also known as fogging, is an architecture that uses one or a collaborative multitude of end-user clients or near-user edge devices to carry out a substantial amount of storage (rather than stored primarily in cloud data centers), communication (rather than routed over the internet backbone), and control, configuration, measurement, and management (rather than controlled primarily by network gateways such as those in the LTE (telecommunication) core).

Fog computing can be perceived both in large cloud systems and big data structures, making reference to the growing difficulties in accessing information objectively. This results in a lack of quality of the obtained content. The effects of fog computing on cloud computing and big data systems may vary; yet, a common aspect that can be extracted is a limitation in accurate content distribution, an issue that has been tackled with the creation of metrics that attempt to improve accuracy.

Fog networking consists of a control plane and a data plane. For example, on the data plane, fog computing enables computing services to reside at the edge of the network as opposed to servers in a data-center. Compared to cloud computing, fog computing emphasizes proximity to end-users and client objectives, dense geographical distribution and local resource pooling, latency reduction for quality of service (QoS) and edge analytics/stream mining, resulting in superior user-experience and redundancy in case of failure.

Fog networking supports the Internet of Everything (IoE), in which most of the devices that are used on a daily basis will be connected to each other. Examples include our phones, wearable health monitoring devices, connected vehicles, and augmented reality using devices such as the Google Glass.

A.2.4 Dew Computing

Dew Computing goes beyond the concept of a network/storage/service, to a subplatform – it is based on a microservice concept in vertically distributed computing hierarchy. Compared to Fog Computing, which supports emerging IoT applications that demand real-time and predictable latency and the dynamic network reconfigurability, DC pushes the frontiers to computing applications, data, and low level services away from centralized virtual nodes to the end users.

One of the main advantages of Dew Computing is in its extreme scalability. The DC model is based on a large number of heterogeneous devices and different types of equipment, ranging from smart phones to intelligent sensors, joined in peer-to-peer ad hoc virtual processing environments consisting of numerous microservices. Although highly heterogeneous, the active equipment in DC is able to perform complex tasks and effectively run a large variety of applications and tools. In order to provide such functionality, the devices in DC are ad hoc programmable and self-adaptive, capable of running applications in a distributed manner without requiring a central communication point (e.g., a master or central device).

Mobile Cloud Programming and Application Platform

Using NIST cloud computing definition [200], PaaS is a good reference model to describe the functional collaboration features, in which it provides a standard Application Platform Interface (API) for functions (or services) to call each other.[1] The main challenge in establishing MCC PaaS is the compatibility issue among many mobile operating systems in the current market, e.g., Android, iOS, Windows 7, Symbian, etc. A general application platform is required to integrate the IaaS delegation and NaaS service model to support different mobile application platforms. To this end, we presented an XMPP [282] plus OSGi [222] (i.e., Extensible Messaging and Presence Protocol plus Open Services Gateway initiative) solution in Section 4.2. XMPP is a set of open technologies. It provides a lightweight middleware solution to coordinate the operations among MCC components. It also supports multimedia data transmissions and presence services that can be easily integrated as general interfaces for MCC PaaS. By interfacing with XMPP, OSGi provides multiplatform supported Java programming capabilities. Standard OSGi bundles supporting MCC basic functions can be created as software development kits for easier programming. Distributed OSGi allows MCC to run applications in a distributed fashion to balance performance and energy consumptions of mobile devices. An example based on OSGi framework is presented in this appendix.

The example includes two parts: an Android app and a surrogate server in VM. The experiment includes two stages: passing the compute code from Android app to the surrogate server, and establishing the service binding between original app and the offloaded code. The experiment example leverages the OSGi framework for code encapsulation and service discovery/binding. Although there are many offloading implementation approaches, we use OSGi and Android to illustrate the compute offloading process as an example to let the reader get the basic compute offloading ideas.

The OSGi framework provides the modular encapsulation. The compute offloading packages the code piece and sends to the surrogate to host it, which requires that the code piece is well packaged. Besides, the mobile application and the surrogate server agree on the code format so that the surrogate can successfully run the offloaded code. We run OSGi framework on

---

[1] We do not differentiate terms *Function* and *Service* since they will not impact our presented analytical models.

Mobile Cloud Computing
DOI: 10.1016/B978-0-12-809641-3.00021-1
245

both mobile device and the VM, which make the code agreement easy. Moreover, the OSGi framework is service oriented, which may help the code discovery and sharing.

In the experiment, we use a PC as VM. But you can use either laptop or PC, or a VM in the cloud if you want, as long as your phone can talk to the surrogate machine. We use TCP instead of XMPP to simplify the implementation. In our experiment, the PC and the phone are in the same local network through a WiFi switch.

This chapter is organized in four sections. Section B.1 sets up the environment and prepares the OSGi on Android application. Section B.2 implements the code transfer from Android application to the surrogate server. Section B.3 implements the service binding to let mobile application to consume the hosted code in the VM. Section B.4 puts all the components together to run the experiment application in offloading mode.

In this chapter, we will build 4 OSGi bundles: *surrogate.jar* in Section B.2 and the other 3 bundles (*provider.jar*, *consumer.jar* and *manager.jar*) in Section B.3. We will run the two OSGi frameworks and four bundles together to demonstrate how the compute offloading works in Section B.4. All the code in this chapter is available on github.[2] The code runs on Nexus 4 with Android 5.1.1 and Windows 10.

B.1 Run OSGi Frameworks

This section demonstrates how to run OSGi framework on both PC and Android to prepare for the following sections.

B.1.1 OSGi on Laptop

There are several OSGi framework implementations, among which Apache Felix is adopted in our experiment. The Felix is available from http://felix.apache.org/downloads. cgi#framework. The *Felix Framework Distribution* is what we need. Download and unzip it into any directory you want. Then start a command line window to interact with the Felix OSGi framework. We assume that Java is already installed.

B.1.2 OSGi on Android

To run the OSGi on a PC is straightforward, but to run OSGi in an Android application is a bit tricky.

---

[2] https://github.com/MobileCloudComputingCode.

Figure B.1: Running Felix OSGi on a PC.

The OSGi framework can be instantiated as an object which can be embedded into the Android application. The Felix subproject *Main* implements an embedded OSGi framework, which helps implement the embedded OSGi framework object on Android.

1. *Create an Android application.* From *Android Studio Create Project wizard*, choose the simple Android application to create an Android application with empty activity; see Fig. B.2.

2. *Runing Felix on Android.* For the Android project, we do not use the Felix OSGi Distribution like we did for the PC. Instead, we download the *Main subproject jar* file.[3] The *Main subproject* is the essential core of the *Felix Framework Distribution*, while *Felix Framework Distribution* provides directory structures and configurations and default bundles for a user to run the Felix framework easily.

---

[3] http://felix.apache.org/downloads.cgi#subprojects.

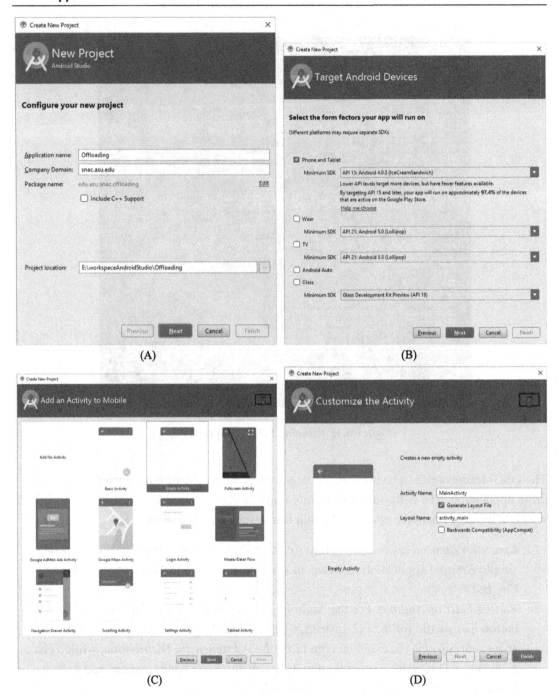

Figure B.2: Creating an Android project. (A) Android Studio–New Project. (B) Choosing API Level. (C) Choosing Activity Template. (D) Finishing Wizard.

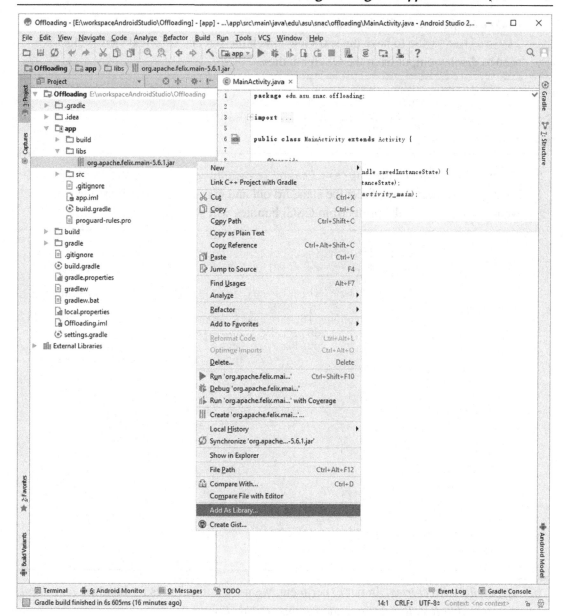

Figure B.3: Adding Felix Main as Dependency.

3. *Setup directory.* To use the downloaded *Main jar* file, we have to put it in the libs folder of Android project and indicate it as dependency library; see Fig. B.3.

4. *Update configuration file.* Update the `/app/src/main/res/layout/activ-ity_main.xml` file to have the text view match the screen. This TextView widget is used to display output from the OSGi bundles.

```
<TextView
          android:layout_width="match_parent"
          android:layout_height="match_parent"
          android:id="@+id/log"
          android:scrollbars = "vertical" />
```

5. *Setup logging.* Update the `app/src/main/java/edu.asu.snac.offloading/-MainActivity` file to redirect the standard out and err stream to the TextView widget we just set. Thus, all the prints from OSGi bundles will show up on the screen.

```
// set out & err
private void redirectStd() throws UnsupportedEncodingException {
        PrintStream ps = new PrintStream(new OutputStream() {
                @Override
                public void write(final int oneByte) throws IOException {
                        // in UI thread
                        runOnUiThread(new Runnable() {
                                @Override
                                public void run() {
                                        text.append(String.valueOf((char)
                                                oneByte));
                                        // append timestamp after every line
                                        if (String.valueOf((char)
                                                oneByte).equals("\n")) {
                                                text.append(new
                                                        Date().toString() +
                                                        "\n--------------------\n");
                                        }
                                }
                        });
                }
        }, true);
        System.setOut(ps);
        System.setErr(ps);
}
```

6. *System files directories.* In our experiment, we need 3 directories for bundles: *auto-load directory*, *file-install directory*, and *runtime-cache directory*.
   - The auto-load directory contains the bundles that will be loaded when the OSGi framework starts, which includes the *remote-shell* bundle and *file-install* bundle.
   - The *file-install* directory is monitored by *file-install* bundle. Any bundles in the file-install directory will be automatically installed in the OSGi framework and removing the bundle jar file from the directory will lead to uninstalling the bundle from OSGi framework. The *file-install* bundle is helpful for easy deployment.

- The runtime-cache directory is for Felix OSGi framework to cache the bundles at runtime. The runtime-cache directory is managed by Felix OSGi framework.

We prepare these directories and clean the runtime-cache directory every time we start the OSGi framework so that it is in a clean state every time.

```
// prepare osgi directories
private void prepareDirs() throws IOException {
    // path root
    File pathRoot = getExternalFilesDir(null);
    // path auto-load
    pathLoad = new File(pathRoot, "bundle-deploy-dir");
    pathLoad.mkdirs();
    // path file install
    pathWatch = new File(pathRoot, "bundle-watch-dir");
    pathWatch.mkdirs();
    // path runtime-cache
    pathRuntimeCache = new File(pathRoot, "bundle-cache-dir");
    pathRuntimeCache.mkdirs();
    // clean runtime-cache
    FileUtils.deleteDirectory(pathRuntimeCache);
    pathRuntimeCache.mkdirs();
}
```

7. *Start the framework.* Set OSGi framework configuration and start it in a new thread.

```
// start osgi thread
new Thread(new Runnable() {
    @Override
    public void run() {
        // pass key-value to osgi framework
        System.setProperty(AUTO_DEPLOY_ACTION_PROPERTY,
            TextUtils.join(",", new
            String[]{AUTO_DEPLOY_INSTALL_VALUE,
            AUTO_DEPLOY_START_VALUE}));
        System.setProperty("osgi.shell.telnet.ip", "0.0.0.0");
        System.setProperty("felix.fileinstall.bundles.new.start",
            String.valueOf(false));

        try {
            prepareDirs();

            try {
                System.setProperty("felix.fileinstall.dir",
                    pathWatch.getCanonicalPath());

                printOneLineLog("starting osgi .. please try
                    'TELNET " + getLocalIpAddress() + "
                    6666'");
                Main.main(new
                    String[]{Main.BUNDLE_DIR_SWITCH,
                    pathLoad.getCanonicalPath(),
                    pathRuntimeCache.getCanonicalPath()});
```

```
                  } catch (Exception e) {
                       e.printStackTrace();
                  }
              } catch (IOException e) {
                   e.printStackTrace();
              }
          }
      }).start();
```

8. *Setup access permissions.* Add permission for network and storage access in the `app/src/main/AndroidManifest.xml` file.

```
<uses-permission
    android:name="android.permission.WRITE_EXTERNAL_STORAGE"/>
<uses-permission android:name="android.permission.ACCESS_WIFI_STATE"
    />
<uses-permission android:name="android.permission.INTERNET"/>
```

9. *Prepare auto-load bundles.* We need several bundles from Felix subprojects to make us access the OSGi inside Android application easily. From http://felix.apache.org/downloads.cgi#subprojects, download the *Shell, Remote Shell, File Install, Bundle Repository, Configuration Admin* bundle jar files in one directory. These jar files cannot be used directly on Android. We have to dex them before Android can recognize them.

    (a) Set the Environment Path so that the command *dx* and *aapt* are available on the command line. The *dx* and *aapt* programs are available from Android SDK build-tools. On the PC, add `AndroidSDKPath\build-tools\<version>` to the System environment path. Type *dx* and *aapt* on command line and make sure the help information is shown.

    (b) Open a command line window in the directory where you put the 5 bundle jar files. Run the following one-line command to *dex* them.

```
FOR %F IN (*.jar) DO dx --dex --output=classes.dex %F && aapt add %F
    classes.dex && echo done %F
```

10. *Connect devices.* Connect the phone to Android Studio through USB connection and run the application. The application shows in the phone similar to Fig. B.4. We ignore the *config.properties* file and last class loader problem.

11. *Transfer files.* Transfer the 5 *dexed jar* files to the phone and put them into the "auto-load" directory shown on the phone screen using any tools you like. Then, restart the application from Android Studio.

12. *Remote access to the Android phone.* Open command line window and try to telnet to the phone by command "telnet <phone ip> 6666". The telnet command shows the Remote Shell of the Felix OSGi, which is exactly like you are accessing the local OSGi frame-

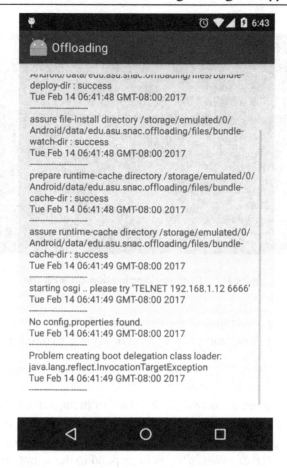

Figure B.4: Running Application on a Phone.

work as shown in Fig. B.5. In this way, we can easily access the OSGi framework on the Android phone through our development PC.

B.2 Running Surrogate Server

The surrogate server runs on the VM. It accepts the code from the Android application and hosts the code. The code is actually an OSGi bundle, which can be fetched from the bundle cache on Android and sent to the VM. The surrogate server accepts the bundle and runs it.

The surrogate server has two TCP servers binding to an address and listening to two ports. In our simple example, it accepts all the coming bundles and all remote invocations. The surrogate server itself is a bundle, which can be installed on the OSGi framework.

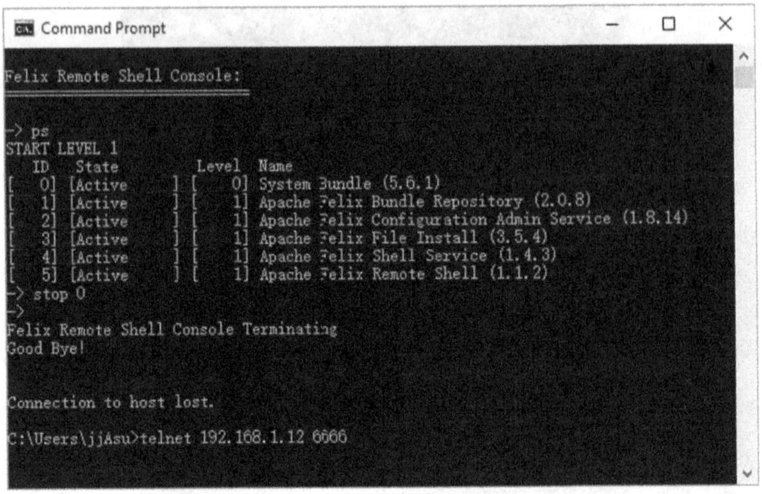

Figure B.5: Running Application on a Phone.

The Eclipse provides easy development environment as Eclipse itself is based on OSGi framework. We will use Eclipse Java Enterprise Edition or JaveEE to develop our bundles.

1. Create OSGi project using Eclipse Plug-in Wizard. We choose simple Hello World bundle template to start; see Fig. B.6.
2. The surrogate server bundle has two servers. One of them, named *JarFileReceiver*, is to accept the bundle jar files from the Android phone and start the received bundle. The *JarFileReceiver* starts TCP server listening on a port and writes to a temporary directory. The other server, named *ServiceCaller*, is to respond to the remote procedure call when the Android phone would like to call the offloaded code. The *ServiceCaller* also starts a TCP server and fetches the local OSGi service object through Java reflection mechanism. The *surrogate* bundle starts the both servers as two threads.
   The TCP server code sketch used by both servers is as follows:

```java
@Override
public void run() {
    // create TCP server on port
    ServerSocket serverSocket = new ServerSocket(port);
    // loop to accept the incoming connections
    do {
        Socket socket = serverSocket.accept();
        // process the connection
        process(socket);
        // close the connection
        socket.close();
    } while (true);
}
```

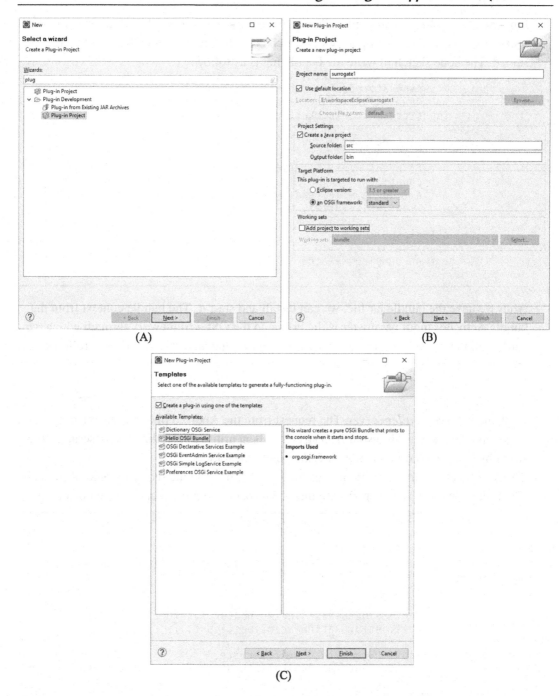

Figure B.6: Creating Eclipse Plug-in Project. (A) Eclipse Plug-in Wizard. (B) Creating a project. (C) Choosing a Template.

3. Implement *JarFileReceiver* server. The *JarFileReceiver* server reads the stream from the socket and writes a local temporary file which is the bundle file and which will be installed. The code sketch to write the bundle file is as follows:

```
private String storeJarFile(Socket socket) {
    // get in stream
    InputStream in = socket.getInputStream();
    // get out stream
    OutputStream out = new FileOutputStream(bundleFilePath);
    // read in, write out
    byte[] bytes = new byte[16 * 1024];
    int count;
    while ((count = in.read(bytes)) > 0) {
        out.write(bytes, 0, count);
    }
    out.close();
    in.close();
    return bundleFilePath;
}
```

After we have the bundle jar file, we can install and start it. The bundle context from the bundle Activator input parameter is the bridge to the OSGi framework through which we can install the bundle file. The code sketch to install and start the bundle is as follows:

```
Bundle b = context.installBundle(bundleFilePath);
b.start();
```

4. Implement *ServiceCaller* server. The request from the Android phone is encoded in a Json string and the response is also a Json string. A Json utility to serialize and deserialize the Java object is adopted in the *ServiceCaller* implementation.

The Java reflection mechanism help us to locate the method the request would like to call. The following code sketch shows the method *invocation* on the local service object:

```
private String invokeLocalService(String input) throws Exception {
    // 1 get object
    Object service =
        context.getService(context.getServiceReference(Util
        .getServiceName(input)));
    // 2 get method
    Method method =
        service.getClass().getMethod(Util.getMethodName(input),
        Util.getInvokationParamTypes(input));
    // 3 invoke
    Object ret = method.invoke(service,
        Util.getInvokationParams(input));
    // 4 return
    return ret.toString();
}
```

The invocation has 4 steps. The first two steps locate the service object as well as the method and the input parameters. The third step makes the invocation to get the result.

5. Package the bundle and run it on the VM; see Fig. B.7. The generated bundle can be installed to the local Felix OSGi distribution through the command line.

B.3 Service Binding

When the surrogate server is hosting the offloaded code, the Android application may access the hosted code through many ways, such as remote procedure call, web service, language binded approach like Java *RMI*, or application customized approach. In our experiment, we use OSGi service binding to make the Android application access the code in the VM.

B.3.1 A Simple Service

Since the OSGi framework is service oriented, we define a very simple addition service just for illustration. In real scenario, more complicated service may be defined.

1. The interface has only one *add()* method. The service interface is presented below:

```
public interface SimpleServiceInterface {
    public int add(int a, int b);
}
```

2. We create a bundle which registers an object that implements the *SimpleServiceInterface*. The registration happens when the bundle starts, and unregistration happens when the bundle stops.

```
public void start(BundleContext context) throws Exception {
    ref =
        context.registerService(SimpleServiceInterface.class.getName(),
            new SimpleServiceInterface() {
                public int add(int a, int b) {
                    System.out.println("service called with params
                        " + a + " " + b);
                    return a + b;
                }
        }, null);
}
```

3. The bundle that contains the service implementation of the previous steps is the service provider, which will be offloaded to the surrogate server. We need a service consumer to call the service, e.g.,

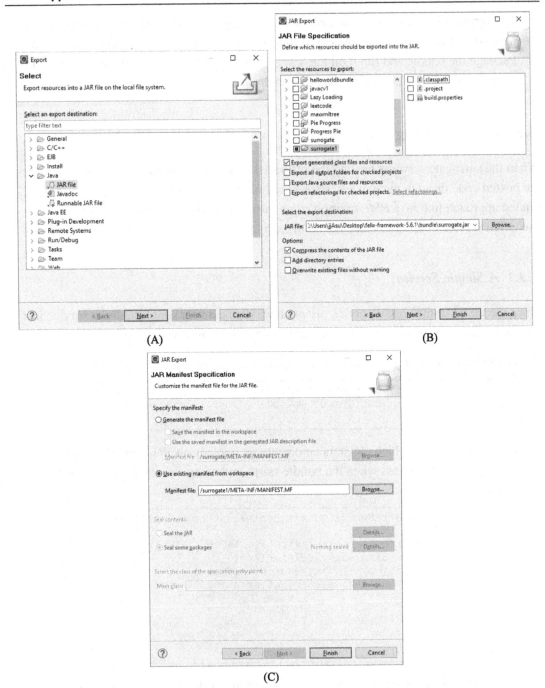

Figure B.7: Generating a Bundle File. (A) Exporting a Jar File. (B) Selecting a Location. (C) Choosing a Manifest File.

```
public void start(BundleContext context) throws Exception {
    ServiceReference ref =
        context.getServiceReference(SimpleServiceInterface.class
            .getName());
    if (ref == null) {
        System.out.println("Service not ready");
        return;
    }
    Object service = context.getService(ref);
    int a = r.nextInt();
    int b = r.nextInt();
    int c = ((SimpleServiceInterface) service).add(a, b);
    System.out.println("Call the service (" + a + ")+(" + b + ")=(" +
        c + ")");
}
```

It calls the service once when the bundle starts and prints the result.

4. Wire the service consumer and service provider. Since the service provider and service consumer are in different bundles, there has to be a way to let them know each other. The *MANIFEST.MF* indicates the export and import packages, so that they know each other's package.

In the service provider bundle, we add

```
Export-Package: edu.asu.snac.simpleservice
```

In the *service consumer bundle*, we add

```
Import-Package: edu.asu.snac.simpleservice
```

5. Update the *MANEFEST.MF* file. The Eclipse plug-in Wizard generates the dependency on JavaSE; however, it is not available on Android. We have to remove the *Bundle-RequiredExecutionEnvironment: JavaSE-1.x* from the bundle *manifest* file.

6. Export, *dex/aapt* and upload the jar file to the phone as we did in Section B.1.2, step 9. There is *bundle-watch-dir* directory for *File-Install* bundle, where we put both the service provider and consumer bundles.

We can start the uploaded bundles from the remote shell and observe the bundle output on the phone screen. Both bundles should work on the PC as well.

When the service bundle is started, starting consumer bundle displays the result of calling the service. When the service bundle is not started, starting the consumer bundle displays a notice saying the service is not ready.

B.3.2 Service Proxy on Android

To bind the service provider in the VM and the service consumer in the Android application, we need a proxy and a stub to make the service binding transparent to the service consumer and provider. The stub on the PC side is implemented in Section B.2.

A manager bundle is created to generate the proxy on the phone. In our experiment, the manager bundle finds the local *SimpleServiceInterface* service object and sends it to surrogate server. Then, it creates a proxy and connects to the remote surrogate server on the PC.

The manager bundle and both simple service bundles are developed in Eclipse and prepared to be uploaded to the Android phone.

Sending Code to Surrogate Server

The Android application needs a client to talk to the surrogate server to send the code to it. A simple TCP client will do the work. The bundle code file is sent as a byte stream.

1. Fetch the bundle file from the bundle cache. The Felix OSGi framework caches the installed bundle in the cache directory which is set when we start the framework.
   The Felix bundle in the runtime cache is versioned. We find the latest version and get the file path given bundle id:

```java
public static String getJarPath(Long id) throws IOException {
    String base_path =
        MainActivity.pathRuntimeCache.getCanonicalPath();
    // get the bundle id directory
    String version_path = base_path + "/bundle" + id;
    String lastest = "0.0";
    File dir = new File(version_path);
    // find the latest version
    for (File child : dir.listFiles()) {
        String dir_name = child.getName();
        String start = "version";
        if (dir_name.startsWith(start)) {
            String sub_str = dir_name.substring(start.length());
            // update the latest version
            if (versionCompare(lastest, sub_str) < 0) {
                lastest = sub_str;
            }
        }
    }
    // the path is like W/bundleX/versionY.Z/bundle.jar
    return version_path + "/version" + lastest + "/bundle.jar";
}
```

2. Initiate the byte stream transfer. On Android, the network operations should be in a thread other than UI thread. We create a new thread to send the bundle file to the surrogate server.

   In the field, the VM has URL to access to. In our experiment, we use IP address directly to simplify the implementation.

```
public static void sendFile(final String path) {
    new Thread(new Runnable() {
        @Override
        public void run() {
            BufferedInputStream bis = null;
            Socket sock = null;
            OutputStream os = null;
            try {
                // connecting ...
                sock = new Socket(surrogateIp, jarFilePort);
                // send file
                File myFile = new File(path);
                byte[] mybytearray = new byte[(int)
                    myFile.length()];
                bis = new BufferedInputStream(new
                    FileInputStream(myFile));
                bis.read(mybytearray, 0, mybytearray.length);
                os = sock.getOutputStream();
                os.write(mybytearray, 0, mybytearray.length);
                os.flush();
            } catch (Exception e) {
                e.printStackTrace();
            } finally {
                bis.close();
                os.close();
                sock.close();
            }
        }
    }).start();
}
```

Since the surrogate server in our example accepts the bundle code blindly, the bundle thread sends the bundle file and exits.

Generate Proxy at Runtime

Once the service bundle is migrated to the PC, there has to be a proxy on the Android phone to proxy the service consumer request to the remote PC so as not to break the service binding. Thanks to the Java reflection mechanism, we can generate the proxy object on the Android phone at runtime.

1. When the bundle starts, it stops the local service bundle, which is sent to the remote, and generates the proxy at runtime.

```
public void start(BundleContext context) throws Exception {
        // stop local service bundle
        b = context.getServiceReference(SimpleServiceInterface.class)
            .getBundle();
        b.stop();
        // send service bundle to remote
        String path = Util.getJarPath(b.getBundleId());
        Util.sendFile(path);
        // generate service proxy
        generateProxy(context);
}
```

2. The Java reflection helps to generate the service proxy which is an object that hooks the service function call and which is registered under the same name as the original service. When the service consumer invokes the function call to the service provider, the proxy is triggered before the real function call happens, so that we have chance to connect to the remote PC. The proxy starts a TCP session to the surrogate server and asks for the remote service object to reply the request.

```
private void generateProxy(BundleContext context) {
    System.out.println("generate service proxy");
    Object p = Proxy.newProxyInstance(SimpleServiceInterface.class
        .getClassLoader(),
        new Class[] {SimpleServiceInterface.class}, new
            InvocationHandler() {
                @Override
                public Object invoke(Object proxy, Method method,
                    Object[] args) throws Throwable {
                    // connect to surrogate server
                    Socket socket1 = new Socket(surrogateIp,
                        invocationPort);
                    // get input stream
                    BufferedReader br = new BufferedReader(new
                        InputStreamReader(socket1.getInputStream()));
                    // get output stream
                    PrintWriter pw = new
                        PrintWriter(socket1.getOutputStream(), true);
                    // get encoded request
                    String str = new
                        Marshalling().setService(SimpleServiceInterface
                        .class.getName())
                        .setMethod(method.getName()).addParams(args)
                        .build();
                    // send to surrogate server
                    pw.println(str);
                    // read response
                    if ((str = br.readLine()) != null) {
```

```
                                    System.out.println("received surrogate reply
                                        " + str);
                                    br.close();
                                    pw.close();
                                    socket1.close();
                                    // return result
                                    return Integer.valueOf(str);
                        } else {
                                    System.out.println("surrogate fail");
                                    return null;
                        }
                }
            });
        // register the proxy to osgi framework
        context.registerService(SimpleServiceInterface.class.getName(), p,
            null);
}
```

3. Similarly to the surrogate server, we will encode the objects in the Json string before sending to the surrogate and decode the Json string from surrogate, which is implemented in the Marshalling class which shares the same key words so that the surrogate can recognize the message correctly.

```
public class Marshalling {
        public static final String SERVICE_NAME = "service";
        public static final String METHOD_NAME = "method";
        public static final String PARAM_LIST = "params";
        // json object contains a map
        JSONObject obj = new JSONObject();
        // generate json string from json object
        public String build() {/* .. */}
        // set pair <SERVICE_NAME, value>
        public Marshalling setService(String s) {/* .. */}
        // set pair <METHOD_NAME, value>
        public Marshalling setMethod(String m) {/* .. */}
        // set pair <PARAM_LIST, value>
        public Marshalling addParams(Object... objects) {/* .. */}
        // add one value in array
        public Marshalling addParam(Object o) {/* .. */}
}
```

B.4 Putting All Together

In the previous sections, we made 4 bundles: *surrogate.jar*, *manager.jar* and 2 service bundles, *provider.jar* and *consumer.jar*, among which *surrogate.jar* runs on the PC while the other three bundles are uploaded to the Android phone. In this section, we run all the bundles to observe how the compute offloading happens.

1. Start OSGi on an Android application and put the *consumer.jar, provider.jar* and *manager.jar* bundles in the directory that the *File-Install* bundle watches so that all the bundles are installed in the OSGi framework. We can verify it from the Remote-Shell as shown in Fig. B.8.

2. We first test the service bundles and observe how the service binding happens in Android phone locally. Through Remote-Shell, we first start service provider bundle and then start *service consumer* bundle. Observe the printout on the phone screen, like shown in Fig. B.9, to verify that the "service called with parameters" shows, which proves that the service function is called locally. After verification, we stop the *service consumer* bundle for the next service invocation.

3. On the PC, we run the Felix OSGi distribution and start the *surrogate* bundle. We can verify it from the command line as shown in Fig. B.10.

4. Once both OSGi frameworks are ready, we can start offloading the bundle from the Android to the PC by starting the manager bundle on Android. The bundle prints the log of proxy and bundle file on the phone screen as shown in Fig. B.11.
    We can verify that the bundle is offloaded to the PC by listing the bundles on PC as shown in Fig. B.12.
    We can also verify that the bundle is stopped on Android by listing the bundles on Remote-Shell as shown in Fig. B.13.

5. After migrating the bundle code to the PC, we let the service consumer call the service again on Android *Remote-Shell*. Since the service provider bundle is not active on Android, the service object is provided by the proxy. The service invocation request is sent to the surrogate server on the PC to run the service function call. We can verify that the service is actually called on the PC by verifying the log printout on the PC as shown in Fig. B.14.

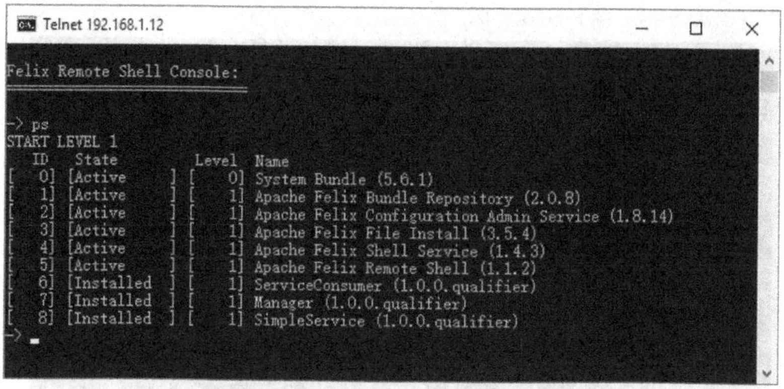

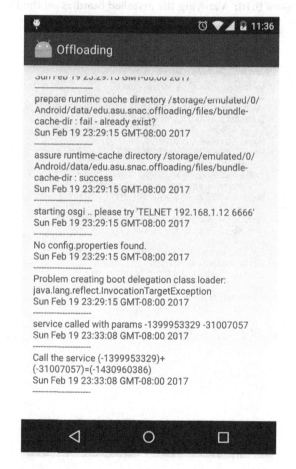

Figure B.8: Verifying the installed bundles on Android.

Figure B.9: Observing service binding on Android locally.

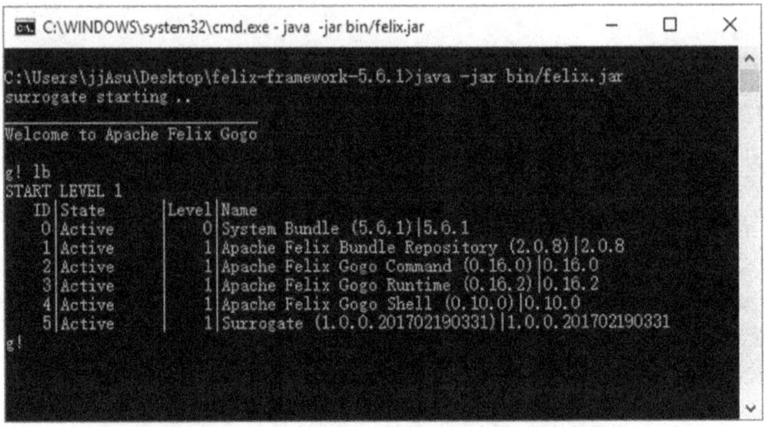

Figure B.10: Verifying the installed bundles on the PC.

Figure B.11: Verifying that the bundle is offloaded.

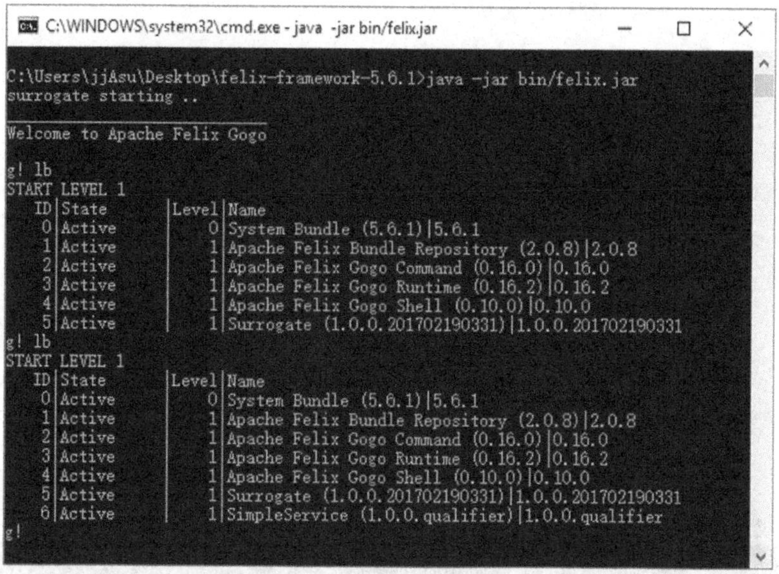

Figure B.12: Verifying that the offloaded bundle is installed and started.

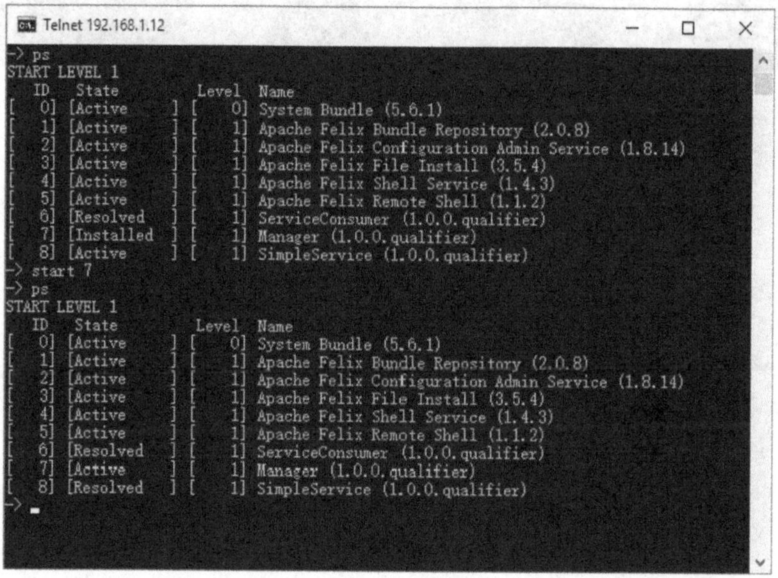

Figure B.13: Verifying that the service bundle is inactive.

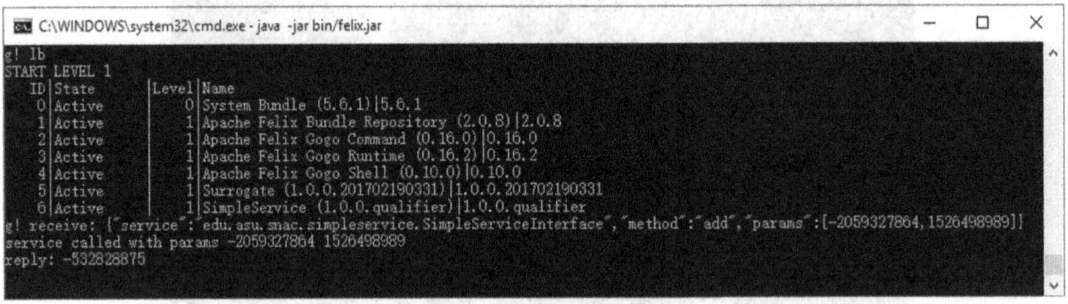

```
C:\WINDOWS\system32\cmd.exe - java -jar bin/felix.jar                                    —    □    ×
g! lb
START LEVEL 1
   ID|State       |Level|Name
    0|Active      |    0|System Bundle (5.6.1)|5.6.1
    1|Active      |    1|Apache Felix Bundle Repository (2.0.8)|2.0.8
    2|Active      |    1|Apache Felix Gogo Command (0.16.0)|0.16.0
    3|Active      |    1|Apache Felix Gogo Runtime (0.16.2)|0.16.2
    4|Active      |    1|Apache Felix Gogo Shell (0.10.0)|0.10.0
    5|Active      |    1|Surrogate (1.0.0.201702190331)|1.0.0.201702190331
    6|Active      |    1|SimpleService (1.0.0.qualifier)|1.0.0.qualifier
g! receive: {"service": edu.asu.smac.simpleservice.SimpleServiceInterface","method":"add","params":[-2059327864,1526498989]]
service called with params -2059327864 1526498989
reply: -532828875
```

Figure B.14: Verifying that the service called on the PC.

Cryptographic Constructions

C.1 Cryptographic Constructions for ICN Naming Scheme

C.1.1 Preliminaries of Bilinear Map

The foundation of ABE-type algorithms is pairing computation. In this appendix, we adopt the design from [297] in terms of algebraic structure. Suppose we have two groups: an additive group G_0 and a multiplicative group G_1 with the same order $n = sp'q'$, where p' and q' are two large prime numbers. We define a bilinear map $e : \mathbb{G}_0 \times \mathbb{G}_0 \to \mathbb{G}_1$. This map has three properties:

- Bilinearity. $e(aP, bQ) = e(P, Q)^{ab}$, for any $P, Q \in \mathbb{G}_0$ and $a, b \in \mathbb{Z}_p$;
- Nondegeneracy. $e(g, h) \neq 1$, where g and h are generators of $\mathbb{G}_0$;
- Efficiency. Computing the pairing can be efficiently achieved.

C.1.2 ABE Security Model

As mentioned in Section 7.2.1, the proposed solution includes an upper-level ontology-based attribute management scheme and a lower-level ABE-based naming scheme. The upper-level is only focused on the relationship between attributes, which has little to do with security. In this section, we only focus on the naming scheme, which can be modeled in the form of a game between a challenger and an adversary. The challenger simulates the operations of the TTP and the attribute authorities, while the adversary tries to impersonate as a number of normal network nodes. The game consists of the following five steps:

- **Setup.** The challenger runs the **GlobalSetup** algorithm and returns to the adversary the parameters.
- **Phase 1.** The adversary can ask for an arbitrary number of user keys from the challenger. The challenger runs the **NodeJoin** algorithm for each user involved in the requests and returns the corresponding secret information. The adversary then plays the roles of these users to request for attributes from the challenger. The challenger runs the **Authority-Setup** algorithm to create parameters for authorities and runs the **KeyGen** algorithm to generate keys on behalf of the authorities and the TTP.

- **Challenge.** The adversary provides two messages M_0 and M_1 to the challenger, together with an access policy A such that none of the users created by the challenger has attributes satisfying A. The challenger flips a coin b and encrypts M_b using A. It sends the ciphertext back to the adversary.
- **Phase 2.** The adversary can ask for more attributes and users from the challenger. But if any single user can gain satisfactory attribute combinations for A, the challenger aborts the game.
- **Guess.** The adversary makes a guess b' for the real value of b.

The adversary's advantage in this game can be defined as $ADV = P[b' = b] - \frac{1}{2}$. The proposed scheme is secure if for all the polynomial time adversaries, the advantage is at most negligible in the game.

C.1.3 ABE-Based Naming Scheme

In this section, we use a composite order group G_0 with an order $n = p^2 q^2$, where p and q are two large prime numbers. In other words, we fix the composite value s in Section C.1.1 as equal to pq. We also choose two subgroups G_s and G_t of G_0 such that $s = pq, t = pq$, and G_s is orthogonal to G_t. We deliberately choose such composite-order group configuration mainly because the proposed scheme is designed to support attribute rankings in G_s. It follows RSA conditions to enforce one-direction deduction between attribute values. This is why the values of s and t are set to be products of two large prime numbers. Details of such process will be illustrated in Section C.1.4.

Attributes of an entity can be any value in strings. In our scheme, each attribute string A_i corresponds to a triplet (I_i, k_i, h_i), where $I_i, k_i, h_i \in \mathbb{Z}_{n'}^*$. S_i and T_i are assigned by the TTP. The mapping from a string to such a triplet is determined by the authority of attribute A_i. An access policy can be expressed in Disjunctive Normal Form (DNF) of attributes. In each conjunctive clause of the DNF, the sequence of attributes is determined by the encrypter. The sequence encrypting a conjunctive clause (encryption sequence) is opposite to the decryption sequence. We define a public attribute A_{Pub} in the scheme. Unlike other attributes, A_{Pub} is associated with a triplet $(S_{Pub}, T_{Pub}, I_{Pub})$. For each conjunctive clause, the encrypter adds A_{Pub} at the end of the encryption sequence. In other words, the special attribute A_{Pub} is always the last attribute in encryption and the first attribute in decryption.

In the proposed scheme, **GlobalSetup** algorithm is run by the TTP to generate global parameters for the system. For each node joining in the network, the TTP runs **NodeJoin** algorithm once to generate a unique secret for the node. For each attribute, the authority in charge runs **AuthoritySetup** algorithm to generate secrets associated with that attribute. Besides, this naming scheme includes the other three basic algorithms: **KeyGen, Encrypt,** and **Decrypt.**

Once set up, the authority of an attribute runs **KeyGen** for each node carrying this attribute to allocate the inherent attribute secrets. **Encrypt** and **Decrypt** are respectively used by encrypters and decrypters for message passing.

The **GlobalSetup** algorithm generates global parameters $\{\mathbb{G}_s, \mathbb{G}_t, \varphi, \psi, \varphi^\beta, e(\varphi, \psi)^\alpha,$ $Enc_k(\cdot), Dec_k(\cdot), (P_{Pub}, S_{Pub}, T_{Pub}), ROOT\}$, and global secrets $\{\beta, g^\alpha\}$, where α and β are random values and $Enc_k(\cdot), Dec_k(\cdot)$ are a pair of symmetric encryption algorithms.

Algorithm C.1 GlobalSetup.

1: Choose two bilinear groups $\mathbb{G}_0$ and $\mathbb{G}_1$ with a composite order $n = p^2 q^2$, where p and q are two large prime numbers. g is the generator of $\mathbb{G}_0$;
2: Choose two subgroups $\mathbb{G}_s$ and $\mathbb{G}_t$ of $\mathbb{G}_0$ such that the order of both $\mathbb{G}_s$ and $\mathbb{G}_t$ is $n' = pq$ and $\mathbb{G}_s$ and $\mathbb{G}_t$ are orthogonal to each other;
3: Choose two generators $\varphi \in \mathbb{G}_s$ and $\psi \in \mathbb{G}_t$;
4: Choose two random values $\alpha, \beta \in \mathbb{Z}_{n'}^*$;
5: Define a constant $ROOT \in \mathbb{G}_1$ as identification of the secret message;
6: Choose a pair of symmetric encryption algorithms $Enc_k(\cdot)$ and $Dec_k(\cdot)$ in $\mathbb{G}_1$;
7: Define a public attribute, $(S_{Pub}, T_{Pub}, I_{Pub})$, $S_{Pub} \in \mathbb{G}_s$, $T_{Pub} \in \mathbb{G}_t$, $I_{Pub} \in \mathbb{Z}_{n'}^*$;
8: The global parameters are $\{\mathbb{G}_s, \mathbb{G}_t, \varphi, \psi, \varphi^\beta, e(\varphi, \psi)^\alpha, Enc_k(\cdot), Dec_k(\cdot),$ $(S_{Pub}, T_{Pub}, I_{Pub}), ROOT\}$, while global secrets are $\{\beta, \psi^\alpha\}$.

The **NodeJoin** algorithm is given in **Algorithm C.2**.

Algorithm C.2 NodeJoin.

1: For each node with UID in network, generate a random number $r_{UID} \in \mathbb{Z}_{n'}^*$;
2: Calculate $D_{UID} = \psi^{(\alpha + r_{UID})/\beta}$;
3: Calculate:

$$X_{Pub,UID} = \varphi^{r_{UID}} S_{Pub}^{r_{Pub}},$$

$$Y_{Pub} = \varphi^{r_{Pub}},$$

$$Z_{Pub,UID} = e(\varphi, \psi)^{r_{UID} I_{Pub}},$$

where $r_{Pub} \in \mathbb{Z}_{n'}^*$ is a random number for each node;
4: Choose a random value $P_{UID} \in \mathbb{Z}_{n'}^*$;
5: Assign to the node $\{D_{UID}, X_{Pub,UID}, Y_{Pub}, Z_{Pub,UID}, P_{UID}\}$.

Each individual authority that manages an attribute A_i will have to run **AuthoritySetup** to set up attribute secrets.

Algorithm C.3 AuthoritySetup.

1: For each attribute A_i, choose random numbers $I_i, k_i, h_i \in \mathbb{Z}_{n'}^*$;
2: For each attribute A_i, generate $S_i \in \mathbb{G}_s$ and $T_i \in \mathbb{G}_t$, where $S_i = \varphi^{h_i}$ and $T_i = \psi^{h_i}$.

Algorithm C.4 KeyGen.

1: The authority passes I_i, S_i, and T_i to TTP;
2: TTP computes and sends back to the authority:

$$X_{i,UID} = \varphi^{r_{UID}} S_i^{r_i},$$
$$Y_i = \varphi^{r_i},$$
$$Z_{i,UID} = e(\varphi, \psi)^{r_{UID} I_i},$$
$$L_{UID} = T_{Pub}^{1/P_{UID}},$$

where $r_i \in \mathbb{Z}_{n'}^*$ is a random number;
3: The authority assigns $X_{i,UID}, Y_i, Z_{i,UID}$, and L_{UID} to the node, together with I_i, h_i, and k_i.

The **KeyGen** algorithm generates the private keys corresponding to each attribute for each node holding this attribute. It is defined in **Algorithm C.4**. When the node receives the keys from the authority, it checks if $L_{UID}^{P_{UID}} = T_{Pub}$ is true. If it's true, it updates P_{UID} with P_{UID}^2 and accepts the keys. This update is intended to prevent from replay attack on L_{UID}. Otherwise, it will discard the keys.

The **Encrypt** algorithm works following the encryption sequence of each clause, by denoting each attribute from I_1 to I_m, where m is the number of attributes in the clause. In the example of Fig. 7.6, $I_1 = MRI$, $I_2 = Physician$, $I_3 = Hospital\ A$, $I_4 = A_{Pub}$, $m = 4$. Choose a random value $s \in Z_p$, set $I_0 = s$, and follow **Algorithm C.5**.

The **Decrypt** algorithm works in the decryption sequence. Note that the first attribute in a decryption sequence is always A_{Pub}. The decrypter follows **Algorithm C.6**.

When **Decrypt** algorithm succeeds, S_k is the random data encrypting key embedded in C.

C.1.4 Attribute Rankings

The proposed ABE scheme extends the capabilities of traditional ABE schemes and is able to support a comparison between the values of the same attribute. In a real world scenario, this

Algorithm C.5 Encrypt.

1: Calculate $C = Ke(\varphi, \psi)^{\alpha s}$, $C' = \varphi^{\beta s}$, and $C'' = Enc_K(ROOT)$;
2: For each attribute A_n, **if** a triplet $(C_{1,n}, C_{2,n}, C_{3,n})$ has already been calculated, move to the next attribute A_{n+1} and restart step 3 with A_{n+1}; **else goto** step 4;
3: Choose a random number $l_n \in \mathbb{Z}_{n'}^*$;
4: Calculate

$$C_{1,n} = \psi^{(I_{n-1} - I_n)l_n},$$
$$C_{2,n} = T_n^{(I_{n-1} - I_n)l_n},$$
$$C_{3,n} = (k_n l_n)^{-1},$$

for $1 \le n \le m$;
5: Calculate $C_{1,m+1} = \psi^{(I_m - I_{Pub})}$, $C_{2,m+1} = T_{Pub}^{(I_m - I_{Pub})}$.

Algorithm C.6 Decrypt.

1: Start from the public attribute A_{Pub};
2: For each attribute A_n that the decrypter possesses, compute

$$\frac{Z_{n,UID_{dec}} \cdot e(X_{n,UID_{dec}}, (C_{1,n})^{k_n C_{3,n}})}{e(Y_n, (C_{2,n})^{k_n C_{3,n}})}$$
$$= e(\varphi, \psi)^{r_{UID_{dec}}(I_{n-1})};$$

3: **If** $e(\varphi, \psi)^{r_{UID_{dec}}(I_{n-1})}$ is the decrypter's private key, go to step 2 with attribute A_{n-1}; **else goto** step 4;
4: Calculate

$$S_k = C/(e(C', D_{UID})/e(\varphi, \psi)^{r_{UID_{dec}}(I_{n-1})}).$$

If $Dec_{S_k}(C'') == ROOT$, then **Success; else Failure**.

means, for instance, that two values, *Physician* and *Nurse*, of attribute **Occupation** can be compared and have the relationship *Physician* > *Nurse*, meaning that the *Physician* attribute subsumes all the privileges that the *Nurse* has, but the *Nurse* does not have any of the additional privileges the *Physician* has. Such capability is applicable when capabilities of the lower-ranking role (*Nurse*) is a subset of that of the higher-ranking role (*Physician*). In traditional ABE solutions, each attribute value (*Physician* and *Nurse* in the above example) corresponds to a set of cryptographic components that are designated for that specific attribute (**Occupation** in the example) of a specific user. Components for different values of the same attribute are not related. In other words, the key components of *Physician* are independent of those of *Nurse*. To establish ranking relations between attribute values, certain connections need to be created between the corresponding key components. Specifically, a one-direction relation between values of the same attribute is supported in the proposed scheme. It allows a higher-ranking user (*Physician*) to be able to legally derive the corresponding lower-ranking role (*Nurse*) key components for himself. However, the lower-ranking role cannot derive anything regarding the higher-ranking role.

Such capability can be achieved by deliberately assigning appropriate values in **KeyGen** algorithm. We assign h_P for *Physician* and h_N for *Nurse* such that $h_P = h^{\alpha_P}$, $h_N = h^{\alpha_N}$, $h \in \mathbb{Z}_{n'}^*$, and $\alpha_P < \alpha_N$. Thus, we have $S_P = \varphi^{h_P}$ and $S_N = \varphi^{h_N}$. This is different from traditional ABE scheme, where both S_P and S_N are randomly chosen. This is the connection we establish between comparable values (*Physician* and *Nurse*) of the same attribute (**Occupation**). Recall that when we defined the order of $\mathbb{G}_s$, it was written as $n' = pq$, where p and q are two large prime numbers. In other words, n' is a composite number satisfying RSA algorithm requirements. If a user U_P is assigned $S_P = \varphi^{h^{\alpha_P}}$, i.e., the key for *Physician*, it is able to calculate the corresponding key S_N for *Nurse* as long as $\alpha_P < \alpha_N$. This can be done as

$$S_N = \varphi^{h^{\alpha_N}} = (\varphi^{h^{\alpha_P}})^{h^{\alpha_N - \alpha_P}} = (S_P)^{h^{\alpha_N - \alpha_P}}. \tag{C.1}$$

This means that when we assign attributes to U_P, we can choose to assign the value $h^{\alpha_N - \alpha_P}$ to the user together with S_P. Thus, when the user needs to decode some message dedicated for *Nurse*, he can easily calculate S_N following equation (C.1). However, if another user U_N has the attribute *Nurse*, he cannot deduce S_P following the same equation in a similar way. This is because in this case, $\alpha_P - \alpha_N < 0$. Under RSA assumption, h^{-1} cannot be efficiently computed due to the secrecy of n'. A benefit of such extension to our original scheme is that it allows the ranking relations among attributes without incurring too much workload on the TTP side. Only eligible users, *Physician* owners in this example, can use such capability, and the value $h^{\alpha_N - \alpha_P}$ is only useful to eligible users.

With such a knowledge, the TTP can assign two more values, Δh and Δr, to user U_P in **KeyGen** algorithms. When needed, the user can derive his key values corresponding to attribute *Nurse* afterwards. The modified step 3 of **KeyGen** is as follows:

$$X_{P,UID} = \varphi^{r_{UID}} S_P^{r_P},$$
$$Y_P = \varphi^{r_P},$$
$$Z_{P,UID} = e(\varphi, \psi)^{r_{UID} I_P},$$
$$L_{UID} = T_{Pub}^{1/P_{UID}},$$

$$\Delta h = h^{(\alpha_N - \alpha_P) r_P},$$

$$\Delta r = \Delta h I_N / I_P.$$

Thus, the r_{UID} for U_P's *Nurse* attribute is changed to $r'_{UID} = r_{UID} \Delta h$. Correspondingly, we have:

$$X_{N,UID} = (X_{P,UID})^{\Delta h} = \varphi^{r_{UID} \Delta h} S_N^{r_P} = \varphi^{r'_{UID}} S_N^{r_P},$$

$$Y_N = Y_P,$$

$$Z_{N,UID} = (Z_{P,UID})^{\Delta r} = (e(\varphi, \psi)^{r_{UID} I_P})^{\Delta h I_N / I_P}$$

$$= e(\varphi, \psi)^{r_{UID} \Delta h I_P} = e(\varphi, \psi)^{r'_{UID} I_P},$$

$$L'_{UID} = L_{UID}.$$

Here, we need to point out that to make sure that the values of h for two comparable attributes are the same, comparable attributes need to be managed by the same authority. This means that one single authority defines the relative order between these attributes. This requirement makes sense in a real-world scenario since in most cases a single authority (the hospital in this example) defines values of the same attribute (job position).

C.1.5 Security Proof Sketch

In this section, we provide a sketch of security proof following the structure in [63]. Before going into details of the proof, we firstly modify the security game described in Section C.1.2. This modification follows the same idea as in [63] and it is intended to change from differentiating two random messages M_0, M_1 to differentiating $e(\varphi, \psi)^{\alpha s_j}$, $e(\varphi, \psi)^{\theta_j}$ so that the generated intermediate results can be represented using the four mappings introduced in Section C.1.5.2. The goal of such modification is essentially to facilitate the following security proof. To differentiate these two games, we call the one in Section C.1.2 as **Game1** and the modified game as **Game2**.

C.1.5.1 Modified Game

Game2 consists of five steps similar to **Game1**. The steps **Setup**, **Phase1**, and **Phase 2** are the same as in **Game1**. The **Challenge** step is different in that the challenger does not choose one message to construct the ciphertext C. Instead, it outputs C_j as

$$C_j = \begin{cases} e(\varphi, \psi)^{\alpha s_j} & \text{if } b = 1, \\ e(\varphi, \psi)^{\theta_j} & \text{if } b = 0. \end{cases}$$

Here, all the θ_j are randomly chosen from Z_n^*, following independent uniform distribution.

Suppose an adversary **adv1** in **Game1** has the advantage of ϵ, the corresponding adversary **adv2** in **Game2** can be constructed according to the following strategy:

- Forward all the messages between **adv1** and the challenger during **Setup, Phase1**, and **Phase 2**;
- In the **Challenge** step, **adv2** gets two messages M_0 and M_1 from **adv1** and the challenge C from the challenger. **adv2** flips a coin δ and sends $C' = M_\delta C$ to **adv1** as the challenge for **adv1** in **Game1**. **adv2** generates its guess based on the output δ' from **adv1**. If $\delta' = \delta$, then the guess is 1; otherwise, it is 0.

The advantage that **adv2** has in this game can be calculated as $\frac{\delta}{2}$.

In the following, we will show that no polynomial adversary can distinguish between $e(\varphi, \psi)^{\alpha s}$ and $e(\varphi, \psi)^\theta$. Therefore, no adversary can have nonnegligible advantage in the security model.

C.1.5.2 Security Guarantee in the Modified Game

In this section, we follow the generic group model introduced in [247] and use a simulator to model the modified security game between the challenger and the adversary. The simulator chooses random generators $\varphi \in G_s$ and $\psi \in G_t$. It then encodes any member in G_s and G_t to a random string following two mappings: $f_0, f_1 : \mathbb{Z}_{n'} \to \{0, 1\}^{\lceil \log n' \rceil}$. It also encodes any member in G_1 to a random string in a similar way: $f_2 : \mathbb{Z}_n \to \{0, 1\}^{\lceil \log n \rceil}$. One additional mapping f_3 is used to convert elements in $\mathbb{Z}_{n'}^*$ to string representations: $f_3 : \mathbb{Z}_{n'}^* \to \{0, 1\}^{\lceil \log n' \rceil}$. The four mappings should be invertible so that the simulator and the adversary can map between the strings and the elements of corresponding algebraic structures in both directions. Four oracles are provided to the adversary by the simulator to simulate the group operations in G_s, G_t, G_1, and the pairing. Only the string representations can be applied to the oracles. The results are returned from the simulator in the string representations as well. The oracles will strictly accept inputs from the same group. The simulator plays the role as the challenger in the modified game.

- **Setup.** The simulator chooses G_s, G_t, G_1, e, φ, ψ, and random values α, β. It also defines the mappings f_0, f_1, f_2 and the four oracles mentioned above. The simulator chooses the public attribute parameters $I_{Pub} \in \mathbb{Z}_{n'}^*$, $S_{Pub} = f_0(\mu) \in G_s$, $T_{Pub} = f_1(\lambda) \in G_t$, and $ROOT \in G_1$, where λ and μ are random strings. The public parameters are G_s, G_t, $\varphi := f_0(1)$, $\psi := f_1(1)$, $\varphi^\beta := f_0(\beta)$, $e(\varphi, \psi)^\alpha := f_2(\alpha)$, $(S_{Pub}, T_{Pub}, I_{Pub})$, and $ROOT$.
- **Phase 1.** When the adversary runs **NodeJoin** for a new user with UID, the simulator generates a random number $r_{UID} \in \mathbb{Z}_{n'}^*$. It returns to the adversary with $D_{UID} = f_1((\alpha + r_{UID})/\beta)$, $X_{Pub,UID} = f_0(r_{UID})f_0(\mu r_{Pub,UID}) = f_0(r_{UID} + \mu r_{Pub,UID})$,

$Y_{Pub} = f_0(r_{Pub})$, and $Z_{Pub,UID} = f_2(r_{UID}I_{Pub})$, here $r_{Pub,UID} \in \mathbb{Z}_{n'}^*$ is a random number chosen by the simulator. When the adversary requests a new attribute A_i that has not been used before, the simulator randomly chooses $I_i, k_i, h_i \in \mathbb{Z}_{n'}^*$ and $S_i = f_0(h_i) \in G_s$, $T_i = f_1(h_i) \in G_t$ to simulate the process for setting up an attribute authority. For each attribute key request made from the adversary, the simulator computes $X_{i,UID} = \varphi^{r_{UID}} S_i^{r_i} = f_0(r_{UID} + h_i r_i)$, $Y_i = \varphi^{r_i} = f_0(r_i)$, and $Z_{i,UID} = e(\varphi, \psi)^{r_{UID}I_i} = f_2(r_{UID}I_i)$, where r_i is a random number chosen from $\mathbb{Z}_{n'}^*$. The simulator passes all these values to the adversary as the attribute keys associated with A_i.

- **Challenge.** When the adversary asks for a challenge, the simulator flips a coin b and chooses a random value $s \in \mathbb{Z}_{n'}^*$. If $b = 1$, the simulator calculates $C = f_2(\alpha s)$; if $b = 0$, it picks a random value $s' \in \mathbb{Z}_{n'}^*$ and calculates $C = f_2(s')$. In addition, it calculates $C' = \varphi^{\beta s}$ and $C'' = Enc_K(ROOT)$. It also computes other components of the ciphertext following **Encrypt**: $C_{1,n} = f_1((I_{n-1} - I_n)l_n)$, $C_{2,n} = f_1(h_n(I_{n-1} - I_n)l_n)$, and $C_{3,n} = f_3((k_n t_n)^{-1})$, where $h_n \in \mathbb{Z}_{n'}^*$ is a random number chosen by the simulator.

- **Phase 2.** The simulator interacts with the adversary similar as in **Phase 1** with the exception that the adversary cannot acquire attribute keys enabling a single user to satisfy the access policy $\mathbb{A}$. The output of this step is similar to that of Phase 1 except that the simulator acquires more user IDs and attributes in this step.

From the above game, we can see that the adversary only acquires the string representation of random values in $\mathbb{Z}_{n'}^*$, $\mathbb{Z}_n$ and combinations of the values. We can model all the queries as rational functions and further assume that different terms always result in different string representations [63]. As shown in [63], the probability that two terms share the same string representation is $O(q^2/n)$, where q is the number of queries made by the adversary. We assume in the rest of the proof that no such collision happens.

Now we argue that the adversary's views are identically distributed between the two cases when $C = f_1(\alpha s)(b = 1)$ and when $C = f_1(s')(b = 0)$. As a matter of fact, what the adversary can view from the modified game with the simulator are independent elements that are uniformly chosen and the only operation that the adversary can do on these elements is to test if two of them are equal or not. Thus, the situation that the views of the adversary differ can only happen when there are two different terms v_1 and v_2 that are equal when $b = 1$. Since αs and s' only occur in group G_1, the results from f_1 cannot be paired. Queries by the adversary can only be in the form of additive terms. Then we have $v_1 - v_2 = \gamma \alpha s - \gamma' s'$, where γ is a constant. By transformation, we have $v_1 - v_2 + \gamma' s' = \gamma \alpha s$. This implies that by deliberately constructing a query $v_1 - v_2 + \gamma' s'$, the adversary may be able to get the value of $e(g, g)^{\gamma \alpha s}$. Now we prove that such a query cannot be constructed by the adversary based on the information it gets from the game.

In fact, the information that an adversary can acquire from this game can be listed as in Table C.1. This table excludes values related to L_{UID} as it has nothing related to αs. To

Table C.1: Query information accessible to the adversary

μ	β	$r_{UID} + \mu r_{Pub,UID}$
r_{Pub}	h_i	$r_{UID} + h_i r_i$
r_i	$(I_{n-1} - I_n)h_n$	$t_n(I_{n-1} - I_n)h_n$
λ	$(\alpha + r_{UID})/\beta$	βs
h_i		
α	$r_{UID} I_{Pub}$	$r_{UID} I_i$
I_{Pub}	I_i	k_i
$(k_n t_n)^{-1}$	h_i	

construct the desired value, the adversary can map two elements from G_s and G_t into one element in G_1. He can also use elements in Z_n to change the exponentials. From this table, we can easily see that to obtain a value containing αs, the adversary can pair βs and $(\alpha + r_{UID})/\beta$ to get $\alpha s + r_{UID} s$ in G_1. In fact, this is the only way to get a term containing αs. But it is not feasible in that both βs and $(\alpha + r_{UID})/\beta$ belong to G_t while the pairing requires one element from G_s and G_t each.

Therefore, based on the information an adversary can get from the proposed scheme, the attacker cannot differentiate a random ciphertext from an authentic one. The security of the proposed scheme is proved. □

C.2 Partitioning CP-ABE

Essentially, the basic idea of P-CP-ABE to outsource intensive but noncritical part of the encryption and decryption algorithm to the service providers while retaining critical secrets. As we can prove later in this section, the outsourcing of computation does not reduce the security level compared with original CP-ABE schemes, where all computations are performed locally.

The encryption complexity of CP-ABE grows linearly in the size of access policy. During the encryption, a master secret is embedded into ciphertext according to the access policy tree in a recursive procedure, where, at each level of the access policy, the secret is split to all the subtrees of the current root. However, the security level is independent on the access policy tree. In other words, even if the ESP possesses secrets of most but not all parts of the access policy tree, the master secret is still information theoretically secure given there is at least one secret that is unknown to ESP. Thus, we can safely outsource most of encryption complexity to ESP by just retaining a small amount of secret information, which is processed locally.

As for the decryption, the CP-ABE decryption algorithm is computationally expensive since bilinear pairing operations over ciphertext and private key is a computational intensive operation. P-CP-ABE addresses this computation issue by securely blinding the private key and outsourcing the expensive Pairing operations to the DSP. Again, the outsourcing will not expose the data content of the ciphertext to the DSP. This is because the final step of decryption is performed by the decrypters.

C.2.1 System Setup and Key Generation

The TA first runs **Setup** to initiate the P-CP-ABE system by choosing a bilinear map: $e : \mathbb{G}_0 \times \mathbb{G}_0 \rightarrow \mathbb{G}_1$ of prime order p with the generator g. Then, TA chooses two random $\alpha, \beta \in \mathbb{Z}_p$. The public parameters are published as

$$PK = \langle \mathbb{G}_0, g, h = g^\beta, e(g, g)^\alpha \rangle. \tag{C.2}$$

The master key is $MK = (\beta, g^\alpha)$, which is only known by the TA.

Each user needs to register with the TA, who authenticates the user's attributes and generates proper private keys for the user. An attribute can be any descriptive string that defines, classifies, or annotates the user to which it is assigned. The key generation algorithm takes as input a set of attributes S assigned to the user, and outputs a set of private key components corresponds to each of attributes in S. The **GenKey** algorithm performs the following operations:

1. Chooses a random $r \in \mathbb{Z}_p$;
2. Chooses a random $r_j \in \mathbb{Z}_p$ for each attribute $j \in S$;
3. Computes the private key as:

$$SK = \langle D = g^{(\alpha+r)/\beta};$$
$$\forall j \in S : D_j = g^r \times H(j)^{r_j}; D'_j = g^{r_j} \rangle;$$

4. Sends SK to the DO through a secure channel.

C.2.2 P-CP-ABE Encryption

To outsource the computation of Encryption and preserve the data privacy, a DO needs to specify a policy tree $\mathcal{T} = \mathcal{T}_{ESP} \bigwedge \mathcal{T}_{DO}$, where $\bigwedge$ is an *AND* logic operator connecting two subtrees $\mathcal{T}_{ESP}$ and $\mathcal{T}_{DO}$. $\mathcal{T}_{ESP}$ is the data access policy that will be performed by the ESP and $\mathcal{T}_{DO}$ is a DO controlled data access policy. $\mathcal{T}_{DO}$ usually has a small number of attributes to reduce the computation overhead at the DO, in which it can be a subtree with just one attribute (see the example shown in Fig. C.1).

In practice, if $\mathcal{T}_{DO}$ has one attribute, DO can randomly specify a 1-degree polynomial $q_R(x)$ and sets $s = q_R(0)$, $s_1 = q_R(1)$, and $s_2 = q_R(2)$. Then DO sends $\{s_1, \mathcal{T}_{ESP}\}$ to ESP, which is denoted as

$$DO \xrightarrow{\{s_1, \mathcal{T}_{ESP}\}} ESP.$$

Here, we must note that sending s_1 and $\mathcal{T}_{ESP}$ will not expose any secret of our solution.

ESP then runs the **Encrypt**$(s_1, \mathcal{T}_{ESP})$ algorithm, which is described below:

1. $\forall x \in \mathcal{T}_{ESP}$, randomly choose a polynomial q_x with degree $d_x = k_x - 1$, where k_x is the secret sharing threshold value:
   (a) For the root node of $\mathcal{T}_{ESP}$, i.e., R_{ESP}, choose a $d_{R_{ESP}}$-degree polynomial with $q_{R_{ESP}}(0) = s_1$.
   (b) $\forall x \in \mathcal{T}_{ESP} \setminus R_{ESP}$ set d_x-degree polynomial with $q_x(0) = q_{\textbf{parent}(x)}(\textbf{index}(x))$.
2. Generate a temporal ciphertext:

$$CT_{ESP} = \{\forall y \in Y_{ESP} : C_y = g^{q_y(0)}, C'_y = H(att(y))^{q_y(0)}\},$$

where Y_{ESP} is the set of leaf nodes in $\mathcal{T}_{ESP}$.

At the meantime, the DO performs the following operations:

1. Perform **Encrypt**$(s_2, \mathcal{T}_{DO})$ and derive:

$$CT_{DO} = \{\forall y \in Y_{DO} : C_y = g^{q_y(0)}, C'_y = H(att(y))^{q_y(0)}\}.$$

2. Compute $\widetilde{C} = Me(g, g)^{\alpha s}$ and $C = h^s$, where M is the message.
3. Send $CT_{DO}, \widetilde{C}, C$ to the ESP:

$$DO \xrightarrow{\{CT_{DO}, \widetilde{C}, C\}} ESP.$$

On receiving the message from the DO, ESP generates the following ciphertext:

$$CT = \langle \mathcal{T} = \mathcal{T}_{ESP} \bigwedge \mathcal{T}_{DO}; \widetilde{C} = Me(g, g)^{\alpha s}; C = h^s;$$
$$\forall y \in Y_{ESP} \bigcup Y_{DO} : C_y = g^{q_y(0)}; C'_y = H(\textbf{att}(y))^{q_y(0)}\rangle.$$

Finally, the ESP sends CT to the SSP.

C.2.3 Outsourcing Decryption

CP-ABE decryption algorithm is computationally expensive since bilinear pairing is an expensive operation. P-CP-ABE addresses this computation issue by outsourcing the expensive Pairing operations to the DSP. Again, the outsourcing will not expose the data content of the ciphertext to the DSP.

To protect the data content, the DO first blinds its private key by choosing a random $t \in \mathbb{Z}_p$ and then calculates $\widetilde{D} = D^t = g^{t(\alpha + r)/\beta}$. We denote the blinded private key as $\widetilde{SK}$:

$$\widetilde{SK} = \langle \widetilde{D} = g^{t(\alpha + r)/\beta},$$

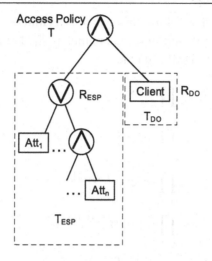

Figure C.1: Illustration of access policy $\mathcal{T} = \mathcal{T}_{ESP} \bigwedge \mathcal{T}_{DO}$.

$$\forall j \in S : D_j = g^r \cdot H(j)^{r_j}, D'_j = g^{r_j}). \tag{C.3}$$

Before invoking the DSP, the DO first checks whether its owned attributes satisfy the access policy $\mathcal{T}$. If so, the DO sends $\{\widetilde{SK}\}$ to the DSP, and requests the SSP to send the ciphertext to the DSP. On receiving the request, the SSP sends $CT' = \{\mathcal{T}; C = h^s; \forall y \in Y_1 \bigcup Y_2 : C_y = g^{q_y(0)}; C'_y = H(\mathbf{att}(y))^{q_y(0)}\}$ and $CT' \subset CT$ to the DSP:

$$SSP \xrightarrow{\{CT'\}} DSP. \tag{C.4}$$

Once the DSP receives both $\{\widetilde{SK}\}$ and CT', it then runs the **Decrypt**$(\widetilde{SK}, CT')$ algorithm as follows:

1. $\forall y \in Y = Y_{ESP} \bigcup Y_{DO}$, the DSP runs a recursive function DecryptNode(CT', $\widetilde{SK}$, R), where R is the root of $\mathcal{T}$. The recursion function is the same as defined in [63] and DecryptNode(CT', $\widetilde{SK}$, y) is proceeded as follows:

$$\begin{aligned} \text{DecryptNode}(CT', \widetilde{SK}, y) &= \frac{e(D_i, C_y)}{e(D'_i, C'_y)} \\ &= \frac{e(g^r \cdot H(i)^{r_i}, g^{q_y(0)})}{e(g^{r_i}, H(i)^{q_y(0)})} \\ &= e(g, g)^{r q_y(0)} \\ &= F_y. \end{aligned}$$

The recursion is processed as follows: $\forall y$ which is a child of x, it calls $DecryptNode(CT'; \widetilde{SK}; y)$ and stores the output as F_y. Let S_x be an arbitrary k_x-sized set of children nodes y, the DSP computes:

$$
\begin{aligned}
F_x &= \prod_{y \in S_x} F_y^{\Delta_{i, S_x'}(0)} \\
&= \prod_{y \in S_x} (e(g; g)^{r \cdot q_y(0)})^{\Delta_{i; S_x'}(0)} \\
&= \prod_{y \in S_x} (e(g; g)^{r \cdot q_{\text{parent}(y)}(\text{index}(y))})^{\Delta_{i; S_x'}(0)} \\
&= \prod_{y \in S_x} (e(g; g)^{r \cdot q_x(i) \cdot \Delta_{i; S_x'}(0)}) \\
&= e(g, g)^{r q_x(0)},
\end{aligned}
\tag{C.5}
$$

where $i = \textbf{index}(z)$ and $S_x' = \{\textbf{index}(z) : z \in S_x\}$, $\Delta_{i; S_x'}(0)$ is the Lagrange coefficient. Finally, the recursive algorithm returns $A = e(g, g)^{rs}$.

2. Then, one computes

$$
e(C, \widetilde{D}) = e(h^s, g^{t(\alpha+r)/\beta}) = e(g, g)^{trs} \cdot e(g, g)^{t\alpha s}.
$$

3. And sends $\{A = e(g, g)^{rs}, B = e(C, \widetilde{D}) = e(g, g)^{trs} \cdot e(g, g)^{t\alpha s}\}$ to the DO:

$$
DSP \xrightarrow{\{A, B\}} DO.
$$

On receiving $\{A, B\}$, DO calculates $B' = B^{1/t} = e(g, g)^{rs} \cdot e(g, g)^{\alpha s}$ and then it recovers the message:

$$
M = \frac{\widetilde{C}}{(B'/A)} = \frac{Me(g, g)^{\alpha s}}{(e(g, g)^{rs} \cdot e(g, g)^{\alpha s})/e(g, g)^{rs}}.
$$

Bring Your Own Device (BYOD) Implementation and Evaluation

In this appendix, we discuss the system setup and user experiments for our BYOD framework. Samsung Exynos 5250 is present in many tablets such as Samsung Chromebook, Nexus 9, etc. The steps for this part are similar to Virtual Open System guide for KVM over Arndale [46] and tutorial from Linaro Linux group [186].

D.1 Hardware Requirements

The hardware requirements for setting up the test environment include:

- System to prepare the host, guest images, QEMU. A system with sufficient disk space and Ubuntu-12.04 is suggested.
- Samsung Exynos 5250 Arndale Board.
- A memory card (16 GB suggested) to load host and guest OS.
- A serial port cable to communicate with the board using Minicom.
- Power supply (5 V).
- LAN cable connected to the Arndale development board.

D.2 Host and Guest Setup

Ubuntu 12.04 LTS is used as a base system to setup Linux Kernel and *rootfs* for both host and guest OS. We will first install the following packages on host system:

- *Qemu* which is a generic opensource machine Emulator [46].
- *debootstrap* which is a tool that installs the base system into a subdirectory of another already installed system.
- An ARM Cross Compiler for cross compiling the packages.

The implementation script can be run as follows:

```
$  sudo apt-get install -y gcc-arm-linux-gnueabihf
$  sudo apt-get install -y QEMU QEMU-user QEMU-user-static
$  sudo apt-get install -y debootstrap
```

D.2.1 *Host File System and Kernel Setup*

We install *arm-precise-root* using *QEMU-debootstrap* and setup root password for *arm-precise-root* [186] as follows:

```
$ sudo QEMU-debootstrap --arch=armhf raring ./arm-precise-root
$ sudo chroot ./arm-precise-root
```

Then, we need to copy the file *etc/init/tty1.conf* to *ttySAC2.conf*, and change *tty1* to *ttySAC2.conf*. Then we also perform the same steps to create a file *ttyAMA0.conf* in the same directory. We also need to change the baud rate to "115200" for serial port login. In addition, we need to add a line *ttySAC2* to file *etc/security*.

The next step is to add the following lines to *etc/source.list*:

```
deb http://ports.ubuntu.com/ precise main restricted universe
deb-src http://ports.ubuntu.com/ precise main restricted universe
```

Now, we need to update the *sources.list* file, reconfigure locales and install the following packages and exit from host *rootfs*:

```
$ locale-gen en_US.UTF-8
$ dpkg-reconfigure locales
$ apt-get install -y ssh gcc make xorg fluxbox tightvncserver
$ apt-get install -y libsdl-dev libfdt-dev bridge-utils uml-utilities
$ apt-get clean
$ exit
```

The following is to setup kernel for the host OS. For this part, we need to download *linux-linaro-lng* version 3.14.32 and unzip it to act as a source tree. We will use it to generate *dtb* and *uImage* for the host file system. Run the commands below on your Linux machine. We need to download sources from "*tar.gz*" repository. If we download from "*git*" repository, we will get errors while installing the Linux Kernel modules on the Arndale development board. The following shows the details of implementation steps:

```
$ wget https://releases.linaro.org/14.06/components
/kernel/linux-linaro-lng/linux-linaro-lng-3.14.3-2014.06.tar.bz2
$ tar -zxvf linux-linaro-lng-3.14.3-2014.06.tar.bz2
$ cd linux-linaro-lng
$ export CROSS_COMPILE=arm-linux-gnueabihf-
$ export ARCH=arm
$ mkdir ../lll-kvmhost ./scripts/kconfig/merge_config.sh
```

```
-O ../111-kvmhost/ linaro/configs/linaro-base.conf
linaro/configs/distribution.conf linaro/configs/kvm-host.conf
linaro/configs/arndale.conf linaro/configs/ovs.conf

$ make O=../111-kvmhost/ uImage dtbs modules

$ cp -t /tftpboot/ ../111-kvmhost/arch/arm/boot/uImage
../111-kvmhost/arch/arm/boot/dts/exynos5250-arndale.dtb

$ sudo make ARCH=arm CROSS_COMPILE=arm-linux-gnueabihf-
O=../111-kvmhost/ INSTALL_MOD_PATH=${KVMHOST_ROOT} modules_install
```

The presented deployment can generate *uImage* in the folder 111-kvmhost/arch/arm/boot and exynos5250-arndale.dtb in 111-kvmhost/arch/arm/boot/dtc, and these two files will be used later.

D.2.2 Guest File System and Kernel Setup

The guest file system that will be used as a VM on top of the host file system can be downloaded from Virtual Open System [35]. We are using *"Versatile Express"* – an ARM release – as the guest kernel. We can download *guest-zImage* and *guest-vexpress.dtb* from the website [46]. We will then need to create a bootable guest OS image and copy the precise file system used for host OS in that image. The following steps are set for this purpose:

```
$ dd if=/dev/zero of=./ubuntu.img bs=1MiB count=512
$ mkfs.ext3 ./ubuntu.img
$ sudo mount -o loop ubuntu.img mnt/
$ sudo cp -a precise/* mnt/
$ sudo umount mnt/
```

The bootloader used for booting up the host file system in *Hypervisor mode* and two additional files can also be downloaded directly from Virtual Open System [46].

```
u-boot.bin
arndale-bl1.bin
smdk5250-spl.bin
```

D.2.3 Qemu for ARM Setup

On the x86 Laptop/PC run the commands below:

```
sudo apt-get install -y pkg-config-arm-linux-gnueabihf

cat | sudo tee /etc/apt/sources.list.d/armhf-raring.list <<END
deb [arch=armhf] http://ports.ubuntu.com/ubuntu-ports precise main
restricted universe multiverse
deb-src [arch=armhf] http://ports.ubuntu.com/ubuntu-ports precise
main restricted universe multiverse
END

sudo xapt -a armhf -m -b zlib1g-dev libglib2.0-dev libfdt-dev libpixman-1-dev
sudo dpkg -i /var/lib/xapt/output/*.deb
git clone git://git.QEMU.org/QEMU.git
cd QEMU
git checkout -b v1.6.0 v1.6.0
git submodule update --init dtc
mkdir build; cd build
../configure --cross-prefix=arm-linux-gnueabihf- --target-list=arm-softmmu
--enable-kvm --audio-drv-list="" --enable-fdt --static
make
```

This will generate QEMU that would be used to emulate the ARM guest OS on top of the host OS using an Open vSwitch bridge.

D.3 Booting up Arndale Board

We will be using Secure Digital (SD) card (16 GB suggested) as a boot-up media to run host OS Ubuntu-12.04 on top of the Arndale board. Use a SD card reader and plug it into a laptop or desktop for copying file system.

Copy *bl1*, *spl*, and *u-boot* to the SD card. The SD card will be present as a storage device on the PC and can be viewed by using the command "*fdisk -l*". In this case, it is "*/dev/sdb*". The following command will be performed:

```
$ sudo dd if=arndale-bl1.bin of=/dev/sdb bs=512 seek=1
$ sudo dd if=smdk5250-spl.bin of=/dev/sdb bs=512 seek=17
$ sudo dd if=u-boot.bin of=/dev/sdb bs=512 seek=49
```

Now we will copy the host kernel and DTB file. These values will depend upon the size of the device tree and the Linux kernel. For instance, the Linux kernel size is about 4.6 MB, so that we can copy DTB file, and it does not overlap with the address space of kernel (*uImage*). The following command will be executed:

```
$ sudo dd if=uImage of=/dev/sdb bs=512 seek=1105
$ sudo dd if=arndale.dtb of=/dev/sdb bs=512 seek=13393
```

It is time to format the SD card and copy "*precise*" file system, and source tree onto the SD card. Remember to format from the start block address after DTB file, so leave sufficient space, and do the following:

```
$ sudo fdisk /dev/sdX
$ n
$ p
$ 1
$ 16384
$
$ w
$ mkdir mnt
$ sudo mkfs.ext3 /dev/sdb1
$ sudo mount /dev/sdb1 mnt
$ sudo cp -a ./arm-precise-root/* mnt/
$ sudo umount /dev/sdb1
```

We need to copy the guest file system, guest device tree, guest kernel and QEMU generated for ARM to the SD Card. So simply copy these files to "*root*" folder of the SD card. Alternatively you can use "*scp*" to copy these files once the board boots up and gets an IP address via DHCP. The next step is to insert the SD card into the appropriate slot on the board and then boot it up.

The procedure to boot up the board is provided as follows:

- Connect the serial port cable provided with the Arndale board to a USB port of a PC/Laptop.
- Download and install "*minicom*" or a similar application on the PC.
- Check the DIP switch settings on the Arndale board. It should be "001000" from left to right.
- Press the boot-up key present on the Arndale board. For more details, please refer to the following reference [279], which provides a more detailed version of booting up the Arndale board.
- As soon as the board starts loading the kernel and reads device tree properly, press *escape* key and enter commands below to configure boot arguments and environment variables. These commands will vary depending upon location of your kernel and device tree.

```
$ env edit bootargs
$       root=/dev/mmcblk1p1 rw rootwait earlyprintk
        console=ttySAC2,115200n8 --no-log
$ env edit bootcmd\
$       mmc read 40007000 451 3000;mmc read 42000000
        3451 100;bootm 40007000 - 42000000
$ env save
$ boot
```

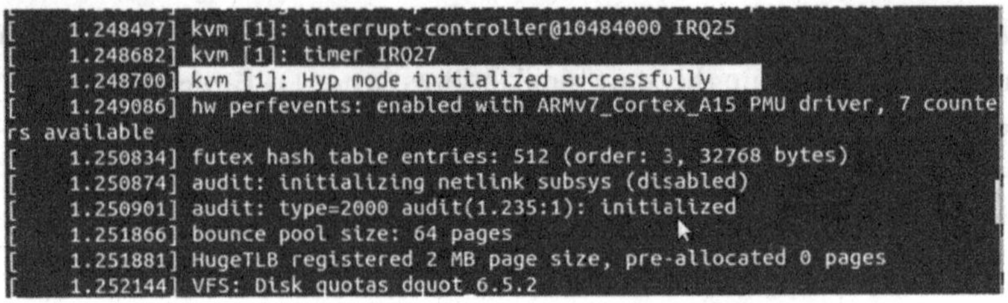

```
[    1.248497] kvm [1]: interrupt-controller@10484000 IRQ25
[    1.248682] kvm [1]: timer IRQ27
[    1.248700] kvm [1]: Hyp mode initialized successfully
[    1.249086] hw perfevents: enabled with ARMv7_Cortex_A15 PMU driver, 7 counte
rs available
[    1.250834] futex hash table entries: 512 (order: 3, 32768 bytes)
[    1.250874] audit: initializing netlink subsys (disabled)
[    1.250901] audit: type=2000 audit(1.235:1): initialized
[    1.251866] bounce pool size: 64 pages
[    1.251881] HugeTLB registered 2 MB page size, pre-allocated 0 pages
[    1.252144] VFS: Disk quotas dquot_6.5.2
```

Figure D.1: Host OS booting in HYP mode.

If the configuration is correct, the board will be booted up in the HYP mode as can be seen in Fig. D.1.

Once this is done, the board will boot up successfully. Enter *username* and *password* to login on the board as a root user. Once the system boots up and gets the IP address, run the following command in root mode. The board has a time skew and this command syncs it with online *ntpserver*.

```
$ ntpdate -s time.nist.gov
```

D.4 Open vSwitch with KVM

This section presents the installation and configuration of Open vSwitch on the Arndale board, and running KVM on top of Open vSwitch. The first step is to check if the KVM driver has been successfully installed by using the command

```
$ ls /dev/kvm
```

The installation of *openvswitch* daemon depends upon the modules: *stp.ko*, *llc.ko*, *bridge.ko*, and *vxlan.ko*. Before configuring Open vSwitch, we need to make sure these modules have been installed properly. A user can use the command "*lsmod modulename*" to check if a module is present or absent.

Next, we need to build Open vSwitch. It requires "*linux-headers*" or a source tree to build *openvswitch.ko* module. For this purpose, we can copy sources from *linux-linaro-lng-3.14.32* into the directory "*/lib/modules/3.14.32/build*" so that Open vSwitch is able to find dependent modules for its build. The version for Open vSwitch used for build is *openvswitch-2.3.10* as it is compatible with Linux kernel 3.14.32.

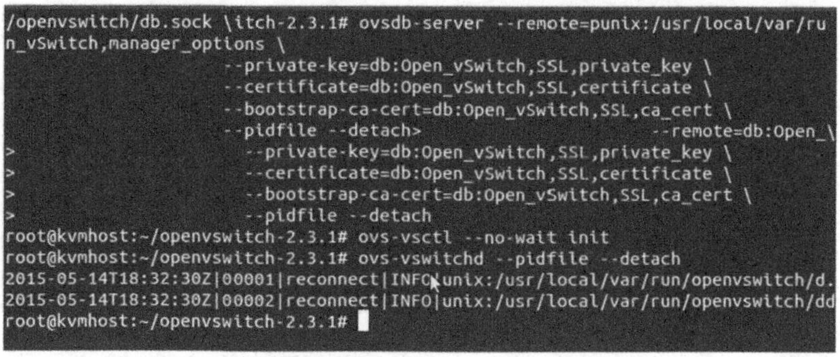

```
/openvswitch/db.sock \itch-2.3.1# ovsdb-server --remote=punix:/usr/local/var/ru
n_vSwitch,manager_options \
                     --private-key=db:Open_vSwitch,SSL,private_key \
                     --certificate=db:Open_vSwitch,SSL,certificate \
                     --bootstrap-ca-cert=db:Open_vSwitch,SSL,ca_cert \
                     --pidfile --detach>                        --remote=db:Open_\
>                    --private-key=db:Open_vSwitch,SSL,private_key \
>                    --certificate=db:Open_vSwitch,SSL,certificate \
>                    --bootstrap-ca-cert=db:Open_vSwitch,SSL,ca_cert \
>                    --pidfile --detach
root@kvmhost:~/openvswitch-2.3.1# ovs-vsctl --no-wait init
root@kvmhost:~/openvswitch-2.3.1# ovs-vswitchd --pidfile --detach
2015-05-14T18:32:30Z|00001|reconnect|INFO|unix:/usr/local/var/run/openvswitch/d.
2015-05-14T18:32:30Z|00002|reconnect|INFO|unix:/usr/local/var/run/openvswitch/dd
root@kvmhost:~/openvswitch-2.3.1#
```

Figure D.2: Open vSwitch Configuration.

The steps below are followed to install Open vSwitch:

```
$ apt-get update
$ apt-get install -y git automake autoconf gcc uml-utilities
  libtool build-essential git
$ wget http://openvswitch.org/releases/openvswitch-1.10.0.tar.gz
$ tar zxvf openvswitch-2.3.10.tar.gz
$ cd openvswitch-2.3.10
$ ./boot.sh
$ ./configure --with-linux=/lib/modules/`uname -r`/build
$ make && make install
$ insmod datapath/linux/openvswitch.ko
$ mkdir -p /usr/local/etc/openvswitch
$ ovsdb-tool create /usr/local/etc/openvswitch/conf.db
  vswitchd/vswitch.ovsschema
$ ovsdb-server -v --remote=punix:/usr/local/var/run/openvswitch/db.sock \
               --remote=db:Open_vSwitch,manager_options \
               --private-key=db:SSL,private_key \
               --certificate=db:SSL,certificate \
               --pidfile --detach --log-file
$ ovs-vsctl --no-wait init
$ ovs-vswitchd --pidfile --detach
$ ovs-vsctl show
```

Fig. D.2 shows the expected outcome after a correct configuration of Open vSwitch.

Now, we need to create custom versions of *qemu-ifup* and *qemu-ifdown* scripts that would be used in KVM configuration of guest OS. The custom versions will make use of Open vSwitch bridges [267]. The configuration files "*/etc/ovs-ifup*" and "*/etc/ovs-ifdown*" should be created for this purpose, which is done as follows:

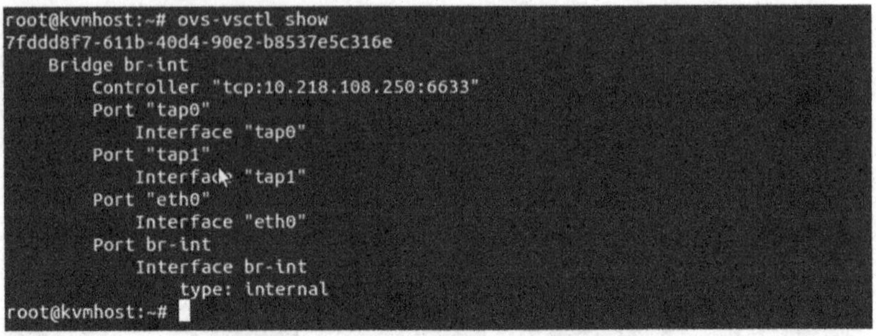

```
root@kvmhost:~# ovs-vsctl show
7fddd8f7-611b-40d4-90e2-b8537e5c316e
    Bridge br-int
        Controller "tcp:10.218.108.250:6633"
        Port "tap0"
            Interface "tap0"
        Port "tap1"
            Interface "tap1"
        Port "eth0"
            Interface "eth0"
        Port br-int
            Interface br-int
                type: internal
root@kvmhost:~# 
```

Figure D.3: Open vSwitch Interface Display.

```
$ vim /etc/ovs-ifup
  #!/bin/sh
  switch='br0'
  /sbin/ifconfig $1 0.0.0.0 up
  ovs-vsctl add-port ${switch} $1

$ vim /etc/ovs-ifdown
  #!/bin/sh
  switch='br0'
  /sbin/ifconfig $1 0.0.0.0 down
  ovs-vsctl del-port ${switch} $1
```

The next step is to add a bridge using Open vSwitch and a port to the bridge over which the guests can communicate. The steps for establishing this connection and configuring IP address for the bridge and gateway are as follows:

```
ovs-vsctl add-br br0
ovs-vsctl add-port br0 eth0
ovs-vsctl add-port br0 tap0
ovs-vsctl list port

#ifconfig eth0 0
ifconfig eth0 0.0.0.0 up
ifconfig tap0 0.0.0.0 up


ifconfig br0 10.218.108.16 netmask 255.255.248.0
route add default gw 10.218.104.1 br0
```

The commands shown in Fig. D.3 are used to verify the correct configuration for Open vSwitch.

The final task for bringing up the guest OS requires that the guest image *ubuntu.img*, guest device tree *guest-vexpress.dtb,* and guest kernel *guest-zImage* are already present on the SD

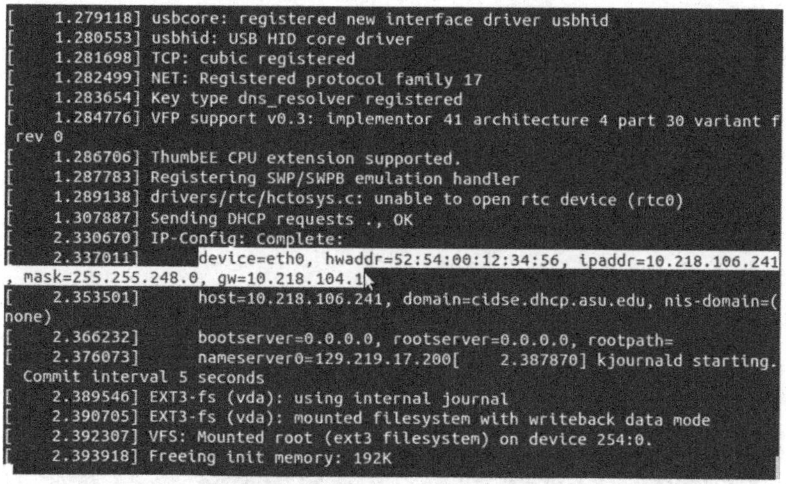

```
[    1.279118] usbcore: registered new interface driver usbhid
[    1.280553] usbhid: USB HID core driver
[    1.281698] TCP: cubic registered
[    1.282499] NET: Registered protocol family 17
[    1.283654] Key type dns_resolver registered
[    1.284776] VFP support v0.3: implementor 41 architecture 4 part 30 variant f
rev 0
[    1.286706] ThumbEE CPU extension supported.
[    1.287783] Registering SWP/SWPB emulation handler
[    1.289138] drivers/rtc/hctosys.c: unable to open rtc device (rtc0)
[    1.307887] Sending DHCP requests ., OK
[    2.330670] IP-Config: Complete:
[    2.337011]     device=eth0, hwaddr=52:54:00:12:34:56, ipaddr=10.218.106.241
, mask=255.255.248.0, gw=10.218.104.1
[    2.353501]     host=10.218.106.241, domain=cidse.dhcp.asu.edu, nis-domain=(
none)
[    2.366232]     bootserver=0.0.0.0, rootserver=0.0.0.0, rootpath=
[    2.376073]     nameserver0=129.219.17.200[    2.387870] kjournald starting.
Commit interval 5 seconds
[    2.389546] EXT3-fs (vda): using internal journal
[    2.390705] EXT3-fs (vda): mounted filesystem with writeback data mode
[    2.392307] VFS: Mounted root (ext3 filesystem) on device 254:0.
[    2.393918] Freeing init memory: 192K
```

Figure D.4: Guest OS boot-up using Open vSwitch.

card. We will issue the command to QEMU to boot up the guest OS on top of Open vSwitch as follows:

```
./QEMU-system-arm \
  -enable-kvm -kernel guest-zImage \
  -nographic -dtb ./guest-vexpress.dtb \
  -m 512 -M vexpress-a15 -cpu cortex-a15 \
  -netdev type=tap,id=net0,script=no,downscript=no,ifname="tap0" \
  -device virtio-net,transport=virtio-mmio.1,netdev=net0 \
  -device virtio-blk,drive=virtio-blk,transport=virtio-mmio.0 \
  -drive file=./ubuntu.img,id=virtio-blk,if=none \
  -append "earlyprintk console=ttyAMA0 mem=512M
  root=/dev/vda rw ip=dhcp --no-log
  virtio_mmio.device=1M@0x4e000000:74:0
  virtio_mmio.device=1M@0x4e100000:75:1"
```

Then, the guest OS will boot up and get IP address via DHCP, as it can be seen in Fig. D.4

Finally, the guest OS terminal will be visible and can be used for communication with other hosts or guest OS; see Fig. D.5.

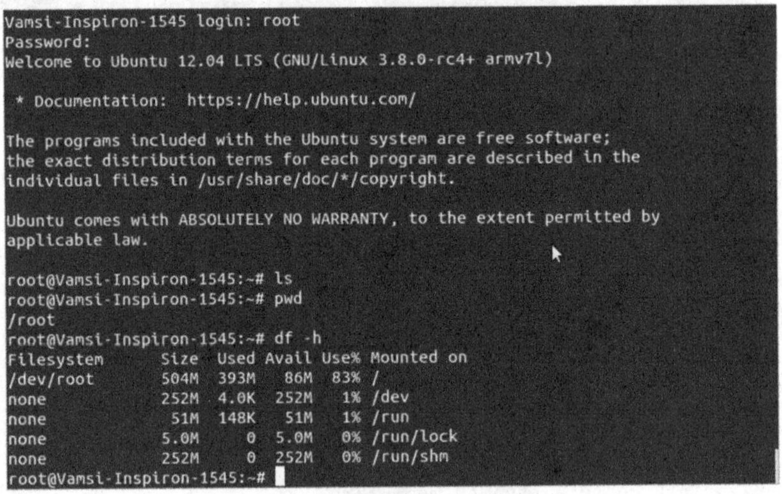

```
Vamsi-Inspiron-1545 login: root
Password:
Welcome to Ubuntu 12.04 LTS (GNU/Linux 3.8.0-rc4+ armv7l)

 * Documentation:  https://help.ubuntu.com/

The programs included with the Ubuntu system are free software;
the exact distribution terms for each program are described in the
individual files in /usr/share/doc/*/copyright.

Ubuntu comes with ABSOLUTELY NO WARRANTY, to the extent permitted by
applicable law.

root@Vamsi-Inspiron-1545:~# ls
root@Vamsi-Inspiron-1545:~# pwd
/root
root@Vamsi-Inspiron-1545:~# df -h
Filesystem      Size  Used Avail Use% Mounted on
/dev/root       504M  393M   86M  83% /
none            252M  4.0K  252M   1% /dev
none             51M  148K   51M   1% /run
none            5.0M     0  5.0M   0% /run/lock
none            252M     0  252M   0% /run/shm
root@Vamsi-Inspiron-1545:~#
```

Figure D.5: Ubuntu guest OS terminal.

Bibliography

[1] KVM, available at https://www.linux-kvm.org/page/Main_Page.

[2] VMware ESXi, available at https://my.vmware.com/web/vmware/info/slug/datacenter_cloud_infrastructure/vmware_vsphere/6_0#open_source.

[3] GPL V2, available at https://www.gnu.org/licenses/old-licenses/gpl-2.0.en.html.

[4] Apache License Version 2.0, available at https://www.apache.org/licenses/LICENSE-2.0.html.

[5] Linux Containers, available at https://linuxcontainers.org/.

[6] Linux VServer, available at http://linux-vserver.org/.

[7] Understanding and Configuring VLANs, available at http://www.cisco.com/c/en/us/td/docs/switches/lan/catalyst4500/12-2/25ew/configuration/guide/conf/vlans.html.

[8] Xvisor, available at http://xhypervisor.org/.

[9] Amazon EC2, https://aws.amazon.com/ec2/.

[10] Apache jena, https://jena.apache.org/index.html. (Accessed 30 January 2017).

[11] Chroot, available at https://en.wikipedia.org/wiki/Chroot.

[12] Facebook Caffe2, available at https://research.fb.com/downloads/caffe2/.

[13] Family educational rights and privacy act (FERPA), website is available at http://www2.ed.gov/policy/gen/guid/fpco/ferpa/index.html.

[14] Federal information security management act (FISMA) implementation project, website is available at http://csrc.nist.gov/groups/SMA/fisma/.

[15] Health insurance portability and accountability act, website is available at https://www.whitehouse.gov/administration/eop/ostp.

[16] Incommon, website is available at https://www.incommon.org/.

[17] Iot-lite ontology, https://www.w3.org/Submission/iot-lite/. (Accessed 30 January 2017).

[18] ISO/IEC DIS 20248: Information technology – Automatic identification and data capture techniques – Data structures – Digital signature meta structure.

[19] Lguest, available at http://lguest.ozlabs.org/.

[20] Linaro Networking Group (LNG), available at https://www.linaro.org/groups/lng/.

[21] Linux Run Project, available at https://en.wikipedia.org/wiki/Lxrun.

[22] lm-sensors, https://github.com/groeck/lm-sensors. (Accessed 30 January 2017).

[23] Mayo clinic, available at http://www.mayoclinic.org/.

[24] OAuth 2.0, the industry-standard protocol for authorization, available at https://oauth.net/2/. (Accessed 1 May 2017).

[25] Open Fog Consortium, available at https://www.openfogconsortium.org/.

[26] Open Virtual Format (OVF), available at https://www.dmtf.org/standards/ovf.

[27] Parrotcode: Parrot documentation, available at http://www.parrot.org/, access in 2017.

[28] Potassco, the Potsdam answer set solving collection, http://potassco.sourceforge.net/. (Accessed 30 January 2017).

[29] QEMU CPU Emulator, available at http://www.qemu-project.org/, and accessed in 2017.

[30] RabbitMQ, https://www.rabbitmq.com/. (Accessed 30 January 2017).

[31] Ruby on Rails, available at http://rubyonrails.org/.

[32] Semantic markup for web services, https://www.w3.org/Submission/OWL-S/. (Accessed 30 January 2017).

[33] Semantic sensor network ontology, https://www.w3.org/TR/vocab-ssn/. (Accessed 30 January 2017).

[34] The translational genomics research institute (TGen), available at https://tgen.org/.

[35] Virtual Open Systems, available at http://www.virtualopensystems.com/.

[36] VMware Workstation Player, available at https://my.vmware.com/web/vmware/free#desktop_end_user_computing/vmware_workstation_player/12_0.

[37] Web service modeling ontology, https://www.w3.org/Submission/WSMO/. (Accessed 30 January 2017).

[38] Weka: data mining software in java, http://www.cs.waikato.ac.nz/ml/weka/. (Accessed 30 January 2017).

[39] Wine Project, available at https://www.winehq.org.

[40] Withings API developer documentation, http://oauth.withings.com/api. (Accessed 30 January 2017).

[41] Withings body, https://www.withings.com/us/en/products/body. (Accessed 30 January 2017).

[42] Xtremelabs Speedtest, available at http://xtremelabs-speedtest.en.aptoide.com/?store_name=apps&app_id=2172058.

[43] SPARQL query language for RDF. [Online]. Available: http://www.w3.org/TR/rdf-sparql-query/, 2008.

[44] News Blog, available at https://searchenginewatch.com/sew/opinion/2353616/mobile-now-exceeds-pc-the-biggest-shift-since-the-internet-began, 2014.

[45] OMAP 5432, available at https://www.isee.biz/products/igep-processor-boards/igepv5-omap5432, visited May 2017.

[46] Samsung-Exynos-5250, available at https://www.notebookcheck.net/Samsung-Exynos-5250-Dual-SoC.86886.0.html, visited May 2017.

[47] E. Abebe, C. Ryan, A hybrid granularity graph for improving adaptive application partitioning efficacy in mobile computing environments, in: 10th IEEE International Symposium on Network Computing and Applications (NCA), IEEE, 2011, pp. 59–66.

[48] E. Abebe, C. Ryan, Adaptive application offloading using distributed abstract class graphs in mobile environments, Journal of Systems and Software 85 (12) (2012) 2755–2769.

[49] L. Allison, O. Tatsuaki, S. Amit, T. Katsuyuki, W. Brent, Fully secure functional encryption: attribute-based encryption and (hierarchical) inner product encryption, in: Theory and Applications of Cryptographic Techniques, Springer-Verlag, 2010, pp. 62–91.

[50] D. Aloni, Cooperative linux, in: Proceedings of the Linux Symposium, vol. 2, 2004, pp. 23–31.

[51] A. Alshalan, S. Pisharody, D. Huang, A survey of mobile VPN technologies, IEEE Communications Surveys & Tutorials 18 (2) (2016) 1177–1196.

[52] Apache Felix. [Online]. Available: http://felix.apache.org/site/index.html.

[53] Apache felix framework and google android, Apache Felix. [Online]. Available: http://felix.apache.org/site/apache-felix-framework-and-google-android.html.

[54] Apache Groovy, available at http://groovy-lang.org/.

[55] Arduino, Arduino UNO, http://www.arduino.cc/en/Main/ArduinoBoardUno, 2011.

[56] ARM, ARM® Architecture Reference Manual ARM® v7-A and ARM® v7-R. ARM Inc., 2013, ch. A1.1.

[57] J. Arnold, OpenStack Swift: Using, Administering, and Developing for Swift Object Storage, O'Reilly Media, Inc., 2014.

[58] J. Barbier, J. Bradley, J. Macaulay, R. Medcalf, C. Reberger, BYOD and virtualization: top 10 insights from Cisco IBSG horizons study, Viitattu 8 (2012) 2016.

[59] P. Barham, B. Dragovic, K. Fraser, S. Hand, T. Harris, A. Ho, R. Neugebauer, I. Pratt, A. Warfield, Xen and the art of virtualization, ACM SIGOPS Operating Systems Review 37 (5) (2003) 164–177.

[60] B. Baron, P. Spathis, M.D. de Amorim, M. Ammar, Cloud storage for mobile users using pre-positioned storage facilities, in: Proceedings of the 2nd Workshop on Experiences in the Design and Implementation of Smart Objects, ACM, 2016, pp. 11–16.

[61] S. Bechhofer, F.v. Harmelen, J. Hendler, I. Horrocks, D.L. McGuinness, P.F. Patel-Schneider, L.A. Stein, Owl web ontology language reference. [Online]. Available: http://www.w3.org/TR/owl-ref/, 2004.

[62] F. Bellard, QEMU, a fast and portable dynamic translator, in: USENIX Annual Technical Conference, FREENIX Track, 2005, pp. 41–46.

[63] J. Bethencourt, A. Sahai, B. Waters, Ciphertext-policy attribute-based encryption, in: IEEE Symposium on Security and Privacy, Washington, DC, USA, 2007, pp. 321–334.

[64] R. Biswas, K. Chowdhury, D. Agrawal, Attribute allocation and retrieval scheme for large-scale sensor networks, International Journal of Wireless Information Networks (2006).

[65] A. Boldyreva, V. Goyal, V. Kumar, Identity-based encryption with efficient revocation, in: Proceedings of the 15th ACM Conference on Computer and Communications Security, ACM, 2008, pp. 417–426.

[66] D. Boneh, M. Franklin, Identity-based encryption from the Weil pairing, in: Proceedings of the 21st Annual International Cryptology Conference on Advances in Cryptology, London, UK, 2001, pp. 213–229.

[67] F. Bonomi, R. Milito, J. Zhu, S. Addepalli, Fog computing and its role in the internet of things, in: Proceedings of the First Edition of the MCC Workshop on Mobile Cloud Computing, ACM, 2012, pp. 13–16.

[68] E. Borgia, The internet of things vision: key features, applications and open issues, Computer Communications 54 (2014) 1–31.

[69] T. Bray, J. Paoli, C.M. Sperberg-McQueen, E. Maler, F. Yergeau, Extensible markup language (XML), World Wide Web Journal 2 (4) (1997) 27–66.

[70] B. Butzin, F. Golatowski, D. Timmermann, Microservices approach for the internet of things, in: Emerging Technologies and Factory Automation (ETFA), 2016 IEEE 21st International Conference on, IEEE, 2016, pp. 1–6.

[71] A. Carzaniga, M. Rutherford, A. Wolf, A routing scheme for content-based networking, in: Proceedings of the IEEE International Conference on Computer Communications, ser. INFOCOM, 2004.

[72] J. Chakareski, Adaptive multiview video streaming: challenges and opportunities, Communications Magazine, IEEE 51 (5) (2013) 94–100.

[73] J. Che, C. Shi, Y. Yu, W. Lin, A synthetical performance evaluation of OpenVZ, Xen and KVM, in: Services Computing Conference (APSCC), 2010 IEEE Asia-Pacific, IEEE, 2010, pp. 587–594.

[74] J. Chen, H.W. Lim, S. Ling, H. Wang, K. Nguyen, Revocable identity-based encryption from lattices, in: Information Security and Privacy, Springer, 2012, pp. 390–403.

[75] M. Chen, Y. Zhang, Y. Li, S. Mao, V. Leung, EMC: emotion-aware mobile cloud computing in 5G, IEEE Network 29 (2) (2015) 32–38.

[76] M. Chen, J. Chen, T. Chang, Android/OSGi-based vehicular network management system, Computer Communications 34 (2011) 169–183.

[77] L. Cheung, C. Newport, Provably secure ciphertext policy ABE, in: Proceedings of the 14th ACM Conference on Computer and Communications Security, ACM, New York, NY, USA, 2007, pp. 456–465.

[78] M. Chiang, T. Zhang, Fog and IoT: an overview of research opportunities, IEEE Internet of Things Journal 3 (6) (2016) 854–864.

[79] S.N.T.-c. Chiueh, S. Brook, A survey on virtualization technologies, RPE Report (2005) 1–42.

[80] B.-G. Chun, S. Ihm, P. Maniatis, M. Naik, A. Patti, CloneCloud: elastic execution between mobile device and cloud, in: Proceedings of the Sixth Conference on Computer Systems, ACM, 2011, pp. 301–314.

[81] C.J. Chung, H. Wu, Y. Deng, V-lab report for fall 2013, Tech. Rep., Arizona State University, 2013.

[82] Cisco, Cisco visual networking index: forecast and methodology, 2014–2019. [Online]. Available: http://tinyurl.com/mev32z8, 2015.

[83] C.V.N.I. Cisco, Global mobile data traffic forecast update, 2015–2020 white paper, 2016.

[84] CloudStack, Apache CloudStack, available at https://cloudstack.apache.org/.

[85] A. Corradi, M. Fanelli, L. Foschini, VM consolidation: a real case based on OpenStack Cloud, Future Generation Computer Systems 32 (2014) 118–127.

[86] B. Costa, P.F. Pires, F.C. Delicato, P. Merson, Evaluating a representational state transfer (rest) architecture: What is the impact of rest in my architecture?, in: 2014 IEEE/IFIP Conference on Software Architecture (WICSA), 2014, pp. 105–114.

[87] A. Covert, Google Drive, iCloud, Dropbox and more compared: what's the best cloud option?, in: Technical Review, 2012.

[88] D. Crockford, The application/json media type for javascript object notation (JSON), 2006.

[89] E. Cuervo, A. Balasubramanian, D. Cho, A. Wolman, S. Saroiu, R. Chandra, P. Bahl, MAUI: making smartphones last longer with code offload, in: Proceedings of the 8th International Conference on Mobile Systems, Applications, and Services, ACM, 2010, pp. 49–62.

[90] C. Dall, J. Nieh, KVM/ARM: experiences building the Linux ARM hypervisor, Tech. Rep. CUCS-010-13, Department of Computer Science, Columbia University, 2013.

[91] C. Dall, J. Nieh, KVM/ARM: the design and implementation of the Linux ARM hypervisor, ACM SIGPLAN Notices 49 (4) (2014) 333–348.

[92] C. Dall, J. Nieh, KVM for ARM, in: Proceedings of the 12th Annual Linux Symposium, 2010.

[93] C. Dall, J. Nieh, Supporting KVM on the ARM architecture, lwn.net, 2013.

[94] C. Dall, J. Nieh, The design and implementation of the Linux ARM hypervisor, in: Proceedings of the 19th International Conference on Architectural Support for Programming Languages and Operating Systems, 2014.

[95] C. Dannewitz, J. Golic, B. Ohlman, B. Ahlgren, Secure naming for a network of information, in: Proceedings of the IEEE International Conference on Computer Communications, ser. INFOCOM, 2010.

[96] A. Davies, A. Orsaria, Scale out with GlusterFS, Linux Journal 2013 (235) (2013) 1.

[97] V. Daza, J. Herranz, P. Morillo, C. Ràfols, Extended access structures and their cryptographic applications, IACR Cryptology ePrint Archive 2008 (2008) 502.

[98] J. Dike, A user-mode port of the Linux kernel, in: Annual Linux Showcase & Conference, 2000.

[99] N. Doshi, D. Jinwala, Hidden access structure ciphertext policy attribute based encryption with constant length ciphertext, in: Advanced Computing, Networking and Security, Springer-Verlag, 2012, pp. 515–523.

[100] N. Dragoni, S. Giallorenzo, A.L. Lafuente, M. Mazzara, F. Montesi, R. Mustafin, L. Safina, Microservices: yesterday, today, and tomorrow, arXiv preprint arXiv:1606.04036, 2016.

[101] DroneCode, Ardu pilot, http://ardupilot.com/, 2014.

[102] B. Eckel, Thinking in Java, 4th ed., Prentice Hall, 2006.

[103] P. Emmerich, D. Raumer, F. Wohlfart, G. Carle, Performance characteristics of virtual switching, in: Cloud Networking (CloudNet) 2014 IEEE 3rd International Conference, 2014.

[104] K. Emura, A. Miyaji, A. Nomura, K. Omote, M. Soshi, A ciphertext-policy attribute-based encryption scheme with constant ciphertext length, in: Information Security Practice and Experience, Xi'an, China, 2009, pp. 13–23.

[105] R. Fakoor, M. Raj, A. Nazi, M.D. Francesco, S.K. Das, An integrated cloud-based framework for mobile phone sensing, in: Proceedings of the ACM SIGCOMM MCC Workshop, 2012.

[106] D. Farinacci, P. Traina, S. Hanks, T. Li, Generic routing encapsulation (GRE), 1994.

[107] N. Fernando, S.W. Loke, W. Rahayu, Mobile cloud computing: a survey, Future Generation Computer Systems 29 (1) (2013) 84–106.

[108] R.T. Fielding, R.N. Taylor, Principled design of the modern web architecture, ACM Transactions on Internet Technology (TOIT) 2 (2) (2002) 115–150.

[109] S. Flur, K.E. Gray, C. Pulte, S. Sarkar, A. Sezgin, L. Maranget, W. Deacon, P. Sewell, Modelling the ARMv8 architecture, operationally: concurrency and ISA, ACM SIGPLAN Notices 51 (1) (2016) 608–621.

[110] N. Fotiou, G.F. Marias, G.C. Polyzos, Access control enforcement delegation for information-centric networking architectures, in: Proceedings of the ICN Workshop on Information-centric Networking, ser. ICN, 2012.

[111] N. Fotiou, P. Nikander, D. Trossen, G. Polyzos, Developing information networking further: from PSIRP to PURSUIT, in: Lecture Notes of the Institute for Computer Sciences, Social Informatics and Telecommunications Engineering, 2012.

[112] K. Frikken, M. Atallah, J. Li, Attribute-based access control with hidden policies and hidden credentials, IEEE Transactions on Computers 55 (Oct. 2006) 1259–1270.

[113] Market Trends: Cloud-Based Security Services Market, Worldwide, https://www.gartner.com/doc/. (Accessed 16 November 2016).

[114] M. Gerla, Vehicular cloud computing, in: 2012 The 11th Annual Mediterranean Ad Hoc Networking Workshop (Med-Hoc-Net), 2012, pp. 152–155.

[115] A. Ghosh, P.K. Gajar, S. Rai, Bring your own device (BYOD): security risks and mitigating strategies, Journal of Global Research in Computer Science 4 (4) (2013) 62–70.

[116] I. Giurgiu, O. Riva, G. Alonso, Dynamic software deployment from clouds to mobile devices, in: Middleware, Springer, 2012, pp. 394–414.

[117] I. Giurgiu, O. Riva, D. Juric, I. Krivulev, G. Alonso, Calling the cloud: enabling mobile phones as interfaces to cloud applications, in: Middleware, Springer, 2009, pp. 83–102.

[118] J. Goodacre, A. Cambridge, The evolution of the ARM architecture towards big data and the data-centre, in: 8th Workshop on Virtualization in High-Performance Cloud Computing, 2013.

[119] Google Inc., http://www.google.com/wallet.

[120] V. Goyal, O. Pandey, A. Sahai, B. Waters, Attribute-based encryption for fine-grained access control of encrypted data, in: ACM Conference on Computer and Communications Security, Alexandria, Virginia, USA, 2006, pp. 89–98.

[121] G. Gruman, Android for work brings container security to google play apps, Infoworld (Feb 25, 2015).

[122] R.P. Guidance, A.E.-I. Credentials, Federal identity, credential, and access management trust framework solutions.

[123] K. Ha, M. Satyanarayanan, OpenStack++ for cloudlet deployment, School of Computer Science Carnegie Mellon University Pittsburgh, 2015.

[124] K. Habak, M. Ammar, K.A. Harras, E. Zegura, Femto clouds: leveraging mobile devices to provide cloud service at the edge, in: Cloud Computing (CLOUD), 2015 IEEE 8th International Conference on, IEEE, 2015, pp. 9–16.

[125] R. Hall, K. Pauls, S. McCulloch, D. Savage, OSGi in Action: Creating Modular Applications in Java, Manning Publications Co., 2011.

[126] B. Han, V. Gopalakrishnan, L. Ji, S. Lee, Network function virtualization: challenges and opportunities for innovations, IEEE Communications Magazine 53 (2) (2015) 90–97.

[127] D. Hardt, The OAuth 2.0 authorization framework, 2012.

[128] J. Herranz, F. Laguillaumie, C. Ràfols, Constant size ciphertexts in threshold attribute-based encryption, in: Practice and Theory in Public Key Cryptography, Paris, France, 2010, pp. 19–34.

[129] J. Hildebrand, P. Millard, R. Eatmon, P. Saint-Andre, XEP-0030: Service Discovery, XMPP Standards Foundation (XSF), http://xmpp.org/extensions/xep-0030.html, 2008.

[130] J. Honeycutt, Microsoft virtual PC 2004 technical overview, Microsoft, Nov, 2003.

[131] C.-Y. Hsu, C.-S. Yang, L.-C. Yu, C.-F. Lin, H.-H. Yao, D.-Y. Chen, K.R. Lai, P.-C. Chang, Development of a cloud-based service framework for energy conservation in a sustainable intelligent transportation system, International Journal of Production Economics (2014).

[132] Samsung Exynos 5250 Dual, http://www.notebookcheck.net/Samsung-Exynos-5250-Dual-SoC.86886.0.html, 2013.

[133] V. Hu, D.F. Ferraiolo, D.R. Kuhn, R.N. Kacker, Y. Lei, Implementing and managing policy rules in attribute based access control, in: Information Reuse and Integration (IRI), 2015 IEEE International Conference on, IEEE, 2015, pp. 518–525.

[134] V.C. Hu, D. Ferraiolo, D.R. Kuhn, Assessment of access control systems, US Department of Commerce, National Institute of Standards and Technology, 2006.

[135] V.C. Hu, D. Ferraiolo, R. Kuhn, A.R. Friedman, A.J. Lang, M.M. Cogdell, A. Schnitzer, K. Sandlin, R. Miller, K. Scarfone, et al., Guide to attribute based access control (ABAC) definition and considerations (draft), NIST Special Publication 800 (162) (2013).

[136] V.C. Hu, D.R. Kuhn, D.F. Ferraiolo, Attribute-based access control, Computer 48 (2) (2015) 85–88.

[137] D. Huang, Pseudonym-based cryptography for anonymous communications in mobile ad hoc networks, International Journal of Security and Networks 2 (3) (2007) 272–283.

[138] D. Huang, Mobile cloud computing, IEEE COMSOC Multimedia Communications Technical Committee (MMTC) E-Letter 6 (10) (October 2011) 27–31.

[139] D. Huang, M. Verma, ASPE: attribute based secure policy enforcement for data access control in vehicular ad hoc networks, Ad Hoc Networks Journal (Special Issue of Privacy & Security in WSNs) (2009).

[140] D. Huang, T. Xing, H. Wu, Mobile cloud computing service models: a user-centric approach, IEEE Network 27 (5) (2013) 6–11.

[141] D. Huang, X. Zhang, M. Kang, J. Luo, MobiCloud: building secure cloud framework for mobile computing and communication, in: Fifth IEEE International Symposium on Service Oriented System Engineering (SOSE), 2010, pp. 27–34.

[142] D. Huang, Z. Zhou, Z. Yan, Gradual identity exposure using attribute-based encryption, in: IEEE Conference on Social Computing (SocialCom), Aug. 2010, pp. 881–888.

[143] D. Huang, Z. Zhou, Y. Zhu, Gradual identity exposure using attribute-based encryption, in: Proceedings of the Second IEEE International Conference on Information Privacy, Security, Risk and Trust (PASSAT), 2010.

[144] J. Hughes, E. Maler, Security assertion markup language (SAML) v2.0 technical overview, OASIS SSTC Working Draft sstc-saml-tech-overview-2.0-draft-08, 2005, pp. 29–38.

[145] J. Hur, D.K. Noh, Attribute-based access control with efficient revocation in data outsourcing systems, IEEE Transactions on Parallel and Distributed Systems 22 (7) (2011) 1214–1221.

[146] IEEE, IEEE Std 802.1Q-1998, IEEE standard, available at http://ieeexplore.ieee.org/xpl/RecentIssue.jsp?punumber=6080, 1998.

[147] A. Inc., Juno ARM development platform, http://www.arm.com/products/tools/development-boards/versatile-express/juno-arm-development-platform.php, 2014.

[148] K. Initiative, et al., Identity assurance framework, 2013.

[149] Intel Corporation, Intel DPDK vSwitch, available at https://github.com/01org/dpdk-ovs, visited May 2017.

[150] S. Jahid, P. Mittal, N. Borisov, EASiER: encryption-based access control in social networks with efficient revocation, in: Proceedings of the 6th ACM Symposium on Information, Computer and Communications Security, ACM, 2011, pp. 411–415.

[151] L.P. Jain, W.J. Scheirer, T.E. Boult, Quality of experience, in: IEEE Multimedia, Citeseer, 2004.

[152] D. Jaramillo, N. Katz, B. Bodin, W. Tworek, R. Smart, T. Cook, Cooperative solutions for bring your own device (BYOD), IBM Journal of Research and Development 57 (6) (2013).

[153] W. Jung, C. Kang, C. Yoon, D. Kim, H. Cha, Devscope: a nonintrusive and online power analysis tool for smartphone hardware components, in: Proceedings of the Eighth IEEE/ACM/IFIP International Conference on Hardware/Software Codesign and System Synthesis, ACM, 2012, pp. 353–362.

[154] P.-H. Kamp, R.N. Watson, Jails: confining the omnipotent root, in: Proceedings of the 2nd International SANE Conference, vol. 43, 2000, p. 116.

[155] G. Kane, MIPS RISC Architecture, Prentice-Hall, 1988.

[156] H. Kang, M. Le, S. Tao, Container and microservice driven design for cloud infrastructure DevOps, in: Cloud Engineering (IC2E), 2016 IEEE International Conference on, IEEE, 2016, pp. 202–211.

[157] D. Karaboga, B. Akay, A comparative study of artificial bee colony algorithm, Applied Mathematics and Computation 214 (1) (2009) 108–132.

[158] J. Katz, A. Sahai, B. Waters, Predicate encryption supporting disjunctions, polynomial equations, and inner products, in: Proc. of EUROCRYPT 2008, Springer-Verlag, 2008, pp. 146–162.

[159] S. Kaur, J. Singh, N.S. Ghumman, Network programmability using POX controller, in: ICCCS International Conference on Communication, Computing & Systems, IEEE, 2014, p. 138.

[160] R. Kemp, N. Palmer, T. Kielmann, H. Bal, Cuckoo: a computation offloading framework for smartphones, in: Mobile Computing, Applications, and Services, Springer, 2012, pp. 59–79.

[161] S. Keshav, R. Sharma, S. Chuang, Dynamically modifying the resources of a virtual server, 2006, US Patent 6,985,937.

[162] A.R. Khan, M. Othman, S.A. Madani, S.U. Khan, A survey of mobile cloud computing application models, Communications Surveys & Tutorials, IEEE 16 (1) (2014) 393–413.

[163] H. Kim, N. Feamster, Improving network management with software defined networking, IEEE Communications Magazine 51 (2) (2013) 114–119.

[164] A. Kivity, Y. Kamay, D. Laor, U. Lublin, A. Liguori, KVM: the Linux virtual machine monitor, in: Proceedings of the Linux Symposium, vol. 1, 2007, pp. 225–230.

[165] M.B. Kjærgaard, J. Langdal, T. Godsk, T. Toftkjær, EnTracked: energy-efficient robust position tracking for mobile devices, in: Proceedings of the 7th International Conference on Mobile Systems, Applications, and Services, ACM, 2009, pp. 221–234.

[166] J. Kjeldskov, Mobile interactions in context: a designerly way toward digital ecology, Synthesis Lectures on Human-Centered Informatics 7 (1) (2014) 1–119.

[167] T. Koponen, M. Chawla, B.-G. Chun, A. Ermolinskiy, K.H. Kim, S. Shenker, I. Stoica, A data-oriented (and beyond) network architecture, in: Proceedings of the Conference on Applications, Technologies, Architectures, and Protocols for Computer Communications, 2007.

[168] S. Kosta, A. Aucinas, P. Hui, R. Mortier, X. Zhang, Unleashing the power of mobile cloud computing using ThinkAir, arXiv preprint arXiv:1105.3232, 2011.

[169] S. Kosta, A. Aucinas, P. Hui, R. Mortier, X. Zhang, ThinkAir: dynamic resource allocation and parallel execution in the cloud for mobile code offloading, in: 2012 Proceedings IEEE INFOCOM, 2012, pp. 945–953.

[170] D. Kovachev, Framework for computation offloading in mobile cloud computing, IJIMAI 1 (7) (2012) 6–15.

[171] D. Kovachev, T. Yu, R. Klamma, Adaptive computation offloading from mobile devices into the cloud, in: Parallel and Distributed Processing with Applications (ISPA), 2012 IEEE 10th International Symposium on, IEEE, 2012, pp. 784–791.

[172] A. Krylovskiy, M. Jahn, E. Patti, Designing a smart city internet of things platform with microservice architecture, in: Future Internet of Things and Cloud (FiCloud), 2015 3rd International Conference on, IEEE, 2015, pp. 25–30.

[173] M. Lasserre, V. Kompella, Virtual private lan service (VPLS) using label distribution protocol (LDP) signaling, 2007.

[174] K. Lawton, Plex86 x86 virtual machine project, Software Package 2004 (2003) 47.

[175] K. Lawton, B. Denney, N.D. Guarneri, V. Ruppert, C. Bothamy, M. Calabrese, Bochs x86 PC emulator users manual, 2003.

[176] L. Xu, L. Li, V. Nagarajan, D. Huang, W.-T. Tsai, Secure web referral services for mobile cloud computing, in: IEEE 7th International Symposium on Service-Oriented System Engineering, 2013.

[177] E. Lee, E.-K. Lee, M. Gerla, S.Y. Oh, Vehicular cloud networking: architecture and design principles, IEEE Communications Magazine 52 (2) (2014) 148–155.

[178] S.-J. Lee, M. Gerla, Dynamic load-aware routing in ad hoc networks, in: Communications, 2001. ICC 2001. IEEE International Conference on, vol. 10, IEEE, 2001, pp. 3206–3210.

[179] J. Lewis, M. Fowler, Microservices – a definition of this new architectural term, 2014.

[180] A. Lewko, A. Sahai, B. Waters, Revocation systems with very small private keys, in: Security and Privacy (SP), 2010 IEEE Symposium on, IEEE, 2010, pp. 273–285.

[181] A. Lewko, B. Waters, Decentralizing attribute-based encryption, in: Advances in Cryptology–EUROCRYPT 2011, 2011, pp. 568–588.

[182] B. Li, D. Huang, Z. Wang, Y. Zhu, Attribute-based access control for ICN naming scheme, IEEE Transactions on Dependable and Secure Computing (2016).

[183] B. Li, A.P. Verleker, D. Huang, Z. Wang, Y. Zhu, Attribute-based access control for ICN naming scheme, in: Proceedings of the 17th ACM Conference on Computer and Communications Security, IEEE, 2014.

[184] B. Li, Z. Wang, D. Huang, An efficient and anonymous attribute-based group setup scheme, in: Global Communications Conference (GLOBECOM), 2013 IEEE, IEEE, 2013, pp. 861–866.

[185] B. Libert, D. Vergnaud, Adaptive-id secure revocable identity-based encryption, in: Topics in Cryptology – CT-RSA 2009, Springer, 2009, pp. 1–15.

[186] Z.S. Lim, Setting up KVM, https://wiki.linaro.org/ZiShenLim/sandbox/SettingUpKVM, 2013.

[187] J. Lin, C. Dyer, Data-intensive text processing with MapReduce, Synthesis Lectures on Human Language Technologies 3 (1) (2010) 1–177.

[188] K. Liu, Applied Markov Decision Processes, Tsinghua University Press, 2004.

[189] Y. Liu, An energy-efficient multisite offloading algorithm for mobile devices, International Journal of Distributed Sensor Networks 2013 (2013).

[190] D. Lu, Z. Li, D. Huang, X. Lu, Y. Deng, A. Chowdhary, B. Li, VC-bots: a vehicular cloud computing testbed with mobile robots, in: Proceedings of the First International Workshop on Internet of Vehicles and Vehicles of Internet, ACM, 2016, pp. 31–36.

[191] L. Lynch, Inside the identity management game, IEEE Internet Computing 15 (5) (2011) 78–82.

[192] B. Lynn, The pairing-based cryptography library. [Online]. Available: https://crypto.stanford.edu/pbc/, 2006.

[193] B. Lynn, Type A internals. [Online]. Available: http://tinyurl.com/gs9s8y9, 2006.

[194] Mark Walshy, Gartner: mobile to outpace desktop web by 2013, Online Media Daily, 2010.

[195] E. McCluskey, Minimization of Boolean functions, Bell System Technical Journal 35 (5) (1956) 1417–1444.

[196] J.C. McCullough, Y. Agarwal, J. Chandrashekar, S. Kuppuswamy, A.C. Snoeren, R.K. Gupta, Evaluating the effectiveness of model-based power characterization, in: USENIX Annual Technical Conf., 2011.

[197] N. McKeown, T. Anderson, H. Balakrishnan, G. Parulkar, L. Peterson, J. Rexford, S. Shenker, J. Turner, OpenFlow: enabling innovation in campus networks, ACM SIGCOMM Computer Communication Review 38 (2) (2008) 69–74.

[198] M. McLarty, Learn from SOA: 5 lessons for the microservices era, InfoWorld, available at http://www.infoworld.com/article/3080611/application-development/learning-from-soa-5-lessons-for-the-microservices-era.html, 2016.

[199] J. Medved, R. Varga, A. Tkacik, K. Gray, OpenDaylight: towards a model-driven SDN controller architecture, in: A World of Wireless, Mobile and Multimedia Networks (WoWMoM), 2014 IEEE 15th International Symposium on, IEEE, 2014, pp. 1–6.

[200] P. Mell, T. Grance, The NIST definition of cloud computing, 2011.

[201] D. Merkel, Docker: lightweight Linux containers for consistent development and deployment, Linux Journal 2014 (239) (2014) 2.

[202] Microsoft, Microsoft Hyper-V, available at www.microsoft.com/HyperV.

[203] Microsoft, Microsoft Hyper-V downloading site, available at https://www.microsoft.com/en-us/evalcenter/evaluate-hyper-v-server-2012-r2.

[204] P. Millard, P. Saint-Andre, R. Meijer, XEP-0060: Publish-Subscribe, XMPP Standards Foundation (XSF), http://xmpp.org/extensions/xep-0060.html, 2010.

[205] J.S. Miller, S. Ragsdale, The Common Language Infrastructure Annotated Standard, Addison-Wesley Professional, 2004.

[206] R. Mittal, A. Kansal, R. Chandra, Empowering developers to estimate app energy consumption, in: Proceedings of the 18th Annual International Conference on Mobile Computing and Networking, ACM, 2012, pp. 317–328.

[207] F. Montesi, J. Weber, Circuit breakers, discovery, and API gateways in microservices, arXiv preprint arXiv:1609.05830, 2016.

[208] A. Mtibaa, A. Fahim, K.A. Harras, M.H. Ammar, Towards resource sharing in mobile device clouds: power balancing across mobile devices, ACM SIGCOMM Computer Communication Review 43 (4) (2013) 51–56.

[209] A. Mtibaa, K.A. Harras, K. Habak, M. Ammar, E.W. Zegura, Towards mobile opportunistic computing, in: Cloud Computing (CLOUD), 2015 IEEE 8th International Conference on, IEEE, 2015, pp. 1111–1114.

[210] M. Nabeel, E. Bertino, Attribute based group key management, Technical Report CERIAS TR 2010, Purdue University, 2010.

[211] Named data, ndn-cxx: NDN C++ library with experimental extensions 0.3.1-6-ga76bbc9 documentation. [Online]. Available: http://named-data.net/doc/ndn-cxx/current/, 2015.

[212] Named data project, NFD – named data networking forwarding Daemon 0.3.1 documentation. [Online]. Available: http://named-data.net/doc/NFD/current/, 2015.

[213] D. Neumann, C. Bodenstein, O.F. Rana, R. Krishnaswamy, STACEE: enhancing storage clouds using edge devices, in: Proceedings of the 1st ACM/IEEE Workshop on Autonomic Computing in Economics, 2010.

[214] S. Newman, Building Microservices, O'Reilly Media, Inc., 2015.

[215] Nike Inc., http://www.nike.com.

[216] T. Nishide, K. Yoneyama, K. Ohta, Attribute-based encryption with partially hidden encryptor-specified access structures, in: Applied Cryptography and Network Security, ser. ACNS'08, New York, NY, USA, 2008, pp. 111–129.

[217] J. Niu, W. Song, M. Atiquzzaman, Bandwidth-adaptive partitioning for distributed execution optimization of mobile applications, Journal of Network and Computer Applications 37 (2014) 334–347.

[218] J. Oberheide, E. Cooke, F. Jahanian, CloudAV: N-version antivirus in the network cloud, in: Proceedings of the 17th USENIX Security Symposium, San Jose, CA, July 2008.

[219] J. Oltsik, A multitude of mobile security issues, 2010.

[220] OpenStack, available at https://www.openstack.org/.

[221] Oracle VirtualBox, VirtualBox, available at https://www.virtualbox.org/.

[222] Open Services Gateway initiative (OSGi), available at http://www.osgi.org/Main/HomePage, Open Source.

[223] OSGi Core Release 5, OSGi Alliance, http://www.osgi.org/Release5/HomePage, March 2012.

[224] S. Ou, Y. Wu, K. Yang, B. Zhou, Performance analysis of fault-tolerant offloading systems for pervasive services in mobile wireless environments, in: IEEE International Conference on Communications (ICC), IEEE, 2008, pp. 1856–1860.

[225] I. Parallels, An introduction to OS virtualization and parallels virtuozzo containers, Parallels, Inc., Tech. Rep., 2010.

[226] C. Pautasso, O. Zimmermann, F. Leymann, Restful web services vs. "big" web services: making the right architectural decision, in: Proceedings of the 17th International Conference on World Wide Web, ACM, 2008, pp. 805–814.

[227] B. Pfaff, J. Pettit, T. Koponen, E.J. Jackson, A. Zhou, J. Rajahalme, J. Gross, A. Wang, J. Stringer, P. Shelar, et al., The design and implementation of open vSwitch, in: NSDI, 2015, pp. 117–130.

[228] T. Pham-Gia, N. Turkkan, System availability in a gamma alternating renewal process, Naval Research Logistics (NRL) 46 (7) (1999) 822–844.

[229] T.C. Project, Sandbox, Last accessed February 2017.

[230] I. Psaras, W.K. Chai, G. Pavlou, Probabilistic in-network caching for information-centric networks, in: Proceedings of the ICN Workshop on Information-centric Networking, ser. ICN, 2012.

[231] M.-R. Ra, B. Priyantha, A. Kansal, J. Liu, Improving energy efficiency of personal sensing applications with heterogeneous multi-processors, in: Proceedings of the 2012 ACM Conference on Ubiquitous Computing, ACM, 2012, pp. 1–10.

[232] D. Recordon, D. Reed, OpenID 2.0: a platform for user-centric identity management, in: Proceedings of the Second ACM Workshop on Digital Identity Management, 2006, p. 16.

[233] M. Rosenblum, VMwares virtual platform, in: Proceedings of Hot Chips, vol. 1999, 1999, pp. 185–196.

[234] M. Ryden, K. Oh, A. Chandra, J. Weissman, Nebula: distributed edge cloud for data intensive computing, in: Cloud Engineering (IC2E), 2014 IEEE International Conference on, IEEE, 2014, pp. 57–66.

[235] A. Sahai, B. Waters, Fuzzy identity-based encryption, 2005, pp. 457–473.

[236] K.M. Saipullah, A. Anuar, N.A. Ismail, Y. Soo, Measuring power consumption for image processing on android smartphone, American Journal of Applied Sciences 9 (12) (2012) 2052.

[237] M. Satyanarayanan, P. Bahl, R. Caceres, N. Davies, The case for VM-based cloudlets in mobile computing, Pervasive Computing, IEEE 8 (4) (2009) 14–23.

[238] M. Satyanarayanan, Elijah: Cloudlet-based Mobile Computing, http://elijah.cs.cmu.edu/. (Accessed 13 May 2016). [Online].

[239] D. Seal, ARM Architecture Reference Manual, Pearson Education, 2001.

[240] N. Shang, M. Nabeel, F. Paci, E. Bertino, A privacy-preserving approach to policy-based content dissemination, in: Data Engineering (ICDE), 2010 IEEE 26th International Conference on, IEEE, 2010, pp. 944–955.

[241] S. Sheikholeslam, C.A. Desoer, Longitudinal control of a platoon of vehicles, in: American Control Conference, 1990, IEEE, 1990, pp. 291–296.

[242] Z. Shelby, K. Hartke, C. Bormann, The constrained application protocol (COAP), 2014.

[243] C. Shi, M.H. Ammar, E.W. Zegura, M. Naik, Computing in cirrus clouds: the challenge of intermittent connectivity, in: Proceedings of the First Edition of the MCC Workshop on Mobile Cloud Computing, ACM, 2012, pp. 23–28.

[244] C. Shi, P. Pandurangan, K. Ni, J. Yang, M. Ammar, M. Naik, E. Zegura, IC-cloud: computation offloading to an intermittently-connected cloud, Tech. Rep., Georgia Institute of Technology, 2013.

[245] D. Shin, K. Kim, N. Chang, W. Lee, Y. Wang, Q. Xie, M. Pedram, Online estimation of the remaining energy capacity in mobile systems considering system-wide power consumption and battery characteristics, in: 18th Asia and South Pacific Design Automation Conference (ASP-DAC), IEEE, 2013, pp. 59–64.

[246] M.-K. Shin, K.-H. Nam, H.-J. Kim, Software-defined networking (SDN): a reference architecture and open APIs, in: ICT Convergence (ICTC), 2012 International Conference on, IEEE, 2012, pp. 360–361.

[247] V. Shoup, Lower bounds for discrete logarithms and related problems, in: Proceedings of International Conference on the Theory and Application of Cryptographic Techniques, ser. EUROCRYPT, 1997.

[248] S. Singh, A trust based approach for secure access control in information centric network, International Journal of Information and Network Security (2012).

[249] K. Sinha, M. Kulkarni, Techniques for fine-grained, multi-site computation offloading, in: IEEE/ACM International Symposium on Cluster, Cloud and Grid Computing (CCGrid), IEEE, 2011, pp. 184–194.

[250] M. Smit, M. Shtern, B. Simmons, M. Litoiu, Partitioning applications for hybrid and federated clouds, in: Proceedings of the 2012 Conference of the Center for Advanced Studies on Collaborative Research, IBM Corp., 2012, pp. 27–41.

[251] A. Scarfo, New security perspectives around BYOD, in: Seventh International Conference on Broadband, Wireless Computing, Communication and Applications (BWCCA), 2012.

[252] Springsource Bundle Repository, SpringSource. [Online]. Available: http://ebr.springsource.com/repository/app/.

[253] O. Standard, OASIS advanced message queuing protocol (AMQP) version 1.0, 2012.

[254] O. Standard, MQTT version 3.1.1. [Online]. Available: http://docs.oasis-open.org/mqtt/mqtt/v3.1.1/mqtt-v3.1.1.html, 2015.

[255] Stanford Open Flow Team, OpenFlow Switch Specification, version 1.0.0, http://www.openflowswitch.org/documents/openflow-spec-v1.0.0.pdf, 2010.

[256] S.R. Steinhubl, E.D. Muse, E.J. Topol, Can mobile health technologies transform health care?, JAMA 310 (22) (2013) 2395–2396.

[257] P. Stued, I. Mohomed, D. Terry, WhereStore: location-based data storage for mobile devices interacting with the cloud, in: Proceedings of the 1st ACM Workshop on Mobile Cloud Computing & Services: Social Networks and Beyond, 2010.

[258] Y. Sun, S.K. Fayaz, Y. Guo, V. Sekar, Y. Jin, M.A. Kaafar, S. Uhlig, Trace-driven analysis of ICN caching algorithms on video-on-demand workloads, in: Proceedings of the ACM International Conference on Emerging Networking Experiments and Technologies, 2014.

[259] V.O. Systems, Virtual open systems, http://www.virtualopensystems.com, 2013.

[260] M. Technology, Bring your own device, 2012.

[261] J. Thönes, Microservices, IEEE Software 32 (1) (2015) 113–116.

[262] S. Tilkov, The modern cloud-based platform, IEEE Software 32 (2) (2015) 113–116.

[263] A. Tootoonchian, Y. Ganjali, HyperFlow: a distributed control plane for OpenFlow, in: INM/WREN'10 Proceedings of the 2010 Internet Network Management Conference on Research on Enterprise Networking, 2010.

[264] W. Tsai, C. Fan, Y. Chen, R. Paul, J.-Y. Chung, Architecture classification for SOA-based applications, in: Ninth IEEE International Symposium on Object and Component-Oriented Real-Time Distributed Computing, 2006. (ISORC 2006), April 2006.

[265] J. Turnbull, The Docker Book: Containerization is the New Virtualization, 2014.

[266] T. Verbelen, T. Stevens, F. De Turck, B. Dhoedt, Graph partitioning algorithms for optimizing software deployment in mobile cloud computing, Future Generation Computer Systems 29 (2) (2013) 451–459.

[267] O. vSwitch, KVM on open vSwitch, http://git.openvswitch.org/cgi-bin/ gitweb.cgi?p=openvswitch;a=blob_plain;f=INSTALL.KVM;hb=HEAD, 2013.

[268] L. Wang, Y. Cui, I. Stojmenovic, X. Ma, J. Song, Energy efficiency on location based applications in mobile cloud computing: a survey, Computing 96 (7) (2014) 569–585.

[269] Y. Wang, X. Lin, M. Pedram, A nested two stage game-based optimization framework in mobile cloud computing system, in: SOSE, 2013, pp. 494–502.

[270] Z. Wang, D. Huang, Y. Zhu, B. Li, C.-J. Chung, Efficient attribute-based comparable data access control, IEEE Transactions on Computers 64 (12) (2015) 3430–3443.

[271] B. Waters, Ciphertext-policy attribute-based encryption: an expressive, efficient, and provably secure realization, in: Public Key Cryptography – PKC 2011, Springer-Verlag, 2011, pp. 53–70.

[272] S.A. Weil, S.A. Brandt, E.L. Miller, D.D. Long, C. Maltzahn, Ceph: a scalable, high-performance distributed file system, in: Proceedings of the 7th Symposium on Operating Systems Design and Implementation USENIX Association, 2006, pp. 307–320.

[273] A. Whitaker, M. Shaw, S.D. Gribble, et al., Denali: lightweight virtual machines for distributed and networked applications, Technical Report 02-02-01, University of Washington, 2002.

[274] R. Wolski, S. Gurun, C. Krintz, D. Nurmi, Using bandwidth data to make computation offloading decisions, in: IEEE International Symposium on Parallel and Distributed Processing (IPDPS), IEEE, 2008, pp. 1–8.

[275] H. Wu, D. Huang, Modeling multi-factor multi-site risk-based offloading for mobile cloud computing, in: 10th International Conference on Network and Service Management (CNSM), IEEE, 2014, pp. 230 235.

[276] H. Wu, D. Huang, MoSeC: mobile-cloud service composition, in: 3rd International Conference on Mobile Cloud Computing, Services, and Engineering (MobileCloud), IEEE, 2015.

[277] H. Wu, D. Huang, S. Bouzefrane, Making offloading decisions resistant to network unavailability for mobile cloud collaboration, in: 9th International Conference on Collaborative Computing: Networking, Applications and Worksharing (CollaborateCom), IEEE, 2013, pp. 168–177.

[278] H. Wu, D. Huang, Y. Zhu, Establishing a personal on-demand execution environment for mobile cloud applications, Mobile Networks and Applications 20 (3) (2015) 297–307.

[279] www.arndaleboard.org, Arndale board manual, Arndale, Tech. Rep., 2013.

[280] xen.org, Xen Hypervisor, available at http://www.xen.org/.

[281] C. Xian, Y.-H. Lu, Z. Li, Adaptive computation offloading for energy conservation on battery-powered systems, in: International Conference on Parallel and Distributed Systems, vol. 2, IEEE, 2007, pp. 1–8.

[282] Extensible Messaging and Presence Protocol (XMPP), available at http://xmpp.org/, Open Source.

[283] Z. Yan, H. Hongxin, A. Gail-Joon, H. Dijiang, W. Shanbiao, Towards temporal access control in cloud computing, in: INFOCOM, March 2012, pp. 2576–2580.

[284] K. Yang, X. Jia, K. Ren, Attribute-based fine-grained access control with efficient revocation in cloud storage systems, in: Proceedings of the 8th ACM SIGSAC Symposium on Information, Computer and Communications Security, ACM, 2013, pp. 523–528.

[285] L. Yang, J. Cao, Y. Yuan, T. Li, A. Han, A. Chan, A framework for partitioning and execution of data stream applications in mobile cloud computing, ACM SIGMETRICS Performance Evaluation Review 40 (4) (2013) 23–32.

[286] C. Yoon, D. Kim, W. Jung, C. Kang, H. Cha, AppScope: application energy metering framework for android smartphone using kernel activity monitoring, in: USENIX ATC, 2012.

[287] S. Yu, K. Ren, W. Lou, Attribute-based on-demand multicast group setup with membership anonymity, in: Proceedings of the 4th International Conference on Security and Privacy in Communication Networks, ACM, New York, NY, USA, 2008.

[288] S. Yu, K. Ren, W. Lou, Attribute-based on-demand multicast group setup with membership anonymity, Computer Networks 54 (3) (2010) 377–386.

[289] L. Zhang, B. Tiwana, Z. Qian, Z. Wang, R.P. Dick, Z.M. Mao, L. Yang, Accurate online power estimation and automatic battery behavior based power model generation for smartphones, in: Proceedings of the Eighth IEEE/ACM/IFIP International Conference on Hardware/Software Codesign and System Synthesis, ACM, 2010, pp. 105–114.

[290] L. Zhang, A. Afanasyev, J. Burke, V. Jacobson, P. Crowley, C. Papadopoulos, L. Wang, B. Zhang, et al., Named data networking, ACM SIGCOMM Computer Communication Review 44 (3) (2014) 66–73.

[291] X. Zhang, J. Schiffman, S. Gibbs, A. Kunjithapatham, S. Jeong, Securing elastic applications on mobile devices for cloud computing, in: Proceedings of the 2009 ACM Workshop on Cloud Computing Security, 2009, pp. 127–134.

[292] X. Zhang, A. Kunjithapatham, S. Jeong, S. Gibbs, Towards an elastic application model for augmenting the computing capabilities of mobile devices with cloud computing, Mobile Networks and Applications 16 (3) (2011) 270–284.

[293] Z. Zhou, D. Huang, On efficient ciphertext-policy attribute based encryption and broadcast encryption, in: Proceedings of the 17th ACM Conference on Computer and Communications Security, ACM, 2010, pp. 753–755.

[294] Z. Zhou, D. Huang, Efficient and secure data storage operations for mobile cloud computing, IACR Cryptology ePrint Archive 2011 (2011) 185.

[295] Z. Zhou, D. Huang, Gradual identity exposure using attribute-based encryption, International Journal of Information Privacy, Security and Integrity 1 (2) (2012) 278–297.

[296] Z. Zhou, D. Huang, Z. Wang, Efficient privacy-preserving ciphertext-policy attribute based-encryption and broadcast encryption, Computers, IEEE Transactions on 64 (1) (2013) 126–138.

[297] Y. Zhu, H. Hu, G.-J. Ahn, M. Yu, H. Zhao, Comparison-based encryption for fine-grained access control in clouds, in: Proceedings of the ACM Conference on Data and Application Security and Privacy, ser. CODASPY, 2012.

[298] Y. Zhu, D. Ma, C.-J. Hu, D. Huang, How to use attribute-based encryption to implement role-based access control in the cloud, in: Proceedings of the 2013 International Workshop on Security in Cloud Computing, ACM, 2013, pp. 33–40.

[299] Y. Zhu, D. Ma, D. Huang, C. Hu, Enabling secure location-based services in mobile cloud computing, in: Proceedings of the Second ACM SIGCOMM Workshop on Mobile Cloud Computing, ACM, 2013, pp. 27–32.

[300] ZScaler Cloud Security, http://www.zscaler.com/, 2011.

Index

Printed in the United States
By Bookmasters